F. HASSO

PALESTINIAN SOCIETY
In Gaza, West Bank and Arab Jerusalem
A Survey of Living Conditions

Authored by
Marianne Heiberg
Geir Øvensen
Helge Brunborg
Rita Giacaman
Rema Hammami
Neil Hawkins
Hasan Abu Libdeh
Camilla Stoltenberg
Salim Tamari
Steinar Tamsfoss
Ole Fr. Ugland
Lars Weiseth

Special adviser
Knud Knudsen

Distributed by
Institute for Palestine Studies
3501 M Street NW, Washington, DC 20007
Tel. (800) 874-3614 • (202) 342-3990

FAFO-report 151

© Fagbevegelsens senter for forskning,
utredning og dokumentasjon 1993

ISBN 82-7422-105-2

Cover: Jon S. Lahlum
Print: *Falch* Hurtigtrykk, Oslo

Contents

Preface 6

Introduction 11
The Gaza, West Bank and Arab Jerusalem survey 14

Chapter 1 The Transformation of Palestinian Society:
Fragmentation and Occupation 21
The Fragmentationof Palestinian Society3 22
Urban-Rural Disparities 23
Poverty, Migration, and Living Conditions 24
Juridical Control and the Israeli Civil Administration 26
Control of Land, Labour and Infrastructure 28
Loss of Control and Reaction to Powerlessness 28

Chapter 2 Population Characteristics and Trends 35
Population 35
Who is "Palestinian"? 36
Palestinian Population History 37
The Population Covered by the FAFO Survey 38
Characteristics of Population in the Occupied Territories 39
Infant and Child Mortality 49
Data Limitations 51
Data Quality 52
Childhood Mortality Estimation 56
Regional Comparison 59
Concluding Remarks 61
Fertility 62
Summary Statistics of FALCOT 92 Input Data 62
Population Projections 66
Limitations on Input Parameters 67
Basic Assumptions 68
Formulation of Alternative Projections 71
Results 71
Projected Developments
in the Occupied Territories Using Projection 4 74
Prospects of Change in Population Size 75

Chapter 3 Housing 81
The Cultural Setting of and Domestic and Public Spheres
inside the Housing Unit 81
Variations in Construction 83
Privacy and housing density 84
Infrastructural Amenities: Water, Sewage and Electricity 87
Indoor Standards 88
Forms of Ownership 92
Housing and Safety with Regard to Children 94
Conclusion 96

Chapter 4 Health ... 99
Acute and Chronic Illness. ... 101
Utilization of Health Services ... 111
Health Insurance ... 117
Symptoms of Distress – Mental Health ... 118
Conclusion ... 127
Summary ... 128

Chapter 5 Education ... 131
Brief Overview of the Evolution of the Palestinian
Educational System ... 132
Literacy Rates ... 134
Educational Attainment ... 136
Education and Economic Mobility ... 139
Education and Leisure ... 141
The Impact of Education on Individual Autonomy and
Perception of Influence ... 143
Education and the Perception of Conflict ... 147
Education's Impact on the Status of Women ... 148
Conclusion ... 153

Chapter 6 Household Income and Wealth ... 155
Household Wealth ... 157
Household Income ... 165
Conclusion ... 177

Chapter 7 Employment and
Under-utilization of Labour ... 181
Supply of Labour; Labour Force Participation ... 183
Under-utilization of Labour ... 188
Use of the Labour Force in the Occupied Territories ... 195
Female Labour Activity ... 207
Conclusions ... 212

Chapter 8 Aspects of Social Stratification ... 221
Socioeconomic Status and HH Background Characteristics 228
Social Status and Economic Wealth ... 234
Attitudes to Social Inequalities ... 236
A Homogeneous Society or Three Different Areas? ... 243

Chapter 9 Opinions and Attitudes ... 249
The Attitudinal Framework ... 249
Attitudes on the Status of Women ... 250
Attitudes to Social Divisions in Palestinian Society ... 256
Religious Attitudes ... 259
Political Attitudes ... 266
Evaluation of the Past ... 276
Attitudes to the Future ... 279
Conclusions ... 281

Chapter 10 Women in Palestinian Society 283
Marriage and Attitudes Towards Marriage Age 285
Marriage Age 288
Preferred Marriage Age 292
Women, Property and Access to Economic Resources 294
Women's Informal Support Networks 298
Freedom of Movement 301
Attitudes Towards Women's Appropriate Work Roles 305
Conclusions 309

Appendix A Sampling Strategy 313
Gaza Strip Sample Design 317
West Bank Sample Design 324
Arab Jerusalem Sample Design 330
Estimators 333
Sampling and Non-sampling Errors 336

**Appendix B Recruitment, Training
and Organisation of the Field Work 346**

Appendix C Processing of Data 355

Appendix A.2 Tables 359

Appendix A.6 Tables 369

Appendix A.7 Labour Table Appendix 383

Preface

The history of the FAFO living conditions survey in the occupied territories (FALCOT 1992) goes back five years, commencing in Cairo, where I had the good fortune of living in 1989. That lively city has lent its hospitality to, among a host of international organizations and institutions, the Palestinian Red Crescent and the Palestinian Hospital in Cairo. On account of Norwegian support of the latter I had the pleasure of getting acquainted with the chairman of the PRC, Dr. Fathi Arafat, and the then director of the Palestinian hospital, Dr. Khalid Shbaeb. They suggested that FAFO take on the challenge of conducting a socioeconomic study of the occupied territories.

At the time, FAFO had just started a pilot study on living conditions in the Daqhaliya province in the Nile Delta, based on our experiences with similar projects in Scandinavia and in Eastern Europe. We were in the process of making ourselves familiar with Middle East affairs and, as it turned out, the Daqhaliya survey would serve as an excellent, indeed indispensable, preparation for what lay ahead.

The professional challenges associated with carrying through a major social survey in an area with no or scarce statistics, and the political challenge of negotiating and maintaining the political space necessary to implement complex field operations in the midst of the intifada were considerable. It was evident that there was an acute need for updated, accurate, comprehensive socioeconomic data which could serve policy-making purposes in the area.

In order to investigate the political and professional requirements, I embarked on hectic visits to the Occupied Territories for consultations. The results were not encouraging. Some frankly warned that we would never get in or, if we did, that we would never get out with anything resembling success. The initial responses were hardly surprising, given the fact that a survey of this nature and on such a scale had not been undertaken before in the area. But the discussions did give us a better idea of where the pitfalls actually were located, how deep they were, and how they might be avoided.

It quickly became apparent that the survey should be as broad as possible. There was general agreement among those involved in the discussions that the various dimensions should be viewed and explored comprehensively and in context. A comprehensive approach would also ensure that relevant actors could be certain to find something in the study that was germane and that addressed their particular concerns. Then there was the question of which areas should be included in the survey. Although it would be exacting, both in scientific and in practical terms, it was decided that the survey should cover all three relevant areas - Gaza, the West Bank and Arab Jerusalem.

As preparations got under way in 1990-91, I became more and more convinced that our project could come up with more than a useful data set. It could help stimulate an identification of common interests in the region, perhaps providing a platform for future concerted efforts to improve living conditions. So I urged, with the consent of both Palestinian and Israeli leaders, that the survey be strongly policy-oriented.

The Norwegian Ministry of Foreign Affairs fully concurred with the aims and general approach that were emerging, and the then deputy minister, Knut Vollebæk, together with the Norwegian Agency for Development Cooperation, NORAD, ensured that we had financial support to start designing the project and implementing a pilot survey. In NORAD, director Per Ø. Grimstad and division chief Elny Bredde took a keen interest in the project. Following assessments and adjustments, we were all set to go in 1990. At this point we could count on funding for a full project from the Norwegian Ministry of Foreign Affairs, who would foot most of the bill. Later the project also received generous backing from the Ford Foundation. Most importantly, we had obtained a high degree of moral and practical support from Palestinian personalities and institutions as well as the acceptance of the Israeli authorities. I could feel confident that we would be given the assistance needed to bypass the obstacles that were bound to materialize. Eventually, field work was carried out successfully in June, July and August 1992.

The outcome was the most comprehensive socioeconomic data set on living conditions in the occupied territories to date. Analytical work by Palestinian and Norwegian staff in the ensuing months was carried out with diligence and enthusiasm. This is reflected, in my opinion, in the present baseline report, much to the credit of the authors.

A few words about the data set. The information gathered is quite extensive; the set contains some 1 million data. The present baseline report provides an overview but does not, and cannot, cover the whole ground. I am happy to say that there is an abundance of material on living conditions in the occupied territories that can be utilized in future analyses. We look forward to setting in motion various in-depth studies.

It is my great pleasure to thank the many individuals who have made FALCOT 1992 possible. I should stress that the whole project, which has been led by Marianne Heiberg with zeal and professionalism, has been a cooperative effort involving a wide range of Palestinians, Norwegians and individuals from other nationalities. They come from a variety of professional and political walks of life.

Let me particularly commend Marianne Heiberg and Geir Øvensen on their excellent work as main authors of the report. They have been aided ably and untiringly by FAFO researchers Ole Fredrik Ugland and Steinar Tamsfoss. The latter was in charge of sampling work, which was carried out successfully under difficult conditions. On the Norwegian side, furthermore, important contributions have been made by Camilla Stoltenberg, Helge Brunborg and Lars Weiseth. Tone Fløtten and Kristine Nergaard have offered valuable comments, as have Leo Eitinger and Gunnar Strøno. Nora Stene worked hard to provide researchers with the necessary literature.

FAFO owes a permanent debt of gratitude to professor Knud Knudsen, who has been a key adviser throughout the project. He has played a crucial role during the final stages of report work. I also wish to thank FAFO coordinator Jan Dietz for his admirable patience and for contributing in numerous ways to maintaining the momentum of the project.

Although many Palestinian academics kindly conferred their support and experience to FALCOT 1992, the contributions of two individuals, who both worked with the project from the beginning, have been indispensable. FAFO feels a very special debt of gratitude to Salim Tamari and Rema Hammami. Without their expertise, wisdom, diplomatic skills and constant encouragement, the project would probably have failed at an early stage.

FAFO is also immensely grateful to Hasan Abu Libdeh and Rita Giacaman. Both have been towers of strength throughout the project. They have not only submitted invaluable contributions to this report but have also lectured in training courses and provided countless other services to the project and to colleagues.

The number of people in the occupied territories who have contributed advice, support and personal effort is truly vast. FAFO's coordinator in Jerusalem, Neil Hawkins, did a genuinely outstanding job setting up and managing the field organization. In the West Bank, I would particularly like to thank supervisors Abdel Rahmam Talahme,

Badia Khreishy, Akram Shaaban el Eisa, Mohsen Abu Ramadan, Affaf Ghazawni, Sobheya el Hilew, Reem Mughraby, Nadim Hammouda, Ghasan Abdallah Nofal, Arij el Asy, Sanaa Asy and Abeer Mansour. FAFO's West Bank office administrator, Maha Sweiss, and data enterers Fahoom Shalaby, Arwa Dana and Randa Tawasheh also deserve mention.

In Gaza, the commitment of our assistant coordinator, Khalid el Sirr, was exceptional. Our Gaza supervisors, Maher Dahlan, Suleiman Ikhriwat, Mohammed el Ashqar, Najwa Jihlip, Rudayna el Smeri, Amami Sabawi, Nasser Jaber and Abeer Jaber made eminent contributions. Our appreciation goes also to Rena Zaqqout, FAFO's Gaza office administrator, and to Nadeel Qazzaz and Hani el Dada, our data enterers. Our thanks also to Mahmoud Okasha who advised and assisted in various aspects of the project.

The competence, patience and loyalty of the project's front line workers, the 100 researchers who collected the survey data, were remarkable and vital to the success of operations. FAFO is indebted to them for their tireless efforts in circumstances which were often execeedingly testing.

A range of Palestinian research organizations have been especially helpful. I would like to take this opportunity to thank Suha Hindiyya, Jerusalem Women's Study Centre, Suleiman Khalil, El Najah University, Gaby Baramki, Bir Zeit University, and Hisram Kohail, Hebron Graduates Union. In addition the assistance of the Hebron Graduates Research Centre and the Arab Thought Forum is gratefully acknowledged. Appreciation is also owed the Gaza YMCA for generously providing FAFO with an efficient field office.

This study would not have been possible without the assistance of E. Palgi of the Israel Central Bureau of Statistics, especially S. Kaddouri and R. Palmon was particularly important in furnishing FAFO with the detailed maps required to draw a representative sample of the Palestinian population. In addition, we are exceedingly grateful to Meron Benvenisti, Dov Randel and Fredy Zach for their kind assistance.

Special thanks are also due to the members of the project's cooperation council, Feisal Husseini and Dr. Haidar Abd el Shafi. Their counsel, backing and thoughtfulness will be remembered with affection. I would also like to mention the valuable support received from UNRWA and UNDP, both of which provided members for the project's international reference group. Former UNRWA director in

Gaza, colonel Zacharias Backer, gave us vital help in the initial phases of the project.

The Norwegian ambassador John Grieg unceasingly went out of his way to facilitate our work. Not only did he extend a warm personal welcome by opening his home to FAFO staff - he also boosted our morale whenever spirits were at a low ebb. His efforts will be fondly remembered. It is my pleasure also to thank the secretaries at the Embassy, Wegger Kristian Strømmen and Kåre Eltervåg, for their valuable support and help.

Of course, FALCOT 1992 would never have been feasible without the benevolence of the Norwegian Ministry of Foreign Affairs. Particular thanks go to Deputy Minister Jan Egeland, who enthusiastically accompanied us on visits in the field, for smoothening the political terrain we had to traverse. We could always call upon him for swift advice and action. Anne Bauer and Hans Lehne of the ministry deserve our gratitude for their support and unflagging belief in the project. I should also like to express our appreciation to my former neighbour in Cairo, Mr. David Nygaard of the Ford Foundation, who supplied additional funding to cover local project costs at a critical juncture. Jon S. Lahlum of FAFO Publishing Department is thanked for efficient and professional handling of the manuscript.

The FAFO survey in Gaza, the West Bank and Arab Jerusalem has been, I feel, a unique experience for all involved. But FALCOT 1992 should not be allowed to turn into an isolated event. Rather, it should be followed by similar endeavours, all adding to our store of knowledge about Palestinian society and the Middle East. I sincerely hope that the fruitful cooperation we have witnessed between Palestinian and Norwegian scholars will continue in the years to come.

Terje Rød Larsen
Director, FAFO
Oslo, May 1993.

Introduction
Marianne Heiberg

Parts of this chapter rely heavily on the work of FAFO colleagues Knud Knudsen and Ole Fredrik Ugland.

Level of living conditions study, the organising concept

This report consists of the base line results of the first level of living conditions study ever conducted among Palestinians in the Gaza Strip, the West Bank and Arab Jerusalem. It offers a panoramic view of the general life situation of Palestinian men and women living in Israel's occupied territories. Data was collected during a two month period in the summer of 1992. A carefully selected representative sample of 2500 Palestinian households were interviewed by some 100 specially trained Palestinian data collectors.

In order to place the results presented in this report into perspective it is critical to understand what is meant by a person's or group's "level of living" or "living conditions". Previously the most commonly accepted indicators of individual and social welfare have been economic ones. Indicators such as personal income and gross national product per capita, to mention a few, have been widely used partly due to the belief by ordinary people and policy-makers alike that human welfare could in essence be deduced from the relative economic prosperity of the society as a whole[1]. The general policy implication of such an approach was, in consequence, fairly straightforward. If increases in GNP per capita translated directly or indirectly into the betterment of the human condition, then the emphasis in development planning should focus almost exclusively on fostering national economic growth, since growth would ultimately benefit everyone.

Over the last generation or so the primacy of economic indicators in the measurement of individual welfare has diminished somewhat. While economic growth is still viewed as essential to human welfare, it is by no means seen as sufficient. Not only was the goal of sustained economic growth more elusive than initially assumed, but the negative effects of economic growth, such as pollution, intolerable urban congestion, social disintegration and so forth, have become abundantly apparent. Very importantly, it also became painfully evident that the benefits of growth could be very unevenly distributed, with some sectors within a society profiting greatly while others experienced a rapid deterioration of their life situation. Consequently, there emerged a growing awareness of the need not only for corrective measures to compensate for the negative side effects of the economy, but also of the need for statistically valid instruments that could measure human welfare directly as well as a given society's performance over time in providing such welfare.

In particular indicators were required in two critical areas, areas which lie at the core of the level of living conditions survey. First, indicators were needed to measure the *degree of equality* in important aspects of life between individuals and groups in a society, indicators that revealed the distribution of the benefits of economic growth within a society at a specific period of time. The major concern was to evaluate whether differences between, for instance, the rich and poor, between men and women, between urban and rural residents with regard to health, education and access to economic resources were increasing or decreasing. The consequent policy goal was that development should be aimed at making substantial improvements in the lives of the maximum numbers of individuals possible within a society.

The implication for a level of living conditions study was that such a study should measure, describe and hopefully explain the variations and inequalities within a society in a policy relevant manner.

The second area dealt with the concept of social mobility. The normative and policy goal was that the social positions which individuals could attain during the course of life should be largely independent of the social position they inherit at birth. The core concern was *equality of opportunity*, the possibility for individuals and groups to change their relative social position over time.

Needless to say, the policy goal of equality, i.e. a relatively even distribution of resources - and the goal of equality of opportunity, i.e. a relatively equal access to those resources, such as education, a prerequisite for social mobility - do not necessarily pull in the same direction[2]. A stress on the latter to the exclusion of the former could imply, for instance, that disproportionate amounts of resources are locked in the permanent control of the educated and healthy to the extreme detriment of the uneducated and ill. Today social planning requires an acute understanding of the delicate balance between these two goals, a balance upon which there is little expert consensus.

However, the key conceptual question concerns what is meant by "welfare" or "level of living". The British sociologist, Richard Titmus, has defined "level of living" as:

> ".. the individual's command over resources in money, possessions, knowledge, psychic and physical energy, social relations, security, etc. by the help of which the individual can control and consciously direct his conditions of life."[3]

In short, an individual's level of living is defined not so much by the economic goods he or she possesses, but by the ability of the individual to exercise choice and to affect the course of his or her own life. Material goods are important only to the extent they provide freedom for the individual to determine his own actions. Even though the analysis of living conditions is preoccupied with the possession of goods, the critical point is to explore people's abilities to choose, to delineate the options that are not available and the limits that restrain individual choice.[4] As now internationally understood, level of living studies are concerned with human capabilities and how such capabilities are used. They try to examine the degree to which people can participate in social, political and economic decision-making and can work creatively and productively to shape their own futures.[5]

Human development and the ability to exercise control over one's own life is a two-sided matter. The first is objective. The fundamental dimension involves access to the resources required for 1) decent material living standards, 2) protection of health and personal security and 3) acquisition of knowledge.

The second is subjective. It relates to an individual's conviction that he or she can participate as a full human being in a meaningful social life. Thus, a full measurement of living conditions has to combine both the dimensions necessary for human physical and psychological welfare and those required for a sense of human empowerment, productivity and self-respect.

Since the level of welfare of a human being is determined by the total life situation, a level of living conditions study aspires to provide a holistic, comprehensive description. Such descriptions, of course, pose daunting theoretical and technical problems. Thus, at best, any one survey can only yield an approximate picture. However, the following items are viewed as vital to any level of living study.

Demographics: The size and composition of a population is regarded as crucial background information for a study of living conditions in a country. Population growth as well as gender, age, religious, ethnic and family composition constitute important dimensions in this respect.

Health: Often regarded as one of the most fundamental aspects of living conditions, good health is a prerequisite for well-being, happiness and general daily satisfaction.

Education: Education is seen as a critical resource enabling an individual to become a full citizen in a modern, literate society. Crucial to personal development and self-esteem, education is also viewed as personal resource with the greatest potential impact on social mobility within a society.

Work, income and consumption: Participation in the work force, and the income secured through it, is often decisive for self-esteem, social contact, a sense of belonging as well as the individual's or household's economic well-being.

Housing: There are no standard norms as to what constitutes good housing, but a dwelling is expected to provide for the reasonable comfort, privacy and protection of the household which resides within it. The dwelling is often an object of considerable emotional attachments since it can act as a physical symbol of the family and its linkage to the wider community.[6]

In addition to these core social indicators, level of living studies might also explore use of leisure time, social contact and sense of influence, perceptions of social conflict, access to political resources as well as religious attitudes. The exact combination of indicators will, of course, vary according to the specific requirements of the study.

The Gaza, West Bank and Arab Jerusalem survey

This level of living conditions study of Palestinians is unique not only in the comprehensive nature of the statistical findings it presents. Additionally, it is the only level of living conditions study ever conducted among a people living under occupation. The implications of this have a fundamental impact on the major conceptual premise underlying such a study. The capacity of an individual to execute control and to exercise meaningful choice over his daily life is in many respects simply incompatible with the fact of occupation. However, this is not a study of the occupation, nor indeed are the effects of occupation on the lives of Palestinians explored in any systematic way. Nonetheless, for Palestinians the occupation forms a rigid frame within which daily life is conducted and a critical perspective shaping all the issues this report examines.

Although the literature on the occupied territories is large indeed, most of it tends to deal with only one, albeit critical, aspect of the Palestinian situation, the Palestinian-Israeli interface. In the post World War II period, no other single conflict has commanded the same level of political, diplomatic and intellectual attention. The amount of documentation, published and unpublished, this attention has generated is truly staggering. Yet despite this, reliable statistics on Palestinian society are relatively scarce. Reasonable statistics relating to, for example, health, housing conditions, labour force participation, the status of women or educational attainment, are limited. Statistics which attempt to relate across these dimensions, say, for instance housing density and psychological welfare, are almost non-existent.

This insufficiency of quantitatively reliable and representative information on Palestinian society has a range of consequences. Two such consequences are particularly significant for this study. First, each year international organizations, like the Norwegian government which funded this survey, provide millions of dollars in humanitarian and development assistance. Yet these organizations operate under a critical disadvantage. To an important extent they are forced to work arbitrarily on a hit or miss basis. Lacking comprehensive information, they are unable to make priorities between development requirements or to identify the groups in Palestinian society who are most deprived. Where are the needs greatest? Should health care or educational services be given preference? Should improvements in housing standards be given priority over improvements in infrastructure? Who are in greatest need? Should refugees living in camps or those refugees who live outside them be especially targeted for assistance - and for what type of assistance? Are levels of deprivation more marked in the north of the West Bank or the south? Is poverty more pronounced in Gaza City or in the villages of the West Bank? In terms of education or health, are refugee women in Gaza worse off than village women in the West Bank? Without adequate information, these types of questions, essential to development planning, cannot be answered. Consequently, resources cannot be distributed and utilized in a rational, efficient manner.

Second, both Palestinians and Israelis hold firm views concerning the nature of Palestinian realities, and these views are often diametrically different. For example, Israeli official statistics state that unemployment in Gaza is around 5 to 6%. UNRWA has suggested that the real figure is somewhere around 60%. Some Palestinian figures for infant mortality are almost three times higher than Israeli figures. The same disparity exists in almost all other spheres, from Palestinian housing standards to political attitudes. In fact, there is no agreement on how many Palestinians actually live in the occupied territories. This gap in perceptions of reality stimulates a war of images, a form of discourse whereby Israelis and Palestinians, while trying to talk to each other, end up talking past each other, partly because they have no shared view of the facts. The search for common ground becomes almost intractably difficult when there is no agreement even on what the ground looks like.

This survey has been undertaken to address both these dimensions. The specific objectives of the survey are:

1. To contribute needed, comprehensive, reliable statistical information on the occupied territories. It should be noted that no official census has been conducted since 1967 and surveys conducted subsequently have been partial and generally viewed as inadequate.
2. To be of assistance to governments and international organizations in designing appropriate development and humanitarian aid programmes for the region.
3. To assist Palestinians in planning and measuring the course of their own social and economic development.

The dimensions of living conditions surveyed are:

- Household composition & demographics
- Housing conditions & amenities
- Education
- Employment, work force & work histories
- Sources of income
- Capital goods, consumer durables & expenditures
- Savings & indebtedness
- Culture & leisure activities
- Health & psychological welfare
- Children & injury
- Political, religious & social attitudes
- Travel & mobility
- Gender relations

- Women's work load & types of work
- Women's control over resources & decision-making
- Women's attitudes to constraints & conventions
- Family planning
- Birth histories

The project was built up in three stages. Each stage was initiated only after the successful completion of the preceding phase.

Stage I consisted of a preliminary investigation to establish whether or not the political and professional parameters for successful project implementation were present in an area which is both volatile and complex. This stage was completed in July 1990.

Stage II consisted of a pilot survey of 300 households in Gaza. Preparation for the pilot consisted of building a *local research organization*, developing the *questionnaire*, designing procedures by which to draw a *representative sample* of the Gaza population and, finally, recruiting, training and organizing a Palestinian *supervisor and data collector corps*. The aim of the pilot study was to provide a thorough trial run of the main instruments of research as well as to test the competence of the data collectors and the adequacy of the project's logistical capacities. The pilot study was completed successfully in August 1991 and showed the need to make significant changes in many aspects of the project design. Based on the results of the Gaza pilot most of the questionnaire was modified, the sampling design was refined, improved training programmes were instituted, SPSS data entry and logical rules and consistency checks were revised, and FAFO's field organization was considerably reinforced. Some eight months were required for the preparation of the main survey.

Stage III was the main survey of 1000 households in Gaza, 1000 in the West Bank and 500 in Arab Jerusalem. Field work took approximately two months. The final data base was available in November 1992. By that time all questionnaires had been processed through an initial SPSS entry program which contained some 500 logical rules and consistency checks and, subsequently, double-punched to uncover errors that might have escaped the first data entry processing.

The final stage involved the analysis of the data base and the interpretation of the statistical findings. It should be emphasized at the outset that, since we here deal with sample data, some fluctuations due to sampling errors will normally occur in all of the following analyses.

Interested readers should consult this book's appendix A, on sampling strategy, in addition to appendices B and C.

Living conditions studies have for the most part been conducted in modern Western societies although their use in developing countries is accelerating. In the West, the analysis of results can usually be based on comprehensive social models which contain the essential relationships and dynamics of the societies involved. Thus survey results can be used to confirm, modify or challenge pre-existing policies and/or models. To some extent such surveys tread ground that already has been ploughed.

However, in this sense Palestinian society presents an exceptional analytical challenge. The holistic models required for analysis have not so far been developed and appropriate comparative data is difficult to obtain. Broadly speaking, from a sociological view, a combination of four specific factors are critical to an understanding of Palestinian living conditions in the occupied territories and the forces of change and tension which affect and are transforming them.

1 It is a society under prolonged occupation.
2 A significant portion of Palestinians resident in the area are displaced or refugees with the consequent disruption of traditional social structures.
3 For over four years this society has experienced low intensity warfare, the intifada.
4 Culturally, Palestinian society is a integral part of Middle Eastern society.

Whereas parallels for any one of these factors could, perhaps, be easily found elsewhere, it is the convergence of these central parameters that bestows a distinctive quality upon Palestinian society.

The limitations of the present survey are similar to the limitations of all surveys of this nature. On the practical side respondents were occasionally unwilling to answer questions openly. On some of the economic variables, some respondents under-reported their assets. On some of the attitudinal questions, respondents at times concealed their true opinions and at times failed to understand the question. Despite the two years used on its development, the questionnaire still contained weaknesses which have hampered analysis of some of the results.

On the more theoretical side comprehensive, statistical surveys can provide a representative and comprehensive overview of a society, but the price is often lack of analytical depth. Explanatory power and causal understandings of certain social phenomena can often be better gained through prolonged qualitative study rather than through quantitative methods, however sweeping in scope.

This survey was also subject to another, more specific limitation. During the three years the project lasted, the Middle East witnessed a major war, as well as, in the wake of that war, the most promising attempt hitherto to fashion peace in the region. In the occupied territories violence was frequent and the population was subjected to a range of restrictions and punitive measures including prolonged periods of curfew. Although its initial fury had dimmed, the resistance, sacrifice and discipline of the intifada had become institutionalized in daily life. The problems of conducting a large scale project in such a highly strained and unpredictable environment are obvious. Moreover, the fears, anger and suspicions that are inherent in these circumstances could well have coloured the way the survey was perceived as well as how the more sensitive parts of the survey questionnaire were answered.

Despite these limitations, however, it is hoped that the analysis this report contains will contribute new and useful insights into Palestinian society, into its vulnerabilities and strengths, its constraints and opportunities and into the concerns and aspirations of its people.

The various analyses in this report underline important and critical aspects of the situation of Palestinians in the occupied territories.

Typically, the chapter on Population (Chapter 2) shows that although child mortality still is relatively high, a general improvement has occurred during the last decades. The proportion of very young Palestinians is presently large indeed. This fact, together with expected future fertility levels, give rise to dramatic projections for the population size in the next twenty years.

There are great variations between the main regions in daily living conditions, indoors and outdoors, as demonstrated in Chapter 3 on Housing. Gazans, particularly in camps, score on average low on indicators for, e.g., housing and infrastructure. People on the West Bank, and especially in Arab Jerusalem, are often better off, a pattern illustrated also in Chapters 6, 7 and 10 on Economy, Employment and Women respectively. However, results of services by UNWRA and similar organizations are demonstrated by findings in Chapter 4 (on Health) and Chapter 5 (on Education). Efforts on a broad scale over time seem to have reduced otherwise substantial inequalities.

It is an interesting finding that Gazans, especially in camps, despite their low score on several objective living condition components, still often look at their situation in more positive terms than people in the other regions (see chapter 4 on Health, Chapter 8 on Social Stratification and Chapter 9 on Attitudes). A possible interpretation of this pattern could be that the more direct and intense experience of external conflict prevalent there may strengthen feelings of shared values and common purpose.

Findings and interpretations in this report like those just summarized, are manifold and sometimes, by necessity, complex. They should therefore be read in the proper context, i.e. in the very chapters they are presented. As an introductory background for an understanding of the following survey results, a general description of Palestinian Society is given in the first chapter (Chapter 1). Each subsequent chapter concentrates on specific level of living components.

Notes

1 Gudmund Hernes and Knud Knudsen, *Lithuania: Living Conditions* Oslo: FAFO Report, 1991 p.156.

2 Hernes and Knudsen, op cit, p.157-8.

3 Richard A. Titmus, *Essays on the Welfare State*, London: Allen and Unwin, 1958.

4 Ole Fredrik Ugland, unpublished FAFO memo, August 1992.

5 UNDP, *Human Development Report 1992*, New York and Oxford: Oxford University Press p.12.

6 Ole Fredrik Ugland, op.cit.

Chapter 1
The Transformation of Palestinian Society: Fragmentation and Occupation

Salim Tamari

Introduction

The present level of living conditions study is the first contemporary attempt to present a social and demographic profile of Palestinian society in order to isolate its dynamic variables for the purpose of analysis, comparison, and social planning. The society it describes is one that is dispersed over several social formations and communities, its fragmentation being the product of successive wars (most notably the war of 1948 and the June war of 1967) with the Israelis. The condition of exile, which has affected more than one half of Palestinians, has stamped the collective consciousness, cultural trends, as well as the political behaviour of Palestinians throughout the Middle East and in the diaspora.

The purpose of this chapter is to present the socio-historical context of the material discussed in the survey. The focus is on those segments of Palestinian society which came under Israeli control in 1967. Collectively those segments (with the Galilee) contain the largest global concentration of Palestinians today. Data for 1991 indicate that a full 42% of all Palestinians live in the occupied territories and in Israel (18.6% in the West Bank and Jerusalem, 10.8% in Gaza, and 12.6% in Israel).[1] The bulk of the rest are distributed in Jordan (31.6%), Lebanon (5.7%), Syria (5.2%), and the rest of the Arab world (7.7%).[2] This pattern of dispersal is particularly crucial for our analysis in this survey, not only because the future of the Palestinians is being determined on part of their historic land in the current peace negotiations, but also because these territories constitute a historic continuity with Mandatory Palestine of the pre-1948 period.

The Fragmentation of Palestinian Society[3]

One major consequence of the 1948 war was that a whole segment of the rural highlands of Central Palestine (which came to be known as the West Bank) became isolated from its cultivable land, coastal markets and metropolitan centres. Its population became land-locked. Those areas of Palestine that were not incorporated into the state of Israel, were incorporated into new political formations: Jordan and Egypt. That integration continues to affect the administrative apparatus, the educational system, the economy, and the social structure of the two regions – more than a quarter century after Israel took control over the West Bank and Gaza.

In order to place into context the data discussed in this survey it is important to appreciate the *differential* impact of this historical heritage: while Jordan incorporated the West Bank under its constitutional rule, extending its franchise to its residents and establishing a common civil service to administer the Jordanian and Palestinian regions of the state, Egypt – by contrast – set the Gaza Strip aside as a trusteeship.

But aside from the *administrative* impact of the Egyptian and Jordanian administration, the two areas exhibit significant topographic and social structural variations. With respect to the latter it should be noted that there are marked differences in the relationship of the refugee population to the resident population, the density of population, its distribution, and its occupational patterns. To appreciate the magnitude of this contrast the salient socio-economic features of each area are summarized in table 1.1.

The West Bank as a region is distinguished from the Gaza Strip by its geographic expanse (5.8 million dunums vs 0.36 million dunums in Gaza), and by the immense variation in its topography – both features that allow for a more balanced social formation and a lower population density.[4] The decisive element in this imbalance is the stifling population density in the Gaza Strip, resulting from the mass influx of refugees from the coastal regions south of Jaffa during the 1948 war, and their concentration in the city of Gaza, where the bulk of the urban population resides: the rest live in 8 refugee camps and in about a dozen townships and villages (table 1.1).

By contrast the approximately one million people living in the West Bank are distributed over 12 main medium-sized urban centres – ranging from 90,000 to 35,000 inhabitants each – and 430 villages.

Urban-Rural Disparities

The social structure of the population in the occupied territories exhibits considerable differentiation between the urban and rural sections, as well as within village and urban societies. Rural differentiation is high in Gaza where large citrus plantations (now in decline) used to employ the bulk of the agricultural labour force as wage workers.[5] The West Bank, by comparison, is, as a rural society, dominated by a smallholding peasant population and very few big landholdings (concentrated mostly in the Jordan Valley). Average landholdings per rural household is less than 50 dunums (this category includes 84% of all landholders, and covers 34% of all possessed land).[6] On the other extreme we observe that less than 1% of holders possess 38% of the land, with holdings in excess of 100 dunums each.

When examining sources of income in this survey the reader should note that, for dry farming land, any cultivated area under 100

Table 1.1 The West Bank and the Gaza Strip Disparities in Socio-Economic Structure

	Social Feature	Gaza District	The West Bank
1	Population Density	Very high (1400/sq km)	Low density (135/sq km)
2	Ratio of rural to urban population	About 20% of total population	62% of total population
3	Distribution of urban population	Concentrated in one major urban conurbation (Gaza)	11 urban centres medium-sized (35-90,000 each)
4	Distribution of rural population	8 refugee camps, and 9 villages	430 villages
5	Mode of agriculture	Irrigated (48%) Wage labour predominant	Rain-fed agric. (95% of land), small farmers
6	Land tenure	Large and medium-sized plantations	Medium and small-sized owned plots
7	Social stratification	Sharp class and social disparities	Relative social homogeneity
8	Refugees as a % of total population	63%	18%

Sources: (1) K. Nakhleh and E. Zureik, (eds.) *Sociology of the Palestinians* (London, 1980); (2) Sarah Roy, *The Gaza Survey* (Jerusalem, 1986); (3) *Statistical Abstract of Israel*, no. 38 (Jerusalem, 1987); Lisa Taraki (ed.) *Palestinian Society in the West Bank and Gaza*, (Akka, 1990); M. Benvenisti and S. Khayat, *The West Bank and Gaza Atlas* (Jerusalem, 1989); FAFO Household Survey (Oslo and Jerusalem, 1993).

Note: The reader will notice some discrepancy between some of the data above and those in the survey. Those discrepancies are primarily due to conceptual differences in the definition of social categories (e.g. what is urban and rural) by the several authors listed above.

dunums would be used for subsistence and marginal farming. Hence the extent of agricultural disparities is less than would seem to be indicated by the figures. Ownership of irrigated land, on the other hand (which constitutes less than 5% of total arable land), would indicate greater disparities.

There is considerable urbanization among Palestinians by the standards of developing countries. Our survey suggests that 60% of the Palestinians in the three regions under study live in urban areas (see also chapter 2 on Population). But there are significant contrasts within the three regions. For the West Bank, 1987 Israeli data suggests that 47% of the population live in urban areas, distributed in 11 townships, the average size of which is 43,000 inhabitants.[7] The household survey identifies 62% of West Bankers as 'rural' (living in over 400 villages and rural refugee camps). However, there is an uneven dispersal of the urban population, with fully 75% of those concentrated in 3 major conurbations: Nablus, Hebron, and the greater Jerusalem area (including Bethlehem and Ramallah-Bireh). Almost all West Bank towns act as centres of services and retail trade for their rural hinterlands, and are noted for their small, and weak, manufacturing sector (with the average employment per establishment amounting to 4.28 persons).[8] Over the last few decades there has been a steady and even growth in the size of rural and urban localities due to the proximity of district centres to satellite villages.[9] The main social divide within the townships continues to be the one found between refugee camp dwellers and residents outside these camps.

By contrast Gaza is overwhelmingly urban, with 75-80% of the population living in the Gaza-Khan Yunis-Rafah conurbations. Gaza is also distinguished by the preponderance of its refugee population, constituting 2/3 of the total, of which about 1/3 are camp dwellers. Within all of the Palestinian regions only 18% of the population live in refugee camps.

Poverty, Migration, and Living Conditions

The social and economic trends which emerge from this survey could suggest both a higher rate of social homogeneity and a lower rate of social mobility than has been perceived in the existing literature on Palestinians.[10] This may be, in part, due to the process of *selective* out-migration and depletion of resources which preceded and was accelerated by the Gulf War. In 'Household Income and Wealth' it appears that disposable income has declined since the war. Wage income has emerged, in consequence, as the major source of family income, emphasizing household demographic factors, such as the ratio of men to women, and adults to dependent children and older people.

From our analysis of households it appears that the most deprived of the social segments are the urban poor who, in both the West Bank and Gaza, constitute a significant section of the town population living in refugee camps.

The low level of rural to urban migration, caused by the proximity of villages to their district centres, has prevented these camps from expanding and developing into urban slums made up of refugees and rural immigrants. Only in Gaza, therefore, do we see this process of squalor produced by demographic pressure and housing congestion, permeating the urban scene as a whole.

Our data shows discrepancy with figures used by the Israeli Central Bureau of Statistics (CBS) on levels of wealth and employment. These discrepancies can only partly be explained by changes brought about by the Gulf War and restrictions on (Arab) labour mobility to Israel. Some of the differences are caused by conceptual differences as to what constitutes employment, unemployment and underemployment of individuals in the labour force. The data in 'Employment and the Underutilization of Labour' (chapter 7) suggests that conventional unemployment indicators may reflect serious flaws in assessing levels of unemployment and underemployment, and misconceives the nature of female labour, which – in the case of Palestinian society – involves a high degree of put-out work within the household economy.

The data further indicates important variations by region, with Jerusalem ranking the highest in income levels and full employment among household members (one out of five fully employed) with Gaza, at the extreme end, supporting one out of twenty as fully employed (one out of thirty for southern Gaza – see chapter 6).

Loss of land and property as a result of war conditions enhanced the value of education and emigration as sources of social mobility. The vehicle of that mobility was the extended family, which invested heavily (proportional to its income) in the education of its younger members, especially sons.[11]

During the initial period of Israeli rule (up to 1988) the demand for unskilled wage labour in Israeli industries (the services and construction) transformed the whole relationship between family expectations, children's education and the demands of the labour market.[12]

Whole village communities, as well as residents of refugee camps, became completely dependent for their survival on employment in Israel. The relationship between earlier migrants who left the country before 1967 and their remaining relatives, was weakened. The structure of employment in the last 25 years has been such that the labour force as a whole has been "de-skilled" The traditional transfer of knowledge among craftsmen and artisans from generation to generation has been disrupted.

The loss of skilled migrants has had a conservative effect on village society as a whole since it removed the most innovative and educated segments, that might otherwise have been a force for change in rural society.[13] It also led to a "radical re-assessment of occupational priorities" because of risks involved in emigration and in investing family savings in the education of sons. Recent employment figures show, however, that in spite of continued stress on the value of higher education by the Palestinian family, the market has been saturated with high school and university graduates with little chance of employment. This has been the result not only of the lack of employment opportunities in the local establishments, but also of the lopsided system of education, which is heavily oriented to semi-professional and white collar employment, at the expense of a specialization that is more likely to respond to the local labour market conditions.

Juridical Control and the Israeli Civil Administration

Israeli control over the West Bank and Gaza was based on a strategy of enhancing the dependency of the occupied territories on Israel's economy through an elaborate system of political and juridical control. The Israeli Military Government (MG), and since 1981 the Civil Administration (CA), acquired immense powers over the lives of residents in the occupied territories beginning with the first week of occupation in 1967. Military Order no. 2 (June 7, 1967) concentrated these powers in the hands of the Military Governor:

"All powers of government, legislation, appointment and administration in relation to the Area or its inhabitants shall henceforth be vested in me alone and shall be exercised by me or whoever shall be appointed by me to that end or acting on my behalf" (Article 3(A)).[14]

Since 1981 the bulk of these powers have been transferred to the head of the Civil Administration in the West Bank and Gaza. Although ostensibly the MG and the CA formally assumed the powers vested in the hands of the Jordanian District Commissioner (before 1967) and the Egyptian military governor of the Gaza District, in fact there was a qualitative difference in the manner in which the Israelis exercised these powers. The shift lies in the conscious and systematic method the Israelis undertook to subordinate the economy of the two regions to the needs of the Israeli state, and – more significantly – in the appropriation of public land (and substantial private properties) to serve the needs of the Jewish Settlement Councils in the occupied territories.

Raja Shehadeh in his *Occupier's Law* (2nd ed. 1988) outlines four legislative stages in the consolidation of Israel's juridical control over the West Bank and Gaza. These were based on a succession of over 1,200 military orders regulating all aspects of daily life in the territories. In the first stage (1967-1971) the military government established its control over transactions of immovable property, the use of water and other natural resources, the power to expropriate land, and the authority to operate banks and over the regulation of municipal and village councils. In this period, also, the system of control over the movement of individuals was established (identity cards, travel permits, driving licenses, and licenses for professional practices).[15]

The second phase (1971-1979), was primarily aimed at the transfer of Arab lands to the control of Jewish settlement councils. This involved amending Jordanian land laws to facilitate zoning 'public' lands to the benefit of Israeli bodies, and for acquisition of local land by 'foreign' (i.e. Israeli) companies.[16]

The third phase of Israeli legislation (1979-1981), involved the transfer of authority and power from the Military Government to the newly established Civil Administration, and the extension of Israeli law to apply to Jewish settlers so that they will not be subject to the jurisdiction of West Bank (and Gaza) courts.[17]

The fourth phase of legislation (1981 to the present), marked the consolidation of Israeli-Jewish control over expropriated areas. Those, by 1991, constituted more than 60% of the total land area of the occupied territories. In this period, furthermore, Military Orders concentrated on the regulation of the fiscal policies governing the West Bank and Gaza, particularly those pertaining to the collection of taxes and revenue, and of the flow of funds to the territories.[18]

The net effect of these military laws has been to create two systems of legal bodies (one applying to Israeli Jews, and the other to native Palestinians), with a gradual transformation of zoning laws, regional planning, the transfer of land acquisitions to the benefit of the former national group, and to the detriment of the latter.[19]

Control of Land, Labour and Infrastructure

At the structural level Israeli policy was formulated in the early years of occupation (1967-68), and continues to operate along these lines until today.[20] It rests on a system of formal and informal control whose main features are

1. The physical control of land and water resources through a tight system of regional zoning and restriction of Arab building and water drilling permits
2. The integration of the Palestinian water, electrical and road network within the Israeli grid, thus making the Palestinian infrastructure dependent on Israeli services
3. Absorbing unskilled Arab labour into the Israeli economy, most notably in construction and services
4. The subordination of the occupied territories' economy as a tariff-free market for Israeli commodities, without extending the same benefits to goods produced in the West Bank and Gaza in the Israeli market.[21]

The net effect of these features has been to render sources of livelihood and services in Palestinian society dependent on Israel, and consequently, to make it virtually impossible for any future political arrangement to evolve in the direction of separating the two entities from each other. Thus, a system of structural integration has emerged, supported by political control and increased pressure for land confiscation and the building of Jewish settlements. Those pressures created the main conditions which triggered the popular uprising in December of 1987, and have continued during the period covering the present survey.

Loss of Control and Reaction to Powerlessness

The main thrust of the Palestinian intifada has been a call for disengagement from Israeli control after conventional political pressures failed to bring about any change in the systematic annexation of the territories to Israel. Its main achievements, on the positive side, have been to place the Palestinian issue on the international agenda after the many years of neglect it suffered after the invasion of Lebanon in 1982. Internally it gave the Palestinians a sense of empowerment which created a prelude to the Peace Negotiations of 1992, creating the possibility, for the first time since the war of 1948, of a territorial solution, and independence for the Palestinians.[22] However, the intifada also brought profound social changes in the occupied territories which affected the nature of Palestinian society. Perhaps the two most significant features of these changes are (a) the mobilization of youth in organized and spontaneous activities against military occupation; and (b) the growth of politically defined Islamist movements. One consequence of the first development is the manner in which generational conflict has been re-defined, and the disruption of traditional normative behaviour towards elder members of the family by younger ones. The implication of these changes has been examined here in those attitude items of the survey that deal with age and gender conflicts (see for example "Men's opinions concerning western dress by age", in 'Social and Political Attitudes and Values'). The growth of religiously defined political and social norms during the intifada is intriguing because of the significant variation it has elicited in terms of regional, gender and educational differences. The prevalent notion that the intifada has led to a drastic growth of religious fundamentalism across the country is challenged by the data in this study (chapter 9). What is more likely to have happened is that the country is being polarized by secular and religious trends to an extent that has not been witnessed before.[23]

At the level of living standard – as opposed to style of living – the combined effect of the intifada and the Gulf War was devastating for people's daily life. Although at the political level these events brought into the open the question of the nature of structural relation between Israel and the occupied territories, they nevertheless accentuated conflicts in that relationship which were – until 1987 – dormant. The initial brunt of the war-time restrictions described here were felt by farmers, who had to market their crops;[24] it was then extended to the rest of the population. Palestinians were also affected indirectly, as a result of the decline – and then cessation – of remittances coming from Kuwait and other Gulf countries, and directly from the effects of curfews and other military restrictions imposed by Israel.

The comprehensive curfew which was imposed at the beginning of 1991 began a prolonged process of control over the movement of the population which was still official policy two years later, at the beginning of 1993. It continues to affect hundreds of thousands of residents who are barred from entering Israel (i.e. the so-called Green Line) and the city of Jerusalem. Residents were also restricted from moving freely from one district to another. In effect, the current movement restrictions, in addition to excluding workers who do not hold permits from entering Israeli territories, have cut the occupied territories into three parts: Northern West Bank (Nablus, Ramallah, and Tulkarem districts), Southern West Bank (Hebron, Bethlehem), and the Gaza Strip. The city of Jerusalem divides the two first regions, and the pre-1967 borders divide the whole West Bank from Gaza.

Four measures of political control can be identified here as having a detrimental effect on the population's daily lives: two of them (administrative detentions and curfews) restrict the movement of the population; and the other two (land confiscation, and house demolitions) affect their conditions of habitat. In the period from December 9, 1987, (signifying the beginning of the intifada and Israeli measures to curtail it) to the summer of 1992 (when this survey was conducted), 15,240 people were placed under administrative detention.[25] Curfews during the same period confined the inhabitants of the occupied territories for prolonged periods to their homes (or at least to their village and town localities), drastically disrupting their access to work sites.[26]

The other two items directly connected with administrative measures undertaken by the Israeli authorities are land confiscation and house demolitions. For the five year period under review 359,806 dunums were confiscated and 2,193 housing units were destroyed (only about 35% of them for 'security' reasons).[27] Thus the principal factor responsible for the disruption of building activity was directly related to the seemingly wilful restriction of available space for expansion, rather than to punishment for political activity, as is commonly believed.

For the purposes of our analysis in this survey these modes of control have two distinct impacts on the living conditions for Palestinians. Administrative detention and curfews affect people's sources of income (inability to commute to work in the case of the latter, and loss of income due to the incarceration of the breadwinner), as well as their general mobility. The latter has a negative influence on the traditional fabric of society and its cohesiveness since it affects social visits, recreational activity and ritual social duties (prayer, attendance of seasonal festivities, and pilgrimage).

Land confiscation and demolition of houses, on the other hand, directly affect the household's attachment to its community and the individual's security in his or her habitat. In a predominantly agrarian society (or even in an urban society with persisting agrarian values) such as the one under examination, property in terms of land and housing underlines the community's national identity. The continued confiscation of Palestinian land by the military authorities is seen not as a loss of real estate, but as the alienation of national patrimony. More significant is the current confinement of building permits by the Civil Administration to increasingly restricted areas within municipal boundaries and areas of authorized village councils, rendering about 65% of the total land area in the West Bank and Gaza out of bounds for both private and public construction.[28] These restrictions have not only led to increasingly congested housing conditions and limitations on levels of privacy (affecting especially newly married couples), but has also constituted a detrimental impediment on the ability of whole communities to plan for their collective needs, and prohibited local councils from establishing masterplans for regional development.[29]

The overall impact of such measures is the prevalence of a sense of *arbitrariness* and *uncertainty* which permeates the tempo of daily life. At the individual level it creates a sense of powerlessness; at the family level, it obstructs the ability of households to chart a purposeful existence for their members; and at the community and national levels, it prevents systematic planning for the future.

While the authors of this survey were aware of these restrictions when they undertook the research, they did not plan the survey to be a 'demonstration of grievances'. Rather these grievances were derivative of conditions of daily existence which elsewhere might be 'normal'. The purpose of the study was to create an empirical foundation for the examination of the quality of social life, and to monitor (as has been done in similar studies elsewhere) the critical components of social and economic life as they appeared at one point in time.

Notes

1 The Center for Policy Analysis on Palestine, *Facts and Figures About the Palestinians*, (Washington, DC, 1992), p. 5.

2 Ibid., p. 5.

3 Table 1 and the analysis pertaining to it will appear in a forthcoming study written by the author for UNCTAD (Geneva) under the title of 'Social Transformations and Development Prospects in the West Bank and Gaza Strip'.

4 The data in this section is derived from PASSIA, *The West Bank and Gaza Strip*, Jerusalem, 1990, and from Lisa Taraki (ed.) *Palestinian Society in the West Bank and Gaza Strip* (Akka, 1990), pp. 70-82 and 205-207.

5 Dawood Istanbooli et al, *The Agriculture of the Occupied Territories and the Conditions of Development* (Arabic), Arab Thought Forum, Jerusalem, 1981.

6 D. Istanbooli, ibid.

7 CBS, *Statistical Abstract of Israel*, 1988, and The West Bank Data Project (WBDP), *The West Bank and Gaza Atlas* (Jerusalem, 1988), pp. 28-29.

8 UNIDO, *Survey of the Manufacturing Industry in the West Bank and Gaza Strip*, June 1984; WBDP, *The West Bank and Gaza Atlas*, p. 43.

9 WBDP, *The West Bank and Gaza Atlas*, p. 28.

10 See for example the section on 'Society' in Lisa Taraki (ed.), *Palestinian Society in the West Bank and Gaza Strip* (Akka, 1990); and in Elia Zureik and Khalil Nakhleh (eds.), *Sociology of the Palestinians*, (London: Croom Helm, 1980).

11 For a discussion of the relationship between migration and the mobility of the Palestinian family in the 1950s and 1960s, see Abdullah Lutfiyyeh, *Baytin: A Jordanian Village*, Mouton, The Hague, 1966.

12 Linda Ammons, *West Bank Villagers: The Influence of National and International Politics on Village Life*, unpublished PhD thesis, Harvard University, Cambridge, Mass., 1978.

13 Ammons, ibid., p. 224. For an alternative perspective, see Annalies Moors, "Rural Women in the West Bank: Gender, Kinship, and the Domestic Economy", in *Afaq Filistiniyya*, no. 5 (Summer 1990) [in Arabic].

14 Quoted in Don Peretz, *The West Bank: History, Politics, Society, and Economy* (Westview Press, Boulder, 1986), p. 80.

15 Raja Shehadeh, *Occupier's Law: Israel and the West Bank*, Institute for Palestine Studies (2nd ed. Washington DC, 1988), p. viii, 114-115.

16 Ibid., p. ix, 40.

17 Ibid., pp ix-x, 91-95.

18 Ibid., x-xi.

19 Anthony Coon, *Town Planning Under Military Occupation*, Dartmouth Publishing Company, London, 1992 (155-202).

20 For an overview of this system, see Sarah Graham-Brown, "Impact on the Social Structure of Palestinian Society" in Aruri, ed., *Occupation: Israel over Palestine* (second edition), Belmont, Mass. 1989, pp. 361-397.

21 In mid-March, 1991, however, the Israeli Court of Justice rejected an appeal by Israeli farmers to stop Palestinian farm products from 'being smuggled' into the Israeli market. Although the practical significance of this judgement is not yet clear it seems to overturn the de facto control of Arab products into Israel, although restrictions continue to take the form of curtailing water use, land appropriation, and curfews during the harvest seasons. (See *Jerusalem Post*, March 21, 1992, "Court Rejects Quotas for Farmers in the Areas").

22 For a discussion of social aspects of the uprising and its prelude, see Jamal Nassar and Roger Heacok (ed.), *Intifada: Palestine at the Crossroads* (New York: Praeger, 1990); David McDowell, *Palestine and Israel: The Uprising and Beyond* (London: I.B. Tauris, 1989); Naseer Aruri, *Occupation: Israel over Palestine* (Boston: Southend Press, second edition, 1986); Kimmerling, B. and Migdal, J., *Palestinians: The Making of a People* (New York: The Free Press, 1993); Michael Roman and Alex Weingrod, *Living Together Separately: Arabs and Jews in Contemporary Jerusalem* (Princeton: Princeton University Press, 1991).

23 For a discussion of these issues, see my essay "Left in Limbo: Leninist Heritage and Islamic Challenge", in *Middle East Report*, No. 179 (November - December 1992), pp. 16-21.

24 JMCC, *Bitter Harvest: Israeli Sanctions Against Palestinian Agriculture During the Uprising*, Jerusalem, 1989.

25 Palestine Human Rights Information Center (PHRC,Jersualem), *June 1992 Update*, and The Center for Policy Analysis on Palestine, *Facts and Figures on the Palestinians* (Washington), 1992, p. 28.

26 Ibid. These figures do not include the January 16 - February 25, 1991 period when during the Gulf War the entire West Bank and Gaza Strip were closed. According to PHRC these curfews would add up an additional 2,600 days (based on an average of 65 areas covering a population of 300,000 people under curfew for 40 days).

27 PHRC, ibid. The breakdown of demolitions and sealing of houses are as follows: demolished for 'security reasons': 500 units; demolished for lack of building license: 1,319; demolished by settlers 4; sealed buildings for 'security reasons': 370 units.

28 See Anthony Coon, *Town Planning Under Military Occupation, op.7*

29 Coon, Ibid., p. 114-116.cit., pp. 107-154.

Chapter 2
Population Characteristics and Trends

Hasan Abu Libdeh
Geir Øvensen
Helge Brunborg

Geir Øvensen has had the main responsibility for the first part of this chapter. Hasan Abu Libdeh drafted the section about mortality, fertility and population projections, which later on were revised by Helge Brunborg.

Population

Introduction

A country's population is a crucial element in an analysis of living conditions. First, living conditions for various population groups are the very focus of concern for such studies. Second, a country's population is also among its most important resources. It is the skills and knowledge of humans that enable services and welfare in areas like health, housing and education.

One of the main goals of this chapter is to introduce criteria and concepts of importance for the identification of different population groups. Some criteria, like age and gender, are well known and defined. Other criteria, like for example the definitions of "Palestinian" and "UNRWA refugee" are specific for this geographic region and may therefore require further delimitations.

Identification of the composition of the population with regard to geographical distribution, refugee status, age and gender may be considered a pre-requisite both for evaluation of living conditions as well as for public planning and policy implementation. The relevance of different living condition components may vary across region and socio-economic groups. Certain welfare aspects in the occupied territories, like for example the availability of education in Gaza, may be of great importance to young Gazans, but of little relevance to older residents in Arab Jerusalem.

The first part of this chapter consequently deals with the present composition of the population in the occupied territories. The population distribution by region, type of locality, refugee status, age and gender will be discussed, both on a national and on a regional level.

The second part of the chapter deals with one of the most important determinants of future living conditions in the occupied territories, that is the high population growth rate caused by high fertility. There is little reason to doubt that it poses great challenges in terms of future welfare policy. In particular, strains will be put on the ability of the educational system and the labour market to absorb the steadily increasing number of young people wishing to improve their lot.

Who is "Palestinian"?

Who is "Palestinian"? How, and by what criteria, can such an identity be established? The identity issue is central to any discussion of the status and circumstances of the population in the occupied territories. The current survey, which is based on quantitative measurements, has by no means been designed to disentangle or resolve the many difficult and interwoven matters related to the question of national loyalties and affinities in the area. Indeed, such efforts might prove futile even if predominantly qualitative methods were applied. There is, simply put, no consensus on the fundamental issues at hand.

Yet the identity issue cannot be ignored. In order to structure the investigation of living conditions in the occupied territories, it has been necessary to make certain assumptions about identity. These assumptions have been translated into crude operational definitions, using United Nations terms and concepts as reference to the extent possible. First, it has been assumed that although a separate Palestinian state does not exist, thus making it impossible to delineate a Palestinian nationality using citizenship and other formal criteria, a Palestinian national identity nevertheless does exist. Second, it has been thought that while that identity rests on an emotional, political and historical foundation, other and supplementary factors must be utilized when defining the term "Palestinian" for the purposes of the present survey. Hence, to bypass the uncertainties and complexities of the intervening years, the survey has taken residence in the former

British Mandate of Palestine as its point of departure. "Palestinians" will be understood as patrilineal descendants of Moslems, Christians, Druse and other "non-Jewish" citizens who were residents in this area prior to 1947/48.

The assumptions and definitions referred to above are, of course, open to question. Their use in this report do not imply that the authors would rule out other interpretations. As indicated, the present assumptions and definitions serve the purpose of structuring and lending consistency to the ensuing discussion.

Palestinian Population History[1]

Palestinian recent population history can very roughly be divided into three main periods, the two main watersheds being constituted by the 1947-48 and the 1967 wars. After being under Ottoman rule for centuries, Palestine became a British Mandate after the First World War. The pre-1948 Mandate was a traditional, mainly peasant society. Even though a Jewish population segment had lived continuosly in the area, particularly in Jerusalem, the new wave of Zionist immigrants represented a different challenge to traditional Palestinian life and society. Equipped with modern Western technology and organizational skills, the new immigrants gradually achieved a dominant economic position. Increasing amounts of agricultural land were aquired by Zionist organizations and settled by Jewish immigrants. Erosion of the traditional local economy made Palestinians increasingly dependent on the Jewish population for employment and infrastructure. (Most Zionist organizations, however, followed a strategy of employing Jewish workers only).

The 1947-48 war had disastrous consequences for the Palestinian society. The state of Israel was founded on approximately three quarters of the area of the former Mandate of Palestine. During and after the war, four out of five Palestinians in the area that became the state of Israel left the area as refugees[2]. Even if the refugees were scattered around most of the world, the majority continued to live in, or close to, the area of the Mandate.

Until 1967, the "Palestinian" population which continued to live in the area of the former British Mandate was ruled by three separate countries: The Palestinian population in the Negev, the "Triangle" and the Galilee lived under Israeli rule[3]; the population of the West Bank and East Jerusalem lived under Jordanian rule, while the population in the Gaza Strip was ruled by Egypt.

The Israeli occupation of the West Bank and Gaza in 1967 also led to a "reunification" of all Palestinians living in the former British Mandate area, in addition to the displacement of new groups of Palestinians. Their legal status was, however, still significantly different, depending on the area of residence: Palestinians living within the pre-1967 borders of Israel had already been granted Israeli citizenship. Shortly after the occupation in 1967, the borders of East Jerusalem were extended into the West Bank, and the city unilaterally annexed by Israel[4]. The population of Gaza and the West Bank, however, continued to live under military rule.

The Population Covered by the FAFO Survey

The population of the FAFO living conditions survey is defined as "Palestinians" living in the "occupied territories". "Occupied territories" in this connection refers to the areas belonging to the pre-1948 British Mandate of Palestine which were occupied by Israel in 1967, i.e. the Gaza Strip, the West Bank and East Jerusalem.

At this stage it should be emphasized that the FAFO living conditions survey is a sample survey and not a census. Indeed, no census has been taken in the occupied territories since the Israeli census in September 1967. The FAFO survey is thus only able to draw a picture of the relative distribution of population groups and variables. It cannot give separate, exact and absolute numbers for variables like population, labor force, unemployment, etc. Taking into consideration that population figures for the occupied territories, particularly for Gaza, are highly disputed, absolute results in a sample survey like the present FAFO survey will also be vulnerable to precarious estimates of the total population. The total population numbers used for sample design, (i.e. various geographically and socio-economic homogenous groups), stem from the 1987 Benvenisti/ Khayat West Bank and Gaza atlas. It is assumed that the development of the population in the various districts has

Figure 2.1 Distribution of population 15 years or older by region and type of locality

Camps included   Camps excluded

Gaza
West Bank
Arab Jerusalem
Gaza/West Bank camp

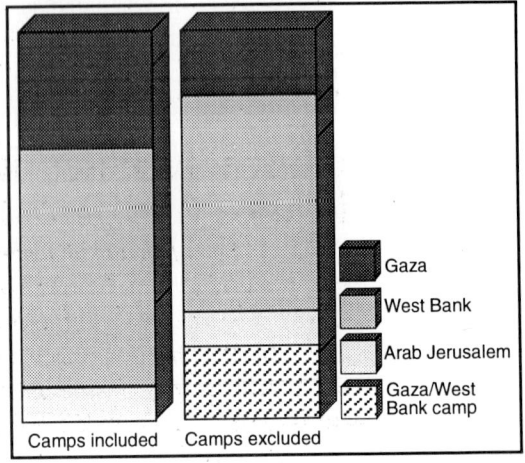

Table 2.1 Head of household's father's birthplace by head of household's present residence

Head of Households present residence	Gaza	West Bank	Arab Jerusalem	Israel	Other Arab country	Total
Gaza	40	-	-	59	1	100
West Bank	-	80	2	17	1	100
Arab Jerusalem	1	18	62	15	4	100
Occupied territories	13	49	7	30	1	100

Head of household's father's birthplace (1992 Geographical areas, all numbers in residence percent of present region of residence

been roughly parallel since 1987. Rough estimates of population growth indicate an average absolute population growth in the occupied territories between 20% and 25% from 1987 to 1992.

Figure 2.1 shows the geographical distribution of the population of individuals over the three main regions covered by the FAFO living condition survey[5].

The dislocation of the Palestinian population since the 1947-48 war has already been discussed above. In table 2.1 the geographical distribution of the households interviewed by the FAFO survey is presented together with the place of birth of the *fathers* of the Head of Households in these households.

In 99% of the households the father of the Household Head was born inside the borders of the pre-1948 British Mandate. A little less than one third of the fathers of the Head of Households were born in the area presently constituting the State of Israel. The table reveals a great difference with regard to local roots between, on the one hand, the West Bank and Arab Jerusalem, and on the other, the Gaza Strip. In the West Bank and Arab Jerusalem the vast majority of the fathers of the Heads of Household were born in the area of present residence. For Household Heads presently residing in Gaza, on the contrary, only two out of five had fathers who were born in the region.

Characteristics of Population in the Occupied Territories[6]

What are the characteristic features of the population composition in the occupied territories? A straightforward answer to this question can hardly be given because the occupied territories, as already stated above (and further documented in the following chapters), comprise three main regions of substantial geographical and socio-economic heterogeneity. This section will give an overview of the three regions with regard to population density, type of locality, age, gender, religious distribution and household composition. The main aim of the section is to introduce and describe regions and socio-economic groups that will be used as references in subsequent chapters.

Population Density

The main demographic feature of the Gaza Strip, physically isolated from the rest of the occupied territories, is a large number of people in a small land area. Gaza comprises less than 6% of the total surface of the occupied territories, but holds 37% of their population. Comprising 93% of the total land area, the West Bank geographically constitutes the bulk of the occupied territories. The West Bank also harbours the majority (55%) of the total population. The last main region covered by the survey, Arab Jerusalem, covers 1% of the area, and 8% of the population[7]. Figure 2.2 shows total and regional 1987 population densities compared to that of Israel.

This figure illustrates the fundamental difference between Gaza and the West Bank with regard to population density. While Arab Jerusalem as a city can be expected to be densely populated, both the Gaza Strip and the West Bank were originally agricultural societies. In spite of an economic transformation through which wage labour gradually has replaced self-subsistence agriculture, large parts of the West Bank still have a rural character. The high population density of the Gaza Strip, on the contrary, has given the area a distinctive urban appearance.

Refugees

As a consequence of the 1948 and (to some extent) 1967 wars, two out of five persons in the occupied territories are UNRWA refugees or descendants of UNRWA refugees. Less than half of the refugees still reside in refugee camps. Refugee camps, which are almost exclusively inhabited by refugees (98%), comprise both "urban" and "rural" camps.

Urban refugee camps are mainly situated around those population

Figure 2.2 Comparative 1987 population density in the occupied territories and Israel

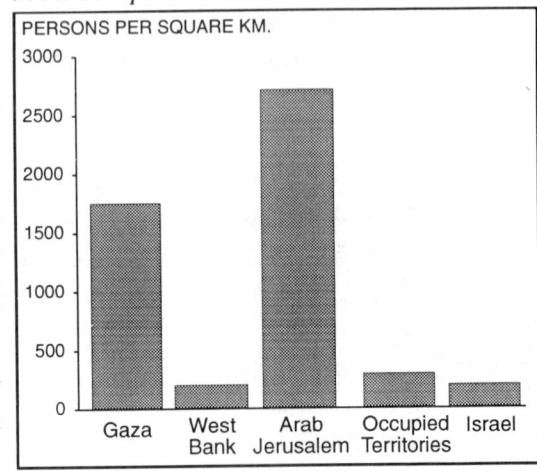

centers which remained under Arab control after the 1947-48 war. Today, most of the urban camps may be characterized as "urban slum areas" due to their physical and socio-economic resemblance to slum areas in other so-called developing countries. Rural refugee camps are situated in rural areas, and offer, in contrast to urban camps, the possibility of some agricultural activity for their inhabitants.

Particularly in Gaza, the population composition was dramatically changed as a result of the 1947-48 war. A huge influx of approximately 200 000 refugees tripled the population in the area that came to be known as the Gaza Strip[8]. The high population density in Gaza is thus to a large extent due to events in 1948. Today, approximately two out of three persons in Gaza are UNRWA refugees. About one out of two refugees live in (mainly urban) refugee camps.

The 1947-48 war had much less dramatic effects for the population composition of the West Bank. Today, one out of four persons in the West Bank is an UNRWA refugee, and more than two out of three refugees live outside camps. In Arab Jerusalem the refugee share is approximately the same as for the occupied territories in total[9]. Figure 2.3 show the distribution of the total population in the occupied territories according to refugee status.

Type of Locality

In contrast to most developing countries, the occupied territories are marked by a very high degree of urbanization. In total three out of five persons live in urban localities. Largely due to the massive influx of refugees in 1948, four out of five persons in the Gaza Strip live in urban areas. In the West Bank only two out of five persons live in such urban areas.

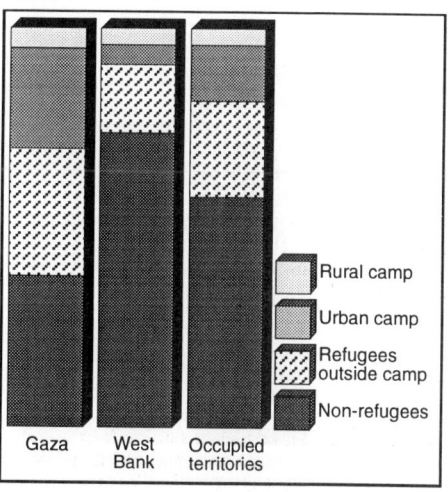

Figure 2.3 Distribution of population by refugee status

Greater Gaza City is, by far, the largest urban area in the occupied territories. Greater Arab Jerusalem (Arab Jerusalem and its West Bank suburbs) is the major urban conglomeration in the eastern part of the occupied territories, but comes out only second to Greater Gaza City in population[10]. Perhaps surprising to some observers, the third largest urban area in the occupied territories is constituted by the towns of Khan Younis and Rafah and adjacent camps, while Nablus, the most populous area in the West Bank proper, comes out fourth.

In Gaza the middle region is the only area which still has a distinct rural appearance. For many so-called "villages" both in Gaza and Arab Jerusalem the label "village" has more historical than contemporary socio-economic relevance. Most of these "villages" (e.g. Silwan and Jabaliya) are in reality urban areas, and have consequently been classified as such.

As opposed to Gaza and Arab Jerusalem the West Bank still contains a large rural population. Three out of five persons live in more than 400 villages and rural refugee camps. Small distances and relatively good communications, however, normally enable most of the rural population to reach larger towns within a few hours.

More than half of the population in Gaza lives around Greater Gaza City in the northern part of the Strip. With more than 5000 persons per km^2, this area has the highest population density in all of the occupied territories. The southern part of the Strip, comprising the towns of Khan Younis and Rafah, harbour approximately one third of the Gaza population.

In the West Bank, too, more than half of the population resides in the northern part (Tulkarem, Jenin and Nablus sub-districts). The central part of the West Bank (Jericho, Ramallah and Bethlehem sub-districts) encircles Arab Jerusalem and comprises one fourth of the population. Somewhat less populated, Hebron sub-district constitutes the southern part of the West Bank.

Figure 2.4 Distribution of population in Gaza and the West Bank by sub-region and type of locality

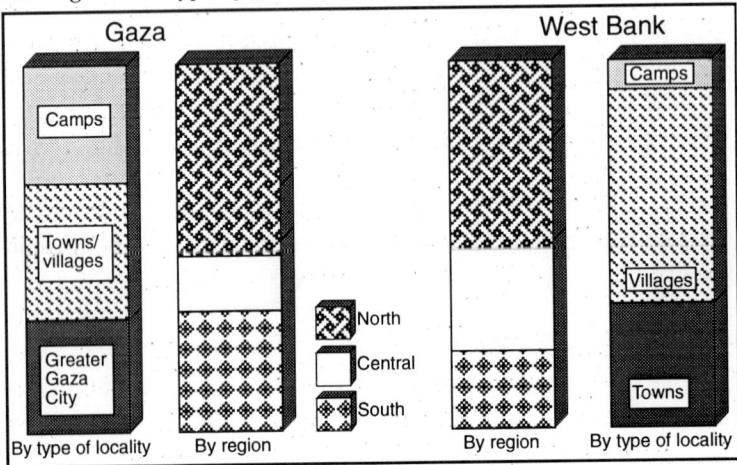

In the present study the Gaza Strip was subdivided into Greater Gaza City (excluding refugee camps), other towns/ villages, and refugee camps. Easier access to the Israeli labor market for the inhabitants of Greater Gaza City, and the particular services provided by UNRWA for the population living in refugee camps, were among the considerations that prompted this classification. In the West Bank localities were grouped into towns, villages and refugee camps. Figure 2.4 show the distribution of the population in Gaza and the West Bank by type of locality and sub-region.

Since 1948 intra-regional migration in the occupied territories has generally been small. Prior to 1967 migration was limited because Gaza, on the one hand, and the West Bank and East Jerusalem on the other, were ruled by Egypt and Jordan respectively. After the "reunification" through Israeli occupation in 1967, new restrictions on regional Palestinian population movements were introduced.

In particular, Palestinian settlement in Arab Jerusalem has been constrained by Israeli restrictions on immigration and building permissions, leading to widespread "illegal" immigration. Even if the Palestinian population of Arab Jerusalem has doubled since 1967, its growth has still been lower than that of other Middle Eastern capital cities. The lack of housing in Arab Jerusalem has stimulated both "illegal" construction as well as out-migration of young Arab Jerusalem families to neighbouring West Bank towns and villages.

Religious Affiliation

The population in the occupied territories is almost exclusively Moslem (96%)[11]. In Gaza the share of Moslems even reaches 99.8%, making Gaza one of the most compact Moslem areas in all of the Middle East. More than 90% of the Christians live in Arab Jerusalem and the Bethlehem and Ramallah sub-districts of the West Bank. Still, they constitute only 15% of the total population in Arab Jerusalem and 11% of the total population in Bethlehem and Ramallah[12]. The Christian population share in the occupied territories is steadily decreasing, partially due to high emigration rates, and partially because of substantially lower birth rates than among the Moslem majority[13].

Age and Gender[14] [15]

In contrast to population factors unique to the occupied territories, such as types of locality and internal migration, the age distribution of the population in the occupied territories shows great similarities with that of other Arab countries.

Figures 2.5a-c shows population pyramids which illustrate the distribution of the respective populations by five year age groups and gender, men to the left-hand side and women to the right. Comparison of results for separate five year age groups must be made with care due to the small sample size, in particular on the regional level. These

Figure 2.5a Distribution of population in Gaza, in five-year age groups by gender

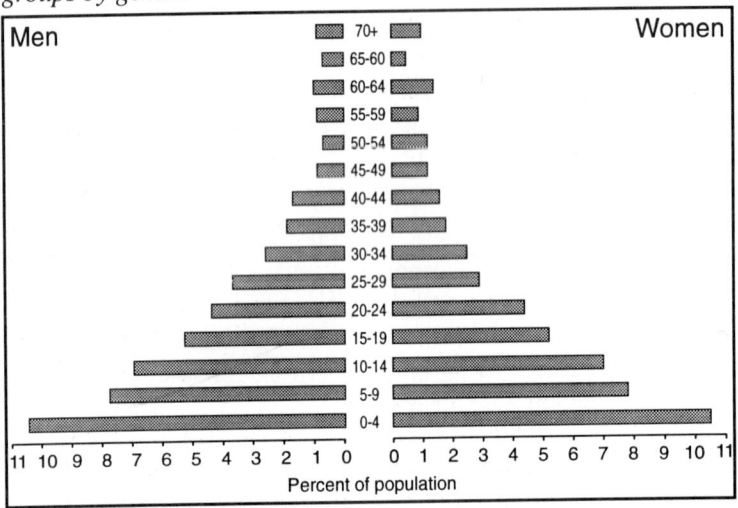

Figure 2.5b Distribution of population in the West Bank, in 5-year age groups by gender

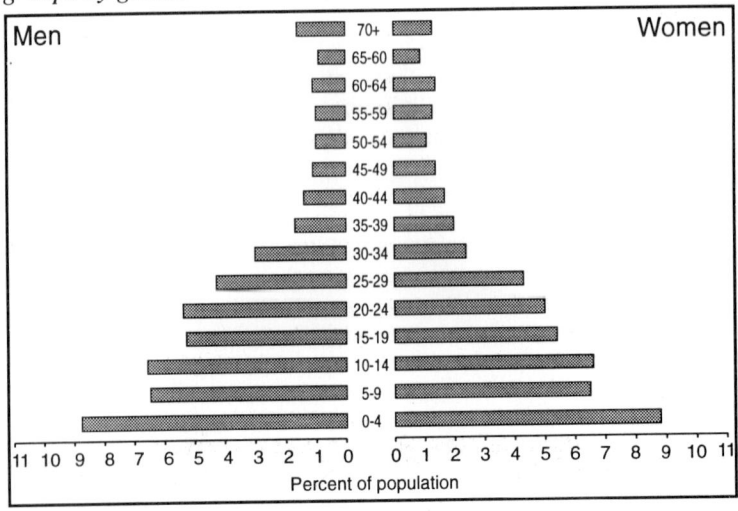

44

regional pyramids can be compared to the overall age-sex distribution for the sample population, see figure 2.11.

The overall gender distribution for Palestinians, *15 years or older,* living in the occupied territories is almost exactly 50% male/female. There is a tendency of male over-representation in age groups 20-34 years, while there is an over-representation of females in the age groups 40-65 years. A possible explanation for the last result is an over-representation of males in labour related emigration during the seventies. Somewhat surprising is the fact that there is a weak male, rather than female, over- representation in the two oldest age groups. Note, however, that the sample size is small.

The survey contains no information on the gender of children younger than 15 years. Assuming an approximately even number of female and male births, distribution on sex for these three five-year age intervals has simply been set to 1/2 male and 1/2 female.

The young age structure of the population in the occupied territories is striking, but not particularly different from other Middle East countries. 46% of the population is aged 14 years or younger, 18% is aged 4 years or younger. In contrast to the distribution on gender, total results for the age distribution in the occupied territories disguise substantial regional differences.

Gaza is the region with the youngest population. 51% of the population is 14 years or younger. As much as 21% of all Gazans are 4 years or younger. At the other end of the scale is Arab Jerusalem, with

Figure 2.5c Distribution of population in Arab Jerusalem, in 5-year age groups by gender

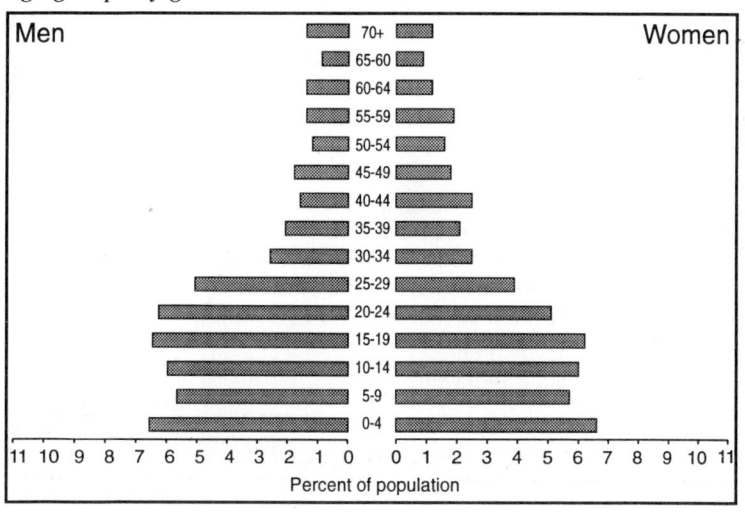

"only" 37% aged 14 years or younger and 13% aged 4 years or younger. The West Bank is the area with a relative age distribution most similar to that of the occupied territories in total. Note, however, that this result to some extent follows automatically because of the West Bank's large share of the total population in the occupied territories (60%). The "low" share of children below 5 years of age in Arab Jerusalem may partially be due to emigration of families with small children from Arab Jerusalem to the West Bank.

Composition of Households[16]

What is the average size of households in the occupied territories? The 1992 FAFO survey estimates an average number of 7.5 persons per household in the occupied territories. The corresponding 1990 numbers for Israeli Jews and "non-Jews" were 3.4 and 5.6 respectively[17].

Gaza has an average of nearly 9 persons per household, while the numbers for the West Bank and Arab Jerusalem are 7 and less than 6 respectively. The average total number of persons per household has also been broken down to average numbers for men, women and children (persons 14 years or younger). While regional variations between the average numbers of adult men and women are relatively small, the average number of children varies substantially by region. Arab Jerusalem on average has 0.58 children per adult household member, the ratio in Gaza is 1.02, i.e. almost twice as high[18]. Figure 2.6 illustrates these findings.

Within Gaza, Greater Gaza City has the highest average number of children per adult household member. In the West Bank variations by sub-region and locality are small, except for a higher average number of children per adult in the southern part.

Figure 2.7 shows household composition by refugee status. For the occupied territories in total camp refugees seem to have a higher average number of persons per household than other groups. This result is, however, due to the high proportion of camp refugees living in Gaza, which generally comprise large households. In both Gaza and the

Figure 2.6 Household composition by region and type of locality

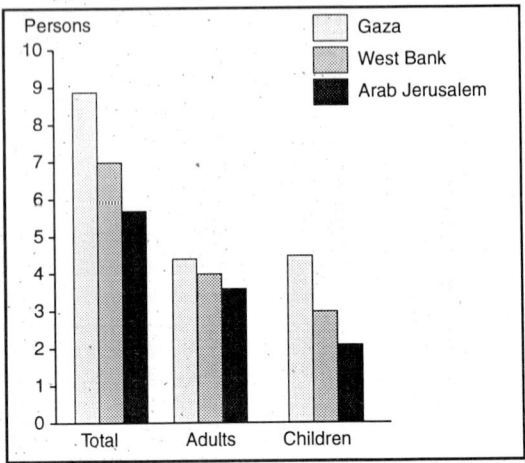

West Bank variations by refugee status are smaller than the general regional variation.

Contrary to the notions of many, both Gaza and West Bank refugee households have a lower average total number of members than do non-refugee households. In the Gaza Strip, households in camps actually have a lower average total number of members than both non-refugee households and refugee households outside camps.

With regard to religious affiliation, Moslem households have on average more members than Christian households (7.6 and 4.7 respectively). In particular, the average number of children is higher in Moslem households (3.5), than in Christian households (1.5). The average number of children in Christian households is the lowest among all socio-economic groups analyzed in this section. However, the number of observations here is low, and estimates should be interpreted with caution.

Household composition also varies systematically with the Head of Household's age. Average household size is smallest for young and old Household Heads, and greatest for middle-aged Heads of Households. As can be seen from Figure 2.8, this observation is valid both for the occupied territories taken as a whole and for each of the three main regions. For all Head of Household age groups Gaza has the highest, and Arab Jerusalem the lowest average number of household members.

The variations in household composition with regard to the Head of Household's age can, of course, be explained by the usual life cycles of the household members. Figure 2.9 illustrates this point by showing the average number of adult males, females, and children for households in the occupied territories according to the age of the Head of Household.

Figure 2.7 Household composition by refugee status

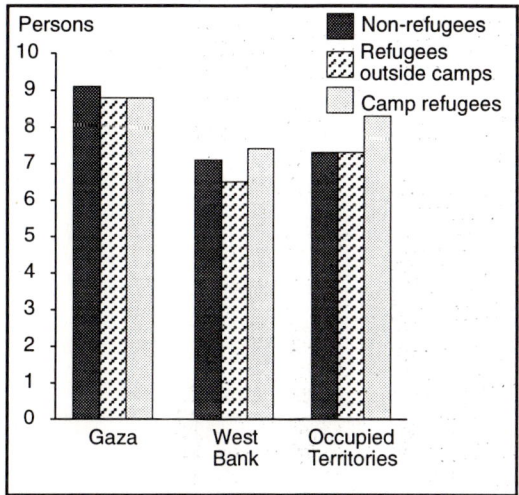

The typical household composition in the youngest Head of Household age group is one of few adults and few children, i.e. a group dominated by young couples with only one or two children. In the next Head of Household age group, the average number of children increases sharply, while the average numbers of adult males and females are stable. This group is likely to be dominated by single couples with an increasing number of own children.

For the two next Head of Household age groups, the average number of children decreases markedly while the average number of adults shows a moderate increase. More and more children are growing older than 15 years of age, and are consequently being counted as adults. Sons may also marry, and their wives move in, hence a number of daughters-in-law are included among adult household members. Even more sons, however, move out to form households on their own.

Head of Household demographics[19]

The Head of Household has the final decision-making authority in family matters[20]. In 96% of the households, the Household Head was the oldest male. In 80% of the households the Head of Household was also the oldest person. To what extent is the status as Head of Household tied to labour activity? The household economy chapter (chapter 6) shows that 28% of the Household Heads have either not worked at all, or worked less than one month the last year prior to the survey. It thus seems that in most cases, age and sex are the main factors that make a person Head of Household, rather than, i.a., income.

Figure 2.8 Total number of persons in households by age of Head of Household

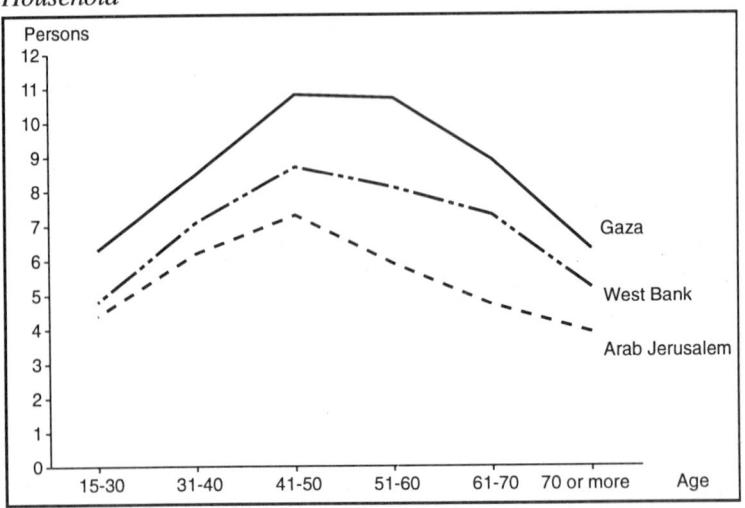

Infant and Child Mortality

The rest of this chapter is more technical than the others. Some readers may therefore prefer to go directly to the concluding sections.

Introduction

Infant and child mortality rates (IMR and CMR) can be interpreted as measures of the well-being of children in any country. Usually, the values of these rates reflect the levels of health and socio-economic status of the population they are used to describe. These two measures of mortality are watched closely world-wide by policy-makers and national program managers. As indicators of general health status, health and children organizations such as WHO and UNICEF have introduced programmes in different countries to reduce these rates at various points in time.

Since 1967, nationwide health surveys have rarely been conducted in the occupied territories. The Israeli-controlled Palestinian health

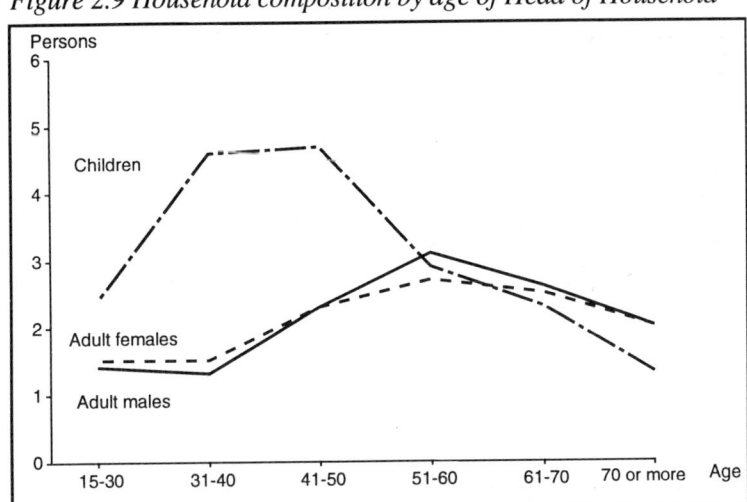

Figure 2.9 Household composition by age of Head of Household

sector suffers from lack of estimates of important health indicators. Infant mortality estimates vary greatly depending on the source providing these estimates. While some Palestinian professionals claim that IMR exceeds 70 deaths in 1000 live births, the Israeli authorities claim that this rate is in the lower twenties.

The Israeli Ministry of Health (IMOH) publishes annual figures for registered infant deaths per registered live births. However, the rate of non-reporting of infant deaths and births is not known. UNRWA similarly publishes registered infant births and deaths. Table 2.2[21] shows the official reported infant mortality rates (IMR) (1970-1990), indicating a steady decline since 1970. The rates for the West Bank exclude Arab Jerusalem.

Indirect demographic methods have been used by different researchers to estimate IMR in small non-representative localities of the occupied territories (table 2.3). In addition, Vermund et al. (1985) have analyzed official records of infant deaths to estimate under-reporting and produced a further estimate of infant mortality rates. Using official records and applying a demographic model, Vermund et al. (1985) have estimated an IMR for 1982 of 53-63 for the West Bank and 53-56 for the Gaza Strip.

At the national level, the only recent estimate of IMR for the total population in the occupied territories is the one obtained through a multi-stage clustered sample survey carried out by UNICEF and the Jerusalem Family Planning and Protection Association (JFPPA) in the winter of 1991 and 1992 (Abu-Libdeh et al. 1992). Estimates of the probability of dying before exact age 1, between ages 1 and 4 and before exact age 5 for the total population, West Bank, Gaza Strip, Urban, Rural, Refugee Camps, North West Bank, Middle West Bank, and South West Bank were provided for both sexes combined and for each sex alone. According to the results of this survey, IMR for 1988 is estimated at 41 and U5MR is estimated at 55 deaths per one thousand live births.

FALCOT 92 has included a standard module questionnaire for indirect estimation of IMR and U5MR using the Brass (1964) methods and their variants (1983). In this section, we derive an estimate of IMR and U5MR using two approaches. In the first approach, we use data on children

Table 2.2 Official Israeli reported infant mortality rates for the occupied territories, selected years

	Reported Infant Mortality Rates[23]	
	West Bank	Gaza Strip
1970	--	86.0
1975	38.1	69.3
1980	28.3	43.0
1985	25.1	33.4
1990	22.0	26.1

ever born (CEB) and children surviving (CS) classified by 5-year age groups of their mothers (15-19 years through 45-49 years). In the second approach, we use data on children ever born (CEB) and children surviving (CS), classified by 5-year duration of marriage groups of their mothers (0-4 years through 30-34 years). Due to the sensitivity of estimators to sampling and non-sampling errors, we start subsection 2 by pointing out some limitations of the data set. In subsection 3 we investigate the quality of data used for estimation. Data quality assessment is necessary to make sure that our estimates are seen in the proper context. We then proceed in subsection 4 to estimate $q(1)$ and $q(5)$ and highlight their trends during the last decade. In subsection 5, we compare the results obtained with those of UNICEF and JFPPA (Abu-libdeh et. al. 1992) and of neighbouring countries.

Data Limitations

The FALCOT 92 was not meant to be a study of childhood mortality rates for this population. Therefore, possible shortcomings of the data set should be evaluated with this in mind. The limitations we are about to present force us to review the results on childhood mortality as rough estimates rather than well established unbiased estimates:

Sample Size Limitations

The sample size needed to estimate the probability of dying before exact age 1, $q(1)$, or the probability of dying before exact age 5, $q(5)$, should ideally have been many times larger than the one actually obtained. Furthermore, the current sample size (1223 females) does not permit elaborate analysis on the regional level, nor does it provide for serious analysis by factors such as gender or level of education. (See also this book's Appendix A on sampling strategy).

Table 2.3 Results of some local studies of infant mortality using indirect methods

	Sample Size of Ever Married Women	IMR	Year	Reference
3 villages in Ramallah area	272	91	1981	Giacaman(1989)
Biddu village, Ramallah area	311	49	1986	UPMRC/BZUCHU (1987)
20 villages in Hebron area	380	97	1988	Shahin et al.(1989)
Khan Younis	--	70	1982	Dahlan(1987)
Beach Camp and Ash-Shajaiyeh	--	32	1982	Scott(1989)

Questionnaire Limitations

Some important questions relating to data collection on children ever born and children dead were missed during questionnaire development. In particular, no questions were asked concerning the status of the last birth, such as date of birth, sex, and whether the child was still alive by the time of interview. Moreover, no questions were asked to allow estimation using birth history or life table methods. The questions missing on the status of last birth will mostly affect fertility calculations.

Parity limitations

For the purpose of parity calculations and analyses, all ever married women of child-bearing age (15-49 years) in each household should have been interviewed for the purpose of inclusion in the childhood mortality and fertility analysis. The exclusion of ever married women (of unknown quantity) from interviewing for this section makes it very difficult to estimate average parities in the manner recommended by demographers.

Data Quality

In the preparatory stage for the FALCOT 92 and during its implementation, every effort was made to ensure strict adherence to the methodology developed and the field protocol designed. However, classic problems may arise in any survey regardless of the control procedures used. The quality of data collected is usually determined by the extent of control on measurement errors (non-sampling errors) as long as the proper methodology is used to insure minimal amount of sampling errors which are uncontrollable. Having made every effort to control non-sampling errors and assuming that the questionnaire is carefully designed and pretested, it is only natural to expect to get a data set of fairly good quality. However, response and field worker bias may result in low quality data. As for the FALCOT 92, the general assessment of data quality is not the subject of this section. However, due to the sensitivity of the parameters we are trying to estimate and the procedures used, we present here a brief investigation of the quality of those variables entering estimates of childhood mortality and fertility. The overall quality of these variables will be assessed by evaluating age structures, average parities, sex ratios of CEB and proportion of dead children.

Age Structure

The data set represents the responses of 1223 females between 15 and 85 years of age at the time of field work. For the purpose of analysis for this and the next section, only 995 (81.4%) female respondents of child-bearing age will be used in the analysis based on data by age groups. Only 665 (54.4%) ever married women (EMW) respondents who reported having a marriage duration of 34 years or less will be used in the analysis using data classified by duration of marriage.

Table 2.4 shows the age structure of qualified females for analysis. The breakdown of the age structure of all females of child bearing age using 5-year categories is almost similar to the overall age structure of females in the same age interval which is compiled from the listing of ages of all household members. The only exception is the share of females in the age groups 20-24 and 25-29. While the first age group is under-represented, the second is over-represented. Assuming that the overall age structure is accurate, this slight misrepresentation may be viewed as an indicator of selection bias during randomization or during field work. The over- (under-) representation in these two age groups will have direct impact on the estimates of IMR and U5MR due to the fact that the average parities of these two age groups will be extensively used in calculations.

Age Reporting

Age misreporting, in particular digit preference for ages ending in 0 or 5, is common in censuses and sample surveys in most developing countries. This is also evident in the FAFO survey. An indicator of the degree of age heaping is the Whipple's Index,

Table 2.4 Age structure of qualified females for child mortality estimation

Age Group	# all Females	Percent	# of EMW	Percent	% EMW of All
15-19	258	25.9	44	7.1	17.1
20-24	184	18.5	134	21.5	72.8
25-29	179	18.0	124	19.9	69.3
30-34	128	12.9	105	16.8	82.0
35-39	90	9.1	75	12.1	83.3
40-44	84	8.4	76	12.1	90.5
45-49	72	7.2	67	10.7	93.1

which ranges from 100 when there is no preference for 0 and 5 and up to 500, when only ages ending in 0 and 5 are reported (Newell 1988: 24). The Whipple's Index for the age range 15-49 in the FAFO survey is 141, which indicates a high but not severe case of digit preference. United Nations describes data with an Index of this magnitude as "rough" (Newell 1988: 25).

There is also a clear case of age misreporting at age 16, with more than twice as many respondents (98) at age 16 as in ages 15 (44) and 16 (45). Over-sampling at other ages seems to have happened to a lesser extent (ages 32, 42 and 48).

Age misreporting may result in a slight bias in parity calculations since the heaping usually occurs at the start of age groups. However, since age heaping seems to have occurred in all categories, we expect the net effect to be negligible. Had field workers been instructed to verify ages from official documents, the effect of this phenomenon could have been reduced.

The data on age at first marriage does not appear to be positively skewed in the smooth manner that it should be. Calculations indicate possible over-sampling of ever married women or age heaping by those sampled in reporting their age at first marriage. The age heaping is very clear at ages ending with 0 or 5. Other ages suspected of heaping or over-sampling are 32, 42, and 48, as is also found in the age reporting of all females.

Sex Ratios and Proportion Dead

An acceptable sex ratio of male (MCEB) to female children ever born (FCEB) usually falls between 1.02 and 1.07. Sex ratios

Table 2.5 Sex ratios of children ever born, dead children and proportion of dead children by age of mother at the time of interview

Age Group	Sex Ratio at Birth (MCEB/FCEB)	Sex Ratio of Dead Children	Proportion of Dead Children (# DEAD/# FEMALES)
15-19	0.82	----	0.0104
20-24	1.02	0.40	0.0512
25-29	1.48	1.06	0.0497
30-34	1.27	0.83	0.0656
35-39	0.86	0.38	0.0921
40-44	1.10	1.55	0.1109
45-49	1.07	1.11	0.1499
Total	1.12	0.92	0.0914

falling outside this interval may indicate errors in sampling or under-reporting of births of one sex – many of these probably died at an early age. The official reports of the Israeli CBS for the occupied territories indicates that the sex ratio at birth is approximately 1.5 for 1991 (ICBS, 1992). The overall sex ratio for CEB in the data set used here is 1.12. This slight deviation is not serious enough to raise concern about the quality of the data. The age-specific sex ratios and proportion dead by age category are presented in table 2.5.

The sex ratios of the table may indicate the existence of under-reporting of female births, but could also stem from sampling error. This would probably be due to ommissions on the part of mothers giving female births who later (in a matter of days or weeks) have died. On the other hand, the sex ratio of dead children could indicate the existence of a severe case of under-reporting of dead males in three age groups. The abnormality of the sex ratios for both births and deaths casts some doubt on the quality of the data set. These abnormalities will directly affect our estimates of childhood mortality, and pave the way for an over- estimation of female infant mortality and under-estimation of male infant mortality. As for the proportion of dead children, we notice a drop in this proportion for the 25-29 age group. Moreover, this indicator does not increase normally for the first three age groups, as opposed to the last three age groups. Both the drop in the proportion of dead children and the slow increase for the three categories are indicators of problems with the data quality.

Average Parity

Questions relating to children ever born were put to all ever married women, EMW. From the investigation of the data it turns out that no EMW were classified as having missing parity. Moreover, 72 (10.8%) EMW were classified as having had no children (zero parity). Most of these are relatively newly wed females. Average parity that systematically increases with the age of the woman with no sharp jumps, is a sign of acceptable data quality. The average parity is calculated by dividing the number of births by the total number of female respondents in each age group, see table 2.11 in the fertility section.

Conclusion

Every measure we have used for checking the data quality has showed us a problem of some sort, the most serious being related to sex ratios. Our conclusion is that the available data – although suitable for many other analytical purposes – maybe are not good enough to produce reliable estimates of parameters of childhood mortality and fertility. Therefore, all estimates and analyses should be treated with caution.

Childhood Mortality Estimation

The infant mortality rate $q(1)$ and under five mortality rate $q(5)$ represent probabilities of dying before exact ages 1 and 5 years ,respectively. Several indirect methods of measuring $q(1)$ and $q(5)$ have been suggested in the literature (UN, 1983). The data at our disposal do not permit the use of methods such as the preceding birth (PB) and life table methods. However, the Brass (1964) method and its variants are applicable in our case. We will arrive at estimates of $q(1)$ and $q(5)$ using two approaches. The first approach uses data on CEB and CS classified by age of mother. The second approach uses data on CEB and CS classified by duration of marriage. Once estimates are obtained, they will be compared with estimates of OT, made by UNICEF and JFPPA, and of neighbouring countries.

Preliminaries

The results of this section should be read bearing the following considerations in mind:

a When estimating mortality levels we need a so-called mortality model. We have chosen the West model life table (Coale and Demeny 1983) because it has been shown by the UNICEF and JFPPA regional office to fit Middle East populations reasonably well. Moreover, in the absence of literature on mortality trends in the region, the West model, being an average model based on a large number of empirical life tables, is a primary choice.

b The methods being used to estimate $q(1)$ and $q(5)$ usually produce better results for $q(5)$ than for $q(1)$. Hence, one should always treat estimates of $q(1)$ with caution.

c Estimates of $q(x)$, $x=1,5$, based on the first and to some extent the second age groups (or duration groups), are normally discarded on account of their instability.

d In the case of this data set, a single estimate of $q(x)$, $x=1,5$, will be produced by calculating the weighted average of $q(x)$ for the second and the third groups with weights being the proportion of CEB in each group.

e Trends of q(x), x=1,2, will be presented in common indices to facilitate comparisons.

f The data are weighted and the effect of weighing can be seen from the CEB values since they are given with decimals and not as integers.

Estimates Using Data Classified by Age Group of Mothers

Table 2.6 presents input data for analysis. Disregarding gender, the above table shows that 9%1 of reported CEB have survived by the time of field work. Using data of the above table and the methodology described in UN (1983), the calculated mean age at child-bearing is 26.35 years for both sexes, 27.91 years females, and 25.84 years for males.

Further calculations show that the probability of dying before age x is almost identical for the two standard alternative procedures (Palloni-Heligman, Trussel). The only slight difference is in the estimated reference dates. However, the differences between the reference dates are not of a large magnitude. For trend assessment, estimates of q(1) and q(5) can be converted to common indices as shown in table 2.7 together with life expectancy at birth, e_0.

Inspection of the estimates of q(1) and q(5) shows a clear mortality decline during the last 15 years. The high estimate of q(x) for May 1990 is expected since it is based on an age group (20-24) where many

Table 2.6 Number of children ever born and children surviving by age group of mothers and sex of children

Age Group	Number of responde	Children Ever Born (CEB)			Children Surviving (SC)		
		Both	Males	Females	Both	Males	Females
15-19	258	34.46	15.53	18.93	34.10	15.17	18.93
20-24	184	232.77	117.67	115.10	220.86	114.28	106.58
25-29	179	459.26	273.76	185.50	436.42	185.50	174.42
30-34	128	624.08	349.19	274.89	583.15	330.63	252.52
35-39	90	500.60	231.50	269.10	454.49	218.71	235.78
40-44	84	520.84	272.49	248.35	463.08	237.42	225.78
45-49	72	629.96	325.29	304.67	535.53	275.57	259.96
Total	995	3001.97	1585.43	1416.54	2727.63	1453.78	1273.85

women marry and have their first child, there is usually a surplus mortality for first births.

Life expectancy at birth is calculated using values of q(1), which explains the upward trend in life expectancy.

To get a single estimate for q(1), q(5) and e0, we use the weighted average of the estimates of each parameters for age groups 20-24 and 25-29. The weights suggested here are the proportion of CEB in each age group (0.336 for 20-24 and 0.664 for 25-29). This is done to avoid discarding the mortality experience for the 20-24 age group altogether, and to obtain estimates that are fairly recent.

Our estimate of q(1) is 43 deaths per one thousand live births for both the Palloni-Heligman and Trussell approaches. The Palloni-Heligman estimate refers to February 1989 and the Trussell's estimate refers to December 1988, both of which in practice refer to the same time period. The estimate of q(5) for the same reference dates is 56 deaths per one thousand live births. The two procedures also give very similar estimates of q(1) and q(5) for each sex.

We have also estimated child mortality using children ever born and children surviving by *duration of marriage* of mothers, using Trussell's procedure, see table 2.8.

Generally, estimates of q(x) based on data by duration of marriage are expected to be more reliable than those derived from data by age of mother, due to a higher accuracy in reporting age at first marriage (being a memorable experience). However, for this data set, the sample size is not large enough to permit reliable estimation. Therefore, since we are looking for trends in IMR and U5MR rather than specific point estimates, both approaches show a decline in q(1) and

Table 2.7 Estimates of probability of dying by exact age 1 and 5 and life expectancy at birth (in common indices) using two different versions

Age of woman	United Nations Models (Palloni-Heligman) General model				Coale-Demeny Models (Trussel) West model			
	Reference date	q(1)	q(5)	e(0)	Reference date	q(1)	q(5)	e(0)
15-19	May 1991	.024	.029	75.0	Oct 1991	.018	.021	73.1
20-24	May 1990	.048	.062	67.1	May 1990	.048	.063	65.0
25-29	Jul 1988	.041	.053	69.0	Mar 1988	.041	.053	66.7
30-34	Jan 1986	.050	.066	66.5	Jul 1985	.049	.064	64.8
35-39	Jan 1983	.063	.086	62.7	Aug 1982	.062	.089	61.9
40-44	Oct 1979	.069	.096	61.2	Jul 1979	.068	.094	60.5
45-49	Mar 1976	.083	.120	57.3	Jul 1976	.082	.121	57.5

q(5) during the last fifteen years, but the decline based on the age-of-mother data is more systematic. Moreover, the decline in q(1) and q(5) resulting from the age group method agree quite well with that reported by UNICEF and JFPPA for the same period. Based on these arguments, we recommend adopting the q(x) values based on data by age of mother.

Regional Comparison

Although the infant and child mortality rates are falling, they are still relatively high. In general q(x) also varies by gender and region of the occupied territories (Abu-libdeh et.al 1992). For example, in both the UNICEF and FALCOT 92 studies, girls seem to be at a higher risk of dying before ages 1 or 5 than boys are. This indicates that boys are

Table 2.8 Estimates of probability of dying by exact age x, 1 and 5 and life expectancy at birth, Trussell version

Duration of marriage	Age x	Reference date	q(x)	q(1)	q(5)	e(0)
0-5	2	Mar 1991	.020	.019	.022	72.9
5-10	3	Apr 1989	.080	.064	.087	61.5
10-15	5	Mar 1987	.066	.050	.066	64.6
15-20	10	Jan 1985	.079	.055	.073	63.6
20-25	15	Sep 1982	.096	.061	.083	62.1
25-30	20	Dec 1979	.098	.057	.077	63.0
30-35	25	Jan 1977	.203	.101	.146	53.7

TRUSSELL Version WEST Model Life Table — Converted probabilities Common Indices

Table 2.9 Comparisons of estimates of probability of dying by exact age 1 and 5 for FALCOT 92, UNICEF and JFPPA and Israeli reported figures for West Bank

Age of woman	FAFO Living Condition Survey (June-July 1992) Reference date	q(1)	q(5)	UNICEF IMR Survey (Nov. 1991-Feb. 1992) Reference date	q(1)	q(5)	Israeli reported IMR Reference date	q(1)
15-19	Oct 1991	.018	.021	Jan 1991	.034	.041	1989	.0194
20-24	May 1990	.048	.063	Oct 1989	.045	.057	1988	.0208
25-29	Mar 1988	.041	.053	Jan 1988	.039	.048	1987	.0224
30-34	Jul 1985	.049	.064	Jan 1986	.047	.061	1985	.0270
35-39	Aug 1982	.062	.089	Nov 1983	.054	.072	1982	.0256
40-44	Jul 1979	.068	.094	May 1981	.059	.080	1979	.0263
45-49	Jul 1976	.082	.121	May 1978	.074	.103	1976	.0279

treated better than girls, as mortality is normally higher for boys than for girls, although the reverse is found in some developing countries. Moreover, the UNICEF results indicate that mortality estimates for West Bank are consistently higher than those for the Gaza Strip. Within the West Bank, q(x) is the highest in the southern region and in rural areas. Looking at patterns of decline in q(1) and q(5), table 2.9 presents point estimates obtained from the FALCOT 92, UNICEF and JFPPA surveys and official Israeli reported q(1) for West Bank excluding Arab Jerusalem.

As can be seen from the table, the decline of q(x) is more systematic for the UNICEF and JFPPA than for the FAFO estimates. The reflections of the estimates of q(x) on the well-being of the Palestinian population in the occupied territories is emphasized by comparison with neighbouring countries. Table 2.10 presents trends in q(x) for FALCOT 92 as compared to that of Jordan (UNICEF 1990), Syria (UNICEF 1988), Israeli Jews of Israel and Palestinian Arabs in Israel (ICBS, selected years).

Recently published estimates for Jordan 1990 are 36.4 and 37.3 for q(1) and 42.2 and 42.7 for boys and girls, respectively (Zou'bi, Poedjastoeti and Ayad 1992).

We see (table 2.10) that the FAFO estimates for the occupied territories fall between the mortality rates for Jordan and Syria. On the other hand, they are considerably higher than the Israeli estimates for the occupied territories. Moreover, but not surprisingly, they are fully 5-6 times higher than the infant and child mortality rates for the Jewish population in Israel.

Table 2.10 Comparisons of estimates of probability of dying by exact age 1 and 5 for FALCOT 92, Jordan, Syria, and Israel. Deaths per 100 births

FAFO (1992)			Jordan (1990)			Syria (1988)23			Israel			
										Jews	Arab
Year	q(1)	q(5)	Year	q(1)	q(5)	Year	q(1)	q(5)	Year	q(1)	q(1)
1990	48	63	1988	40	50	1986	55	73	1990	7.8	15.4
1988	41	53	1987	34	42	1984	50	65	1988	8.4	16.4
1985	49	64	1986	37	46	1982	41	51	1987	9.0	17.1
1982	62	89	1984	43	54	1980	62	84	1982	11.8	22.5
1979	68	94	1981	57	75	1977	63	85			
1976	82	121	1978	56	74	1975	67	92	1977	15.0	31.1

Concluding Remarks

The Brass methods of estimating $q(x)$ are known to provide lower boundaries of parameter estimates only. Further, an average age at marriage exceeding 19 years invites us to attach less weight to estimates of $q(x)$, $x=1,5$, using the second age group (20-24). Although we have used weighted averages to arrive at univariate estimates of $q(1)$ and $q(5)$, we tend to believe that a more realistic lower bound for $q(x)$ should be taken from the age group 25-29.

In this section we have presented indirect estimates of infant and under five mortality rates. The rates are at the same level as in neighbouring countries, but are, however, much lower than for the Jewish population in Israel. Childhood mortality in the occupied territories seems to have been declining rapidly in the last 15 years. The decline is not expected to continue as fast in the future since health-related improvements become harder to achieve after they reach a certain level.

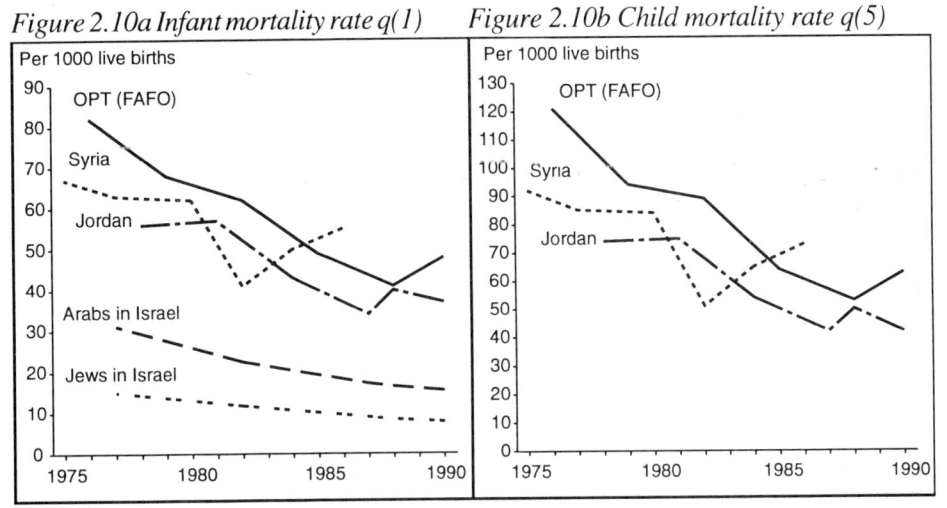

Figure 2.10a Infant mortality rate q(1)

Figure 2.10b Child mortality rate q(5)

Fertility

Introduction

The Palestinian population in the occupied territories is characterized by a very high birth rate. The Israeli CBS (1992) reports a birth rate of 46.5 per 1000 population for the West Bank and 56.1 for the Gaza Strip during 1991.[24] Moreover, the FALCOT 92 results on age structure show that more than 45% of the population is younger than 15 years of age. The pattern of annual births reported by ICBS for the years 1968-1991 shows no specific decline in the birth rate during the 1970s and early 1980s. It suggests, on the other hand, a rising birth rate since the outbreak of Intifada. As for the total fertility rate (TFR), Israeli published results show a rise in the TFR during the 1970s and a pattern of decline later on (ICBS, 1987). These estimates are provided for the period 1968 – 1984. For more recent years we have not been able to locate any published results on TFR and age specific fertility rates (ASFR). Moreover, the ICBS annual publication on population dynamics cannot be used in its present format to estimate these indicators.

Fertility indicators for the occupied territories have not been estimated by any independent source so far. The only exception is UNICEF JFPPA (1992).[25] Being a major determinant of trends in family and future population size, the lack of reliable fertility estimates seems disturbing.

In this section, we use data on children ever born (CEB), classified by age of mother or duration of mother's marriage, to estimate various fertility measures.

Summary Statistics of FALCOT 92 Input Data

A total of 1219 women were interviewed, excluding those with missing information on data needed for this section. Of those females who completed the interview, 830 (68.1%) reported being ever married (EMW).

These 830 women have given birth to 4724 living children (2470 boys and 2254 girls, with a sex ratio of 1.10, which indicates a small over-reporting of boys – or under-reporting of girls – as the sex ratio at birth is usually between 1.02 and 1.06). Women who were less than

50 years at the time of the interview had borne 4,8 children on average, with a maximum of 17 births, which indicates high fertility among Palestinian women of child-bearing age.

The mean age of child-bearing is estimated at 26.4 years in the infant mortality section.

The period total fertility rate is a synthetic measure of completed family size. Since TFR combines the current fertility experience of females 15-49 years, it can be interpreted as a hypothetical measure of completed cohort fertility.

Period TFR estimates for the population in the occupied territories have not been published for the last 8 years.[26] Data needed for direct estimation of this measure using birth registration records are not available for Palestinians since they are controlled solely by Israel.

Two methods were used to estimate the TFR from children ever born. The first method (the P/F Ratio Method) uses data on CEB classified by age of the women and the number of births in the year preceding the survey. The second method (the P/P* Ratio Method) uses data on CEB classified by duration of marriage of the women. Both methods compare lifetime with current fertility and adjusts for typical errors, like omissions of children who died a long time ago. Current fertility may be distorted by a misperception of the length of the period preceding the survey, or in our case, by assumptions about the number of births in the year preceding the survey based on marriages with one or more children ever born. If the data on current fertility is roughly constant with respect to age, the age pattern of current fertility can be accepted as correct although its level may be distorted (UN 1983: 31).

Table 2.11: Number of children ever born and estimated number of children born during the year preceding the survey.

Group number	Age Group	Number of women	Children Ever Born (CEB) Both sexes	Females	Average Parity	Births in the past year
1	15-19	258	34.46	18.93	0.13	12.86
2	20-24	184	232.77	115.10	1.27	31.56
3	25-29	179	459.26	185.50	2.57	44.76
4	30-34	128	624.08	274.89	4.88	15.85
5	35-39	90	500.60	269.10	5.56	7.73
6	40-44	84	520.84	248.35	6.20	0.65
7	45-49	72	629.96	304.67	8.75	4.22
	Total	995	3001.97	1416.54	3.02	117.63

The P/F Ratio Method uses the number of births of EMW in the sample during the year preceding the survey to estimate a preliminary schedule of age specific fertility rates (ASFR). Unfortunately, no questions on this variable were posed in the survey. Instead, a question relating to the age of the youngest child was asked. To correct for this problem, we investigated all EMW in the sample with a marriage duration not exceeding two years and whose CEB was at least one. These women were classified as having given birth to a child during the year preceding the survey if they were less than 30, see table 2.11.

Using the data in table 2.11 and steps 1 through 6 of UN (1983: 35-36), we arrive at table 2.12.

The so-called P/F-ratio (parity/fertility ratio) is used to adjust the preliminary period fertility schedule. Disregarding this ratio for age groups 15-19 and 45-49, the ratios are fairly similar except for a drop

Table 2.12: Estimates of period fertility rates, cumulated fertility and P/F ratios.

Group number	Age Group	Period Fertility Rate	Cumulated Fertility	Parity Equivalent, F	P/F ratio
1	15-19	0.0504	0.2519	0.104	1.268
2	20-24	0.1739	1.1215	0.701	1.807
3	25-29	0.2514	2.3785	1.919	1.336
4	30-34	0.1250	3.0035	2.770	1.760
5	35-39	0.0889	3.4479	3.309	1.682
6	40-44	0.0119	3.5075	3.356	1.848
7	45-49	0.0556	3.7852	3.720	2.352

Table 2.13 Age specific fertility rates for conventional age groups and adjusted ASFR for different choices of K.

Age Group	Conventional	$K = P(2)/F(2) = 1.807$	K = weighted average of $P(2)/F(2)$ and $P(3)/F(3) = 1.576$	$K = P(4)/F(4) = 1.760$	K = arithmetic average of $P(2)/F(2), P(3)/F(3)$ and $P(4)/F(4) = 1.635$
15-19	0.0620	0.1120	0.0977	0.1091	0.1014
20-24	0.1871	0.3381	0.2949	0.3293	0.3059
25-29	0.2445	0.4418	0.3853	0.4303	0.3998
30-34	0.1180	0.2132	0.1860	0.2077	0.1929
35-39	0.0804	0.1453	0.1267	0.1415	0.1315
40-44	0.0077	0.0139	0.0121	0.0136	0.0126
45-49	0.0575	0.1039	0.0906	0.1012	0.0940
Total	0.7570	1.3682	1.1933	1.3327	1.2381
TFR	3.79	6.84	5.97	6.66	6.19

in the value for the age group 25-29. This deviation is probably due to problems with the data for this age group, possibly a large number of birth omissions, as indicated by the large sex ratio of 1.48 male to female births. Disregarding the P/F ratio for age group 25-29, we are left with P/F ratios that vary between 1.7 and 1.8. From these ratios we derive an adjustment factor K which is used to adjust the period fertility rates of various age groups in order to get estimates of age specific fertility rates. Because of the problem encountered in age group 25-29, four alternative sets of values for K are suggested, resulting in four sets of age specific fertility rates, see table 2.13. We see that the conventional fertility rates are adjusted upwards by a factor varying between 57.6 and 80.7 per cent.

For population projection purposes (next section), we may use a TFR value of 6.19, as this adjustment factor has been determined by the P/F ratios of age groups 20-24, 25-29, and 30-34. This choice of initial TFR value for population projection purposes can be considered a conservative choice which will lead to a conservative set of projected population totals over the projection period.

As for the remaining estimates of TFR, we are inclined to adopt a value of 6.84 births per woman as our estimate of TFR for 1992. This choice is guided by the unsupported evidence of a rising trend in early marriages since the outbreak of the Intifada and a general tendency among Palestinians in the occupied territories to have more children during the last five-year period. Using the P/P* ratio method, an estimated TFR value of 7.04 was obtained. This estimate further demonstrates that a realistic estimate of TFR for the occupied territories is roughly around 7 births per woman in 1992.

Population Projections

Introduction

The dynamics of population growth in the occupied territories depend basically on the development of mortality, fertility and migration. Moreover, the end result of the current peace process is expected to have a direct influence on the size and direction of population growth in the future. In the absence of census-taking and local demographic data collection and research, we are left with a bare minimum of information regarding the elements affecting population size and structure in the coming years. The only census of the population since the occupation of the occupied territories was conducted in September 1967 by Israel. Since then, demographic parameters of the population have been estimated every now and then by ICBS, local researchers and others. For example, many population figures are available through educated guessing[27], projections[28] or sampling[29] (in rare cases).

Various estimates of possible developments in the population structure have been suggested in ways that invite controversy. There is basically no consensus on any of these estimates[30].

Currently, several estimates of population totals are being used by researchers. In this section, however, we are interested in two estimates which are presented by WBDP (1987) and ICBS (1992). The first estimate, which was used in the sampling stage of FALCOT 92 is that of WBDP which comes to 1,836,000 persons in the occupied territories in 1987. Taking the annual growth rate published by ICBS for the years 1988-1991 into account, this total is estimated (for the mid-year of 1992) at 2,117,391 persons. As for the other estimate, ICBS (1992) estimates the population total at the end of 1991 to be 1,838,200. Assuming a continuation of the 1991 rate of increase through the first half of 1992, this estimate becomes 1,885,070 persons for mid-year 1992. These two estimates will be used in this section as base populations for our projections.

In this section, we use the findings of the FALCOT 92 concerning age structure, mortality and fertility to introduce our own estimates and projections of possible developments for the population in the occupied territories. We do not aim here at more than presenting the findings of these projections. Analyses of implications and comparisons are left for future research.

The projections are based on extensive use of the cohort component method. This method uses age structure and patterns of change in mortality, fertility, and annual net migration balance to estimate future changes of the projected population and its demographic characteristics. Except for assumptions concerning population total in 1992 and trends in the net migration balance, all input parameters are estimated by the FALCOT 92.

Limitations on Input Parameters

The results in this section should be viewed cautiously due to the limitations pertaining to the input parameters that are used in the population projections. In particular, one should keep in mind the following constraints involving input data for projections:

a   There is no information regarding the reliability of the estimated population total for the year 1992. Whether such an estimate over- or under-estimates the actual population will not be known as long as no new census is conducted.
b   Being an estimate resulting from a sample survey, the FALCOT 92 age structure used in the projections is subject to both sampling and non- sampling errors.
c   Due to prevailing political conditions in the occupied territories, no particular pattern of migration can be assumed with any degree of realism. Therefore, no matter how the assumptions concerning trends of future net migration are put, they will represent an educated guess only.
d   Our estimates of the total fertility rate and the infant mortality rate are themselves limited and not very reliable due to data limitations (see the discussion in the infant mortality section).
e   The assumed future trends of mortality and fertility decline are not based on any systematic study of past trends. There is no local literature on this issue except for the Israeli produced estimates, which might be suspected of being unreliable due to under-reporting.
f   Due to lack of enough information on most parameters, we will not be able to present projections by region (West Bank, Gaza Strip, and Arab Jerusalem).

Basic Assumptions

The projections are given for 20 years representing four periods of five years each: 1993-1997, 1998-2002, 2003-2007 and 2008-2012. In deriving these projections, the following assumptions have been made:

Base Population

The mid-year population in the occupied territories of 1992 is estimated at 2,117,391 persons with 1,069388 males and 1,048003 females, based on a sex ratio at 102 males per 100 females. These estimates are taken from WBDP (1987) and adjusted by annual growth rates reported by ICBS (1992) for the period mid-1992.

Age Structure

The age structure for the same mid-year population of 1992 is estimated by FALCOT 92 with adjustments being made for the sex ratio of children in the 0-14 age group. For this particular age group, it is assumed that the sex ratio is 105 males per 100 females.

Fertility

The Total Fertility Rate (TFR) is estimated by FALCOT 92 using the P/F method (see the fertility section) to be 6.19 births per woman. The distribution of age specific fertility rates were smoothed using the Gompertz Relational Fertility Model (Newell, 1988). The following assumptions have been made concerning future fertility:

Assumption 1: Sharp Fertility Decline

TFR will decline from 6.19 during the first projection period (1993-1997) to 3.10 during the last projection period (2008-2012). This represents a reduction of 50% in TFR over a period of 20 years.

Assumption 2: Moderate Fertility Decline

TFR will decline from 6.19 during the first projection period (1993-1997) to 4.13 during the last projection period (2008-2012). This represents a reduction of 33% in TFR over a 20-year period.

Assumption 3: Constant Fertility

TFR will remain constant at its present rate of 6.19 during the projection period (1993-2012). Of course, it is quite unlikely for TFR to remain constant at this high level for the next 20 years. However, this assumption will most probably provide for an upper limit for the total population by the year 2012.

Mortality

Using FALCOT 92 results, it is estimated that IMR for both s~~ 43 deaths per 1000 live births in 1988 (West Model). Moreover been shown in the infant mortality section that females are at a higher risk of dying during infancy. Using the FALCOT 92 findings and the UNICEF and JFPPA (1992) results on IMR, the following pattern (table 2.14) of decline for IMR and the corresponding value for e_0, the life expectancy at birth, is assumed for the projection period.

The underlying hypothesis is that it is possible to reduce IMR by 50% in 20 years given the current interest of international and local health organizations in improving the health status of the population in the occupied territories. Moreover, the current gap in IMR between the two sexes will gradually be closed through improved services and more attention to female infants during the coming 20 years. This decline in IMR will be assumed for all projections.

Net Migration

The only figures available on the annual net migration balance are those published by ICBS. The 1991 figure for net immigration for the occupied territories (excluding Arab Jerusalem) is 9300 persons (5 persons per 1000). This figure has fluctuated during the past years, apparently with no systematic pattern. As for our projections, we assume that the net annual migration balance will fluctuate around 9 persons per 1000 in either direction during the projection period. This assumption is based on two hypotheses:

a The current economic and political situation will influence people to try to move out for a better future.

b. The current peace process is giving the local population some hope of a better future and attracting some Palestinians to come back and invest in the local economy.

Table 2.14 Assumed IMR and Corresponding Life Expectancy at Birth For The Projection Period

Period	Infant mortality ratio (IMR) per 1000 live births Females	Males	e0 life expectancy at birth Females	Males
1993-1997	45	40	66.29	66.23
1998-2002	35	32	68.92	67.51
2003-2007	27	25	71.18	70.21
2008-2012	22	20	72.71	71.68

...hree assumptions concerning net annual migration balance are made:

Assumption 1: The Optimist
An annual net immigration balance of 9 persons per 1000 throughout the projection period.

Assumption 2: The Neutral
An annual net immigration of 0 (zero) persons per 1000 throughout the projection period.

Table 2.16 Distribution of projections by assumption on TFR and net migration balance

Assumptions On Net annual immigration	Sharp decline 6.19 to 3.1	Moderate decline 6.19 to 4.13	Constant 6.19
Net Annual +9 per 1000	----	projection 5	Projection 6 Upper Limit
-9 per 1000	Projection 1 Lower Limit	Projection 3	----
0 per 1000	Projection 2	Projection 4	----

Table 2.17 Assumptions of projections 1 through 6.

	Pr 1	Pr 2	Pr 3	Pr 4	Pr 5	Pr 6
Assumptions						
Base population in 1000	Lower Limit 2117.4	2117.4	2117.4	2117.4	2117.4	Upper Limit 2117.4
Fertility						
1993-1997	6.19	6.19	6.19	6.19	6.19	6.19
1998-2002	5.16	5.50	5.50	5.50	6.19	6.19
2003-2007	4.13	4.81	4.81	4.81	4.81	6.19
2008-2012	3.10	3.10	4.13	4.13	4.13	6.19
IMR (M/F)						
1993-1997	40/45	40/45	40/45	40/45	40/45	40/45
1998-2002	32/35	32/35	32/35	32/35	32/35	32/35
2003-2007	25/27	25/27	25/27	25/27	25/27	25/27
2008-2012	20/22	20/22	20/22	20/22	20/22	20/22
Net Annual immigration per 1000						
1993-1997	-9	0	-9	0	9	9
1998-2002	-9	0	-9	0	9	9
2003-2007	-9	0	-9	0	9	9
2008-2012	-9	0	-9	0	9	9

Table 2.15 Assumed age structure of migration

Age group	%
0-14	5.0
15-19	5.0
20-24	15.0
25-29	20.0
30-34	20.0
35-39	15.0
40-44	10.0
45-49	5.0
50-54	5.0
55 +	0.0

Assumption 3: The Pessimist

An annual net immigration of minus 9 persons per 1000 throughout the projection period.

No information is available on the age structure of migrants. However, the following assumptions are made:

1. Due to the labour force dynamics and traditions of the Palestinian society in the occupied territories, 70% of migrants are assumed to be males and 30 % females.
2. The percentage of migration from each age group is assumed to be as in table 2.15

The distribution (table 2.15) of migrants is designed to reflect a greater tendency of those in the age group 20-39 to migrate in either direction.

Sex Ratio at Birth

The sex ratio at birth is held constant at 105 male births per 100 female births throughout the projection period.

Formulation of Alternative Projections

Based on these assumptions, a series of six projections were chosen, as summarized in the tables 2.16 and 2.17.

Results

The most striking aspect of the projections is that they indicate a very rapid population growth in the next 20 years, with nearly a doubling of the population, see table 2.18 and figures 2.11 and 2.13. This is the case for all alternative projections, almost regardless of fertility decline and migration assumptions. The reason for this is that the high past and current fertility rates have resulted in a large number of young people in the population. The total number of children borne by these persons in the future will be large, even if each individual has few children on average.

The annual growth rate for 1987 is estimated at 3.7%. For the end of the projection period, projections 1-5 show that an annual growth rate of 2%-3% is likely, even when fertility is assumed to decline.

Projection number 6 shows the largest growth (119 % since 1992), as expected by virtue of the assumptions it is based upon. This is, however, an unlikely development. It is presented here only to provide a likely upper limit for the projected population size. Similarly, projection 1 presents the smallest growth (73 %), providing a lower limit for the projected population size. The remaining projections (2-5) show a growth of 78% to 95% by the end of the projection period.

The broad age structure of the population varies according to the underlying assumptions for each projection. Table 2.19 presents the

Figure 2.11 Age pyramid for the 1992 OT population, as estimated by FAFO living conditions survey

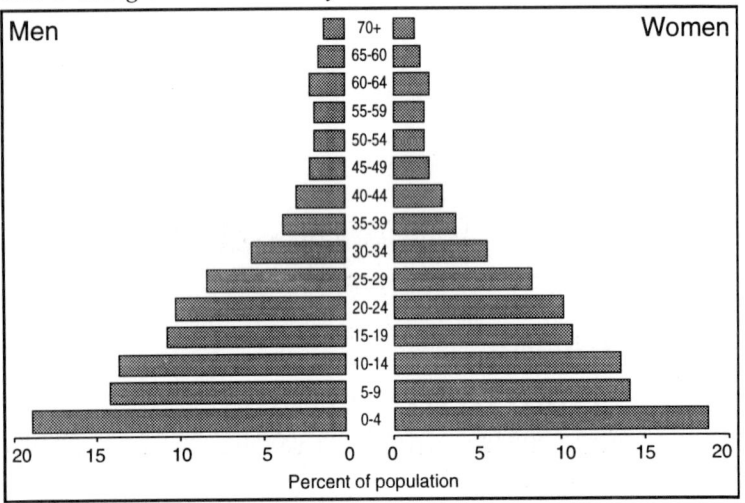

Figure 2.12 Age pyramid for the 2012 OT population, as estimated by projection 4

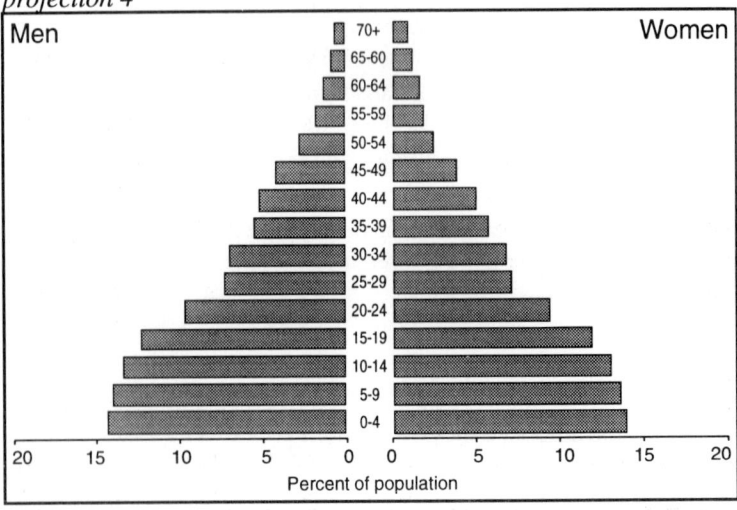

distribution in three broad age groups (0-14, 15-64, and 65 +) together with the dependency ratio (number of persons 0-14 and 65+ per 100 persons 15-64) for 1992 and 2012.

Even if one assumes that no drastic change in the political and economic situation will occur, job opportunities together with other conditions prevailing outside the area will probably continue to make people want to leave the occupied territories. However, given the

Figure 2.13 Projections of OT population. Six alternative series

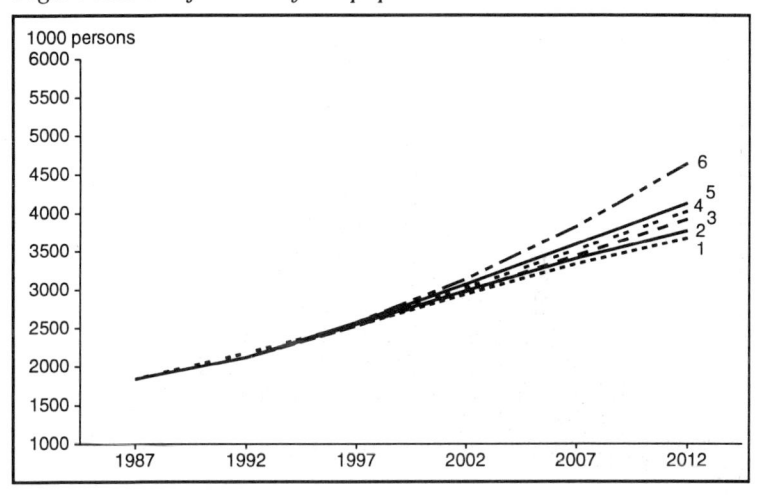

Table 2.18 Population projections

	Projection number					
	1	2	3	4	5	6
Year	Population size in 1000					
1987	1836	1836	1836	1836	1836	1836
1992	2117	2117	2117	2117	2117	2117
1997	2527	2549	2527	2549	2572	2572
2002	2941	2988	2974	3021	3071	3138
2007	3332	3405	3443	3518	3595	3824
2012	3670	3769	3921	4023	4127	4644
	Annual growth rate					
1993-1997	3,6	3,8	3,6	3,8	4,0	4,0
1986-2002	3,1	3,2	3,3	3,5	3,6	4,1
2003-2007	2,5	2,6	3,0	3,1	3,2	4,0
2008-2012	2,0	2,0	2,6	2,7	2,8	4,0
	Growth 1992-2012					
Absolute (in 1000s)	1553	1651	1803	1906	2010	2526
Per cent	73	78	85	90	95	119

Table 2.19 Dependency ratios at year 2012 for projections 1-6

Age Group	1992	Projection for year 2012					
		1	2	3	4	5	6
0-14	45.7	37.6	37.1	41.6	41.1	40.7	47.3
15-64	50.3	59.4	59.8	55.6	56.0	56.5	50.2
65 +	4.0	3.1	3.0	2.9	2.8	2.8	2.5
Dependency ratio	98.9	68.5	67.1	80.0	78.4	76.9	99.1

restrictions imposed by both Israel and other countries on the free movement of Palestinians, the net emigration may be low. Although it is likely that fertility will continue to fall, increasing attachment to Islamic values may slow down the rate of decline.

Based on these and other arguments, we believe that projection 4 is the most realistic one, i.e., a moderate fertility decline and no net immigration. In the rest of this section, we will limit the presentation to results obtained from this projection unless otherwise stated.

Projected Developments in the Occupied Territories Using Projection 4

The total population in the occupied territories will grow to 4,023,000 persons in 2012. Assuming that the current population share of each of the three regions will remain unchanged for the next 20 years, the population in 2012 is estimated at 2,200,000 persons for West Bank, 1,480,000 for Gaza Strip, and 343,000 persons for Arab Jerusalem.

The age composition of the population will differ in year 2012 from that of 1992 (as estimated by FALCOT 92). Due to the assumed fertility decline, the population will not be quite as young in the future as it is now, with 41% under age 16 in 2012 vs. 45 % in 1992. On the other hand, the relative size of the age group 30-44 will be larger in 2012, see table 2.20.

Table 2.20 shows that the largest growth will be in age group 30-44, followed by age group 45-

Table 2.20 Relative size of specific age groups and amount of growth by year 2012.

		Projection 4	
Age Group	FLCS 1992	2012	% Growth (1992-2012)
0-14	45.7	41.1	71
15-29	28.8	28.8	89
30-44	12.3	17.5	171
45-64	9.2	9.8	103
65 +	4.1	2.8	33
15-64	50.3	56.1	112

74

64. The weakest growth is expected in that of old people (65 +).

The relative size of females of child-bearing age (ages 15-49) is estimated by FALCOT 92 in 1992 at 43.6% of the female population. This is expected to change to 49.9% in year 2012. In other words, almost one half of the female population will be in child-bearing ages in twenty years. The size of the female population of child-bearing age is expected to have grown 116% by 2012. The main age group of child-bearing women (15-34) will grow by a full 172%, i.e., it will almost have doubled.

The following summary statistics (see table 2.21) are derived using the stated assumptions on fertility and mortality for projection 4. West model life tables for each gender and for both sexes combined are also used (Coale and Demeny 1983).

Prospects of Change in Population Size

The official estimate of population size published by ICBS (1992) for the end of 1991 is 1,005,600 for the West Bank excluding Jerusalem, 676,100 for the Gaza Strip, and 156,500 for Arab Jerusalem. Based on the assumption that the 1991 growth rate continues through the first six months of 1992, the official estimated population total will be

Table 2.21 Summary assumptions and results for projection 4

	Year			
	1997	2002	2007	2012
Birth rate	44.4	40.0	35.1	30.9
Death rate	7.3	6.0	4.7	4.1
Growth rate	3.71	3.40	3.04	2.68
Total fertility	6.19	5.50	4.82	4.13
NRR	2.73	2.49	2.22	1.93
e(0) - Both sexes	66.3	68.2	70.7	72.2
IMR - Both sexes	42.9	35.3	26.2	21.2
q(5) - Both sexes	55.0	43.8	31.4	24.9
Dep. ratio	99.9	100.6	92.0	78.4
Avg. ann. births	103360	111185	114632	116234
Avg. ann. deaths	17032	16707	15293	15261
Infant deaths	4433	3924	2999	2460
Deaths age 1+	12599	12783	12294	12801

75

1,885,070 persons. This estimate differs from the one we have used by 232,300 persons. A relevant question is what the population total would be in year 2012 if we proceed from the official Israeli estimate. This question will be further investigated in a later report.

Although it lies outside the scope of this discussion to speculate on the political prospects for the occupied territories in the coming 20 years, the fact that the Palestinian and Israeli sides have been negotiating a settlement since November 1991 cannot be discarded. If negotiations are completed successfully during the course of the next 2-3 years, it is expected that many thousands of displaced Palestinians (as a result of 1967 war, deportations, loss of residence, etc.) will return to area. This would strongly affect the future population growth.

References

Abu-Libdeh, H. C. Smith, K. Nabris, M. Shahin (1992). A Survey of Infant And Child Mortality in The West Bank And Gaza Strip. UNICEF and JFPPA: Jerusalem.

Alloush, K. and I. Ali (1988). Syrian Arab Republic Infant And Child Mortality Survey. Unicef Office For The Middle East And North Africa.

Bennvenisti, M. and S. Khayat. (1988), The West Bank and Gaza Atlas. Jerusalem, West Bank Data Base Project. Jerusalem

Biddu Survey (unpublished data);

Brass, W. (1964). Uses of Census And Survey Data For The Estimation of Vital Rates. Paper presented for the African seminar on vital statistics. United Nations Document.

Coale, Ansley J. and Paul Demeny (1983): "Regional Model Life Tables and Stable Populations." Second edition, with Barbara Vaughan. Academic Press: New York.

Dahlan, A.S.M (1987), Population Characteristics and Settlement Changes in the Gaza Strip. Ph.d. Thesis. University of Durham, p. 167.

Giacaman, R. (1988). A Profile of Life and Health in Three Palestinian Villages. London, Ithaca Press;

Government Health Services, The Gaza Strip (1990), Annual Report of Health Statistics.

HABITAT (1989). Housing Requirements in the Future Independent Palestinian State: 1987-2007. A Study for the United Nations Center for Human Settlements (HABITAT).

ICBS (1987): Projections of Population in Judea, Samaria and Gaza Area Up to 2002. Special Series No. 802. Jerusalem.

ICBS (1987). Projections of Population in Judea, Samaria and Gaza Area Up to 2002. Special Series No. 802. Jerusalem.

ICBS (1992): Statistical Abstract of Israel. No. 43.

Israeli Ministry of Health (1991), Health in Judea, Samaria and Gaza: 1990-1991, Jerusalem.

Ministry of Health And Unicef-Jordan (1991). Jordan EPI/CDD And Child Mortality Survey. Amman.

Newell, C. (1988): Methods And Models in Demography. Belhaven Press: London.

Shahin et al. (1989), A Baseline Descriptive Study on Selected Health and Health Related Conditions of Designated Villages in the Hebron Area. Arab College of Medical Professions Al-Bireh.

The Union of Palestinian Medical Relief Committees/Birzeit University Community Health Unit (1988), Ain Al-Dyuk: A Village Health Study;

The Union of Palestinian Medical Relief Committees/Birzeit University Community Health Unit (1987), Interim report,

UNICEF Middle East and North Africa Regional Office and London School of Hygieneand tropical Medicine (1990). Measuring Childhood Mortality: A Guide for Simple Surveys. Al-Ra'i Press: Amman.

United Nations (1983): Indirect Techniques for Demographic Estimation. Department of International Social and Economic Affairs. Population Studies No. 81. United Nations: New York.

Vermund, S.H., S.G. Miller, and Cohen, S.P. (1985), Health Status and Health Services in the West Bank and Gaza Strip. Institute for Middle East Peace and Development.

Zou'bi, Abdallah Abdel Aziz, Ari Poedjastoeti and Mohamed Ayad (1992): "Jordan Population and Health Survey 1990." Department of Statistics and Ministry of Health, Amman, and IRD/Macro International Inc., Columbia, Maryland.

Notes

1 For an extensive presentation of the establishment of the State of Israel, see Ian Lustic, "Arabs in the Jewish State", University of Texas Press 1980.

2 The UNRWA definition of "refugee" refers to patrilineal descendants of persons who fled from the area that became the state of Israel in 1948.

3 The "Triangle" refers to a small, but densely populated area, on the costal plain in the region between Hadera and Haifa.

4 The FAFO living conditions survey has used the official Israeli borders for East Jerusalem when defining main regions. Application of the Israeli borders for Arab Jerusalem are, however, neither intended as a legitimization nor as a recognition of these borders in a legal sense. The justification for use of the Israeli borders is, on the contrary, their socio-economic impact on the Palestinian population living within them, taking the different legal status between Jerusalem and West Bank residents into account.

Towards West Jerusalem, "East Jerusalem" has been defined as Arab neighborhoods east of the 1949 Green Line. After the war in 1948, Beit Safafa South remained the only area in West Jerusalem with compact Palestinian settlement. Except for this small area, 95% of the "Non-Jews" in Jerusalem live in the eastern part of the city, i.e. in areas covered by the FAFO survey.

Since 1967 approximately 120 000 Jews have moved into Jewish neighbourhoods in the (geographical) area of "East Jerusalem", (i.e. the Jordanian part of Jerusalem prior to 1967). In contrast to the pre-1967 period, the extensive Jewish presence in East Jerusalem means that the geographical label "East" Jerusalem no longer refers to a part of the city exclusively populated by Palestinians. We have thus found the label "Arab Jerusalem" more appropriate for the Palestinian neighborhoods of the city comprised by the survey.

5 Palestinian individuals

"Palestinian" individuals are defined as all individuals in Gaza, the West Bank and East Jerusalem who are *"residents"* and *not "foreigners"*, (i.e. "Palestinians"). A *"resident"* is defined as a person who has been permanently living in Gaza, the West Bank or East Jerusalem for at least the past 4 months prior to the interview. People meeting this criteria are considered residents regardless of whether they hold a formal residency or not. Persons who have not lived in Gaza, the West Bank or East

77

Jerusalem for at least the past 4 months prior to the interview are not considered as "residents" even if they hold an Israeli ID-card. A *"foreigner"* (i.e. in most cases an Israeli), is defined as an individual who has:
 1 A foreign passport
 and
 2 At least one of the following:
   a) No parents of Palestinian heritage
   b) Who does not use Arabic as his or her primary language
All other persons are considered "non-foreigners" (Palestinians), and should be surveyed if they are "residents".

Palestinian households
A "household" is defined as persons who are living together, and who pool their economic resources together, i.e. persons who live in the same housing unit, and share the same working kitchen.

"Palestinian" households are defined as all households in the Gaza Strip/ West Bank/ East Jerusalem, where the majority of the inhabitants, 15 years or older, are considered as "Palestinians" according to the definition above.

6 See Table A.2.1 and Table A.2.2 in the Population Appendix for further references to the discussion in this section.

7 See end note 4 for definition of "Arab Jerusalem".

8 The borders of the Gaza Strip and Israel were, as those of the West Bank, determined by the 1949 ceasefire lines between the Israeli and the Arab armies, rather than by topographic features.

9 Refugee camps in Arab Jerusalem have not been placed in a separate stratum, but grouped with other areas in strata along a north/ south dimension. By chance, neither Shufat nor Kalandia refugee camps were selected when preparing the Arab Jerusalem sample. As a consequence, none of these two Arab Jerusalem refugee camps are covered by the survey. Results for refugees in Arab Jerusalem are thus strictly valid for the groups of refugees outside camps only.

10 It is here referred to towns like Bethlehem and Ramallah which form part of Greater Jerusalem, but are situated on the West Bank.

11 Jewish settlers are not included in this figure. For a detailed discussion of the population included in the survey, see end note 5.

12 This survey's estimate for the Christian population share in Arab Jerusalem exceeds CBS results by 3-4% A possible explanation may be the inclusion of the Old Town "Christian Quarter" in the sample. When estimating the Christian population share in Arab Jerusalem it is worth noting that the results of this survey are different for the population of households, the population of individuals, 15 years or older, and the (total) population of individuals. Small average household size and low average numbers of children per adult household member in Christian households make the Christian population share vary from 21% to 18% and 15% for the three statistical populations respectively.

13 See average number of children per adult in Christian households in Table A.2.8 in the Population Appendix.

14 See Table A.2.3, Table A.2.4 and Table A.2.5 in the Population Appendix for further references to the discussion in this section.

15 A common feature observed in many developing countries is a tendency of persons aged 40 years and more to state their age in "round" numbers. This means to some extent that there is a tendency to let ages end with 5, but in particular to give an age ending with 10. Age intervals containing the values 50, 60 and 70 are thus probably the most inflated ones compared to the "true" age distribution.

16 See Table A.2.6, Table A.2.7, Table A.2.7, Table A.2.8 and Table A.2.9 in the Population Appendix for further references to the discussion in this section.

17 Statistical abstract of Israel 1991, A. Main Series p.4. The basic definitions of "household" are parallel in the two surveys, but may of course have been implemented somewhat differently in the field.

18 If regional variations had been due to parallel variations in adults and children, this ratio should have been constant over main regions.

19 See Table A.2.10 in the Population Appendix for further references to the discussion in this section.

20 The FAFO survey uses the concept Head of Household in two different ways. The starting point was the *"acknowledged/ expected"* Head of Household, the person being determined on the basis of the subjective opinion of the household members. In about 30% of the households the acknowledged Head of Household was not available or capable for doing the Head of Household interview. Among the not available or not capable Household Heads we distinguished between absence spanning a "short" time (less than 3 months) and a "long" time (more than 3 months). Two thirds of the 30% of Household Heads who were absent, were so for a short time only, while one third was absent for a long time.

When the absence of the Household Head was of a *short* duration, (e.g. Head of Household was at work, etc), a "substitute" was used as respondent speaking on behalf of the Household Head. Any household member well informed about the economic affairs of the household could act as substitute for the Household Head, even though the spouse or oldest son of the Household Head were preferred. Approximately 80% of the substitutes were spouse of the Household Head, while 8% were the oldest son. In the households where the interview was made with a substitute, all information about the Head of Household as a person still refers to the *acknowledged* Household Head (and not the substitute).

When the absence of the Head of Household had a prolonged character, e.g. when the accepted Household Head was senile, working abroad, in prison, etc., survey definitions overruled the subjective opinion of the household members. In these cases the concept of the *functioning* Head of Household was introduced to include the person in actual fact in charge of running daily household affairs.

Approximately 90% of the *acknowledged* Household Heads were also in charge of the daily affairs of the household, i.e. they were also the *functioning* Household Heads. In 10% of the households, the functioning and the acknowledged Household Head was not the same person. In these households the personal information about the Head of Household refers to the *functioning* Household Head, and not to the *acknowledged* Household Head. In more than 7 out of 10 cases where the acknowledged and the functioning Head of Households were different persons, the functioning Head of Household was the spouse of the acknowledged Head of Household.

21 Israeli Ministry of Health (1991). Health in Judea, Samaria and Gaza: 1990-1991, Jerusalem.

22 Figures represent reported number of deaths of infants of ages between 0 and 12 months per 1000 live births.

23 Calculated by the author using unweighted aggregated data.

24 The reported birth rates have always been more than 40 births per 1000 population since 1968.

25 Research in progress, results are expected to be published in July, 1993.

26 To the best of the author's knowledge.

27 The Arab Thought Forum has published an estimate of the population total for each of the West Bank localities. Their estimates of population size for each locality were derived by direct interviewing of well informed persons in each locality.

28 HABITAT (1989) has published population projections for OPT using ICBS estimate of input parameters. Planning and Research Center of Jerusalem (PRC) is

currently working on a set of population projections for OPT localities using a combination of ICBS and Jordan data.

29 UNICEF and JFPPA (1992) has conducted a nationwide sample survey and estimated the age structure of the population in the West Bank and the Gaza Strip.

30 See the discussion of various estimates of population totals presented in WBDP (1987).

Chapter 3
Housing

Marianne Heiberg

The author wishes to thank Rema Hammami for her many useful comments on this chapter, particularly those which relate to kinship structure, consumption patterns and house investments.

The Cultural Setting of and Domestic and Public Spheres inside the Housing Unit

The house – *al dar* – comprises the fundamental framework which surrounds family life and separates the private domestic realm from the public domain. The house is a physical representation of the family which resides within it and the importance of the house reflects the prominence of the family within Palestinian society. It is an indicator of its status and the permanence or transiency of its anchoring to the local community. It also signals some of the central values and priorities within the society. The size and subdivision of rooms and the investment made in their furnishing tend to reflect the internal hierarchy within the domestic sphere, the relationship and ranking between the domain of men and the domain of women. It also reflects conceptions of privacy both between family members and between the family and the outside world. The structure of the house often reveals not only critical features of the family within, but just as importantly that family's anticipations. In a sense, building a house is also a statement concerning future expectations. Looking toward the development of the family over time, families often build houses that are larger than they can live in and more than they can furnish or even finish.

Traditionally Palestinian villages contained a number of residentially based patrilineal descent groups – *hamuleh* – each of which in turn were subdivided into separate extended families. Members of each *hamuleh* lived in a group of adjoining houses grouped around one or more interconnected courtyards.[1] To a certain extent the spatial relationship between houses was an indication of the kinship relation between households. The more distant the kinship link, the further separated the houses.[2]

The architectural and social unity of the traditional compact Palestinian village has undergone major transformations. The marginalisation of agriculture and the massive shift toward wage labour has splintered family groups and introduced new architectural styles and spatial distributions, reflecting, on one hand, an increase in economic prosperity and, on the other, a trend toward a more nucleated family organisation.

Because architecture and internal environment mirror cultural preferences, specific social structures as well as processes of economic and social transformation, comparisons of housing standards across cultural boundaries can often be misleading. Different concepts of privacy, for instance, imply different thresholds concerning physical human separation and thus acceptable levels of human density. Different and changing notions of status affect patterns of domestic consumption since items that give prestige in one set of circumstances may differ radically from items that mark status in others.

Nonetheless, the house, its furnishings and amenities, the nature of its ownership and the protection and comfort it provides, is a critical dimension of living conditions. In the occupied territories the house has gained an uncommon importance because people tend to spend a good deal more of their time within it. Modern public social arenas, such as cinemas, theatres, restaurants, parks and play grounds, are either relatively undeveloped or have in recent years

Table 3.1 Main material used in house construction by region

	Gaza	West Bank	Arab Jerusalem	Camps
Cement/cement roof	68	53	22	33
Cement/zinc or asbestos roof	32	1	1	64
Stone/stone facing	-	43	76	2
Other	-	3	-	1

Table 3.2 Type of dwelling by region[4]

	Gaza	West Bank	Arab Jerusalem	Camps
Villa	7	6	4	1
Independent small house	22	49	17	26
Terraced house	29	13	11	58
Mansion block apartment	13	9	9	7
Apartment in large building	20	17	39	3
Apartment in high rise building	4	3	12	
Apartment above workshop	3	3	1	1
Other	3	1	7	5

become underdeveloped due to closure. For cultural reasons, married women, in particular are often confined to the house for large parts of the day. Moreover, many social activities traditionally enjoyed by Palestinians have ceased with the intifada. The constant evening gatherings of men in the main village square is a thing of the past and even men's coffee houses, where they still exist, are usually open only during daytime hours. Political strikes, intifada closings, protracted curfews and general fears have further increased the amount of time Palestinians spend within their homes.

Variations in Construction

Traditionally the main material used in house construction in the occupied territories was either limestone or adobe. While limestone, taken from local quarries, is still favoured by more prosperous Palestinians and is required by law in most of Arab Jerusalem, cement has become the main material used in more recent construction. All cement is imported from Israel and most is processed locally. Production methods in construction tend to be labour intensive, often using unpaid family labour, capital short and, consequently, less industrialised and mechanised than in Israel. It has been estimated that building costs in the territories are about one half of costs in Israel.[3]

Table 3.1 shows the regional variations in the use of construction material in housing. It should be noted that West Bank and Gaza camps have been separated into a single category.

One significant aspect of these different building materials is that they also have dissimilar qualities in regard to the insulation they provide and the solidity of the construction they brace. Generally speaking, a house built primarily of stone (associated with Jerusalem) tends to have a more sound structure and can be expected to last longer than one built of cement with zinc or asbestos used as roofing material, a form of housing common in the camps.

There are also notable variations in the types of dwellings in which people live (table 3.2).

A terraced house, typical of camps in the occupied territories, is one that shares walls with an adjoining house. It is the preponderance of this style of housing which is largely responsible for the maze-like character of the refugee camps.

Privacy and housing density

The usual international measurement of housing density is the number of persons per habitable room within a housing unit. For a discussion of the mean household size by type of locality in the occupied territories, see chapter 2 of this report.

Survey figures for the mean number of rooms per housing unit, excluding kitchens, bathrooms and hallways, but including glassed-in verandas, are shown in table 3.3.

On the basis of these figures and average household size, the average number of persons per room in the various types of localities covered by the survey is shown in figure 3.1.

Three or more persons per inhabitable room is a fairly common international criterion for over-crowdedness. Comparable figures for neighbouring countries are scarce. Nonetheless, figure 3.2 can provide one basis for comparison.

As mentioned, however, persons per habitable room can be a misleading indicator because allocation of space within a house is culturally variable. In the occupied territories a disproportionate amount of space is often occupied by one room only, the living room or salon.

Another measurement of density involves the mean square meters of total living space, including

Table 3.3 Number of rooms/housing unit by locality

	Mean
Entire Population	3.6
Greater Gaza City	3.9
Gaza town/village	3.6
Gaza camp	3.4
West Bank town	3.7
West Bank villages	3.7
West Bank camp	3.4
Arab Jerusalem	3.3

Figure 3.1 Persons per room by locality and in neighbouring countries[5]

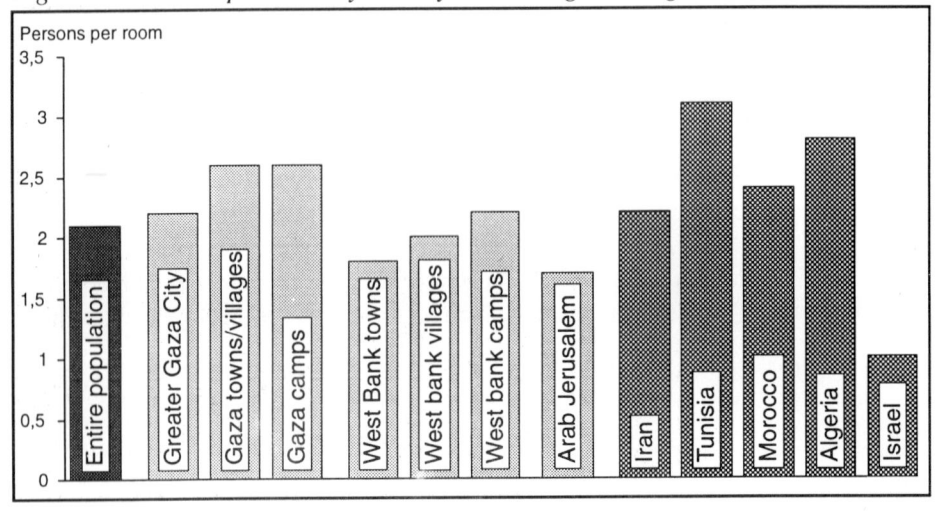

Table 3.4 Mean square meters per housing unit

	Per Unit	Per Person
Entire Population	66	9
Greater Gaza City	91	11
Gaza towns/villages	76	8
Gaza camps	50	6
West Bank towns	66	10
West Bank villages	66	9
West Bank camps	46	6
Arab Jerusalem	51	9

Table 3.5 Percentage of palestinian households with gardens, courtyards or roof areas by type of locality

	Courtyard	Roof area
Greater Gaza City	41	67
Gaza towns/villages	45	49
Gaza camps	26	8
West Bank towns	62	77
West Bank villages	69	82
West Bank camps	61	67
Arab Jerusalem	55	66

kitchens and bathrooms, available to each person. The survey estimates for this measurement are shown in table 3.4.

Density is also modified by other types of private space which provide household members with closed-off room for socializing and conduct of daily activities. The most important of these are useable roof areas and courtyards, a common architectural feature in Palestinian house construction.

Table 3.5 indeed underlines the special difficulties Gaza camps.

In order to make some general comparison of human density between the different localities in the occupied territories, the various elements that affect living density were assembled into one index.[6] The main weighing is on the number of persons per

Figure 3.2 Percent with three persons or more per room

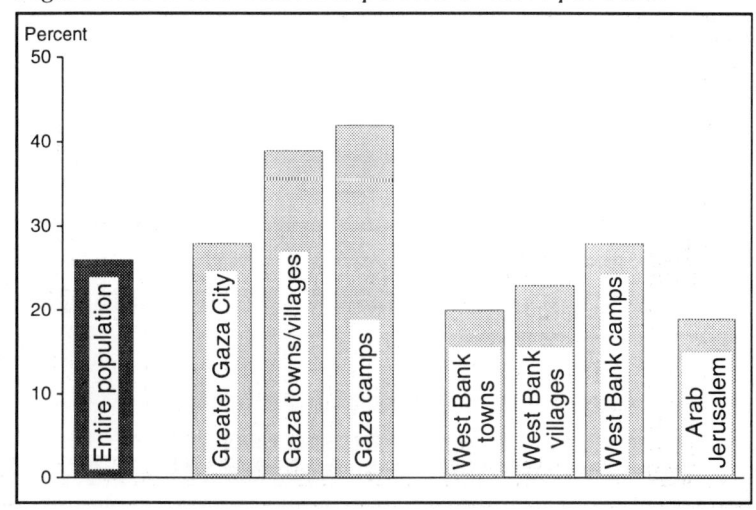

85

room. One person or less is considered low density, three or more high density. However, taking into consideration the manner in which Palestinian homes are actually constructed and utilized, the presence of a courtyard and a roof terrace used for domestic activities and frequently, also, for sleeping in the warmer months, is also included in the index. Thus, if house density is three or more persons per room, but the house contains both a courtyard and a roof area, the household will be classified as having medium density rather than high density occupancy. The resulting density index shows the following distribution for the various Palestinian localities.

Figure 3.3 shows the distribution of household density rates within the different types of localities considered and makes comparisons between locality types feasible. Because courtyards and roof areas are included in the index, it can be noticed that West Bank villages, for instance, in which 23% of all households have houses which contain three or more individuals per room, have the same percentage of high density occupancy as Arab Jerusalem where the presence of these private spaces is less prevalent. The figures show that human crowdedness is highest in Gaza and most acute in the Gaza refugee camps.

However, human density on private space is also dramatically effected by human density on adjoining space. It makes a great deal of difference to a person's sense of over-crowdedness if an over-crowded household is surrounded by large, tranquil areas of agricultural land or is tightly and noisily entrapped between other overcrowd-

Figure 3.3 Relative density of palestinian households by type of locality

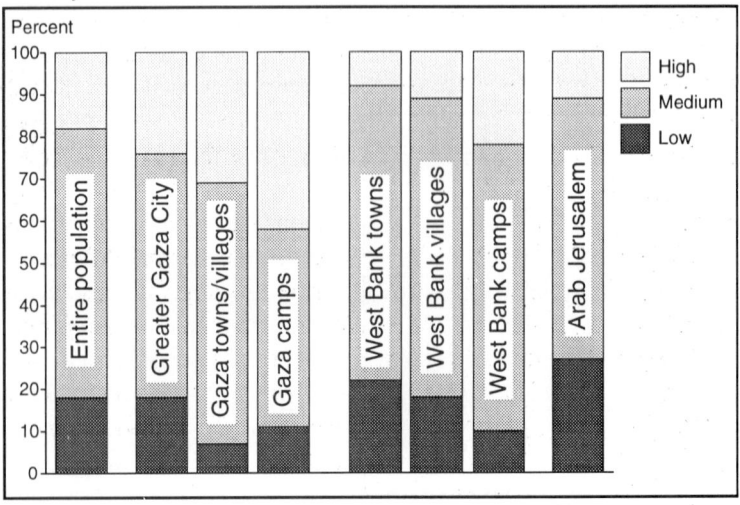

ed households. The survey figures for population per square kilometre have been presented previously in this report. Therefore, it should be noted that the human congestion of Gaza households is exacerbated by the high degree of human congestion in Gaza generally.

Infrastructural Amenities: Water, Sewage and Electricity

Housing standards are highly reliant upon an external infrastructure of electricity grids, sewage disposal systems, sanitation facilities and, in the modern world, telecommunications, in particular connection to a telephone net. Although the survey did not collect data on, for instance, rubbish disposal, the aspects the survey did consider indicate that infrastructural services are very good in relation to developing countries in general (table 3.6).

The survey did not measure the regularity of the electricity supply. Particularly in West Bank rural areas supply is erratic and less than 50% of rural households have around the clock electricity. On average in the West Bank only some 63% of households have electricity on a 24 hour basis (1985 figures).[7]

Again, the survey did not measure the quality of water provided. Several reports suggest that the quality is deteriorating, especially in Gaza, where increasing salinity rates are a cause for concern. A study undertaken for the Dutch government on water in Gaza[8] concludes that the Gaza aquifer has been over-exploited for at least the last two decades resulting in declining water levels, increased salinity and permanent damage to existing reserves of fresh water.

In addition to the amenities already mentioned, the type of sewage system available also has potential impact on the health of individuals. The answer categories provided in the questionnaire are very broad ones. Consequently, it should be noted that within any one category actual differences can be very large. For instance, a "sewage network" can range from the enclosed, underground system of Arab Jerusalem to the open, surface networks found in large parts of Gaza (table 3.7).

Table 3.6 Percentage of households with mains electricity, piped potable water and telephone by locality

	Grid electricity	Piped water	Telephone
Greater Gaza City	98	100	30
Gaza towns/villages	99	98	14
Gaza camps	99	99	4
West Bank towns	99	95	24
West Bank villages	73	90	7
West Bank camps	84	98	3
Arab Jerusalem	100	100	65
Total	90	95	20

Based on survey data concerning potable, piped water, electricity, telephones and sewage system, an infrastructural index has been constructed which facilitates a comparison between different localities in relation to the extension of infrastructural services. The scoring on this index is complex since different facilities have been given different weights. The possession of indoor piped potable water, for instance, is regarded as much more critical for living conditions than the possession of a telephone. But broadly speaking, a good score on the index indicates that the household has mains electricity, piped water, a telephone and is connected to a sewage network. A poor score means that the household lacks at least two of these facilities. Again it needs to be stressed that vital municipal services, such as sanitation, rubbish disposal and roads, have not been taken into account.

This index (table 3.8) shows that infrastructural services are least developed in the more rural areas of the West Bank and especially underdeveloped in the West Bank refugee camps.

Table 3.7 Type of household sewage system by locality in percentage of households

	Septic tank	Sewage network	Other
Greater Gaza city	21	78	2
Gaza towns/villages	57	34	10
Gaza camps	52	37	11
West Bank towns	60	40	
West Bank villages	96	4	
West Bank camps	33	25	42
Arab Jerusalem	17	83	

Table 3.8 Infrastructural index by locality

	Poor	Average	Good
Greater Gaza City	3	75	23
Gaza towns/villages	12	81	7
Gaza camps	13	85	2
West Bank towns	5	81	14
West Bank villages	34	66	
West Bank camps	54	46	1
Arab Jerusalem	1	41	58
All households	18	70	12

Indoor Standards

Indoor standards are partly dependent on the facilities the house contains as well as its furnishings. Needless to say, the quality and quantity of both are indicators of the household's economic resources. Nonetheless, household facilities indicate the degree of comfort and convenience a house affords its occupants. Among the key facilities are a separated bathroom, an inside flush toilet, a fitted kitchen, and sufficient heating to provide warmth and a shield against damp during the winter season. The insulating qualities of the building materials utilised also, of course, have an impact on the provision of warmth.

With regard to heating, in Arab Jerusalem 56% of households depend on kerosine heaters and 20% have electrical bars as the main source for heat. In the towns of the West Bank kerosine heaters, wood/charcoal burning stoves and braziers are the main forms. In the villages and camps of the West Bank wood burning stoves are predominant, as they are throughout Gaza. Some 20% of the households in Gaza report that they have no form of heating whatsoever. Although Gaza does not experience the same cold winters as the West Bank, winters can nonetheless be both chilly and very damp.

Again an index of household facilities has been constructed to measure the relative combined distribution of these amenities among the Palestinian population.

Once more (figure 3.5) it is in the rural areas and camps of the West Bank, rather than in Gaza as might have been expected, that internal housing standards are the least satisfactory.

Household furnishings and equipment tend to reflect the socio-economic standing of the household as well as gender relations within it. They also provide a certain measure of changing social values. Traditionally in Palestine, as throughout large parts of the Middle East, the status of families was more often expressed by the spaciousness of the salon than by the lavishness of kitchens or sleeping quarters.[10] The salon was where the men of the household received and entertained guests and relatives. Status was reflected by the generosity

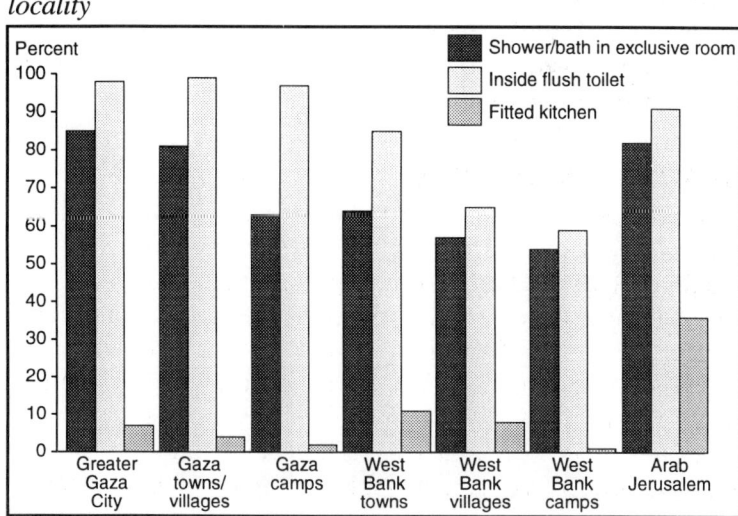

Figure 3.4 Percentage of households with internal facilities by locality

of hospitality, the comfort provided by the divans and chairs placed along the walls of the room and the size and luxuries of the room itself.

Although these patterns have to some extent been modified by social and economic changes, the kitchen remains the domain principally of women. In a society where women are largely confined to the house, have responsibility for most domestic tasks and have access to money only through the forbearance of men, women's labour is cheap. Thus, investment in parts of the house defined as the woman's realm makes little economic sense and solicits little social esteem.[11] Moreover, the values which underlie the consumption preferences of men are mostly shared by women. They tend to favour directing investment toward the most socially prominent areas of the house.

Historically, the groom's family was obliged to furnish the house to be used by the bridal couple. The furnishings provided were detailed in the wedding contract. For peasants this was usually limited to long, flat cotton mattresses and storage chests. Today, for couples moving in with the groom's family, still common in the camps, villages and in poorer urban areas, the groom's obligation is confined to furnishing the bedroom of the couple. In high density households the bedroom is the only room that provides any degree of privacy for couples living in extended households. Among middle class Palestinians furniture is usually needed for a whole house and consequently constitutes a notable additional cost to getting married.

Westernisation of tastes started in the Mandate period and is now almost complete among the urban and rural middle classes. The first

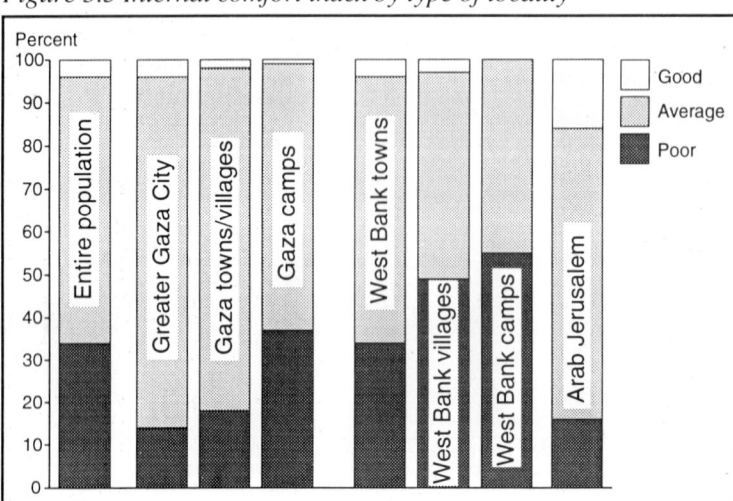

Figure 3.5 Internal comfort index by type of locality[9]

shift, reflecting increased prosperity, focused on bedrooms, the second on fitted kitchens. Westernisation of tastes has begun penetrating the poorer sectors of the population in the form of elaborate bedroom furniture acquired upon marriage. However, few poor households have rooms which are mainly reserved for a single activity. Instead, rooms are multi-purpose. Among the poor, the same space serves for socialising, children's games, food preparation and sleeping quarters for unmarried household members.

The list of selected household possessions in table 3.9 mirrors to some extent the relative economic resources of households as well as trends toward the westernisation of consumption patterns. A critical aspect of the table (3.9) is that it lists not only the percentage of households that own a given item, but also the percentage which purchased that item new rather than used. New items are frequently 4 to 5 times more expensive than used ones. Thus, comparison of items owned and purchased new gives both an economic indication of consumer preferences and an indication of the quality of possessions. Notably, for instance, neither colour televisions nor fridges are cutting edge commodities indicating that the owner belongs to a more elevated economic strata. However, if a household owns a colour television, a prestige item nonetheless, it is much more likely to have been purchased new than a fridge, an item most Palestinians own, but an item connected to the kitchen.

The survey also asked about ownership of a range of other household items such as freezers, dishwashers and air conditioners.

Table 3.9 Percentage of households that own:[12]

	Gaza Used	Gaza New	West Bank Used	West Bank New	Arab Jerusalem Used	Arab Jerusalem New	Camps Used	Camps New
Radio/cassette player	68	37	71	54	76	61	64	33
Colour TV	40	24	48	26	84	66	37	15
Video	11	7	11	7	39	32	6	3
Stereo	3	2	5	3	17	15	3	2
Fridge	91	14	87	17	98	55	87	5
Fully automatic washing machine	16	7	22	12	50	42	14	3
Modern oven	10	9	20	12	51	38	7	4
Modern bathroom	20	13	24	20	56	44	5	3
Car/truck	16	2	23	4	29	8	9	0

However, the number of households who owned these items were 2% or less and, therefore, are not included here.

Forms of Ownership

Property ownership is highly emphasized among Palestinians for a range of reasons. Real estate has traditionally been a favoured form of investment throughout the Middle East. Moreover, in the occupied territories there is a lack of alternative targets for investment and uncertainties about the future place an additional break on investment. Additionally, fathers have been under obligation to provide a house for their sons upon marriage. 24% of the households report that they have taken up loans to finance house construction. House construction is the second most important reason reported for household indebtedness. The first is support of daily consumption.

In the occupied territories there are few credit institutions which extend loans or mortgages for house building. Consequently, the extended family continues to be a principle financial base for construction although survey data suggests that loans from individuals who are not kin might be playing an increasing role in house financing, particularly in Arab Jerusalem. Nonetheless, because financial resources mobilized through kin groups or personal relations are usually fairly limited, this form of financing has clear implications for the quality of the housing stock and the size of units constructed.

The nature of house ownership varies with locality, indicating in part the differential availability of land for construction in the areas concerned and in part a trend toward a more fragmented family structure with urbanisation (table 3.10).

Table 3.10 Forms of ownership by type of locality

	Resident owned	Owned by extended family	Leased	Leased UNRWA	Other
Greater Gaza city	58	28	9	4	23
Gaza towns/villages	37	33	5	22	2
Gaza camps	13	12	2	72	1
West Bank towns	59	18	23	-	-
West Bank villages	81	14	5	-	2
West Bank camps	31	7	5	35	22
Arab Jerusalem	40	26	28	2	5
All households	56	19	11	12	2

Survey data on forms of ownership is both complex, rich and merits a detailed study. A full consideration of this issue has not been possible within the confines of this baseline report. However, it should be noted that UNRWA housing is probably even more widespread in the camps than indicated by these figures since many refugees regard the homes they have leased from UNRWA for several generations as their own and may report them as such.

As mentioned, house building, both in terms of capital invested and labour expended, tends to be a family affair. Except in large urban areas, it is relatively unusual to find multi-household buildings occupied by households that are not part of the same extended family. Even in large cities, families tend to live with non-related households only in large apartment buildings with four floors or more. What is almost non-existent outside Jerusalem and the large West Bank towns is multi-household buildings where kin and non-kin live together. This reflects, among other factors, the role and expectations of the kin group in house construction. Historically, the head of the household was obliged to build, if not an adjacent house, at least an adjacent apartment for his sons. This patrilocal pattern persists in the "large building" type of architecture in which the family builds a number of self-contained apartments for themselves and their sons' future families.

However, there are notable regional variations which partly relate to the impact of urbanisation on family structure.

Table 3.11 Kinship relations between households in multi-household buildings

	Brothers	Other kin	Not kin	Both kin & not kin
Greater Gaza city	46	39	13	1
Gaza towns/villages	63	30	7	-
Gaza camps	38	51	12	-
West Bank towns	39	23	34	4
West Bank villages	46	48	7	-
West Bank camps	38	53	10	-
Arab Jerusalem	18	30	45	7
All households	40	36	22	3

Housing and Safety with Regard to Children

Perceptions concerning the physical safety provided by the house and its surroundings with regard to children tend to mirror attitudes concerning the relative safety of the world outside the home versus the world inside it. In all cases the inside of the house is reported to be safer than the outside environment, but differential perceptions concerning relative safety come into play. It is necessary to take a closer look at how Palestinians evaluate the adequacy of their own homes and the security offered by its external surroundings.

It is only in Arab Jerusalem (figure 3.6) that a majority of households report that the local environment provides safe playing areas for children. Notably, West Bank camp residents find their houses some two times safer than Gaza camp residents. One reason could be that there is a clear correlation between the human density of the house and perceptions concerning the safety the house affords young children, i.e. the more crowded, the less safe (table 3.12).

However, perceptions concerning children's security and the areas in which they are protected from injury, do not necessarily correspond to the realities of children's injury. Respondents were asked if any of the children in the household 12 years of age or younger had been seriously injured during the previous two months. Some 17% of households state that they have children who had been so

Figure 3.6 Availability of safe playing areas for children 12 years or less inside and outside house in percentage of households by locality

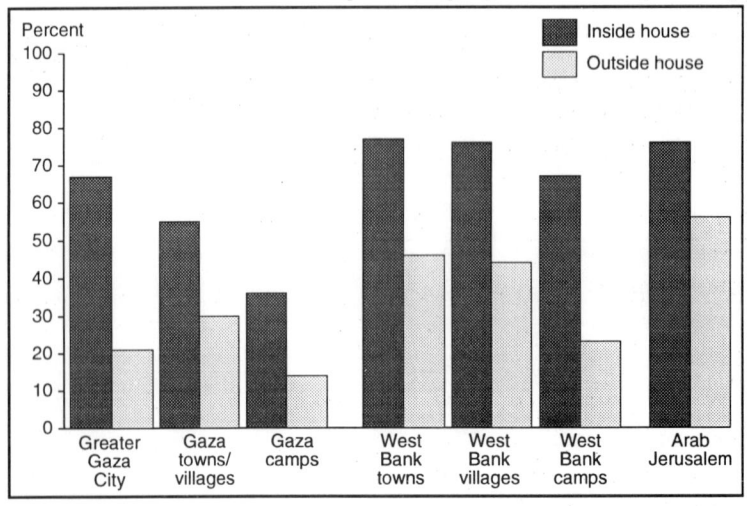

injured, the fewest injuries occurring in Jerusalem (9% of households), where average household size is in any case smaller, and the most in the refugee camps (19% of households). The overwhelming majority of these children had been injured inside the home. Table 3.13 refers only to those households with children who had been seriously injured in the two months prior to the survey period and is broken down on the regional level with both West Bank and Gaza camps placed into a separate category.

Household density does seem to be a significant contributory factor in children's injuries, but in a somewhat indeterminant manner. Whereas, 22% of high density households reported children injured in the two month period, only 13% of families living in low density household report injured children. However, it is uncertain whether household density contributes directly, as one might expect, to increased injuries to children inside the house.

A certain correlation does exist, but it relates not so much to children's injuries as to the respondent's knowledge concerning where the injury has taken place. Respondents from overcrowded households seem to have less awareness of what happens to the household's children. Instead of overcrowding per se, children's accidents inside the house seem much more closely related to poverty. In general, the poorest third of Palestinian households is twice as likely as the richest third to have children who had been injured either inside or outside the house. Controlling for this factor, indoor accident rates are some 70% higher among the poorest third of Palestinian households compared to the richest third.

Table 3.12 Availability of safe playing areas inside house by density of house

	Available	Not available
High density	47	53
Middle density	73	27
Low density	82	18

Table 3.13 Where was the child injured in percentage of households by region

	Gaza	West Bank	Arab Jerusalem	Camps
Inside house	66	78	68%	78
Outside house	19	16	22	9
Don't know	15	6	11	13

Table 3.14 The place of child's injury by density of household

	Inside home	Outside home	Don't know
High density	74	12	14
Middle density	74	18	8
Low density	87	8	5

Conclusion

So far the elements that comprise housing standards have been considered separately. However, in order to give an overall view of the variations of housing standards within the occupied territories, some of the elements discussed have been assembled into a single housing index, which includes main building material, density of dwelling, external infrastructure and internal amenities. In this index building materials, household density and infrastructural facilities have been given more weight than the internal comfort and protection offered by the home. It should be stressed again, however, that the human density of the surrounding environment and certain municipal services, such as rubbish disposal and roads – both of which indirectly impact on housing standards and the general welfare of residents – are not included in the index.

The results indicate that urban residents have better general housing standards than the rural population and that camp residents have the poorest housing standards of all. They also indicate, not surprisingly perhaps, that the worst housing standards are found in Gaza. However, the single most important factor that produces the poor score for the camps, towns and villages of Gaza in relation to their West Bank equivalents is the substandard building materials, particularly zinc and asbestos roofs, that are widely used. If the quality of building materials were not included in the measurement of general housing standards, West Bank villages would rank as badly as the

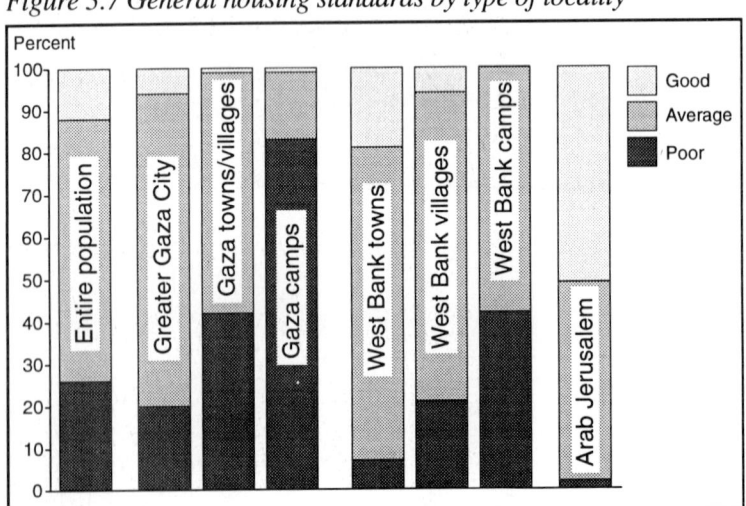

Figure 3.7 General housing standards by type of locality

Gaza camps and West Bank camps would emerge as the areas worst afflicted by unacceptable housing standards. In particular, the lack of a comprehensive sewage network, grid electricity, as well as generally poor internal amenities, combine to pull down general housing standards in the West Bank.

Notes

1 Amiry, S. & Tamari, V., *The Palestinian Village Home*, London: The British Museum, 1989.

2 Amiry and Tamari, ibid.

3 Kressel, G.M. "The cultural-economic variable in the use of disposal personal income: patterns of consumption on the West Bank and in the Gaza Strip, 1967-1977", *Asian and African Studies*, 1986.

4 A terraced house is a house that shares walls with another house. A mansion block is a large house that has been sub-divided into separate apartments. Apartment in large building means domicile in building of less than 4 floors, while high rise indicates 4 floors or more.

5 Figures from *Human Development Report 1992*, UNDP except for Israel. Israeli figure from *Statistical Abstract of Israel 1991*.

6 All indexes are to some degree arbitrary since any one index can be constructed in a range of different manners producing different results. The same is applicable to all the indexes used in this report. However, it should be noted that the various housing indexes are constructed to be descriptive rather than based on a fixed statistical distribution. The indexes are constructed from a series of items or facilities and the index indicates the actual distribution of these items among Palestinian households.

7 Statistical Abstract of Israel, 1987.

8 Bruins, H.J. & Tuinhof, Ir.A., *Water in the Gaza Strip: Hydrology Study*, Government of the Netherlands, 1991.

9 The construction of this index is somewhat complex since each facility, including bathroom, toilet, kitchen and heating, was graduated according to the quality of the amenity. However, a good score means that the household has all of these facilities at an acceptable standard, while a poor score indicates that the family has only one or less.

10 Kressel, G.M. "The cultural-economic variable in the use of disposal personal income: patterns of consumption on the West Bank and in the Gaza Strip, 1967-1977", *Asian and African Studies*, 1986, p.291

11 Kressel, op. cit.

12 It should be noted that official CBS statistics are not necessarily compatible since the items measured may be somewhat different.

13 The observations in Arab Jerusalem are small, therefore, margins of error are correspondingly large.

Chapter 4
Health

Rita Giacaman
Camilla Stoltenberg
Lars Weiseth

Introduction

An important question in the perspective of a living conditions survey is whether there are indications of social welfare systems – particularly in the field of health and education – in the occupied territories that may to some extent counteract general economic and social inequalities and insecurity. In the analysis of employment, household economy and social stratification (chapters 6, 7 and 8) it is shown that important divisions in the Palestinian community exist between camp refugees and refugees outside of camps, and, on the other hand, between Gaza and other areas. To what extent is this true also for the distribution of illnesses, for the utilization of health services, and for symptoms of distress?

Another major question is how and to what extent health conditions are influenced by the Israeli occupation, the social uprising – the intifada – and the sometimes warlike situation that Palestinians experience. Under such circumstances, individuals will experience traumatic events like injuries caused by confrontations with military personnel, arrest and perhaps even torture. Others will react to the general stress of living induced by curfews and restrictions on movement. This topic will be elaborated further in the section on symptoms of distress.

This chapter will first present data on patterns, prevalences and consequences of self-reported acute and chronic health problems, as well as on utilization of health services and health insurance coverage. Second, we will present major concepts concerning psychological and psychosomatic distress, as well as results of the questions on symptoms of distress.

All individuals in the sample were asked questions about their health and health behaviour (were they absent from work or other duties, did they consult health personnel, were they able to go out on their own?). Women answered additional questions focusing on utilization of health services during pregnancy.

The intention here is mainly to report the data collected in the FAFO survey. Only brief references will be made to other studies from the area and international sources. For an overview of literature on health in the occupied territories, see 'Health in the West Bank and the Gaza Strip, an annotated bibliography' (Health Development Information Project, 1992).

Health Transition

Concepts of health and disease, as well as the behaviour and roles related to illness, are cultural inventions. They change through time, and from one community to another. Biological, demographic, economic and social factors determine, and are influenced by, the patterns of mortality and morbidity and of perceptions and behaviour related to health.

The concept of *health transition* (Feachem et al, 1992) parallels the concept of demographic transition, referring to changes in levels and causes of illness and death that occur in the course of social and economic development. The health transition is the net result of a demographic component (the demographic composition and development of a society), a risk factor component (smoking, alcohol, diet, physical activity, traffic, uprising/conflict and violence) and a therapeutic component (availability and quality of health services). In a recent World Bank Report (Feachem et al, 1992), analysis of the health of adults in the developing world indicates that age-specific rates for both communicable and non-communicable diseases are declining in these countries, while the number and relative importance of non-communicable diseases (hypertension, diabetes, coronary heart disease, etc.) are increasing.

The present survey has not been designed to analyze health transition, but the concept is useful to keep in mind when interpreting the results.

Self-perceived Illness

Measurements of health are traditionally obtained through data on demography, mortality, morbidity and utilization of health services. In level of living conditions studies self-perceived symptoms, functional disability and utilization of services are often measured. In the living conditions survey conducted in the occupied territories, data on mortality or observed measures of morbidity (clinical investigations like weight/height/blood pressure etc., or laboratory tests) has not been collected. Nor do such studies normally include categories of self-perceived illness that can be directly translated into medical diagnoses. Measures of self-perceived morbidity are determined both by the underlying diseases and by perceptions of illness. The ratio of clinically diagnosed morbidity in relation to self-perceived morbidity is not easily predictable, and varies from one medical condition to the other, as from community to community. Rates of self-perceived illness may even be inversely correlated to clinically diagnosed morbidity. This is found in several studies where poor people with high prevalences of clinically diagnosed diseases report less illness than rich people, who may tend to categorize a wider range of conditions as illnesses (Feachem et al, 1992). Studies of self-perceived illness lead to results that are difficult to interpret, and the World Bank report states that on the basis of such studies, 'meaningful comparisons of disease burdens over time or across communities cannot be made' (Feachem et al, 1992). The report nevertheless draws comparisons between studies of self-perceived illness for want of other, more reliable information on the same topic. In this chapter, such comparisons will be made as well.

In spite of these inherent problems, studies of self-perceived illness serve useful purposes. They offer the possibility of relating perceived health problems in a representative sample with a broad range of social and economic factors.

Acute and Chronic Illness.

Acute Illness and Injury
All respondents were asked whether they had experienced any illnesses or injuries during the last month. 25% had been ill and less than 1% had been injured (table 4.2). This corresponds roughly to 3 episodes per man per year and 3.1 episodes per woman per year (Feachem et al, 1992).

For illustrative purposes we will briefly cite results from similar studies conducted in other countries. In a Norwegian health survey (Norwegian Central Bureau of Statistics, 1987) that was conducted in 1985, respondents were asked whether they had been ill during the last

14 days. The survey included children. Men reported 2.4 episodes per year and women 2.9. In the Pakistan National Health Survey (Pakistan, Federal Bureau of Statistics, 1986) respondents were asked about illness during the previous month. 14 % of the men and 17% of the women reported having been ill, which translates into 1.7 episodes per man per year and 2.1 episodes per woman per year. In the Thai Health and Welfare Survey (Thailand, National Statistics Office, 1983) the result was 0.7 episodes per man per year and 0.8 per woman per year (table 4.1). The criteria were the same as in the Pakistan survey.

Since the salience criteria vary between the different studies, caution is called for when results are to be compared. In the surveys from Pakistan and Thailand the criteria were stricter than in the surveys in the occupied territories and in Norway. It is difficult to determine the exact extent to which the differences shown in the table are caused by differences in criteria. However, it seems reasonable to assume that the level of perceived illness in the Palestinian population is not lower than in Norway. There can be many different explanations to this. However, if rates are actually lower in Pakistan and Thailand, it is probable that the high rates in the occupied territories are not caused by actual higher prevalences of disease, but rather by factors like feelings of distress, factors related to the role of being ill or access to health care services. Interpretations are by no means conclusive, as the data and the populations they are derived from cannot easily be compared.

Those who report that they have had illnesses or injuries during the last month were also asked whether their illness or injury was so serious as to prevent them from carrying out their normal duties for a period of three days or more (table 4.2). Nearly 3/4 were prevented from carrying out their normal duties. This result indicates that almost 1 out of 5 adults in the Palestinian population were away from regular work and other duties at least three days during the last month before the interviews were conducted.

Table 4.1 Self-reported incidences of acute illness and/or injury per woman per year and per man per year in different countries

	Women	Men
Occupied Territories	3.1	3.0
Pakistan	2.1	1.7
Thailand	0.8	0.7
Norway	2.9	2.4

Sources:
Feachem RGA. et al. *The Health of Adults in the Developing World* A World Bank Book: Oxford University Press, 1992.
Norway, Central Bureau of Statistics. *Health Survey 1985* Oslo 1987.
FAFO 1993.

Prolonged Illness and Handicaps

All respondents were asked whether they had any illnesses of a prolonged nature, or any afflictions due to an injury or a handicap. 30% report having prolonged illnesses or handicaps (table 4.3). In contrast, in the Norwegian health survey (Norwegian Central Bureau of Statistics, 1987) 40% of the respondents between 16 and 24 years of age reported that they had illnesses at the time of the interview. The result indicates that the concept of illness is more inclusive in Norway than in the occupied territories. In Lithuania (Hernes and Knudsen, 1991), FAFO found that 30% of the population reported some kind of chronic affliction. Compared to the present findings this seems to be a low rate since the demographic composition of Lithuania is similar to the Norwegian one,

Table 4.2 Illness and/or injury and absence from normal duties 3 days or more last month, per cent.

	Respondents	Acute illness and/or injuries	Absence from duties		Respondents	Acute illness and/or injuries	Absence from duties
All	2440	25	18	**Refugee status**			
Age				Non-refugee	1359	26	18
15-19	373	17	10	Urban camp	319	27	18
20-39	1244	22	14	Rural camp	77	36	36
40-59	526	29	25	Refugee, not camp	644	23	15
60+	297	45	34	**Camp status**			
Sex				Gaza ex camps	646	14	11
Men	1214	25	18	WB ex camps	916	29	20
Women	1226	26	18	Arab Jerusalem	478	23	14
Main region				Camps	400	29	21
Gaza	959	17	13	**Wealth**			
West Bank	1004	31	21	0-30%	740	31	24
Arab Jerusalem	477	23	14	31-66%	872	25	17
Region				67-100%	827	21	12
Greater Gaza City	313	17	14				
Gaza town/village	332	12	9				
Gaza Camp	313	21	15				
WB town	399	31	20				
WB villages	517	28	20				
WB camp	87	50	38				
Arab Jerusalem	478	23	14				

both of which are characterized by a high per centage of people in the older age groups.

13% of those who have prolonged illnesses have severe difficulty going out without assistance of others, and to 27% it is a bit difficult (question 222). In table 4.3 those who report some difficulties and severe difficulties are grouped into one.

Specific Groups of Prolonged Illnesses

Pains in joints, in the back, in legs and in muscles, are the major causes of prolonged illness among Palestinians (table 4.4). More than half (55%) of the women and more than one third (39%) of the men reporting to have chronic illnesses suffered from pain in the musculo-skeletal system. This corresponds to a prevalence in

Table 4.3 Prolonged illness and problems going out on his/her own, per cent

	Respondents	Prolonged illness	Problems going out on his/her own		Respondents	Prolonged illness	Problems going out on his/her own
All	2440	30	12	**Refugee status**			
Age				Non-refugee	388	29	10
15-19	373	10	3	Urban camp	94	29	11
20-39	1244	21	5	Rural camp	29	43	20
40-59	526	46	17	Refugee, not camp	211	33	15
60+	297	74	44	**Camp status**			
Sex				Gaza ex camps	646	27	13
Men	1214	30	12	WB ex camps	916	31	11
Women	1226	30	12	Arab Jerusalem	478	29	8
Main region				Camps	400	31	13
Gaza	959	27	12	**Wealth**			
West Bank	1004	32	11	0-30%	740	38	19
Arab Jerusalem	477	28	8	31-66%	872	29	10
Region				67-100%	827	24	7
Greater Gaza City	313	30	12				
Gaza town/village	332	25	13				
Gaza Camp	313	27	11				
WB town	399	32	9				
WB villages	517	31	12				
WB camp	87	42	15				
Arab Jerusalem	478	29	8				

the population of 12% for men and 16% for women. In the Lithuanian survey the rate was almost the same, as 14% of the population reported musculo-skeletal diseases and bodily pains, this being the major cause of chronic illness. In the Norwegian Health Survey such pain was an even more dominating cause of illness with a prevalence of 21%.

Men tend to have higher rates of physical handicaps as well as of hearing, speech or sight impairment than women do. In most international studies (Feachem et al, 1992), injury is an important cause of mortality and morbidity among male adults. Hence, injuries may also be the main cause of the high prevalence of disability among men in the occupied territories.

It seems that the prevalence of non-communicable diseases is relatively high, as witnessed by the frequencies of hypertension, heart disease and diabetes. Diabetes is regularly underreported by at least 20–50% (clinically diagnosed) in studies of self-perceived illness. A prevalence of 10% (95% confidence interval: 8–12%) in the age group of 40-59 is comparatively high, but still not surprising in the Middle East (King and Rewers, 1991). Apparently the high frequencies of gastrointestinal diseases (9%), respiratory diseases and 'other diseases' (5%) reflect instances of infective and parasitic diseases as well as of non-communicable diseases.

Table 4.4 Specific groups of prolonged illnesses Cases of selected prolonged illnesses and afflictions due to injury or handicap. Per cent of total population (respondents)

	Women (1198)	Men (1243)	Total (2441)
All	30	30	30
Hypertension	7	3	5
Heart disease, diseases of the cardiovascular system	3	2	3
Diabetes	4	3	4
Pain in joints, back pains, leg pains, muscle pains	16	12	14
Gastrointestinal	10	8	9
Respiratory	6	6	6
Physical handicap	1	4	3
Hearing, speech or sight impairment	2	4	3
Mental disability, epileptic seizures, severe stress, nervous breakdown	2	2	2
Other	4	5	5

Variations in Rates and Patterns of Illness

There are differences in rates and patterns of illness between men and women, different age groups, and different geographic and socio-economic groups in the Palestinian community.

Differences and inequalities between men and women are salient features of Palestinian society. This is reflected in the health problems and the utilization of health services. Some results, nevertheless, show less differences between men and women than what could be expected (table 4.5). There are no differences between men and women in the rates of acute or chronic illness. Nor is there any difference between the sexes in the seriousness of acute episodes as measured by the rate of absence from normal duties. Only 1% of the adults in the total sample were injured during the last month. Out of these, 2/3 are men, indicating that injury is a more common problem among men than among women. The rate of injured adults is particularly low in view of the very high rate of children that have been seriously injured in the last two months before the interviews took place (see below).

Age is a major determinant of health conditions, and no results concerning health should be interpreted without control for age. The rate of acute illness rises from 17% among those aged under 20 to 46% among those aged over 59. Prevalence of prolonged illness steadily increases from 10% in the youngest (15-19 years) to 74% in the oldest group (60 years or more). All specific causes of long term disease, and problems inflicted by these, also increase in frequency with age.

In Gaza, 16% of the respondents had suffered illness or injury during the last month, and all had in fact consulted a doctor. In the West Bank, 32% had experienced illness or injury, and in Arab Jerusalem the rate was 22%. There are no significant differences

Table 4.5 Years of education, illness last month, prolonged illness. By age. Per cent (respondents)

Age 20-39				Age 40-59			
Years of education	Respondents	Illness last month	Prolonged illness	Years of education	Respondents	Illness last month	Prolonged illness
0	46	36	24	0	141	39	52
1-6	258	5	31	1-6	125	38	55
7-9	339	22	20	7-9	78	22	39
10-12	365	19	19	10-12	114	16	40
13+	236	23	13	13+	68	19	30

between the West Bank (32%), Gaza (27%) and Arab Jerusalem (28%) when it comes to prevalence of prolonged illness. If there is, nevertheless, a real difference, this would probably be accounted for by the lower average age of respondents in Gaza as compared to the West Bank. In Gaza, however, there is a closer correlation between reported acute illness and both utilization of health care services and absence from regular duties, than there is in Arab Jerusalem and the West Bank. A possible explanation is that people in Gaza tend to consider themselves ill only when their ability to perform regular duties is affected. People in Gaza may therefore have a higher threshold for reporting illnesses, implying that low levels of reporting do not necessarily reflect low actual rates of disease.

Refugee status does not seem to influence the rate of reported illness and injury. Nor do refugees in camps report significantly different rates of illness than others living in the same area, be it Gaza or the West Bank. When assessing these results, one should bear in mind that a possible tendency to report more illnesses among people that are better off may outweigh possible higher prevalences of clinical diseases in camps. On the other hand, people belonging to households in the lowest wealth group report more acute and chronic illnesses than those in the upper third. This indicates that within the Palestinian community there is not a tendency towards more liberal definitions of illness among the rich than among the poor. About one third of those in the lowest third and one fifth of those in the upper third had been acutely ill last month. Approximately one third in the lower and one fourth in the upper wealth group have prolonged illnesses. This finding is difficult to explain in view of the regional differences mentioned earlier, but these are probably not so important when corrected for age. Persons with chronic diseases in the lower wealth group report having great difficulty going out on their own nearly 3 times more often than persons in the upper wealth group. The same pattern appears when people are asked about absence from normal duties because of acute illness. One out of four persons with acute illness are prevented from performing their normal duties if they belong to the lower third stratum, while only one out of eight in the upper wealth category could not carry out their regular tasks. The present data cannot tell whether this reflects that the duties of the latter are easier to perform, or that their illnesses are less serious.

The rate of acute and chronic illness falls dramatically with an increase in years of education. However, this correlation is much weaker when corrected for age.

When corrected for age, people who live alone tend to have a higher mortality and morbidity than people living in families (Feachem et al, 1992, Norwegian Central Bureau of Statistics). In Palestinian society almost everybody lives in households with more than one person. Only 1% report living alone, and half of these people suffer from prolonged illnesses. With increasing family size there is a fall in the reported rate of both acute and chronic illness among women, but not among men. This finding needs further analysis in order to be interpreted.

The connection between marital status and health is also difficult to depict, since almost everybody aged over 39 is married, and even when they are not married they do not live alone. There are no obvious differences in rates of reported health problems between married and unmarried people, even when corrected for age. This is a remarkable finding in view of what is regularly found in international studies.

In European and Northern American studies, employment and the role that a person plays in the labour market are regularly found to relate to health problems. The correlation between employment and health is more complicated in the occupied territories because of the complicated structure of the labour market and labour activities in this area.

Acute Illness, Chronic Illness and Symptoms of Distress

There are strong correlations between acute and chronic illness, and between illness and symptoms of psychological distress. Half (49%) of the people with chronic illnesses have experienced acute illness during the last month, versus 15% of those without chronic illnesses. This probably represents both active periods during chronic illness, and sporadic episodes of other illnesses. There is also a strong

Table 4.6a Acute and prolonged illness and degree of distress, per cent

	Degree of distress			Row table	N
	High	Moderate	No		
All	30	50	20		2439
Acute illness					
no	23	53	24	75	1816
yes	54	40	6	25	623
Prolonged illness					
no	20	54	26	70	1708
yes	55	40	5	30	731

correlation between somatic illness and symptoms of distress (tables 4.6a, 4.6b). Somatic illness, and in particular prolonged illness, is probably one of the strongest determinants of mental health (Moum et al, 1991). This will be discussed more thoroughly in the section on distress.

Smoking

Smoking is increasingly considered to be an important risk factor, in part because it has an impact on a wide range of medical conditions governing the occurrence of diseases, and in part, of course, because it is a target of preventive programmes. Smoking patterns reflect social and cultural perceptions and conditions. The habit of smoking tends to undergo a characteristic evolution within a society, first spreading among male members of the upper classes, then moving down the social scale and, finally, reaching women in a parallel way. Historically, smoking is considered modern and radical when first introduced in a community. Later on the attitudes change, much in accordance with the pattern of the habit of smoking itself. The men in the upper classes begin to consider smoking as a threat to health and fitness, and thus, as it becomes a lower class habit, those who first introduced the habit are the ones who quit first. In Palestinian society it seems that smoking habits reflect values and moral standards rather than economic circumstances. The very different prevalences of tobacco smoking among men and women exemplify the important division between the two genders in Palestinian society.

In the FAFO survey (table 4.7), very few women (2%) and nearly half (47%) of the men report that they smoke. Smoking is more prevalent among women in Arab Jerusalem (9%) than outside camps in Gaza (0%) and in the West Bank (3%). In camps only 2% of women smoke. Among men there are no differences between the different areas. The rate of smoking among women increases with the degree of exposure to the outside world, but, interestingly, it does not correlate with their status in the labour market, years of education or religious attitudes and behaviour. About 1 out of 2 men tend to smoke, irrespec-

Table 4.6b Prolonged illness and degree of distress by age, per cent

	Degree of distress					
	High		Moderate		No	
Prolonged Illness						
Age	no	yes	no	yes	no	yes
15-29	19	51	53	39	28	10
30-49	23	52	54	41	23	7
50+	24	59	59	39	17	2

tive of social background. Religiosity is the only variable showing a significant correlation with the degree of smoking among men. 60% of men with secular attitudes and behaviour smoke, while only 40% of those who are religiously active and express religious attitudes (see chapter 9) do.

The differing smoking habits of Palestinian men and women are striking, deviating radically from the much smaller differences found in European studies (Schuval, 1992). In Sweden, 24% of the men and 28% of the women aged 15 years or older were smokers in 1986. In Italy, the rates were 46% for men and 18% for women in 1983.

Table 4.7 Smoking, per cent

	Men (1214)	Women (1225)		Men (1214)	Women (1225)
Total(2439) 25	47	3	**Wealth**		
Age			0-30%	51	2
15-19	16	-	31-66%	46	2
20-39	56	3	67-100%	46	4
40-59	53	4	**Years of Education**		
60+	36	-	0	43	-
Main region			1-6	53	3
Gaza	47	-	7-9	48	3
West Bank	46	3	10-12	42	-
Arab Jerusalem	54	9	13+	50	-
Region			**Labour Force**		
Greater Gaza City	47	0	Full time employed	49	-
Gaza town/village	46	0	Part time employed	51	-
Gaza Camp	49	-	Temporarily absent	57	0
WB town	52	6	Unemployed	61	-
WB villages	44	-	Not in labour force	33	2
WB camp	40	-	**Religiosity**		
Arab Jerusalem	54	9	Secular	60	2
Camp status			Observant	45	2
Gaza ex camps	47	0	Activist	40	-
WB ex camps	47	3	**Degree of distress**		
Arab Jerusalem	56	9	High	56	5
Camps	46	-	Moderate	48	1
- = less than 10 persons			No symptoms	37	-

Smoking is the sole risk factor covered in the questionnaire. Alcohol and drug consumption are sensitive topics in all societies, and even more so in Islamic communities. It would have been difficult to get valid data on these topics with the method employed in the FAFO study.

Utilization of Health Services

Health Personnel and Institutions

A vast majority of those who are acutely ill or injured use health services (tables 4.8). 89% consult a doctor during illness, meaning that as much as 23% of the total study population have consulted a doctor during the last month before the interviews took place. 22% of those who reported to be ill or injured consulted a nurse or a pharmacist, 12% consulted a traditional healer and 14% treated themselves (table 4.9). These alternatives are not mutually exclusive. The consultations took place at private clinics in 45% of the cases, at UNRWA clinics in 16%, at government clinics or hospitals in 14%, and at charitable clinics or hospitals in 10% (question 207) of the cases. Less than 1% say that they have been ill without consulting medical personnel at all, and very few state expenditures as the reason for not doing so.

The results show a very close connection between what people perceive as illness and injury and the actual use of medical services. Academic medicine – doctors, nurses, etc – dominates, just as it generally does in industrialized countries. Traditional healers are only contacted by about 1 in 10 (12%) of those who perceive themselves as being ill, and most of these people also contact a physician.

Israeli Jews normally have very high rates of utilization of primary health care services (Schuval, 1992). According to data from the Israeli Central Bureau of Statistics (Israel, Central Bureau of Statistics, 1988), an average member of the Jewish population in Israel visits a physician about 10 times per year, while amongst the non-Jewish population each person goes to see a physician about 3 times per year on average. In the occupied territories, the rate of visits to physicians is 6 per adult per year, according to the FAFO survey. Because of differences in demographic composition and health care systems, one should be wary of direct comparisons between countries. It is still interesting to note that data from the United States (US Department of Health and Human Services, 1989) shows rates for selected western countries varying between 2.4 in Portugal and 2.7

in Sweden, and 7.4 in Belgium and 10.7 in Italy. In other words, the rates found in the occupied territories seem well within the range normally found in European countries.

Utilization rates do not necessarily reflect health conditions in a population, and may not say much about the quality, the appropriateness and the effectiveness of the health care services that are offered. A major determinant of the utilization of primary health care services is, simply, availability. The present data indicates that the availability is satisfactory for most of the population, although there is, of course, some variation between groups and areas.

Women and men alike tend to utilize health services once they have defined themselves as ill or injured. Inter-

Table 4.9 During your illness – have you consulted somebody? Answers are not exclusive. Per cent.

Physician	89
Nurse/pharmacist	22
Traditional healer	12
Treated yourself	14
Other	1
N= 623	

Table 4.8 During your illness, did you consult a physician: Per cent (cases)

	Per cent (cases)	Acute illness and/or injuries	Consulted physician		Per cent (cases)	Acute illness and/or injuries	Consulted physician
All	2441	25	23	**Refugee status**			
Age				Non-refugee	1359)	26	23
15-19	373	17	13	Urban camp	319	27	24
20-39	1244	22	19	Rural camp	77	36	34
40-59	526	29	26	Refugee, not camp	644	23	19
60+	297	45	42	**Camp status**			
Sex				Gaza, ex. camps	646	14	14
Men	1214	25	22	WB ex camps	916	29	25
Women	1226	26	23	Arab Jerusalem	478	23	15
Main region				Camps	400	29	26
Gaza	959	17	16	**Wealth**			
West Bank	1004	31	27	0-30%	740	31	27
Arab Jerusalem	477	23	15	31-66%	872	25	23
Region				67-100%	827	21	18
Greater Gaza City	313	17	17				
Gaza town/village	332	12	12				
Gaza Camp	313	21	19				
WB town	399	31	28				
WB villages	517	28	24				
WB camp	87	50	46				
Arab Jerusalem	478	23	15				

nationally it is often found that women utilize health services more than men do, but this is not the case in the present survey, when excluding visits connected with pregnancy and childbirth (table 4.10). Women are more inclined to seek help at private clinics than men are (50% vs 40%), while men are treated at government clinics and hospitals more often than women are (17% vs 10%). This probably owes to the fact that many men work in Israel. The tendency to utilize health services is strong in all age groups, but it also increases with age.

Refugees both inside and outside camps seem to consult health personnel and institutions as frequently as others do. The difference is that they utilize UNRWA services to a greater extent. UNRWA services are particularly important to those living in camps and to refugees in Gaza. However, private clinics and government clinics are used also by refugees, although less so by camp dwellers.

Charitable clinics play a certain role for some groups, while popular committee clinics and home visits play only a minor role. Pharmacies are without importance as places to go for consultation. The category labelled 'other' is quite large, but it is not clear what this signifies.

Recent descriptions and assessments of the health care services in the occupied territories are provided in both Israeli (Schuval, 1992, Israel Ministry of Health 1992) and Palestinian reports (Barghouti and Daibes, 1990, 1991a, 1991b, 1991c). To a certain extent, these documents evaluate the quality of health care services, although their conclusions are conflicting.

As a conclusion, the availability of health care services seems good and quite fairly distributed both socially and geographically. This may be an indication of a social welfare system which serves to counteract inequality and a skewed distribution of other resources. UNRWA seems to play an important role in this process, being an organization that serves many of those who have the least resources – i.e. the many refugees and poor in Gaza, and refugees in camps.

Maternal and Child Health Care Services

It is generally assumed that the provision of maternal and child health care services can have an impact on fertility behaviour by reducing infant mortality, and by providing family planning and counselling services to couples. However, only a small share of health services provide family planning assistance. In addition, it should be noted that most of the health care resources are found in the urban areas and the centre of the West Bank, leaving especially the north and south of the West Bank with a shortage of basic health services (Barghouti and Daibes 1990, 1991a, 1991b, 1991c). For instance, 64% of the commu-

Table 4.10 Where did the consultation take place? Per cent (cases)

- = less than 10 persons	Respondents	Private clinic	UNWRA clinic	Government clinic or hospital	Charitable clinic or hospital	Popular committee clinic,	Consultant came to my home	Other
All	567	45	16	14	10	3	4	8
Age								
15-19	57	36	19	19	-	-	-	16
20-39	246	49	12	9	13	4	5	6
40-59	137	40	19	16	11	-	-	10
60+	127	49	16	18	-	-	-	-
Sex								
Men	251	40	15	17	10	2	4	10
Women	316	50	16	10	10	-	3	6
Main region								
Gaza	153	29	36	25	-	-	-	-
West Bank	296	52	9	9	11	4	5	9
Arab Jerusalem	118	29	-	27	-	-	-	-
Refugee status								
Non-refugee	322	53	-	15	13	4	5	8
Urban camp	72	22	56	14	-	-	0	-
Rural camp	23	44	44	-	0	-	0	-
Refugee, not camp	148	41	21	11	9	-	-	12
Camp status								
Gaza ex camps	92	42	19	28	-	-	-	-
WB ex camps	261	53	4	9	13	5	5	10
Arab Jerusalem	118	29	-	27	-	-	-	-
Camps	96	28	54	12	-	-	-	-
Wealth								
0-30%	197	34	28	14	7	-	-	12
31-66%	206	53	12	14	7	5	-	-
67-100%	164	49	-	12	17	-	-	8

nities in the Jerusalem and 53% in the Ramallah districts have access to prenatal care services, whereas numbers are but 30% in the Jenin, 38% in the Tulkarm and 20% in the Hebron districts. This information has been obtained from the Health Development Information Project Data Base for 1992. Note that the Gaza Strip is generally well served by UNRWA-operated clinics and has a good system of pre- and postnatal care, with the exception of family planning services.

This section is based on the reports of women under the age of 50 years who have one or more children under the age of five. These women represent 56% of the total number of married women that are studied. Of these, 32% have one, 36% have two and 32% have three or more children under the age of five. When asked about their pre- and post-natal history in relation to the last child, 69% report having had pre-natal care, making 3 or more visits during the pregnancy, whereas 22% made 1-2 visits and the rest made but a referral visit or had no care at all (9%).

No correlation has been found between age or family wealth status and regular pre-natal care. The women's educational level, however, is a relevant factor. 59% of those with 0-6 years of schooling have made 3 visits or more, the number increasing to 71% among those with 7-19 years of schooling. This finding has not been corrected for age or number of children.

Geographical residence also appears to be of importance. 67% of the urban women, 63% of the village women and a high 79% of the camp women, report receiving adequate care, reinforcing the notion that when services are accessible, as in the case of UNRWA services, women tend to use them. What adds further weight to this argument is the finding that 87% of the women from the central West Bank area and 70% of the Gaza Strip women report receiving adequate care, as opposed to 59% of the women from the north and a low 54% of the women from the south of the West Bank. This is in line with the previously noted distribution of health services, reconfirming the lack of basic services in the northern and the southern parts of the West Bank.

A surprising 64% of those who have received pre-natal care report having been examined by a gynaecologist/obstetrician, followed by 38% by certified midwives, 15% by a general practitioner and 1% by a traditional birth attendant. This indicates the end of the era when traditional birth attendants figured prominently in local communities. 33% of these women have made use of UNRWA clinics. We note that a high per centage (46%) were given assistance in private clinics, and a low, but not surprising percentage (18%) by governmental health services – the majority of primary health care services in 1992 were provided by the Palestinian non-governmental and private sector –, and that 5% were given assistance at charitable societies, 13% in hospital (probably referral), 1% through committee services and the rest at home.

An attempt to identify those who seek pre-natal care in private practice reveals no correlation to age, education or wealth status. However, 51% of the women in urban areas, 48% in villages and 32% in camps seek private services for pre-natal care. Likewise, 27% of the women in the Gaza Strip, 43% of the women from the central area of the West Bank, 71% of the women from the north and a very high 88% of the women from the south of the West Bank seek private practice for pre-natal care. Those who seek private care differ little from those who do not as to regularity – three visits or more.

This analysis does suggest that financial considerations do not actually determine where care is sought. The primary determinant of where to seek care appears to be accessibility related to distance from domicile.

To summarize: First, the use of regular pre-natal care is influenced by education. The more educated the woman, the more likely that she will receive regular care. Second, regular pre-natal care is in part contingent upon area of residence. Village women and women from the south of the West Bank have a drawback, reflecting the overall skewed distribution of health services in the occupied territories. Geographical distance clearly affects women's willingness to seek regular care during pregnancy. Third, and supporting this argument, pre-natal care in private practice is not associated with age, education or family wealth status, but rather with residence. Urban women seek private care to a greater extent than other women, as most of the private practitioners are found in urban areas. Gaza Strip women use private care less than others, reflecting the readily accessible and regular services provided by UNRWA.

These results combined thus support the notion that when a system of adequate pre-natal care is available, women are in fact likely to utilize such services. Otherwise, they may skip medical follow-up.

Health Insurance

All respondents have been asked if they are covered by Health Insurance.

Government health insurance covers expenses connected to the utilization of government health services (IGHS) (Israel Ministry of Health, 1992). Government health services are not available in all districts in the occupied territories (Barghouti and Daibes, 1990, 1991a, 1991b, 1991c). Refugees are covered through the UNRWA system. Relatively many refugees report having health insurance, and they probably mean government health insurance.

Only 30% of the total population are covered by health insurance, that is, 33% of the men and 27% of the women. Among young people (15-19 years) the rate is 23%. The rate increases gradually

Table 4.11 Health insurance coverage rates. Per cent (respondents).

	Respondents	Percent		Respondents	Percent
All	2440	30	**Refugee status**		
Age			Non-refugee	1359	26
15-19	373	23	Urban camp	319	24
20-39	1244	25	Rural camp	77	37
40-59	5269	40	Refugee, not camp	644	41
60+	297	44	**Camp status**		
Sex			Gaza, ex. camps	646	27
Men	1214	32	WB ex camps	916	28
Women	1226	27	Arab Jerusalem	478	49
Main region			Camps	400	27
Gaza	959	26	**Wealth**		
West Bank	1004	29	0-30%	740	25
Arab Jerusalem	477	50	31-66%	872	27
Region			67-100%	827	37
Greater Gaza City	313	37	**Employment**		
Gaza town/village	332	19	Full time		43
Gaza Camp	313	24	Part time		25
WB town	399	29	Tempor.absent		36
WB villages	517	28	Unemployed		19
WB camp	87	34	Not in labour force		27
Arab Jerusalem	478	49			

up to 44% among those above 60 years of age. Health insurance coverage varies with socioeconomic factors. In the lower third wealth group only 25% are insured, versus 37% in the upper third of the wealth scale. This contrasts with the rates of acute and chronic illness and with the amount of problems created by illnesses in the different wealth groups, as measured in terms of absence from normal duties and difficulties in going out without help from others.

Interestingly, the coverage is at the same level in camps as it is in Gaza and the West Bank outside camps – approximately 27%. In Arab Jerusalem 49% are covered through health insurance.

Results from the FAFO survey (table 4.11) indicate a lower coverage rate than do official figures from Israel (Israel Ministry of Health, 1992). The Ministry of Health reports that 'Gaza has experienced a marked increase in coverage in the IGHS health insurance plan from 22% of the population at the beginning of 1991, to over 50% in early 1992.' There is a discrepancy between these figures and the FAFO figures, although they cannot be compared directly as children are not included in the FAFO study, and the method is not described in the Israeli report. But the low coverage among people aged 15 to 19 may indicate that the coverage would have been lower in the FAFO study also if children had been included. The West Bank Rural Primary Care Survey (Barghouti and Daibes, 1990, 1991a, 1991b, 1991c) reports dramatically low rates of health insurance, but it has data from rural areas only, and at an aggregate level, which makes comparison difficult.

Symptoms of Distress –Mental Health

Although there exist some studies on mental health effects of uprisings, civil strife and conflict, as well as numerous works on refugee populations and military occupations, few of these, if any, can be directly compared with the present report. There are a few other studies of mental health among Palestinians in the occupied territories, but differing research methods and aims limit the value of comparison (Hein 1993, Baker 1990, Punamaki 1990a, Punamaki 1990b).

Stress and Health

Most illnesses have multiple causes. Stressful conditions and life events may have positive effects, neutral effects, or may indeed contribute to the development of an illness. Stress produces illness only when certain other conditions are present, among which the most important are biological susceptibility and individual vulnerability. A stressful event rarely produces a specific disease, mainly influencing the timing of its onset rather than its type, which may be determined by other factors. Life event studies generally show that populations experiencing high numbers of negative life events suffer from high morbidity. In studies of mental disorders, the typical finding is that people who meet diagnostic criteria have experienced stressful life events more frequently in the period preceding the onset of the disorder than others have.

Psychic Trauma

The effects that stressful life events can have on mental health are consistent and strong only with regard to extreme situations. Severe experiences, such as bereavement of loved ones by "unnatural" death, military combat, imprisonment, torture, imminent threat of death, and severe illness, are generally bound to cause distress to nearly all human beings. Subsequently, psychiatric morbidity among people who have experienced such situations may be very high. The rate of morbidity in severely distressed populations depends on protecting factors, but it frequently reaches 20% or more (Weiseth, 1991). Psychic trauma is understood as a confusion of thoughts and loss of the sense of coherence and cohesion, overwhelming excitements, psycho-physiological exhaustion, and disturbed behavioural responses, all of which conditions that can be produced by stressful events. Extreme and prolonged stress, lasting for several months or years, may increase mortality and general morbidity for decades thenceforth.

In contrast to the most extreme life conditions, responses to moderate stressors show much greater variability. What is stressful to some, is not so to others. This is even more true during times of uprising, society conflict, occupation or war. The meaning of the event – and the sense of social cohesiveness -is crucial in determining how stressful a situation is to each individual (Lazarus and Folkeman 1984, Antonovsky 1992).

Protective Factors

Stress tolerance in situations involving physical danger, i.e. threats to one's health or life, increases along with the quality of cohesiveness of the group to which one belongs. Similarly, it is influenced by the degree of trust in the leadership of the group, the strength of one's motivation for the cause at hand, the ability of those involved to handle the tasks and challenges that arise, the quality of available protective equipment, of first aid and of medical services, and by several other conditions. In some instances of hardship, such as warlike situations, factors like resilience come more fully into play than under more ordinary circumstances. As a consequence, the mental effects of moderate warfare, or of other conflicts, may be surprisingly small. Mental health has even been shown to improve during war (Ødegaard 1954, Eitinger 1990).

Uncertainty and Lack of Control

Two decisive intervening variables can be identified in most stressful life events, namely experience of uncertainty and of lack of control. Severe and particulary prolonged uncertainty and lack or loss of control, i.e. inpredictability and inability to influence one's environment, strongly reinforce the effects of the stressor. Psychic traumas are called forth in situations characterized by severe helplessness and hopelessness.

Post-traumatic Stress Disorder and Late Psychic Sequels

Stressful life events can be classified as

1. acute and limited in time
2. occurring in series over an extended period of time
3. chronic intermittent stressors
4. chronic permanent stressors

While acute time-limited traumas typically produce immediate reactions and entail a risk of developing *post-traumatic stress disorder* (PTSD) during the first year, chronic stressors allow the individual to mobilize defences and adapt to new circumstances. In this case, if the threat has been severe and constant, so-called *late psychic sequels* may appear after a long period of time. Thus, typically, the final and full-scale consequences of such experiences may only be known after the stressful period is over and some years have passed.

The present study may provide a baseline for generating hypotheses as to how Palestinians in the occupied territories react to the stressful conditions under which they live. Many of them have experienced traumatic events, but, as it has been important to guard the anonymity and security of all respondents, the survey questions were not posed in a way that would make it possible to identify the particular stressors that each respondent has been or is exposed to.

Method

Because subjective factors are important in determining stress responses, the method of recording *self-perceived symptoms* is considered valid, maybe more so than for the study of somatic illnesses. The reliability of the report may, however, be reduced by motivational and other factors, and one has to recognize the problem of objectivity confronting the respondents. As in all self-reporting the answers may be influenced by the wish or need to be seen as a socially acceptable person. In the case of recording psychiatric problems, this may cause under-reporting. On the other hand, specific post-traumatic stress reactions may be less stigmatizing if they reflect stress exposures that are seen as admirable or heroic by the surroundings.

Seven Symptoms of Distress

In this study, relatively few psychic symptoms or stress reactions have been recorded, and no standardized instruments have been used that could measure the severity of symptoms or define cases. Seven symptoms have been recorded (table 4.13), and presence or absence of each symptom noted. Headache and fatigue were included because these symptoms frequently express psychological or psychosomatic distress. None of the symptoms are specific. Thus they may reflect underlying conditions of various kinds, such as physical illness, organic brain conditions, psychosocial problems, or psychiatric conditions such as neurosis, post-traumatic stress disorder or clinical depression.

Measuring Degree of Distress

In order to obtain a quantitative measure of the dependent variables, we have used the following procedure: An *index* has been calculated for each respondent by assigning equal weights (i.e. zero = absence of symptom, one = presence of symptom). Based on the frequencies and distributions of the symptoms and the index in the population, and on clinical experience, the index scores are divided into three subgroups (table 4.12).

Persons with no symptoms are assigned to the group with 'no distress'. Persons with 1-3 symptoms are grouped as having a 'moderate degree of distress', and persons with 4-7 symptoms fall into the group with a 'high degree of distress'. The term distress is used in order to avoid misinterpretations. The degree of distress does not imply any simple causal relations, it does not reflect a particular division between somatic and psychic factors, and it does not reflect clinical psychiatric diagnoses. Although we expect people with psychiatric conditions to be present in the highly distressed group, this survey does not allow specific estimations of prevalences of psychiatric illnesses.

Table 4.12 Construction of index expressing degree of distress

Degree of distress	Number of reported symptoms 0 - 7	Percent
No symptoms	0	20
Moderate	1 - 3	50
High	4 - 7	30
N=2441		

Table 4.13 Frequencies of symptoms of distress by gender. Per cent (number of persons affected)

	Women (1198)	Men (1243)	Total (2441)
Sleep disturbances and/or nightmares	36	34	35
Irritability, nervousness and/or anxiety	49	44	46
Impaired concentration	27	25	26
Headache	47	36	42
Impaired memory	28	20	24
Depression	30	28	29
General tiredness	52	47	50

Table 4.14 Frequencies of symptoms of distress in the occupied territories and in Norway Per cent (respondents)

	Norway n=8096	Occupied Territories n=2441
Sleep disturbances and/or nightmares	16	35
Irritability, nervousness and/or anxiety	15	46
Headache	25	42
Depression	10	29
General tiredness	16	50

High Degrees of Distress

The frequencies of various symptoms of distress appear to be relatively high in Palestinian society (tables 4.13, 4.14).

Rough comparisons can be made with the results of the Norwegian Health Survey of 1985 (Norwegian Central Bureau of Statistics). The Hopkins Symptom Check List (HSCL) has been employed in this survey, and some of the questions are similar to those used in the occupied territories. In Norway, a representative sample of the population aged over 16 was interviewed (n=8096). 25% of the Norwegians reported having headache, in contrast to 42% among the Palestinians, 15% of Norwegians and 46% of Palestinians reported nervousness, 16% of Norwegians and 35% of Palestinians reported sleep disorders, and 10% versus 29% respectively, reported being depressive. While 16% of Norwegians reported lack of energy, as much as 50% of Palestinians claimed general tiredness. This means that the Palestinians report between 1,5 and 3 times higher rates of symptoms than Norwegians do (table 4.13). Considering the very different age distributions of the two populations, the differences in frequencies of psychological symptoms become even more striking.

In the study of the occupied territories the rates of men and women do not differ as much as is often found in other studies (Moum et al 1991, Hernes & Knudsen 1991).

Even young people report high frequencies of distress. In the age group 15 – 30 years only 26% report no symptoms (table 4.15). The effects of increasing age are considerable, particularly amongst women. While the number of moderate scores is practically constant in all age groups, the number of persons reporting no distress is very low in the highest age bracket.

The steady increase with age almost disappears, however, when controlled for prolonged illnesses. Among people who do not report prolonged illness, the proportion of persons having a

Table 4.15 Degree of psychological distress by age and gender. Per cent

Age	High Men	High Women	High Total	Moderate Men	Moderate Women	Moderate Total	No Men	No Women	No Total	Total
15-30	22	25	24	52	51	51	27	24	26	51
31-50	29	37	33	48	52	50	23	11	18	32
51+	42	55	48	48	42	45	10	4	7	17
Total		30			50			20		

high degree of distress increases only slightly, from 19% in the lowest age group to 24% in the highest. Among those who do report prolonged illness, the increase with age is from 51% to 59%. This indicates that the main reason why the highly distressed group increases with age is probably the rising prevalence of prolonged illness. Although somatic diseases are known to be strong determinants of psychiatric symptoms (Moum et al 1991), the interpretation of this finding is not clear. Among the diseases reported as prolonged illnesses, all may in principle include illnesses that are symptoms of, or results of, psychological distress. This is particularly so for musculoskeletal syndromes and for the category including mental disorders. On the other hand, the symptoms included in the degree of distress index may well be expressions of somatic disorders. The frequency of high degrees of distress among those who do not have any specific prolonged illnesses is approximately 20%, regardless of age. This is a high rate, requiring other explanations than somatic disease.

Geographical Area, Refugee Status and Residency in Camps

The Gaza population reports lower levels of distress than does the population in the West Bank and in Arab Jerusalem (table 4.16). This is partly explained by the higher average age in the West Bank and Arab Jerusalem, and partly by the fact that people in Gaza report less somatic illness as well. However, results reported in other chapters clearly indicate that living conditions in Gaza are generally worse than in the West Bank. So why do Gazans report fewer symptoms of distress? One possible explanation may indeed be that people in Gaza have a clearer sense of collective meaning and common purpose. A greater sense of cohesiveness, originating in a more traditional family structure, may also contribute as a protective factor. The population in Gaza may enjoy greater protection against distress as the perception of an external enemy becomes exceedingly strong. Then again, the explanation could well be that Gaza residents are less prone to recognizing and expressing symptoms of psychological distress. The degree of perceived conflict in Palestinian society is high (see chapter 9), particularly amongst women in Arab Jerusalem, where living conditions tend to be better than elsewhere in the occupied territories, and this may be seen as an expression of distress.

Refugee status does not influence the degree of distress in itself, but refugees seem to follow the trend of the population in the geographical area they belong to. Living in camps does not make a difference in itself either. However, people in rural camps in the West Bank report higher degrees of distress than others do.

A low educational level and a low economic status relate to high levels of distress. Wealth is here measured in a wealth index (chapter 6) and in respect to weekly consumption of meat. Educational level is measured in terms of years of education.

Arrest of Household Member and Serious Injury of Child. Traumatic Events?

The questions whether the respondent has experienced arrest of a household member and whether a child in the household has been seriously injured, cover events that are stressful to most people, and probably traumatic to many (American Psychiatric Association, 1987).

Table 4.16 Geographical area, refugee status, camp residency and degree of distress. Per cent

	Degree of distress				Degree of distress		
	High	Moderate	No symptoms		High	Moderate	No symptoms
Main region				**Refugee status**			
Gaza	20	56	24	Non-refugee	31	51	18
West Bank	36	47	17	Urban camp	29	55	16
Arab Jerusalem	37	42	21	Rural camp	40	37	23
Camp status				Refugees outside camps	30	46	24
Gaza without camps	20	53	27	**Wealth**			
West Bank without camps	34	50	18	0-30%	35	48	17
Arab Jerusalem	37	42	21	31-66%	31	47	22
Camps	32	51	17	67-100%	27	54	20
Region				**Weekly consumption of meat**			
Greater gaza city	23	58	19	<1kilo	36	49	15
Gaza town/village	17	50	33	1-2 kilo	31	49	20
Gaza camp	21	59	20	3-4 kilo	21	51	28
West Bank town	30	49	21	>/5 kilo	16	56	28
West Bank villages	35	49	16				
West Bank camp	58	31	12				
Arab Jerusalem	37	42	21				

About 1 out of 3 respondents have a household member who has been arrested. A respondent who has experienced the arrest of a household member is more likely to report high degrees of distress than others (table 4.17). Interestingly, the difference is significant only among men, possibly because more men than women are arrested. Several of these may, in fact, be among the respondents.

Table 4.17 Possible effects of trauma of arrest of household member on degree of psychological distress.

Household member arrested	High	Moderate	No symptoms
Men			
Yes	33	51	16
No	25	49	26
Women			
Yes	36	46	18
No	32	52	16

The relation between reported distress and experience of arrest is similar in all socio-economic groups. Thus, a high socio-economic level does not seem to be a protective factor in this case.

A very high per centage of the respondents with children aged under 12 have a child that has suffered serious injury during the last two months. These respondents also report high degrees of distress (table 4.18). Child injury, thus, significantly affects the number of symptoms for both men and women. If this is not a spurious effect, it is still impossible to say in what direction it works. As for the correlation between chronic disease and injury of children, one can assume that the chronic disease of the adult comes before the serious injury of the child. Again, there is a strong correlation between having a seriously injured child and the number of reported symptoms of distress, particularly for men. 77% of the respondents have children in the household aged 12 years or less. 18% of these respondents have children in the household who have recently (during the last 2 months) sustained serious injuries requiring prolonged medical attention. 30% of the households with injured children have more than one child that has been injured. 45% of the injured children are from 0 to 3 years old. 78% of the injuries took place inside the house and 13% outside the house, and 9% do not know where the child has been injured. Serious injury of young children seems to be an important health problem in the occupied territories.

Table 4.18 Serious injury of children. Relationship between high degree of distress and serious injury of children in the family. Per cent of persons with high degree of distress (4-7 symptoms). Only respondents with children below the age of twelve

	Women	Men
Children injured	44	35
No children injured	28	25

Conclusion

Patterns and prevalences of self-reported health problems reflect both underlying diseases and cultural concepts of illness. High reported rates of certain illnesses may reflect a high prevalence of the corresponding disease(s), or a broad definition of the illness, or both. This calls for caution when analyzing self-reported health problems. Utilization of health care services is measured more easily through interviews. Symptoms of distress are always measured through self-reporting, although the methodology may, of course, be more or less refined.

The data on health draws a broad and general picture of what people perceive as health problems and how prevalent these are, where and to which extent they seek medical services, and whether they suffer from symptoms of psychological distress. This presentation gives but a rough baseline for further and more refined analysis of particular questions of interest. Consequently, interpretations must be made with reservations at this stage.

One important question to discuss on the basis of these results is the following: Is there a well-functioning health care system in the occupied territories that serves people equally, independent of their economic resources?

Another major question is: How and to what extent does the Israeli occupation and the intifada influence people's health, and in particular their mental health?

None of these questions can be answered directly. However, the data provides indirect evidence that can be of use when discussing these problems.

It seems that although illnesses and health problems are unequally distributed in the population (that is, illnesses and problems caused by illness are more prevalent among the poor than among the rich), people tend to seek medical services once they have defined themselves as ill, and such services seem to be relatively equally distributed in the sense that nearly all groups have access to health care. UNRWA serves refugees both in- and outside camps, and appears to be an important factor in counteracting social inequality in health care. Low health insurance coverage does not prevent people from using health care services. The appropriateness and quality of the health care may of course vary along social gradients.

The second question needs further analysis as well, but the impression is that reported rates of symptoms of psychological distress are very high, and the few indications we have of stressful and possibly traumatic experiences show strong correlations with high degrees of distress. These events are partly related to general living conditions, and partly to the social uprising and occupation. Further analysis of these problems would be useful for assessing the quality of life in the occupied areas.

Summary

Very briefly, the main results from the preceding analyses can be summarized in the following way:

Acute illness and injury
* 25% report that they have had an illness or an injury during the last month before the interview took place.
* 72% of those who report illnesses during the last month had been prevented from carrying out their regular duties for 3 days or more, which corresponds to 18% of the total adult population.

Prolonged illness and handicaps
* 30% report that they have illnesses of a prolonged nature, or afflictions due to an injury or a handicap.
* Pain in the musculo-skeletal system is the most frequent reason for prolonged illness. 16% of all women and 12% of all men suffer from such conditions.

Determinants of illness
* Age is the strongest determinant of the prevalence of illness. Prevalence of illness increase along with age.
* Women and men report the same rates of both acute and chronic illness, but there are some differences when it comes to specific groups of prolonged illnesses.
* Frequency of acute and prolonged illness is higher when the wealth of the household is low, and when the educational level of the individual is low.
* It seems that refugee status and camp residency has a limited influence on rates of self-reported illness.

Utilization of health services
* More than 96% of those who have been ill consulted a physician (89%) and/or other kinds of health personnel. Once people

define themselves as ill, they tend to consult health personnel. This is true for all subgroups, indicating that availability of health services is good. The quality and appropriateness of the health services offered cannot be evaluated in this survey.
* Utilization of maternal and child health care services shows the same pattern. The utilization increases along with the educational level of the mother, but is not dependent on the wealth of the household. Geographical accessibility seems to be the most important factor determining the use of these services.
* Utilization of primary health care services is much lower than it is in the Jewish population in Israel, but well within the limits of what is found in Western Europe.

Health insurance:
* Health insurance coverage rates a low 30%.
* Coverage does not seem to be determined by refugee status or camp residency. In camps the rate is 27%.
* Important determinants of coverage rates are age, wealth, residency in Arab Jerusalem, and full time employment. In Arab Jerusalem the rate is 50%, in Gaza 26%, and in the West Bank 29%.

Mental health
* Only 20% of the population report no symptoms of distress. 50% report 1-3 symptoms, and 30% report a high degree of distress (4-7 symptoms).
* Comparison with studies in other countries is difficult, but the proportion of people who report symptoms of psychological distress seems relatively high.
* Somatic illness is a strong determinant of psychological distress. When corrected for illness, the degree of distress increases slightly with age.
* Does the high degree of distress in the population indicate stress caused by traumatic events? More symptoms of distress are reported by individuals who have somebody in the household that has been arrested during the intifada, or who have a child that has been seriously injured during the last two months. This may indicate that trauma is a possible reason for the very high numbers of symptoms reported.

References

Feachem RGA. et al. *The Health of Adults in the Developing World* A World Bank Book: Oxford University Press, 1992.

Norway, Central Bureau of Statistics. *Health Survey 1985* Oslo 1987.

Pakistan, Federal Bureau of Statistics. *National Health Survey 1982 – 83.* Karachi: Government of Pakistan, 1986.

Thailand, National Statistics Office. *Health and Welfare Survey 1981.* Bangkok, 1983.

King H, Rewers M. *Global estimates fo prevalence of diabetes mellitus and glucose tolerance in adults.* World health Organization Ad Hoc Diabetes reporting Group. Diabetes Care MS No. 91-142.

Schuval JT. *Social Dimensions of Health. The Israeli Experience.* Praeger. London 1992.

Central Bureau of Statistics. *Monthly Bulletin of Statistics.* Supplement 3. Jerusalem. 1988.

United States Department of Health and Human Services. *Health Care Financing Review.* Annual supplement 1989. Baltimore, Md: DHHS. 1989.

Hein FA *Mental Health in Traumatized Children.* Abstract submitted for the 3. European Conference on Traumatic Stress, Bergen June 6.-10. 1993.

Baker AM. *The Psychological Impact of the Intifada on Palestinian children in the occupied West Bank and Gaza: an exploratory study.* American Journal of Orthopsychiatry 60(4) October 1990.

Punamaki RL. *Impact of Political Change on the Psychological Stress Process among West Bank Palestinian Women.* Medicine and War. Volume 6, 169-181. 1990.

Punamaki RI, Suleiman R. *Predictors and effectiveness of coping with political violence among Palestinian children.* British Journal of Social Psychology. 29,67-77. 1990.

Lazarus RS, Folkeman S. *Stress, Appraisal and Coping.* Springer. New York 1984.

Antonovsky A. *Can Attitudes Contribute to Health?* Advances, The Journal of Mind-Body Health. 8(4), 33-49. Fall 1992.

Ødegård O. *The incidence of mental disease in Norway during World War II.* Acta Psychiatr Nevrol. 29, 333-353. 1954.

Eitinger L. *World War II in Norwegian Psychiatric literature.* In Lundeberg JE, Otto U, Rubeck B (Eds). Wartime Medical Services, Forsvarets forskningsanstalt. 413-425. Stockholm 1990.

Moum T, Falkum E, Tambs K, Vaglum P. *Sosiale bakgrunnsfaktorer og psykisk helse.* In Moum T (Ed) Helse i Norge. Gyldendal. Oslo 1991. (Norway)

American Psychiatric Association. *Diagnostic and statistical manual of mental disorders.* 3rd revised edition. Washington DC 1987.

Chapter 5
Education

Marianne Heiberg

Since 1948 and the first mass dislocation of Arabs from the former Mandated Palestine, Palestinians have placed a special emphasis on the value of education. Education is seen as a durable, but moveable asset that can be used in whatever circumstances a person eventually finds him or herself in, in order to gain social standing and economic well-being. Especially for the dispossessed sectors of the population, education is prized as the major avenue to a better income and enhanced status.

Although Palestinians assign uncommon value to the education of children generally, parents still place the greatest emphasis on the education of sons both as a source of family pride and identity and as an investment in economic security later on[1]. Advanced education for women continues to meet a certain resistance. Many families fear that attendance at mixed institutions of advanced education can lead women into situations which potentially reflect poorly on family honour. More importantly, the traditional expectation of women is that their ultimate fulfilment comes through marriage and children, not through educational and professional achievement.[2] Moreover, the economic rewards gleaned through education will become the property of the daughter's husband and thus will not function as a return on investment for her family. Among many Palestinians, advanced education for women is often viewed as an impediment to marriage. It is the roles obtainable through marriage, rather than the opportunities opened by education, that primarily define a woman's place in Palestinian society.

A major effect of the educational process is that customary knowledge and norms come under challenge by exposure to attitudes, events and experiences which originate outside the local community. Put in other words, education makes the boundaries of local communities increasingly porous and the hold of traditional local elites more tenuous. Those individuals who have had most exposure through education to the world outside local boundaries also tend to become channels for funnelling new ideas and social attitudes back into the local community. They tend to become agents for a type of change that often challenges and redefines local assumptions and practice.

Frequently, the educational process not only produces change and mobility but also an increased intellectual tolerance. A comprehensive educational system which ensures high educational attainment for the vast majority of individuals builds its own intellectual checks and balances against the possible dominance of small, intransigent intellectual minorities. Attempts to impose ideological dogma tend to be confronted by the countervailing force of an educated population that acts as discriminating consumers in an international super market filled with competing dogmas, ideologies and ideas. The broadened and more informed range of intellectual discourse produced by such a system of quality mass education ensures that most ideas, conventions and intellectual assumptions have to withstand the scrutiny of constant questioning and debate.

Brief Overview of the Evolution of the Palestinian Educational System

Limited mainly to primary education, an official educational system in historical Palestine was first instituted at the beginning of this century under the Ottoman Empire. Under the British Mandate Authority education facilities were expanded and endeavours were made, largely unsuccessful, to establish a system of compulsory education. Although possibilities for female education were enlarged, this initial expansion of educational facilities during the Mandate period was primarily of benefit to men.

In 1948 the Gaza Strip became a trusteeship of Egypt. Consequently, the Gazan school system was transferred from British to Egyptian authority and placed under the Egyptian system of education and curriculum. Similarly, the incorporation of the West Bank into Jordan meant the extension of Jordanian educational authority into the region. Thus, until 1967 the educational systems of the West Bank and Gaza operated under the auspices of two independent states. With the establishment of Israeli occupation in 1967, the structure of education in the territories was subjected to an additional complication. While the Israeli military authorities retained the Jordanian and Egyptian educational systems and curricula in the West Bank and Gaza respectively, actual control of educational institutions was placed firmly under Israeli jurisdiction.[3] The Israeli military government has complete authority over matters relating to the financing of, and the hiring and firing of, staff in government schools.[4] Moreover, Israeli authorities have compiled a long list of books which are banned from the schools. Any explicit references to versions of Palestinian history and culture of which the authorities disapprove are suppressed. Needless to say, these restrictions make teaching, particularly in the social sciences, problematic.

Since 1967 the number of educational facilities as well as student numbers have grown significantly. In 1967-68 West Bank schools numbered just over 800. Currently, over 1300 schools exist. In Gaza the number of schools has increased from 166 in 1967 to approximately 340 today.[5] The expansion of educational services has been especially notable on the post-secondary level of community colleges and universities.

The school system in the West Bank and Gaza is based on the four cycles: kindergarten for children 4 to 5 years old, 6 years of elementary school, 3 years of preparatory school and 3 years of secondary school. At the end of 12 years schooling students take the General Secondary Education Certificate Examination (the *tawjihi* exam). Admission into institutions of advanced education is determined largely by *tawjihi* exam results. Education in the occupied territories is provided by three principal sectors: government schools, private schools and UNRWA schools. Government schools, which were established after 1967, are by far the largest sector of the school system. Students pay a nominal tuition and, as mentioned, both financial control and the curriculum are entirely under the auspices of the Israeli government. Private schools are operated by various local and foreign institutions, most of which are of a religious nature. Some of these schools provide only kindergarten although others offer educational courses through secondary level. UNRWA, which is particularly important in the Gaza Strip, provides education only through primary and preparatory levels and tuition is free. All further education has to be provided by either the private or governmental sectors.

Since the beginning of the intifada, however, the five main universities of the West Bank and Gaza and most of the preparatory and secondary schools and even primary schools have been subject to frequent and prolonged closures. The effects of these closures could mean a decline in educational attainment among the current school age sector of the Palestinian population. It should be noted, however, that this survey is unable to measure this potential decline. However, in a subsequent chapter which deals with political and social attitudes, survey results are presented that could suggest that the extensive disruption of education, which has had its greatest impact on those who are currently from 15 to 25 years of age, may be producing a discernible surge of intolerance among younger Palestinians.

Specifically, this chapter will explore changes in literacy rates, educational attainment and the impact of education on economic mobility, use of leisure and attitudes. It should be noted that within the framework of a base line study, only some of the survey data collected can be presented here. Again, the reader is also advised to consult this book's appendix A, on sampling strategy.

Literacy Rates

The critical element in literacy is not only the ability to read, but the ability to write statements concerning daily life. It is the ability to write, rather than just read, that equips the individual with the essential qualification for full membership in modern literate society. Most international definitions of functional literacy take the ability to write, rather than to read, as the pivotal threshold.

In terms of general literacy rates Palestinians score in the middle ranges for developing countries. Some comparative figures are shown in figure 5.1.[6]

The Palestinian rate can be broken down by gender (figure 5.2).

The differentials in the literacy rates between men and women in the current Palestinian population is almost entirely due to the high illiteracy rates among older women, especially those in the rural areas of the West Bank. Although male literacy rates over the past 30 to 40

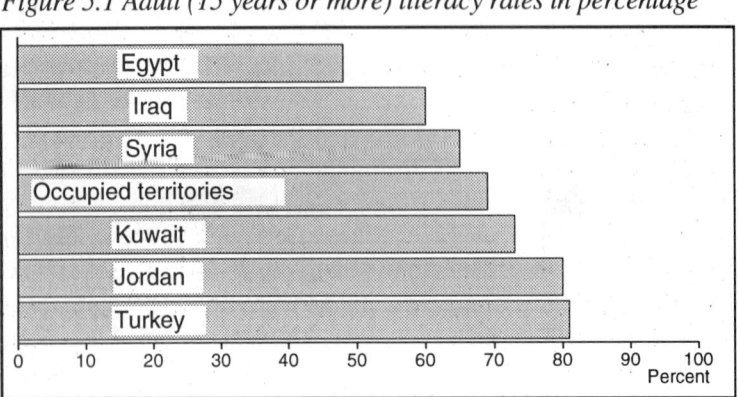

Figure 5.1 Adult (15 years or more) literacy rates in percentage

Figure 5.2 Adult literacy rates by gender

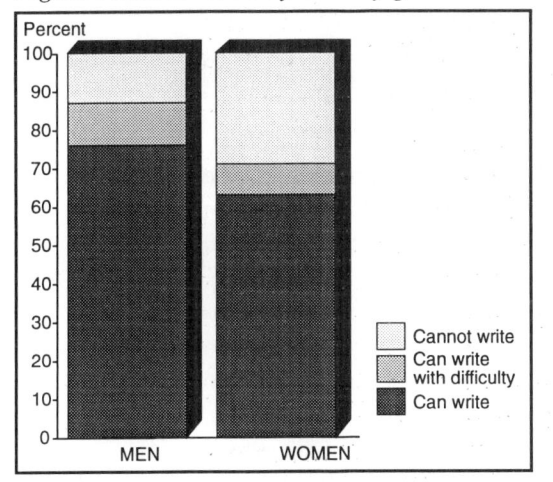

Table 5.1 Adult literacy rates by region and gender

	Can write	Can write with difficulty	Can't write
Male Gaza	72	7	21
Female Gaza	69	5	27
Male West Bank	77	15	8
Female West Bank	57	11	32
Male Arab Jerusalem	78	9	13
Female Arab Jerusalem	75	6	19

years have doubled, women's literacy has grown some 8-fold in the same period. Figure 5.3 present literacy rates by gender and age.

When broken down by region (table 5.1), survey figures indicate that literacy rates are lowest among women in the West Bank, the region in wich disparities between men and women in terms of literacy are the greatest.

Survey results also indicate that the Christian population have a higher literacy rate than Muslims (78% versus 69% for Muslims) and UNRWA refugees have about the same rate (70%) as non-refugees (69%).

Six years schooling is often considered the threshold for functional literacy. In the case of Palestinians, survey results would suggest that six years schooling may be sufficient for rudimenta-

Figure 5.3 Adult (15 years or more) literacy rates by gender and age

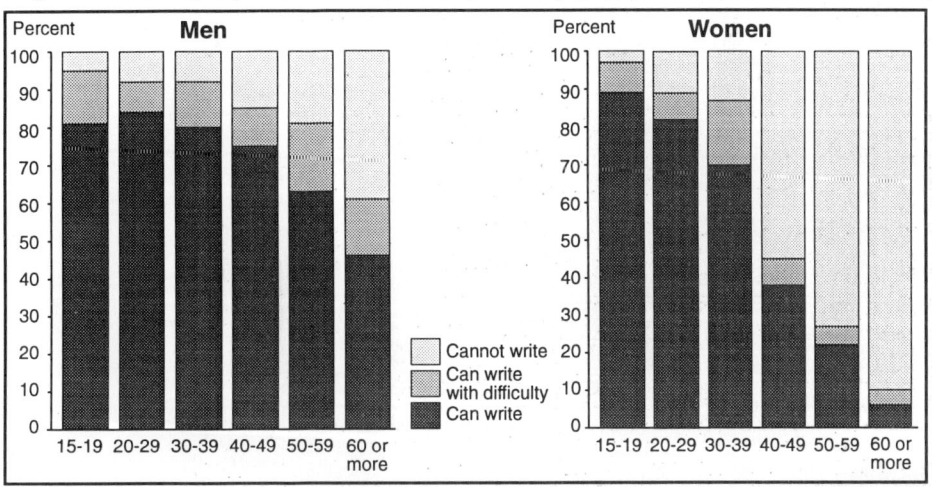

135

ry literacy, but is not the equivalent of literacy in relation to the ability to write (table 5.2).

Educational Attainment

The sharp increase in literacy of the Palestinian population corresponds to the marked increase in the number of school years the younger generations of Palestinians have completed and the closing of the gender gap between the amount of education received by men and women.

Figure 5.4 reflects the evolution of Palestinian educational attainment over at least the past 40 years. It indicates a sharp jump in educational attainment separating those who are currently from 50 to 59 years from those who are older. However, it also indicates that men, much more so than women, were the beneficiaries of the initial improvement in general educational levels. The gender gap, the average length of female education in per cent of male education, did not significantly begin to narrow until some 20 years ago. This could suggest that it was only at this point that, first, Palestinian attitudes to female education began to change radi-

Table 5.2 Literacy rates by mean number of years of schooling

	Mean school years
Can write	10.3
Can write with difficulty	5.8
Cannot write	1.3

Figure 5.4 Mean number of completed school years by gender and age groups

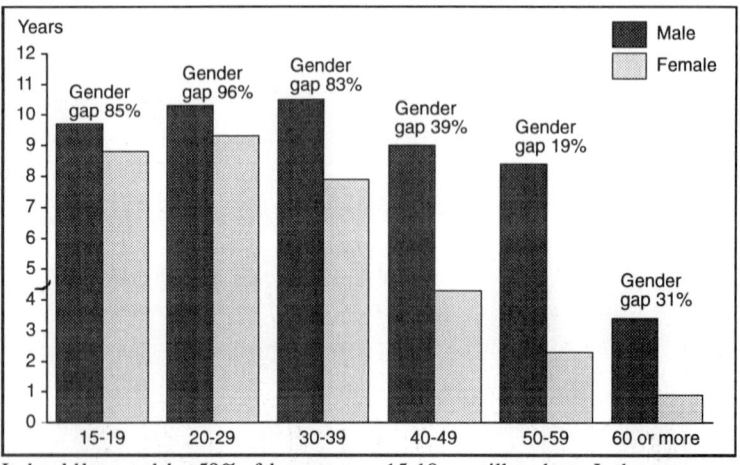

[Bar chart showing mean years of schooling by age group for males and females:
- 15-19: Gender gap 85%
- 20-29: Gender gap 96%
- 30-39: Gender gap 83%
- 40-49: Gender gap 39%
- 50-59: Gender gap 19%
- 60 or more: Gender gap 31%]

It should be noted that 59% of the age group 15-19 are still students. In the age group 20-29 years some 8% are still students.
The gender gap is female education as a percentage of male education.

cally and, second, Palestinian families felt they could afford to send their daughters to school.

The survey data also indicates that UNRWA refugees stay in school somewhat longer than non-refugees (an average of 8.3 years versus 7.8). Again Christians enjoy on average longer educations (9.7 years) than Muslims (7.9). There are also significant variations between regions. In figure 5.5 refugee camps have been separated as a distinct category.

Notably, if the older generation of camp refugees who have little or no education are overlooked, the educational attainment of camp refugees is as high as for Palestinians living in Arab Jerusalem. In fact, other survey data suggests that West Bank camp refugees are more likely than any other single group to have advanced education. Some 21% of them have schooling beyond the secondary level compared to only 9% of those who live in West Bank villages and 17% of the residents of Arab Jerusalem. UNRWA refugees in general have a significantly higher educational level than their non-refugee counterparts. Some 45% have at least 10 years schooling compared to 36% of other Palestinians.

On the other end of the spectrum, however, the survey data indicates that among the younger age groups, there still exists a significant percentage who are illiterate. In the West Bank, Gaza and Arab Jerusalem, camps excluded, some 7% of Palestinians between 20 and 29 years of age say they have had no schooling whatsoever. For camp refugees in this age group the figure is 2%.

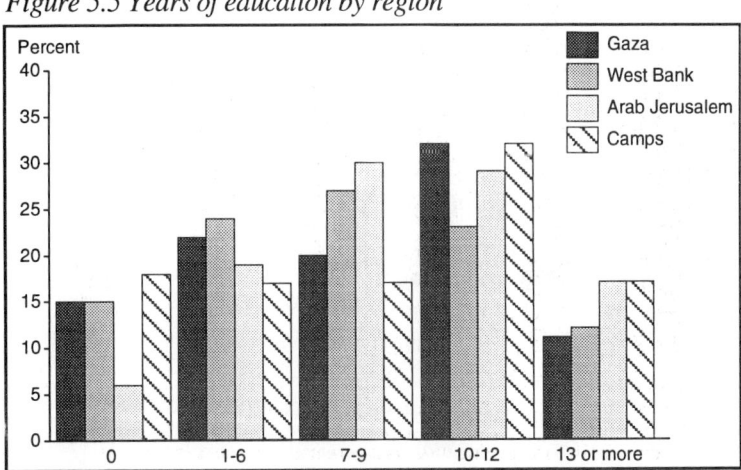

Figure 5.5 Years of education by region

It is widely believed that UNRWA and private schools provide a better education than that provided by the Israeli government system. Partly this may reflect the resentment many Palestinians experience over Israeli control of the educational curriculum. The survey data shows that some 9% of those who had attended UNRWA schools were not in fact UNRWA registered refugees although whether they were attracted by the quality of education or the lack of tuition fees (or both) is uncertain. Survey results suggest that those who had attended UNRWA schools had somewhat higher literacy rates (87%) than those who had attended government schools (83%) and stayed in school somewhat longer (UNRWA mean = 10.2 years, government mean = 9.7 years). On these criteria private schools seem to demonstrate the best performance. 90% of those who had attended private schools were fully literate and the average number of years of school attendance was 10.9. However, the differences are small and should be treated with caution. Except with reference to literacy rates, it needs to be stressed, moreover, that the survey data cannot be used to make judgements on the quality, in contrast to the quantity, of education.

The survey was also interested in determining why those Palestinians who had left school having completed only 9 years or less had not continued their educations. Of most interest is the data collected for those currently of school age. This data indicates that women are the most frequent early school leavers (table 5.3).

When the reported reasons for leaving school are examined, men and women seem to discontinue their educations for somewhat different reasons. Because the number of observations among those between 15 and 19 are rather small, table 5.4 can only serve to identify general trends.

The results reveal a fairly complicated picture which is difficult to interpret clearly. Although among women early marriage seems to be a factor in school leaving, for the youngest group of women, a reported lack of academic ability appears to be the single most important reason

Table 5.3 Percentage of Palestinians leaving school with 9 years or less of education by age

	Men	Women
15-19 years	22	37
20-29 years	37	51

Table 5.4 Main reason for leaving school with 9 years or less of education by age, percentage

	Men		Women	
	15-19	20-29	15-19	20-29
Marriage	-	11	28	-
Work	-	15	5	-
Helping family at home	11	16	15	20
Not clever enough	56	41	29	19
Not enough money	17	20	11	12
Because of intifada	3	1	11	4
Transport problems	-	6	3	-
Other	10	7	11	14

for leaving school. The same is true for the youngest group of men. However, why men should feel less clever than women and both men and women in the youngest age group feel less clever than those in the preceding age group is unclear. The costs of education, both in terms of direct costs and opportunity costs, such as lost labour, appear to be a major cause inhibiting the continuation of schooling. The intifada, and the accompanying fear that parents harbour for their children's safety, seems to be having a more disruptive effect on the education of women than of men.

Education and Economic Mobility

Another factor that correlates with educational attainment among current school age youth is the educational level of their fathers. In order to examine this relationship, a very specific sub-sample needs to be constructed because of, among other reasons, the nature of the life cycle of the Palestinian family. This sub-sample consists of those who are currently between 20 to 29 years, have completed their educations, are still unmarried and who are still living in their father's home. The relationship between these individuals' educational attainment and the education received by their fathers (or heads of households) reveals – as expected – a positive relationship between the two (table 5.5). Because the sample in question consists of only 117 individuals, it is not possible to provide a detailed breakdown.

The effects of education on employment and income will be examined in subsequent chapters. However, it can be noted that, unlike Western societies, in which increased education correlates strongly with increased income, in Palestinian society this correlation is weaker. Table 5.6 is based on an economic classification of the Palestinian population into the thirds ranging from the poorest third (0-33%) to the richest third (67-100%). (This classification will be discussed at length in chapter 6.)

Table 5.6 indicates the comparative weakness in the correlation between education and economic resources. In a Western society it would be unusual to find that almost 20% of those with no education at all, individuals who one can assume are probably illiterate, nonetheless belong to the upper economic third of society.

Table 5.5 Educational attainment of 20-29 age group by the educational attainment of their heads of household

Educational level head of household	Years of education of 20-29 age group	
	9 years or less	10 years or more
9 years or less	50	50
10 years or more	12	88

Reversely, for those in the bottom third of Palestinian society, except for those with no education, increasing educational attainment does not seem to be reflected in increasing possession of economic assets. This pattern may indicate a lack of possibilities for translating education into wealth, although there are strong regional variations. In Gaza, for instance, 24% of the heads of households with post-secondary education are among the poorest one third and 39% are among the top one third. In Arab Jerusalem only 2% of the most educated household heads are found among the poorest third and a full 83% are among the richest third. However, notably in Arab Jerusalem, of those household heads who have no education at all, a full 44% of them are also among the richest third of the population.

This data suggests the persistence of traditional stratification patterns in which economic position is to an important extent determined by the social status of the family and the access such status gives to other resources. Economic institutions in the occupied territories continue to be deeply embedded in kinship structures. Family connections remain decisive in obtaining employment particularly in the white collar category. The relation between education and economic

Table 5.6 Wealth categories by educational attainment

Educational level Head of Household	Lower third	Middle third	Upper third
0	46	36	19
1-6	27	43	30
7-9	32	40	28
10-12	25	31	44
13 or more	22	30	48

Table 5.7 Wealth categories for refugees and non-refugees by educational attainment

Wealth Categories	Educational Level of Head of Household				
	0	1-6	7-9	10-12	13 or more
Lower third					
Refugees	59	36	46	40	34
Non-refugees	37	22	24	15	13
Middle third					
Refugees	27	40	34	36	34
Non-refugees	41	45	43	28	28
Upper Third					
Refugees	14	25	20	24	32
Non-refugees	22	33	34	57	58

mobility becomes clearer when the differential effects of education on the refugee and non-refugee populations are examined (table 5.7).

As expected, UNRWA refugees are heavily over-represented in the lowest wealth income category and even those with the highest educational level remain somewhat over-represented in the lowest category in relation to the general population. Except for those refugees with no education, increased education seems to have only limited impact on economic standing. The pattern for non-refugees is of a different nature and there is a correlation between increasing wealth and increasing education. While 58% of non-refugees with advanced studies are in the highest income category, only 13% are in the lowest. This correlation, however, should not be interpreted as a straightforward causal relationship. Instead, the figures for both refugees and non-refugees suggest that the role of intact kinship groups, and especially the links between these groups and property, are more critical than education in determining the household's economic position. While refugees might retain large networks of kinship relations, the connection between these networks and property was to a large extent severed in 1948.

These issues will be explored more fully in the chapters dealing with household resources, employment and social stratification.

Education and Leisure

Another way of elucidating the impact of education is to examine the relationship between education levels and the use of leisure time. The assumption is that the more varied and numerous leisure activities are, the better the general quality of life. The picture that emerges from the survey data on leisure activities examined, by gender, is as shown in table 5.8.

With regard to having hobbies, enjoying nature and, not surprisingly, reading books, the pattern is the same. Education correlates with increased activity and the net increase is statistically somewhat greater for men than for women. The same holds generally true for a wide range of activities, such as taking educational courses, participation in voluntary societies, sports and so forth. Increased activity for both men and women correlates with educational level, but participation differs between men and women. In contrast to men, women's participation in activities that take place outside the home remains more limited regardless of education.

Religious observance is affected by educational levels, but according to survey results, in a particular manner. On average some 33% of men attend a religious study group, in which religious texts are discussed, at least weekly, but the rate of attendance declines steadily with increasing educational level. However, for the most educated sector of Palestinian men the percentage who attend religious study groups weekly jumps dramatically. While only 27% of those men with 10 to 12 years attend such groups, 43% of those with post-secondary education reportedly attend them. Although more men than women attend these study groups, the pattern of attendance is similar for women. Attendance is most frequent among those women with no education and those who are most highly educated. The same pattern is repeated with reference to mosque attendance. While men attend some 6 times more often than women, for both men and women this form of religious observance is most common among those with least education and those with most.

Interestingly, with increasing education the desire to participate in cultural and leisure activities seems to grow dramatically. While only some 6% of the least educated men and women claimed there were activities which they would like to, but were unable to participate in; more than 65% of the men and women with most education expressed a desire for more leisure activities. The principle constraints listed by men were political reasons (27%), work (24%), lack of facilities (23%), and lack of money (18%). The main constrains listed by women were lack of facilities (24%), restraints imposed by social conventions (21%), and child care (17%). Only 7% of women mentioned political reasons as the main obstacle to participation in

Table 5.8 Percentage of Palestinians who pursue selected leisure activities by years of education

	0	1-6	7-9	10-12	13+	Total
Weekly hobbies						
Men	3	12	28	35	50	28
Women	10	19	43	49	49	33
Take weekly walks in countryside						
Men	17	35	44	40	50	40
Women	13	18	42	32	32	27
Read books weekly						
Men	0	22	35	57	84	45
Women	0	22	47	67	81	38

leisure activities. In short, a majority of youth and a large majority of the more educated youth express a dissatisfaction with their inability to take part in leisure activities they find meaningful.

The Impact of Education on Individual Autonomy and Perception of Influence

Education has often been accredited with the introduction of westernised notions and practice leading to marked shifts in attitudes, the norm of achievement replacing the weight of ascription, the drive toward individual independence eroding the value of group solidarities and obligation. In this context the relationship between educational levels and a sense of individual influence and perceived control over one's own life will be examined.

It is generally assumed that the well educated feel a greater sense of personal control over their lives and of influence over the forces that shape their future. Is this also the case in Palestinian society? Does education provide for a sense of individual autonomy?

The survey posed various questions concerning how much influence the individual felt he or she had within different realms of daily

Table 5.9 Degree of perceived influence within family by education of respondent

	Decisive	Considerable	Occasional	Not at all
Mens' responses				
0	56	34	8	2
1-6	48	32	17	3
7-9	47	26	23	5
10-12	33	33	29	5
13 or more	47	34	16	2
Total men	44	32	21	4
Women's responses				
0	16	45	27	12
1-6	14	37	34	15
7-9	10	24	49	17
10-12	14	31	44	11
13 or more	27	32	32	9
Total women	15	33	39	14

life – the family, the neighbourhood, the wider community and so forth. Answer categories ranged from decisive influence to none whatsoever. The results are indicative of some of the critical organising principles shaping Palestinian society.

Table 5.9 shows, not unexpectedly, that the degree of influence within the family felt by men across all educational levels is far in excess of that felt by women regardless of education. They also indicate a certain correlation between influence and education, but with the exception of the most educated men and women, the correlation is slightly negative.

With reference to influence within the wider community, again the differential between men and women is clear (table 5.10). But once outside the domestic sphere, education does seem to give men a slightly increasing sense of authority, as measured by responses to "not at all". Education tends to have no similar empowering impact upon women. This pattern is repeated on all levels outside the domestic sphere.

The seemingly weak correlation between education and perceived influence, especially inside the domestic realm, is probably related to the hierarchical manner in which authority is organised. Two separate dimensions in particular are germane; gender and age

Table 5.10 Degree of perceived influence within neighbourhood by education of respondent

	Decisive	Considerable	Occasional	Not at all
Men's responses				
0	4	17	41	39
1-5	5	23	38	34
7-9	5	24	40	31
10-12	3	26	43	28
13 or more	3	23	53	21
Total	4	24	43	29
Women's responses				
0	1	13	33	53
1-6	0	13	29	58
7-9	2	10	20	68
10-12	3	10	25	62
13 or more	2	18	23	57
Total	2	12	26	61

or, more precisely, household position. Authority resides mainly with the household head.

A sense of empowerment among men climbs steeply with age, with a sharp drop in the feeling of influence among the highest age group (table 5.11). The pattern is similar for women although the changes are not so marked and is repeated with reference to influence within the wider community. Men have more influence than women, the middle aged more than the very old or the young. In short, in Palestinian society education seems so far to have done little to erode ascribed status as the prime determinant of authority.

Although education appears not to affect the distribution of authority in Palestinian society, does it nonetheless provide the individual with a sense of release from the forces of family ascription and fate? Do the well educated more often than the poorly educated feel that life is more determined by individual endeavour than by family background and the vagaries of unrevealed destiny? The survey asked several questions in order to explore this dimension. The one shown in table 5.12 was one of them.

Table 5.11 Degree of perceived influence within family by age of respondent

	Decisive	Considerable	Occasional	Not at all
Men's responses				
15-19	4	23	56	17
20-29	24	44	29	3
30-39	63	29	9	0
40-49	76	21	3	
50-59	70	22	6	2
60 or more	59	31	9	2
Total men	44	32	21	4
Women's responses				
15-19	4	16	54	26
20-29	11	32	46	11
30-39	18	41	33	8
40-49	26	48	21	5
50-59	24	42	25	10
60 or more	20	33	29	19
Total women	15	33	39	14

For men and women there seems to be a slight decline in the belief in the importance of family background with increasing educational attainment. However, strikingly, the most educated Palestinian men and women seem to place much more emphasis on family background as a determinant of achievement suggesting that they view family background as very relevant to the position they have acquired.

However, the significance of family can also be understood in a manner that relates to family as a source of protection and safety rather than as a basis for ascribed status. The following question attempted to explore this dimension (table 5.13).

The differences between these tables is revealing. In relation to individual achievement, Palestinians seem to stress the critical importance of the solidity of kinship bonds far more than the kinship unit as a transmitter of social status to its members. While family solidarity is viewed as a key contributor to success, the tables suggest that success in life is claimed by Palestinians to be more achieved than ascribed regardless of the actual facts of the matter.

Table 5.12 What one achieves in life is mainly dependent on his or her family's social background

Men's responses by educational level				Women's responses by educational level			
	Disagree	Agree	Don't know		Disagree	Agree	Don't know
0	57	39	4	0	60	29	11
1-6	59	35	6	1-6	61	36	4
7-9	64	34	2	7-9	56	39	4
10-12	68	30	2	10-12	74	25	0
13 or more	55	45		13 or more	59	41	
Total men	62	35	3	Total women	62	33	4

Table 5.13 One's achievements in life depend on family solidarity

Men's responses by educational level				Women's responses by educational level			
	Disagree	Agree	Don't know		Disagree	Agree	Don't know
0	8	91	1	0	10	81	9
1-6	6	91	4	1-6	8	91	2
7-9	10	89	1	7-9	6	93	2
10-12	12	85	3	10-12	12	87	.5
13 or more	14	86		13 or more	8	90	2
Total men	10	88	2	Total women	9	88	3

However, certain beliefs concerning the forces that shape individual futures are clearly influenced by education. Another question involved the power of destiny (table 5.14).

In the Arabic questionnaire this question was phrased slightly differently from the well-known Arabic proverb in order to ensure that respondents would reflect on the substance of this often repeated adage. Among men belief in the power of fate decreases rapidly with increased education. Nonetheless, a full 20% of the most educated men still seem to retain a fatalistic approach to life's challenges.

The picture that emerges from women's responses is somewhat different. Because of the dependent status of most women in Palestinian society and their relative domestic confinement, the picture is also somewhat surprising.

Women's belief in the power of destiny is not particularly affected by educational levels, except among the most educated where it declines abruptly. However, in comparison to men, women generally seem to find the power of fate notably less compelling.

Education and the Perception of Conflict

Education also seems to affect perceptions concerning the degree of conflict in society. The survey posed a range of questions concerning perception of conflict between various sectors of society (tables 5.15, 5.16); between the young and old, management and workers, the rural and urban population, men and women, etc. In all cases the pattern was similar although degree of intensity varied. Those with the highest levels of education were in least doubt about the existence of conflict and were most prone to describe the degree of conflict as very strong.

Table 5.14 Man's destiny is written in advance

Men's responses by educational level				Women's responses by educational level			
	Disagree	Agree	Don't know		Disagree	Agree	Don't know
0	44	52	5	0	81	15	4
1-6	58	39	4	1-6	81	16	2
7-9	61	36	3	7-9	72	22	5
10-12	71	27	2	10-12	82	16	2
13 or more	77	21	2	13 or more	94	6	0
Total men	65	32	3	Total women	80	17	3

The increased propensity, associated with increased education, to view these various relations as conflictive, suggests that education functions in the occupied territories, as elsewhere, to question and challenge established hierarchies and conventions and to provide a critical attitude to one's own society.

This pattern is broken along only one conflict dimension, that between men and women. This dimension will be discussed in more detail in chapter 9.

Education's Impact on the Status of Women

Survey results indicate that educational levels among Palestinians have improved remarkably over the last decades. The slope of improvement has been particularly steep in relation to women's education. It is generally assumed that improved education provides women with a greater degree of self-sufficiency in terms of expanding the realms of choice, control over resources and freedom of movement. Has one outcome of dramatically increased educational levels for Palestinian women been a movement toward increased freedom of

Table 5.15 Perceived degree of conflict between management and workers by education of respondent

	Very strong	Strong	Not strong	No	Connot choose
0	6	31	24	10	30
1-6	13	35	26	14	13
7-9	14	35	28	14	9
10-12	17	37	25	13	9
13 or more	26	39	21	9	5
Total	15	36	25	12	12

Table 5.16 Perceived degree of conflict between young and old by education of respondent

	Very strong	Strong	Not strong	No	Connot choose
0	6	36	26	15	17
1-6	7	37	31	15	10
7-9	9	35	37	17	2
10-12	7	35	39	16	2
13 or more	16	37	37	9	0
Total	8	36	35	15	6

choice? The survey asks women if they are allowed to move outside the home at will or if their movement is constrained (see also chapter 10). The general expectation would be that more educated women have more freedom of movement than others.

There is a correlation between education and freedom of movement, but except for the most educated women, it is negative (table 5.17).

Further analysis (see chapter 10) indicates that it is age, not education, that is vital in regard to freedom of movement. In relation to age there appears to be two thresholds. The lower one divides unmarried women from married women. The upper threshold separates married women, still of child-bearing age, from those who are post-menopausal.

Although their range of movement is restricted, do highly educated Palestinian women spend, nonetheless, more time on average outside the house? The survey asks women how many hours they had actually spent outside the house on the previous day. Again actual hours spent outside the home seem more determined by age than education, except for those women with post-secondary educations who on average spend 3.4 hours outside the home. It should be noted, however, that this group of women are also those most likely to have jobs outside the home. Otherwise the young and the very old spend least time outside the house, on average only two hours per day, and the middle aged, the most time, on average some two and a half hours per day.

One of the prime functions of education is to equip women with the skills to participate in the public sphere of employment. In Palestinian society there have traditionally been severe moral restrictions against women working outside the household. Are these attitudes changed by increased education? The survey asks both men and women whether they believe it is acceptable for women to work outside the home (table 5.18).

Table 5.17 Women's freedom of movement by education of women

	Can move at will	Can't move at will
0	64	36
1-6	50	50
7-9	39	61
10-12	41	60
13 or more	55	45
Total	49	51

Table 5.18 suggests that despite the strong norms against it, a large majority of women, and an overwhelming majority of the more educated women, feel that it is acceptable for them to be employed outside the home. However, since authority in these matters is normally the prerogative of men, it tends to be men's attitudes that

149

determine whether or not women are actually free to seek employment.

Table 5.19 indicates that men's attitudes differ strikingly in relation to the amount of education they have enjoyed. The two tables taken together suggest that women's ability to participate in the public domain might be affected to a much greater degree by the education of their fathers and husbands than by their own educational level. Men's answers to a range of questions concerning appropriate behaviour for women, ranging from placing their children in day care to driving a car, all show the same clear propensity. Increasing education is associated with less restrictive attitudes.

It might be suspected that it is not men's education which is the factor determining attitudes to the acceptability of working women, but their age. The argument would postulate that younger men have more liberal attitudes in reference to women than their fathers or grandfathers. However, it is the middle aged, rather than the very young or old, who have more liberal attitudes in this respect. While 56% of men in the age group 15 to 19 years feel it is unacceptable for women to work outside the home, 56% of men aged 60 or more feel exactly the same. The same pattern exists for women, albeit less marked. Younger women are somewhat less liberal on this issue than their grandmothers. While 18% of women 60 years or more feel working women is unacceptable, 28% of women between 15 and 19 share this view.

The common assumption that increased education provides women with increased access to resources also seems doubtful among Palestinians. Women's potential access operates on two levels: their access to the joint resources of the household kin group, resources that are usually under the management of men, and access to their own inde-

Table 5.18 Women's attitudes concerning the acceptability of women working outside the home by educational levels

	Acceptable	Not acceptable	Don't know
0	75	22	3
1-6	68	30	2
7-9	71	27	2
10-12	86	13	1
13 or more	94	6	0
Total women	76	22	2

Table 5.19 Men's attitudes concerning the acceptability of women working outside the home by educational levels

	Acceptable	Not acceptable	Don't know
0	22	73	5
1-6	31	68	1
7-9	37	62	1
10-12	46	54	0
13 or more	66	34	0
Total men	42	57	1

pendent resources gained through inheritance, employment and so forth.

Inside the family unit the data suggests that again it is age, not education, that facilitates women's access. The survey poses numerous questions which attempt to map women's access to resources both inside and outside the household (see also chapter 10). Women are asked whether they can borrow money from their husbands, fathers, relatives outside of the household or friends if they really need it. Women are also asked if they own a range of commodities that can be transformed into money, such as jewellery, land, bank savings and so on. The pattern of replies is similar along all dimensions. Increased education does not provide women with increased access to household resources or to the resources of the wider family. To the extent there is a correlation, it is negative. Nor do educated women own more resources than their less educated counterparts. In almost all cases women's access to resources is heavily dependent on age and, in particular, their position inside the household.

Currently in Palestinian society attitudes concerning women's dress, particularly western and Islamic forms of dress, are linked to particular political and social attitudes. Both men's and women's attitudes to dress seem clearly linked with education (tables 5.20 and 5.21). The survey asks respondents if they think it is acceptable for women to wear Western forms of dress.

When women are asked the same question, the same pattern appears with an even stronger tendency. While only 14% of women with no education think western dress is acceptable, this figure increases to 44% among those women with post-secondary education. Respondents are also asked how they would react if the women in their household appeared in public without a head scarf. Of those men with no education a full 87% reply they would be insulted. 54% of men with advanced education give this reply. Among women, 77% of the least educated say they would feel insulted while only 34% of the best educated give this response.

Table 5.20 Men's attitudes to the acceptability of western clothes for women by educational level

	Acceptable	Not acceptable	Don't know
0	7	92	1
1-6	17	83	0
7-9	22	78	0
10-12	21	79	1
13 or more	30	69	1
Total men	21	79	1

Since the acceptability of western dress increases with education, do women, as they attain more education, more frequently

151

wear Western forms of dress (table 5.21)?

This table is analyzed in more detail elsewhere (chapter 9). But it can be noted here that whereas Western forms of clothing are more frequently used by better educated Muslim women and are considered acceptable attire by 44% of the best educated, only a small minority wear it.

A critical area affecting women's autonomy is the right to select their own husbands. In a society in which this choice historically has been the jurisdiction of parents, has increased education altered attitudes in favour of women?

The pattern revealed by the survey data is similar to the pattern found in relation to women's roles generally. Among women, 71% of those with no education feel that a woman has the right to choose her own husband. This increases to 93% of the most educated women. The impact of education on men's attitudes is much more decisive (table 5.22).

Again it is education and not age which produces more liberal attitudes. The youngest group of men are in fact more restrictive on the issue than those between 20 and 49, but the differences are not great. Notably, however, even the most educated men are more unwilling to give women the right to choose their own husbands than the most uneducated of women.

Finally, does advanced education for women, as widely believed, operate as an impediment against marriage? Does "too much" education reduce a woman's attractiveness in the marriage market? The survey results would suggest that this is to a certain extent the case. Table 5.23 includes all respondents who are no longer students and who are either currently married or have been married in the past.

Table 5.23 indicates that generally more men than women have been married and thus for every educational level, except one, a

Table 5.21 Forms of dress worn by women by women's educational levels

	Thobe	Strict Islamic	Modified Islamic	Western
0	76	20	4	
1-6	25	56	16	4
7-9	11	48	30	11
10-12	10	49	31	11
13 or more	2	50	30	17
Total women	28	43	21	7

Table 5.22 Men's attitudes on a woman's right to choose her own husband by educational levels

	Women should choose	Women shouldn't choose	Don't know
0	28	71	1
1-6	48	51	1
7-9	48	51	1
10-12	55	44	1
13 or more	63	37	1
Total	51	48	1

gender gap exists. Interestingly, it is only for those with 10 to 12 years of education that no gender gap exists. However, the gender gap is by far the largest for those women with advanced education. This finding seems to be consistent with general Palestinian attitudes concerning education and the marriageability of women. In terms of marriage a certain amount increases attractiveness, too much is counterproductive. It would seem that Palestinian society in this respect is similar to Western societies, in which men tend to marry women who are

Table 5.23 Percentage of men and women who are or have been married educational level

	0	1-6	7-9	10-12	13 or more
Men	97	84	74	80	80
Women	91	75	71	80	58

younger than themselves and who are either as educated as or less educated than they are, but not more educated. Thus, advanced education for women functions to reduce the chances of marriage for at least two reasons. First, advanced education delays the age of marriage for a women, particularly since in Palestinian society it is not acceptable for a women to be both married and a student. Second, the percentage of men with equal or higher educations is significantly reduced. Both these factors operate to reduce the pool of potential husbands.

Conclusion

Like in many other regions of the Middle East, the survey data indicates that educational attainment in the occupied territories has improved remarkably over the past decades for both men and, particularly, women. The effect of greatly improved educational levels on social mobility among Palestinians is open to debate. Among other factors, there are only very limited opportunities to transform education into middle class employment, especially for women, as will be shown in a subsequent chapter. Although for men education seems to induce less fatalistic attitudes to life's tribulations, for neither men nor women do increased educational skills seem to diminish significantly the importance of social solidarities, especially those to the family, in determining eventual individual success and achievement. Nor does educational attainment seem to counteract to any degree deeper organizational principles based on the ascribed attributes of gender and age in affecting a sense of empowerment and the distribution of authority.

In relation to attitudes towards women, the attitudes of women themselves seem forcefully to contest prevailing norms which operate to limit their independence of choice and which are adhered to by a large majority of men. Education seems to function mainly to reinforce this opposition. With regard to men's attitudes, in all areas the survey explores, the acceptability of women working, of dress style, of the right to choose their own husband and so forth, it is education rather than age that shifts men's attitudes in a more liberal direction and education seems to influence attitudes greatly. One conclusion that might be drawn from this data could be that measures to affect improvements in the status of women and attitudes toward them should be chiefly directed toward men. The aspiration among women of all age groups and educational levels to a life style which is less subservient and more under their own control seems already to exist.

Notes

1 Haddad, Y. "Palestinian women: Patterns of legitimation and domination", in Nakhleh K. & Zureil E. (eds.) *The Sociology of the Palestinians*, London: Croom Helm, 1980, p.154.

2 Haddad, Y. "Palestinian women: Patterns of legitimation and domination", in Nakhleh K. & Zureil E. (eds.) *The Sociology of the Palestinians*, London: Croom Helm, 1980, p.154.

3 *Educational Network*, No.1, June 1990, Ramallah.

4 *Educational Network* No.2 September 1990, Ramallah.

5 Khawla Shakhshir, "The Educational System in the West Bank and Gaza Strip, Summary and Conclusion", unpublished.

6 Except for Palestinian figures, remaining figures are taken from *UNDP Human Development Report, 1992*.

Chapter 6
Household Income and Wealth

Geir Øvensen

Introduction

This chapter will discuss the type and amount of economic resources available to Palestinian households. Access to economic resources affect living conditions both directly and indirectly. Most assets, in particular consumer durables, yield immediate and tangible welfare benefits for users. The distribution of economic resources over households and individuals is also highly correlated with the distribution of other living condition components. On the one hand, economic resources, in the strict sense, can be transformed into living conditions benefits such as health, education and leisure activity. On the other hand, income-generating activities may be conditioned by education and good health.

Economic resources may, of course, have both private and public origins. In many countries an important goal in public policy has been to break or modify the connection between private economy and other crucial living condition components through the establishment of a so-called welfare state. In the fields of health and education, there has often been a public desire to secure minimum standards for all persons, regardless of access to (private) economic resources. In this context, identification of deprived socio-economic groups with regard to economic resources should be considered a prerequisite for public compensatory measures. In Palestinian society, as well as in other Middle Eastern communities, kinship structures, however, play a dominant role in the allocation and distribution of economic resources. Local authorities have usually lacked an adequate financial base for financing public welfare. In the occupied territories, the lack of political institutions recognized by the population has further reduced the importance of the public sector, in particular during the intifada.

The family-based Palestinian household constitutes a strong network of economic obligations and privileges. By contrast to Western societies, decisions on consumption and income generating activity are considered as household rather than individual matters. The share of household resources available to an individual is mainly determined by age and sex. In most cases, the patriarchal imprint evident in Palestinian households implies that the final decision-making authority rests with the Head of Household. (The informal influence of women, in particular the wife of the Household Head, on decision-making should, however, not be underestimated).

The authority of the Head of Household is based on his formal position and his knowledge about household economic affairs, usually being the main provider of household income[1]. He disposes of the lion's share of the economic resources that may be characterized as "individual". Due to their dependence on income-earners for obtaining economic means, housewives and other unpaid family workers usually dispose of a relatively small share of individually attributable household economic resources. In spite of their often significant labour activity, the purchasing power of youth and children is close to naught except in some urban upper-class households.

Due to the close and complex economic relations between family members, FAFO has decided to focus on indicators related to the economic resources of households rather than those of individuals. The discussion above shows that the relation between individual and household economic welfare is not, and cannot, be clear-cut. In most cases it is reasonable, however, to assume a positive correlation between household and individual economic resources.

The Problem of Under-reporting of Economic Resources

The strength of kinship groups has traditionally been accompanied by, and has also enabled, extensive opposition to taxation. The lack of national and local authorities acceptable to the Palestinian population under Israeli occupation, has deepened this resistance. The strong fear of taxation, and the resulting scepticism towards strangers asking about economic affairs, have also led to common under-reporting and concealment of assets[2].

On the basis of experiences gained during the pilot survey, the original rather high ambitions as to measurement of wealth and income levels were adjusted, notwithstanding the desire for exact information. The main indicator for measuring differences in household economic resources between regions and between groups, has been a wealth index especially constructed for this purpose. Household wealth, rather than household income, has been chosen as principal point of reference for two main reasons: First, most items comprised by the household wealth index are verifiable, thus reducing the problem of under-reporting. Second, because of the unstable economic situation prevailing in the occupied territories, wealth is probably a more valid expression of household economic resources than various kinds of income.

In the first part of this chapter there will be a discussion of the distribution of the wealth index by region and socio-economic group. In particular, attention will be given to the identification of deprived segments in the population. The second part of the chapter will deal with household income, and discuss possible explanations of variations in household wealth.

Household Wealth

The wealth of a household can be defined as its net balance of economic assets measured at a given point in time. As mentioned in the introduction, household wealth affects living conditions in at least two ways. First, real capital or physical items like consumer durables, have a direct "user value" for the household members. Second, liquid assets indirectly yield welfare benefits if transformed into other living condition components[3].

Household wealth may be acquired through saving of income, inheritance, or appreciation of household economic assets. Apart from receipt or inheritance of gifts, the ability of a household to generate wealth depends on the size of the income which remains after daily consumption expenditures like food and clothing have been deducted. Indispensable for human physical survival, absolute expenditure on such basic items is less dependent on the household income level than other goods are. Their share of the budget is consequently greater the lower the household income is. The residual character of wealth leads to greater variation in household wealth than in household income. Household wealth is thus particularly useful as an indicator for identification of households which suffer economic deprivation.

The lower the level of a household's economic resources, the greater the vulnerability its members will be towards economic fluctuations. The sedimentary nature of household wealth makes it less vulnerable to sudden changes in the economic environment than for example (continuous) labour income. The relative short-term stability of wealth makes it an important buffer against the insecure economic situation in the occupied territories, especially since the outbreak of the intifada.

A comprehensive index, more fully documented in a technical report available from FAFO, has been constructed to measure household wealth. The population of households in the occupied territories has been divided into three equal-sized groups, yielding a low, middle and high wealth group. A region or socio-economic group may be characterized as under-privileged, relative to the occupied territories on average, when its share of households in the lowest wealth group exceeds 1/3 *and* its share in the upper wealth group is less than 1/3. It is worth emphasizing that even if the wealth index allows a ranking of households according to wealth, it does not aspire to measure the absolute level of household economic resources or economic deprivation for any region or socio-economic group[4].

Distribution of Wealth over Region, Type of Locality, Refugee Status and Religion[5]

Investigation of whether any geographical region is economically deprived is of particular use for policy making, because compensatory

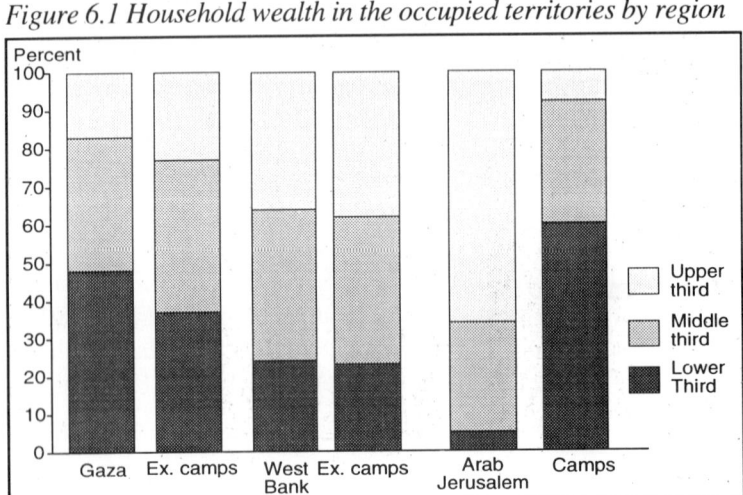

Figure 6.1 Household wealth in the occupied territories by region

policy measures then more easily can be directed to the target population. Can any one of the three main regions in the survey be characterized as relatively deprived with regard to household wealth? Figure 6.1 shows that the regional variations in household wealth are substantial.

Gaza is clearly the region worst off, being over-represented in the lower wealth group, and under-represented in the higher group. Arab Jerusalem, on the contrary, is over-represented in the higher, and under-represented in the lower group. The wealth score of the West Bank is somewhat higher than for the occupied territories in total.

When dividing the West Bank into sub-regions clear variations in household wealth within the main regions are revealed. Central West Bank (Ramallah and Bethlehem sub-districts) has a high score on household wealth, similar to that of Arab Jerusalem. The wealth scores of the northern and southern part are practically identical, and clearly lower than the score for central West Bank.

There are also substantial regional differences in the wealth score within the Gaza Strip. The northern part, dominated by Gaza city, comes out significantly better than the southern area, dominated by the towns Rafah and Khan Yunis[6]. This difference may partially be caused by geographical distances to the Israeli labour market, which is more accessible from the northern part of the Gaza Strip than from the southern part. Figure 6.2 sums up intra-regional variations in household wealth for Gaza and the West Bank.

Figure 6.2 Household wealth in Gaza and the West Bank by sub-region

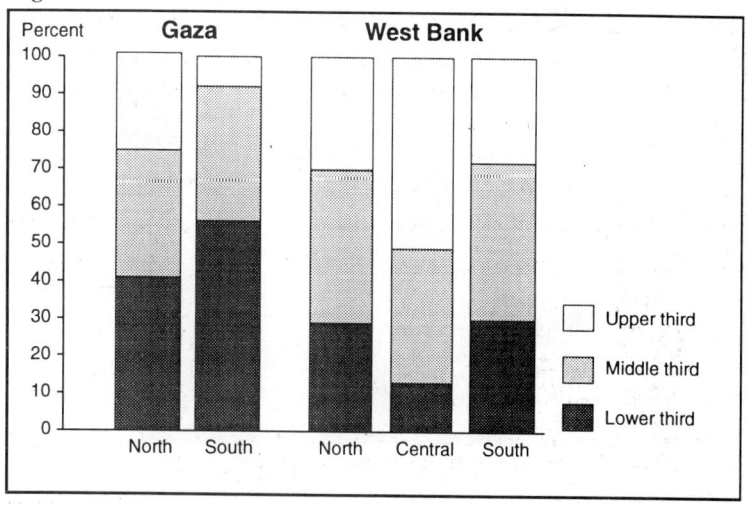

159

In contrast to most developing countries, the urban-rural dimension is less relevant for the distribution of wealth in the occupied territories. Because of the high degree of urbanization in the Gaza Strip, a conventional rural-urban classification of localities is mainly applicable in the West Bank. Even in the West Bank, the relatively small geographical distances involved mean that hardly any locality is more than one hour away from a major town. (This holds true even though new Israeli restrictions after the Gulf War have separated the northern and southern part of the West Bank). Figures 6.3 show the distribution of household wealth by type of locality. Refugee camps, which constitute a type of locality distinctive for the Palestinian society, is clearly a (relatively) deprived type of locality.

Almost 40% of the households in the survey are registered as refugees by UNRWA. Refugee camps are found in all three regions investigated by this survey, but the majority of camp refugees resides in Gaza. Since 1948, many refugees have settled down in dwellings outside the camps, and the survey shows that more than 60% of the UNRWA refugees now live outside the camps.

It was expected at the outset that there would be marked differences in household wealth between refugees and non-refugees, since many households in the latter group lost their houses and agricultural land in 1948. The consequences of the Palestinian exodus in 1948 are still highly visible, as is testified by the variations in household wealth according to refugee status.

Figure 6.3 Household wealth in Gaza and the West Bank by type of locality

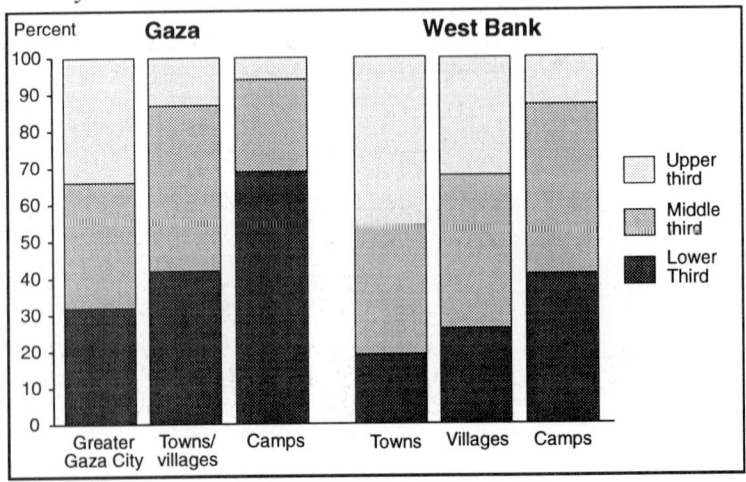

A clear difference in household wealth between, on the one hand, UNRWA refugees, and, on the other, non-refugees, can be observed.

The relevance of this single comparison should, however, be questioned because of the great heterogeneity within the group of UNRWA refugees. As shown in figures 6.4 there are substantial regional and locality variations in the wealth of UNRWA refugee households.

In both Gaza and the West Bank, the household wealth score is higher for refugees outside than refugees inside camps. In Gaza refugee households outside camps have a score clearly below non-refugees. In the West Bank, on the contrary, there is no difference in the wealth score between the non-refugees and refugees outside camps. In both Gaza and the West Bank camp refugees is the group clearly worst off. Finally, West Bank households have a higher wealth score irrespective of refugee status, and the difference is greatest for refugees outside camps.

The relatively small difference in household wealth between Gaza and West Bank non-refugees indicates that regional differences between Gaza and the West Bank to a large extent are related to differences in the refugee situation. The low wealth score of both refugee groups in Gaza, and the large refugee share in the Gaza population, jointly pull the average household wealth score for Gaza downwards.

Figure 6.4 Household wealth in Gaza and the West Bank by refugee status

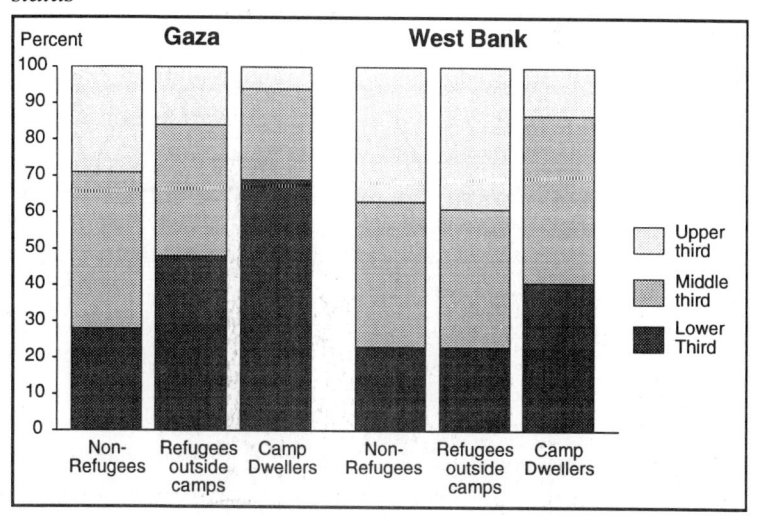

Religious affiliation was considered of minor importance as reference variable for the distribution of household economic resources in the occupied territories. First, the area is almost exclusively Moslem, (96%). Second, a possible correlation between religion and household wealth has more academic interest than policy relevance.

Apparently, Christian households have much higher scores on household wealth than Moslem households. 90% of the Christian population in the occupied territories, however, live in the high wealth score areas of Central West Bank and Arab Jerusalem, while virtually no Christians live in low score Gaza.

Household Wealth and Household Composition

"With every mouth comes a pair of hands". This saying indicates the dual effect of household size on economic resources. On average it seems reasonable to assume that the more household members there are, the higher the household income, but also the household expenditure. In the introduction it was asserted that the ability of a household to generate wealth depends on the size of the income which remains after daily consumption expenditures like food and clothing have been subtracted. Investigation of the correlation between household size and household wealth should thus give a more correct picture of the possible effect of household size on household economic resources than the correlation between household size and household income.

In particular, a high number of adult men in the household could be expected to increase household wealth, because most men receive income from labour activity. A high number of children, on the other hand, could be expected to increase household expenditures more than household income.

What, then, is the correlation between household size and wealth? Because the number of adult males, adult females and children in a household are highly correlated it is difficult to isolate the effect of each group. Household wealth, however, clearly seems to increase with the number of adult males in the houschold, but this relation is weaker in Gaza than in the other regions.

A high number of children, on the contrary, seems to affect household wealth somewhat negatively. The negative effect of a high number of children on household wealth is weaker in the three regions taken separately than for the occupied territories in total. This result is partially a consequence of the high average number of children in low wealth Gaza.

Altogether, in all three main regions, there is a weak increase in household wealth with increasing total household size. From the household's perspective, there is thus no clear indication that large families lead to poverty.

Palestinian society is also characterized by the existence of relatively close economic relations between family members even when living in different households. The survey does not measure the prevalence of "dispersed extended families" explicitly, except for the type of relationship between families behind multi-household entrance doors. No clear correlation between household wealth and for example the number of brothers in the housing unit could be found, neither for the occupied territories in total, nor for each of the three main regions.

Household Wealth and Head of Household Characteristics

What is the relation between individual Head of Household characteristics like sex, age, civil status, education, and household wealth? With respect to gender differences, the 10% of households with female Household Heads are worse off than other households. A probable explanation is that many of these women are widowed, divorced or separated. On the other hand, many women are Household Heads because their husbands are working abroad, and thus receive remittances which should have pulled household wealth upwards.

The influence of the Head of Household's age on household wealth shows marked regional variations. In Gaza and Arab Jerusalem no correlations are found between Head of Household age and household wealth. In the West Bank, however, there is a clear wealth increase from young to middle-aged Heads of Household, but a decline for the two oldest age groups. A reasonable explanation for the initial increase is that older Household Heads have had more time to accumulate capital. A possible explanation for the drop in household wealth for the two oldest age groups may be lack of savings and labour activity which might compensate for this among older Heads. Many old Household Heads lost their property in 1948, and are too old to have profited from relatively advantageous wage employment in Israel.

Household wealth, as expected, increases with Head of Household education, both for the occupied territories taken together and for the three main regions separately. Figure 6.5 shows the correlation between household wealth and Head of Household education for the occupied territories in total.

Further investigation shows that the effect of education is strongest in Arab Jerusalem and weakest in Gaza. A possible explanation is that Arab Jerusalem offers more relevant employment for well educated persons than the other regions do.

Finally, the place where the Head of Household has received his education seemingly has a strong effect on household wealth in the occupied territories. Breaking down data to the regional level, it is, however, revealed that the effect of place of education on household wealth is almost exclusively tied to present region of residence. The only exception is education outside the Middle East, which seems to trigger a higher score on the household wealth index, irrespective of region of residence.

Household Wealth and Meat Consumption[7]

In most Middle Eastern countries meat consumption tends to increase with increasing household economic resources. In this survey households have been asked about their weekly meat consumption, (excluding poultry, etc.). The distribution of meat consumption by region and socio-economic group in the occupied territories shows similarities with the distribution in the household wealth index (correlation coefficient 0.31). The regional variations are illustrated in figure 6.6.

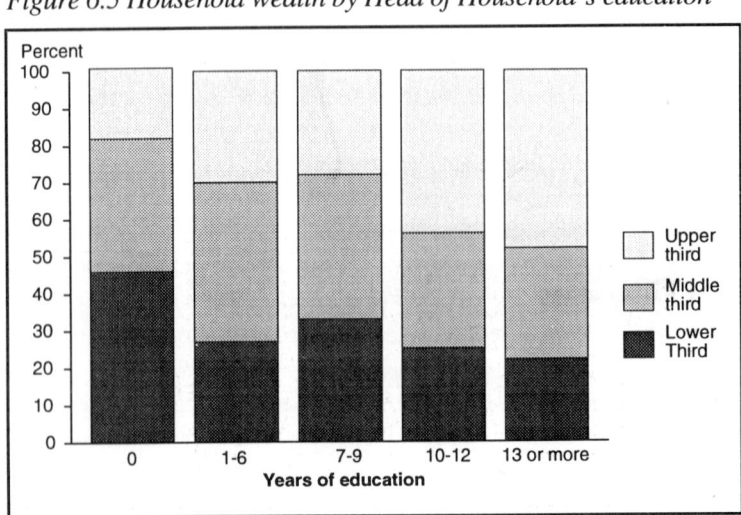

Figure 6.5 Household wealth by Head of Household's education

Meat consumption is not higher in rural than in urban areas, and consequently seems to be determined by household economic resources rather than by type of locality. Both weekly household meat consumption and the household wealth index thus act as measures of household economic resources. As could be expected, meat consumption increases strongly with the number of adult males in the household.

Household Income

Due to assumed under-reporting of household income, household wealth rather than income, has been chosen as main point of reference for household economic resources. For measurement of recent changes in household economic resources, wealth is, however, a less suitable measure due its relative stability over time. The first part of this section thus uses (self-reported) changes in household income to chart the development of household economic resources in the occupied territories since the Gulf War.

Even though the survey does not aspire to record exact levels of household income, the prevalence of various *types* of household income has still been recorded. The second part of this section will thus deal with various household income types, in particular how different income types are correlated with the Head of Households's labour activity and household wealth.

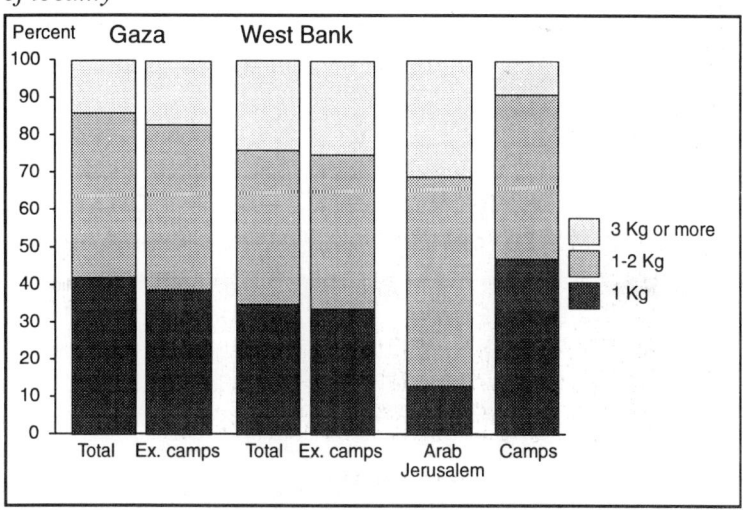

Figure 6.6 Household weekly meat consumption by region and type of locality

165

Recent Development of Household Income in the Occupied Territories[8]

During 25 years of Israeli occupation, the economy of the occupied territories has gradually been integrated into the Israeli economy. Introduction of Israeli currency and economic legislation, as well as extension of water, energy and transportation networks, has created a strong dependence on Israel. Palestinian employment in Israel and unimpeded import of Israeli goods have reinforced the pattern of dependence.

The outbreak of the intifada, characterized by frequent strikes and curfews, has initiated a period of declining household income in the occupied territories. During the Gulf War, a six week curfew paralyzed all economic activity in Gaza and the West Bank. After the Gulf war, new restrictions on employment in Israel deprived many households of their main source of income. Remittances and financial assistance from Arab countries also dropped sharply. Finally, the severe winter of 1991-2 had serious effects on agriculture, particularly in the West Bank.

The recent economic recession in the occupied territories is clearly documented in figure 6.7, which shows (self-reported) changes in household income since the Gulf War.

Two out of three households reported a decline in income, while only one out of twenty households experienced increased household

Figure 6.7 Change in household income since the Gulf War in percent of households by region

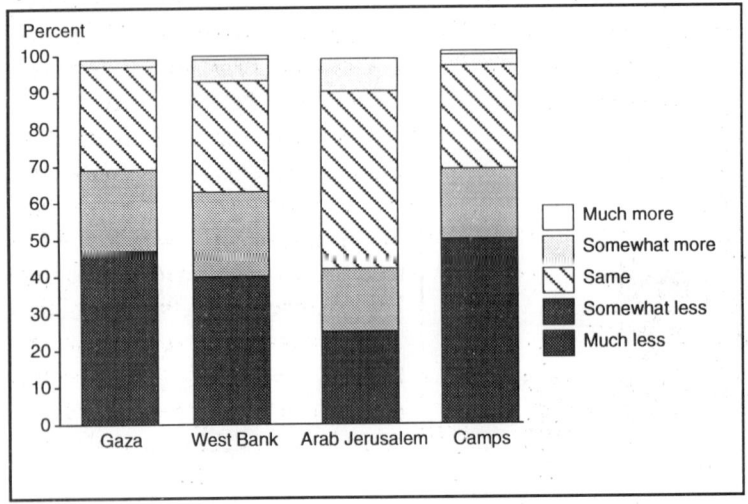

income. Figure 6.7 also reveals that the number of households reporting a substantial decline in household income is particularly high in Gaza and in refugee camps, the areas most affected by the new Israeli restrictions on employment introduced during the war.

Arab Jerusalem has the smallest proportion of households with reduced income, both escaping the curfew during the war and being less dependent on employment in Israel than Gaza and the West Bank. The effect of the Gulf War was thus not only a general recession in household income in the occupied territories, but a decline that hit the groups already worst off (Gaza and camps) the hardest.

Sources of Household Income

Since 1967, a cash economy based on waged labour has gradually replaced self-subsistence as the dominant economic mode of most households in the occupied territories. Employment in Israel has partially substituted local employment, especially in agriculture. The exposure to Israeli influence has also had cogent effects on consumption patterns in the occupied territories, increasing the importance of wage employment.

Household income types may be crudely divided into two main categories. The most important type of household income in the occupied territories by far, is labour activity. The importance of labour activity is particularly great because it is the most evenly distributed type of household income. Private and public transfers to households and capital income constitute the other main category of household income types. As will be shown below, transfers and capital income are, however, of less importance than income from labour activity.

Figure 6.8 Number of income types of households in the occupied territories

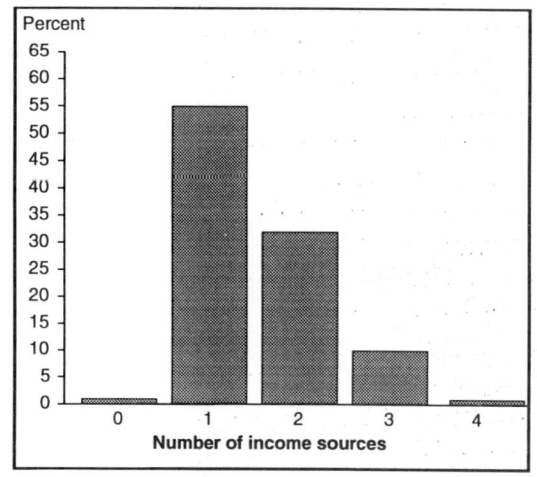

As can be seen from figure 6.8, most households receive only one type of income. (Note, however, that this income type, e.g. wages, may be received by more than one household member). Less than 1% of the households report no income, an interesting result taking the general problem of under-reporting of income into consideration.

Figure 6.9 shows that changes in household income for households receiving only one type of income are very similar to the average for all households. Contrary to what could have been expected, there are no indications that these households have been harder hit by the economic decline since the Gulf War than other households.

Income from labour activity[9]

Income from labour activity comprise wages and salaries, business income, and income from land cultivation and raising of animal husbandry. As illustrated by figure 6.10, wages are, by far, the most frequent type of household income.

The share of households receiving wage income increases, as can be expected, with the number of adult males residing in the house-

Figure 6.9 Change in household income since the Gulf War in households with only one source of income

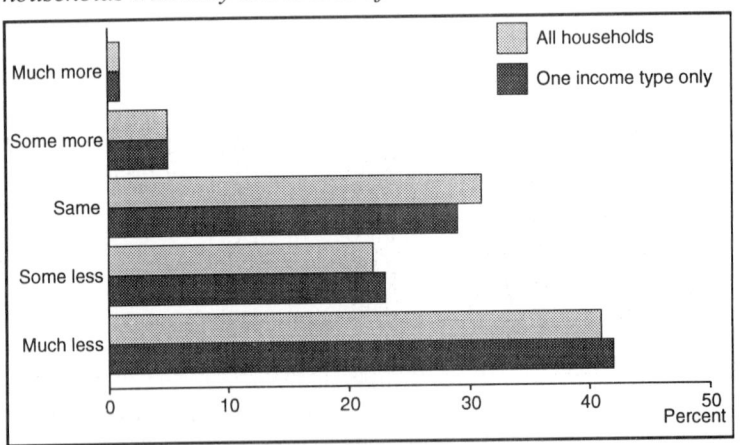

Figure 6.10 Percentage of households receiving labour income types

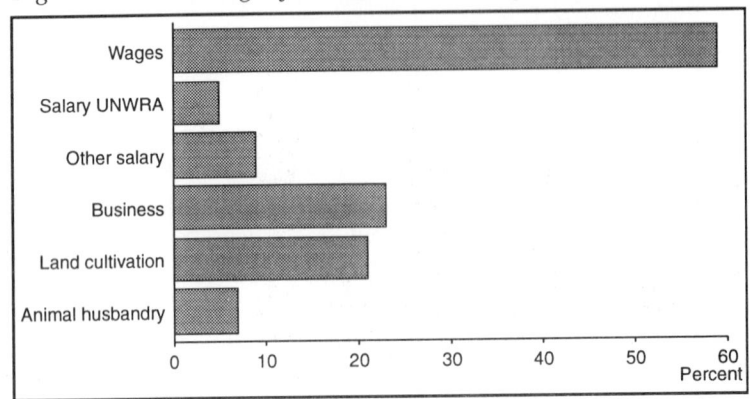

holds. Figure 6.11 shows that Gaza has a lower share of households receiving wage income than the West Bank and Arab Jerusalem. This difference, which persists also when camps are excluded from the respective areas, is most likely caused by the problematic labour market situation in Gaza.

As a further illustration of the employment problems in Gaza, figure 6.12 shows the regional percentages of full-time employed persons out of the *total* population in each area. ("Full-time" work is defined as 7 weeks or more of employment during the last two months prior to the survey).

Figure 6.11 Percent of households earning income from labour activity by region and type of locality

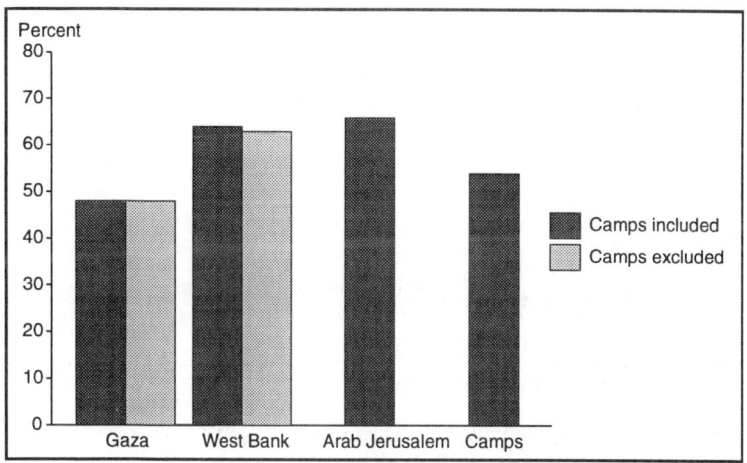

Figure 6.12 Full-time employed persons in percent of total population by region

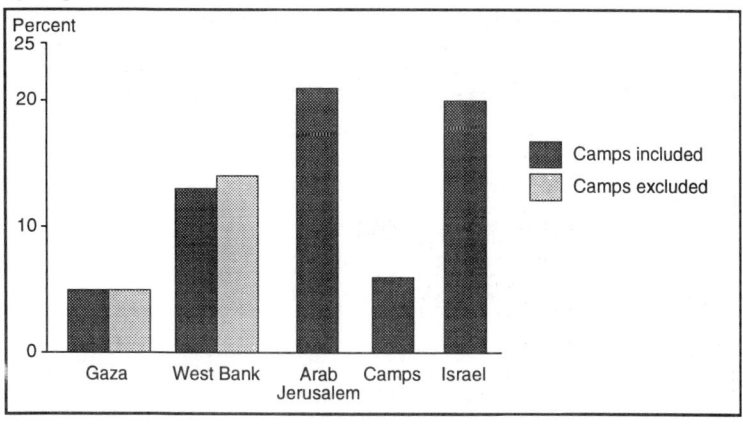

In Arab Jerusalem, one out of five persons is full-time employed, the same figure as for Israeli Jews. In Gaza, on the contrary, only one out of twenty persons is employed full-time. In the southern part of the Gaza Strip this rate even drops to one out of thirty persons.

Figure 6.12 gives an approximate illustration of the ratio of consumers compared to producers in the occupied territories, expressing an important dimension of the prevailing economic problems in the area. While some of the difference between Israel and the occupied territories in total can be ascribed to different age structures in the two populations, age composition falls short of labour market problems as main explanation of the regional differences within the occupied territories. (See the subsequent chapter for a further discussion about employment problems).

There are small variations by region or socio-economic group in the share of households receiving other types of labour income than wages. Salaries from UNRWA and agricultural income constitute the two main exceptions from this rule. The highest share of households receiving salaries from UNRWA are, as one could anticipate, found among UNRWA registered refugees, because UNRWA primarily provides salaried employment to UNRWA registered refugees.

Income from land cultivation and animal husbandry is most frequent in West Bank villages. Quite naturally, shares of households receiving agricultural income are lowest in Arab Jerusalem and in camps, as urban residents usually possess no agricultural land.

Labour income is, as mentioned above, the most common type of household income. In most households the labour activity of the Head of Household provides the bulk of labour income. An index for Head of Household labour activity, documented in a technical report available from FAFO, has therefore been constructed. The index gives a crude estimate of the Head of Household's labour income as a product of the expected wage level for his type of employment, multiplied with the duration of his work the year prior to the survey.

Nearly 30% of the Household Heads had less than 1 month of labour activity the year prior to the survey. These will be referred to as "non-working" or "non-active" Household Heads in the discussion below. The remaining 70% have firstly been ranged according to estimated labour income during the previous year. Secondly, they have been divided into three equally sized groups of low, middle and high estimated income respectively.

The distribution of the index for estimated Head of Household income by region and socio-economic group clearly shows the importance of the Head of Household's labour activity for the acquisition of household economic resources. The variational pattern of the estimated income index shows a fairly close resemblance to the index for household wealth (a correlation coefficient of 0.27 is estimated between the two indices).

What is the share of households receiving labour income when the Head of Household does not work? To answer this question, the households in the occupied territories have been divided into two groups, namely households where the Household Head has no labour activity, and households where the Household Head is working. When a household with a non-working Head receives a particular type of labour income, this income type must stem from the labour activity of other household members.

Figure 6.13 shows that the share of households receiving wages and business income is lower in households with a non-active Head than in other households. For agricultural income, though, there is no difference between the two groups.

A reasonable interpretation of figure 6.13 is that wages, and in particular business income, tend to stem from the labour activity of the Household Head himself. Still, many households receive wages from the labour activity of other household members.

Which types of income from labour activity tend to be the only income type in households in the occupied territories? Figure 6.14 shows the share of households receiving various types of labour

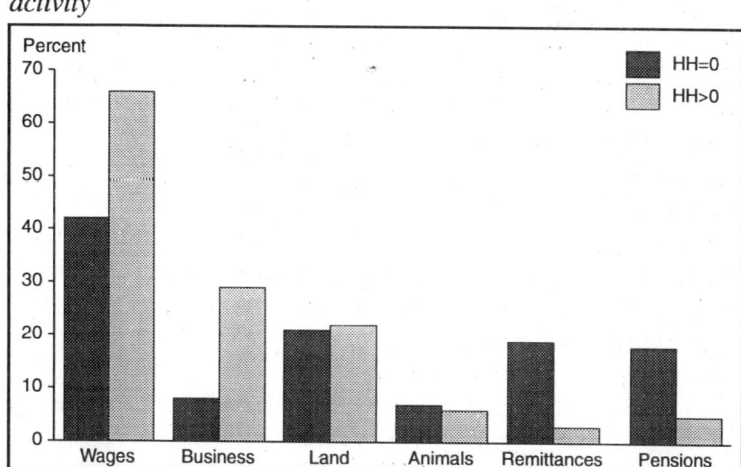

Figure 6.13 Household labour income by Head of Household labour activity

income as their *only* type of income, compared to the total share of households receiving these income types.

Figure 6.14 reveals that most households receiving wages and salaries, rely on these income types as their only source of income. It is less common to find business income as the only type of income. Agricultural income is even rarer as the only source of income, which goes to show that agricultural income generally plays a supplementary role in the household economy.

Transfers and Capital Income[10]

Some types of household income are not directly linked to the labour activity of household members. The most important of these income types are remittances and social benefits. (The category "other" income refers to a number of income types which do not fit into the income classification system). By comparing the share of households receiving non-labour income with the share of households receiving wages, figure 6.15 shows the subordinate role of non-labour income as compared to income from labour activity in the occupied territories.

There are small variations by region or socio-economic group in the share of households receiving non-labour income, except for social benefits. Figure 6.16 shows the regional percentages of households receiving social benefits.

Figure 6.14 Percent of households receiving various labour income types for all households and households receiving only one type of income

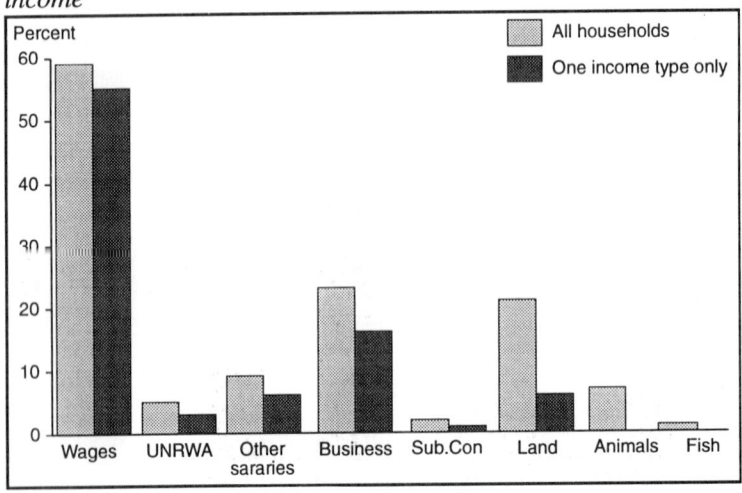

Figure 6.15 Percentage of households receiving non-labour income types

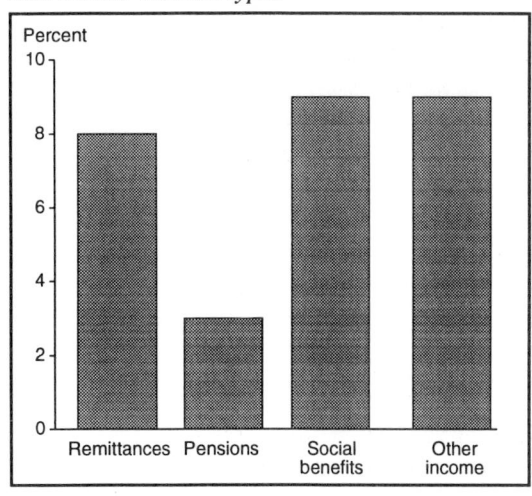

The high rate of recipients of social benefits in Arab Jerusalem is clearly due to easy access to Israeli social security managements. In this connection it should be remembered that Arab Jerusalem enjoys a different status in Israeli law than Gaza and the West Bank. As opposed to these regions, the high share of households receiving social benefits in Arab Jerusalem does thus not necessarily express economic deprivation, at least not when compared to the other regions.

It has been estimated that remittances constitute up to 1/3 of private disposable income in the occupied territories[11]. The share of households receiving remittances is particularly high among households with female Heads, indicating that their spouses are working abroad. As to regions, the share of households receiving remittances seems somewhat higher in the northern and central parts of the West Bank than in other areas.

Capital income, in this survey comprising rent revenues and income from land sale, is received by a small number of households, and is the most unevenly distributed type of income recorded by the

Figure 6.16 Percent of households receiving social benefits by region and type of locality

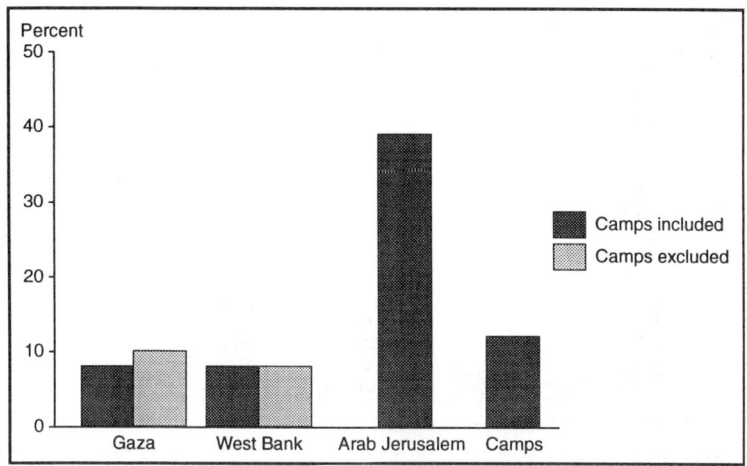

survey. Capital income in the occupied territories, as in most countries, generally increases with household wealth.

What is the share of households receiving non-labour income when the Head of Household does not work? To answer this question, households where the Household Head has no labour activity have been compared to households where the Household Head is working. For transfers like social benefits, remittances and pensions we observe

Figure 6.17 Household non-labour income by Head of Household labour activity

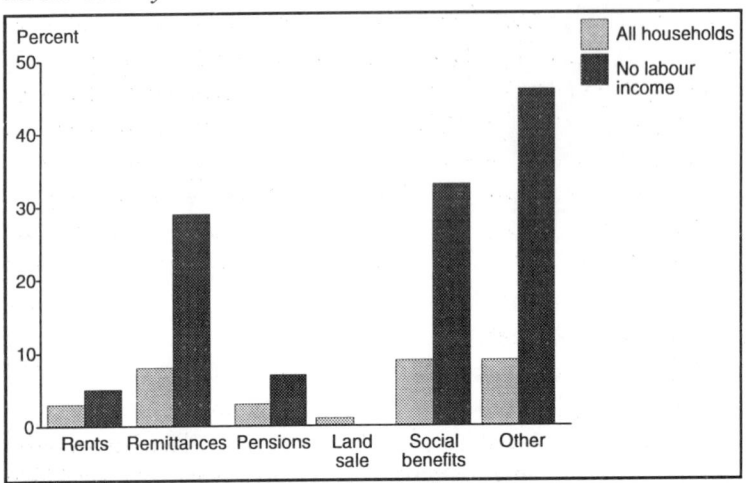

Figure 6.18 Percent of households receiving various non-labour income types for all households and households receiving only one type of income

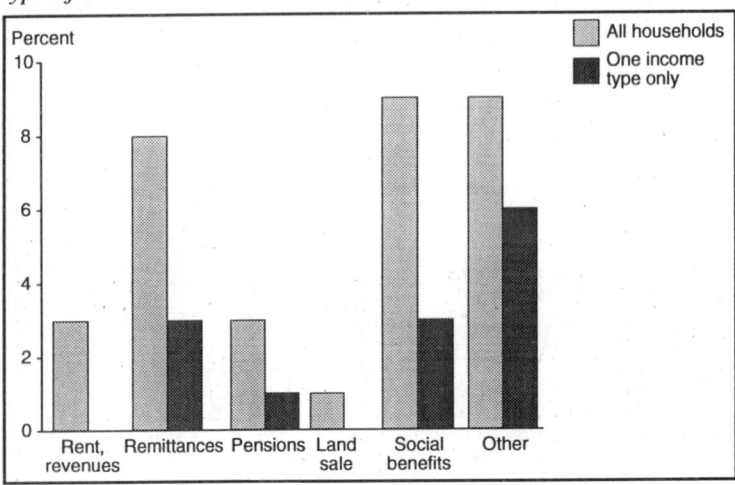

174

the inverse effect of the one found for for wage and business income. Figure 6.17 illustrates these results.

The share of households receiving pensions increases when the Household Head is not working, as pensions obviously replace labour income for older Household Heads. Remittances are also more common in households with non-active Heads, because many of them are women with spouses working abroad. Social benefits are to a large extent received when or if the household lacks alternative income, for example from labour activity.

Which types of non-labour income tend to be the only source of household income? Figure 6.18 shows the share of households receiving various types of non-labour income as their **only** type of income, compared to the total share of households receiving these income types.

Many households receiving capital income and transfers, also have other sources of income. One out of three households receiving remittances and social benefits, however, have no other means of income.

Household Wealth and Types of Family Income[12]

How are the recipient households of various income types distributed over the household wealth groups? If more than 1/3 of the households receiving one particular income type fall into the lowest household wealth group, and less than 1/3 in the highest, this type of income can

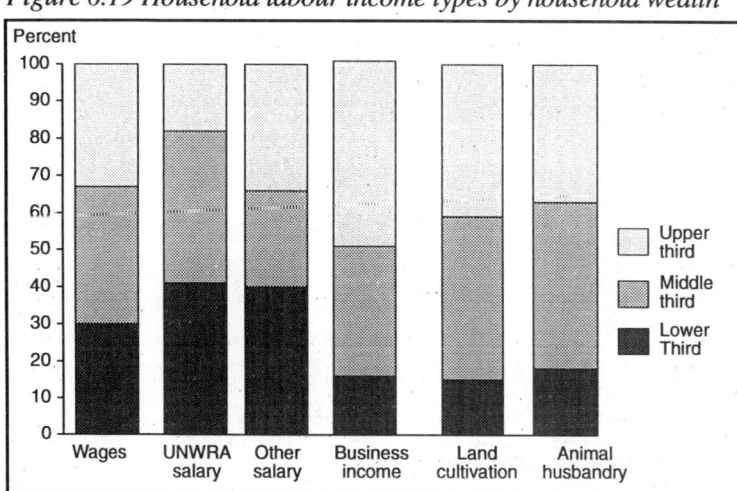

Figure 6.19 Household labour income types by household wealth

be said roughly to be associated with low status. Figures 6.19 and 6.20 show the distribution of households receiving labour income and non-labour income respectively, by household wealth groups.

UNRWA salaries, social benefits, "other salaries" and "other income", are income types mainly received by households belonging to the lowest household wealth group. Most UNRWA employees are refugees, thus explaining the high share of recipients in the lowest wealth group.

As many as almost one out of three households receiving social benefits falls in the upper household wealth group. This result is most likely due to the high share of Arab Jerusalem households receiving this income type. Recipients of social benefits would probably have been even more concentrated in the lowest wealth group if Arab Jerusalem had been excluded. "Other salaries" and "other income" refer to miscellaneous income types, typical of the temporary kind of employment frequently found among persons from poorer households.

Figure 6.20 Household non-labour income types by household wealth

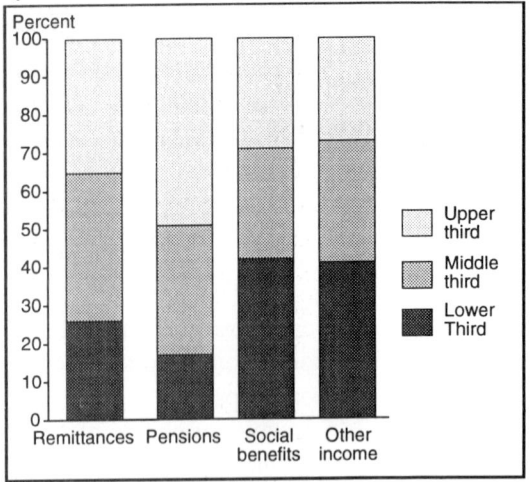

Wages, which comprise everything from daily to monthly wages, are evenly distributed among the three household wealth groups. Note, however, the large size and the strong heterogeneity of this group, which comprises several substantially disparate sub-groups.

Remittances, and in particular agricultural income, are over-represented in the middle household wealth group. Agricultural activity thus seems to secure households a satisfactory minimum level of economic resources.

Pensions, rent revenues and business income are mainly received by households in the upper group of household wealth. For these types of income, the picture is the same as can be found in other countries in the region. (A high share of households receiving income from sub-contracting in the upper wealth group may be due to random variation caused by small sample size).

Conclusion

The primary goal of this chapter has been to identify deprived regions and socio-economic groups with regard to household economic resources. Identification of such groups must be considered a prerequisite for implementation of public compensatory measures in other fields in which possession of economic resources is important, like for example health and education. For reasons discussed in this chapter's introduction, the main indicator for measuring differences in household economic resources in the survey is a wealth index especially constructed for this purpose. The household wealth index shows relative but not absolute differences in the level of household economic resources.

The household wealth index clearly demonstrates that Gaza is the region worst off in the occupied territories. The deprivation of Gaza as a region is, however, closely related to its high share of economically deprived refugees. In particular, refugees living in camps are at a disadvantage compared to other groups, both in Gaza and the West Bank.

Analyzing results on a *household* level, there is no clear indication that poverty increases with the size of families. Household wealth, as expected, clearly increases with Head of Household education.

Accurate statistical measurement of income levels for households in the occupied territories would require a much larger questionnaire, and possibly extensive application of time-use studies. The section about household income has thus dealt with *types* of household income rather than the level of household income as such.

Income from labour activity is by a wide margin the most important type of household income. It is frequently also the only income type received by the households. Gaza has the lowest regional share of households receiving income from labour activity. It is reasonable to believe that lower labour activity in Gaza than in the West Bank and Arab Jerusalem is one of the major explanations of Gaza's low score on the household wealth index. Taking the importance of employment as a source of household income into consideration, providing employment for deprived groups is probably the most cost-effective remedy available if one wishes to correct the present economic inequalities in the occupied territories.

As to recent developments in household economic resources in the occupied territories, two out of three households report a decline in their income since the Gulf war. The share of households that report a reduction is highest among the groups already worst off (Gaza and refugee camps).

As a concluding remark it may be stressed the extent to which political events outside the direct influence of household members may have an impact on the economy of households in the occupied territories. The most important type of household income, earnings from labour activity, is rendered unstable by curfews, strikes and restrictions on employment in Israel. The lack of state-directed economic security arrangements as well as prevailing political uncertainties, have thus apparently enhanced the importance of the economic network constituted by the family.

Notes

1 The economic transition presently taking place in the occupied territories, which entails that the traditional subsistence economy is gradually being replaced by a market economy, may in the long run also challenge the traditional structure of authority in economic matters within the households. In particular, access to the Israeli labour marked has enabled many young males to establish their own economic base beyond the direct control of the Head of Household, thus challenging his superiority in such questions.

2 Non-intentional under-reporting of economic resources is also widespread. Particularly women's and children's work is usually not considered as economic activity, even when considered as such according to survey definitions. For a further discussion of this problem, se the section about women's work in the employment chapter.

The relatively high number of local and foreign organizations providing material support to the population also encourages under-reporting of economic resources. Some respondents may regard it as in their interest to paint their economic situation in dark colours, in order to be entitled to social benefits.

3 Wealth or net fortune may be split into real and finance capital. Real capital is composed of (physical) capital goods and consumer durables, while finance capital can be defined as the net balance between financial savings and debt. The two types of wealth each pose their characteristic measurement problems. In contrast to finance capital, real capital can to a large extent be observed. Value assessment of reported items is, however, more problematic for real capital than finance capital. The survey made a crude value assessment of real capital by asking when the item was bought and whether the items were bought new or used. The outbreak of the intifada was chosen as time reference because of its strong impact on people's minds.

The real capital a household dispose of reflects both the household's past consumption priorities and its contemporary level of economic resources. Different types of real capital have different depreciation rates and liquidity, (i.e. ability to be transformed into other types of resources). Some types of real capital like machinery, cars or land also have productive potential, and may thus reflect development of sources of income as well as development of consumption habits.

Non-productive real capital items like consumer durable may be classified according to their potential as status symbols, their liquidity, or by their user value for different types of household members. The user value of a consumer durable is not necessarily dependent on its age or liquidity. It is for example reasonable to assume that refugee camp dwellings, even if formally rented from UNRWA, represent the same user value for residents as privately owned houses of similar standard. The relationship between user value of consumer durable and household composition is also not always clear-cut. The number of persons in a household may have great influence on individual user value of for example a house of a given size, but not for the user value of a colour television set. Different types of consumer durables, for example kitchen amenities, may have different user value for men and women.

4 The wealth index is based on five sub-indices: 1) A Income generating capital goods; 2) Consumer durables which have a status display function because they usually are allocated in the "public" sphere of the house; 3) Consumer durables which particularly relieve women of manual housework (but have limited value as status symbols as they are allocated in the "private" sphere of the house); 4) A crude value assessment of the family house; and finally, 5) The balance of household debt and savings.

For each of the five sub-indices, the population of households has been divided into three equal-sized groups as for the (aggregate) household wealth index. Finally, the latter index has been constructed from a weighted sum of the five sub-indexes.

As an indication of the properties of the five sub-indexes it should be mentioned that while the first and the third sub-index referred to above show greater variation than the aggregate wealth index over most regions and groups, the second, fourth and fifth sub-indexes yield less variation than the aggregate index.

The relationship between user value and household composition, the amount and types of consumer durables in a household are likely to increase over time, and thus likely to be particularly low for newly established households like recently married couples living alone.

5 Results for the distribution of the household wealth index by region and socio-economic group are presented in Table A.6.1, Table A.6.2, Table A.6.3 and Table A.6.4 in the Household Economy Appendix.

6 The northern part of Gaza, however, also includes Shatti Refugee Camp which has the lowest score on household wealth among all areas included in the survey.

7 See Table A.6.5 and Table A.6.6 in the Household Economy Appendix for further references to the discussion in this section.

8 See Table A.6.7 in the Household Economy Appendix for further references to the discussion in this section.

9 See Table A.6.8, Table A.6.9, Table A.6.10, Table A.6.11 and Table A.6.12 in the Household Economy Appendix for further references to the discussion in this section.

10 See Table A.6.11, Table A.6.12 and Table A.6.13 in the Household Economy Appendix for further references to the discussion in this section.

11 There is likely to be a high number of under-reporting for remittances. While 20% of the households had close contact with relatives abroad, only 8% say they have received remittances. This difference, is however, not only caused by under-reporting, but also by the high number of Palestinian workers losing jobs in the Gulf countries after the 1991 Gulf War.

12 See Table A.6.14 in the Household Economy Appendix for further references to the discussion in this section.

Chapter 7
Employment and Under-utilization of Labour

Geir Øvensen

Labour Activity and Living Conditions

The purpose of this chapter is to investigate important aspects of the labour activity of Palestinians residing in the occupied territories. Both the present data and the limited space available have prohibited any exhaustive account of this comprehensive subject. The aim is rather to provide an overview of the situation, and draw attention to some topics which need further investigation.

The overall perspective applied is one of living conditions, which should be understood as encompassing both material and non-material elements. Labour activity directly and indirectly affects a long range of living condition components. This chapter will, however, primarily deal with employment in relation to household economic resources[1].

Labour activity, normally, is the most important source of household income. It is often also more uniformly distributed than other income types. The economic importance of employment is particularly great in economies without extensive social welfare arrangements. When alternative sources of income are scarce, lack of employment represents a serious threat to the material welfare of households. In a living conditions perspective, particular attention must thus be given to the nature and manifestations of underemployment[2].

This chapter is subdivided into two main parts. The first part will discuss the nature and manifestations of certain types of under-utilization of labour in the occupied territories. The second part will focus on the employed, and their distribution over area, type and economic branch of work. A separate discussion of female labour activity is also conducted in this section.

Labour Force Definitions

For measurement of supply and utilization of labour in household surveys the ILO has endorsed application of the so-called "labour force framework". This classification system uses standardized employment definitions to allow for consistent cross-country comparison of data. A somewhat adapted version of the labour force framework is used by FAFO to fit specific living conditions requirements. The labour force framework system is also used in the annual Israeli labour force surveys of the occupied territories. Figure 7.1 gives an overview of the main categories used in the FAFO living conditions survey:

Based on a person's activities in the so-called "determinant week" the labour force framework divides the population, 15 years or older, into three exhaustive and mutually exclusive categories[3]. "Employed" (box Ia, Ib and Ic above) comprise all persons who worked at least one hour in the reference week, or persons who were temporarily absent[4]. "Unemployed" (box II above) are persons who did not work even one hour, but who at the same time actively sought work. Employed and unemployed persons together make up the "currently economic active population" or "labour force". Persons 15 years or older who are not "currently economic active" and persons outside the survey population together make up the "not in the labour force" category (box III and IV above).

Note that the concept of "work" does not refer to paid work or work outside the home exclusively, as is commonly thought. Non-market

Figure 7.1 Labour survey definitions used by FAFO

Total population						
Working age population persons 15 year or older						Persons under 15 years
Persons included in labour force					Not in labour force	
Employed persons			Unemployed persons	i.e. not "employed" or "unemployed" and did not seek work in the determinant week	
Full time	Part time	Temporarily absent	not "employed" but sought work in the determinant week		
7 or 8 weeks last two months	1 - 6 weeks last two months				
Ia	Ib	Ic	II	III		IV

activities like unpaid work in family farms or business, and several types of home production, are also included. Unpaid housework, like child care, cleaning, washing and cooking are, however, generally not considered as work[5].

Supply of Labour; Labour Force Participation

The size of the labour force refers to the amount of labour available in the economy. For macro-economic needs, focus is thus naturally placed on the composition of the labour force. A living conditions survey, however, should be as much concerned with persons *not* working. Because involuntary non-activity represents a serious welfare problem, the possible reasons for a person's inactivity must be investigated.

Labour Force Participation - an International Comparison[6]

Labour force participation is influenced, of course, by numerous economic, political and cultural factors, working together in a complex interplay. It may thus be instructive to compare labour force participation in the occupied territories with other countries and population groups. Figure 7.2 shows labour force participation as percentage of total population, percentage of adults, adult males and adult females for the occupied territories, for Israeli Jews and "Non-Jews" and for Norway. The share of the total population below 15 years is also indicated in the figure[7]. (Note that labour force participation usually is expressed in per cent of the "working age population", i.e. persons 15 years or older).

Figure 7.2 clearly illustrates the inverse relation between the share of the total population in the labour force and the share of the population below 15 years of age. The very young age structure in the occupied territories is thus a major explanation of the relatively low labour force participation as per cent of the total population[8].

In addition to the effect of the population's age structure, the estimates for labour force participation ratio are determined by three main factors:

First, as is the case in all surveys, measurement methods and definitions are likely to have a strong influence. Respondents tend to understand work as regular employment, which frequently leads to under-reporting of many kinds of labour activity typical of developing countries. Casual work, unpaid work, and work rewarded in kind are often omitted, even when explicitly considered as "work" in line with survey definitions. Under-reporting of labour activity is usually higher for women than for men, in particular in developing countries. Married women are customarily regarded as "housewives" in Palestinian culture, and their labour activity is normally not considered as "employment"[9].

Second, socio-cultural factors play a decisive role in shaping labour force participation. In contrast to Western countries, Middle Eastern culture regards labour activity primarily as a household affair[10]. There are relatively strong cultural norms governing the places and types of work that can be considered "acceptable" according to sex, age and social status. The cultural dimension is particularly important when explaining Palestinian women's lack of (formal) labour activity.

Third, the political and economic situation obviously influences the extent and character of actual labour force participation. The occupied territories are subject to rather exceptional political and economic conditions, having been under military rule for 25 years. In a situation characterized by legal restrictions, strikes and curfews, the local economy, and hence employment opportunities, are by necessity constrained. The integration into the Israeli economy and infrastructure which has taken place during the years of occupation, has profoundly changed the labour markets of the occupied territories. While new employment opportunities have opened up for certain

Figure 7.2 International comparison of labour force participation ratios

social strata, other groups have experienced an erosion of employment possibilities.

Labour Force Participation - Regional Variations within the Occupied Territories[11]

Figure 7.3 (as also figure 7.2) shows labour force participation as percentage of total population, percentage of adults, adult males and adult females for the occupied territories in total and for the three main regions separately. The regional shares of total population below 15 years are also included in the figure.

Only one out of every four persons in the occupied territories belongs to the labour force. Figure 7.3 shows, however, that this result disguises substantial regional variations. The proportion of the total population who are labour force members is as much as 50% greater in the West Bank and Arab Jerusalem than in Gaza. As is the case when accounting for dissimilarities in labour activity between the occupied territories and other countries, regional variations in age structure go some way towards explaining this difference. Controlling for the high share of persons younger than 15 years in Gaza, the ratio with which adult labour force participation in the West Bank and Arab Jerusalem exceeds that of Gaza, drops to about 1/3.

Figure 7.3 also shows that women in the occupied territories generally have a very low participation ratio compared to men in all three areas. Female labour force participation ratio, further, is particularly low in Gaza. While the generally low labour activity of women

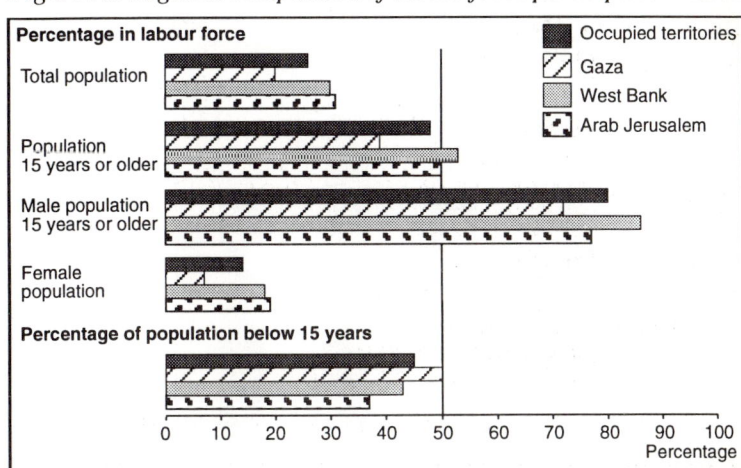

Figure 7.3 Regional comparison of labour force participation ratios

to some extent may be explained by specific difficulties in measuring women's employment accurately, this is not a credible explanation of *regional* differences in female labour force participation. Such differences are most probably caused by regional differences in female employment opportunities. There may, however, also be stronger cultural inhibitions against female employment in Gaza than in the other regions.

Regarding the group of adult males only, figure 7.3 still shows a lower labour force participation ratio in Gaza than in the West Bank and Arab Jerusalem. Further analysis confirms that the West Bank has higher labour force participation among adult males than Gaza, regardless of socio-economic group[12]. Figure 7.4 illustrates the regional differences by presenting age-specific labour force participation ratios for adult males in Gaza and the West Bank separately[13].

How, then, can regional variations in adult male labour force participation be explained? Differences in *age composition* has been considered of great importance when looking at labour force participation as a percentage of the *total* population. Looking exclusively at the adult male population, regional differences in age structure turn out to be relatively small. The only exception is Arab Jerusalem, which has a somewhat older population than the other regions. The total effect of the various age structures is further weakened because labour force participation is low both for the oldest and youngest age groups.

Gender specific *measurement problems* may as already mentioned above explain some of the gender difference in labour force

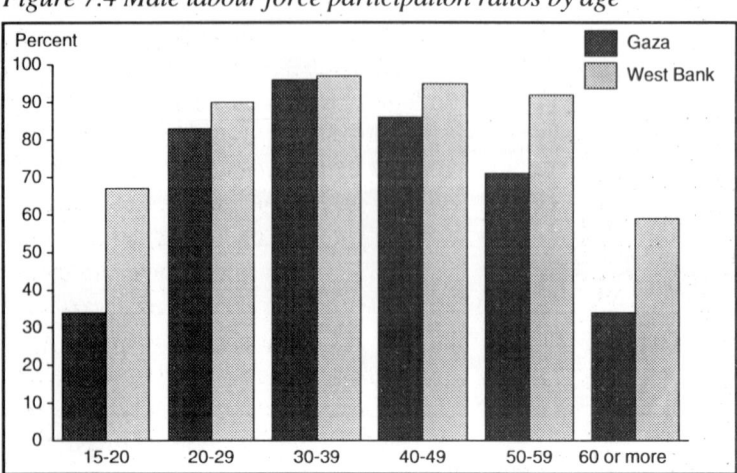

Figure 7.4 Male labour force participation ratios by age

participation. Measurement problems do not, however, provide a plausible explanation for the observed regional differences in adult male labour force participation.

As for measurement problems, *cultural norms* cannot explain the regional differences in male labour activity satisfactorily either. While the cultural norms influencing women's labour activity may vary among regions, there are no restrictive norms in respect to the labour activity for adult males. On the contrary, adult males regardless of area of residence, are explicitly expected to generate economic resources for their families through labour activity.

It is reasonable, therefore, to think that overall differences in male labour force participation between regions and socio-economic groups are due to *economic and political factors*, rather than age composition, measurement problems and cultural factors. While economic and political factors hardly can be measured directly, there are many indicators which support this hypothesis. Variations in male labour force participation are very similar to the variations in household wealth, as pointed out and discussed in the household economy chapter. In Arab Jerusalem and the central parts of the West Bank, employment opportunities are relatively good (outside camps)[14]. The local economy seems to be able to absorb most individuals seeking work. The reasons for non-activity among males, it transpires, are primarily education, i.e. lack of work compatible with training and status, sickness and old age. Labour activity is found to be at its lowest in Gaza and in refugee camps, i.e. the environments most strongly affected by the Israeli occupation[15]. Figure 7.5 illustrates the effect of refugee status on adult male labour force participation. In Gaza labour force participation among refugees is low, regardless of whether they live inside or outside camps. In the West Bank, by contrast, labour force participation is higher and there are small variations in labour force participation according to refugee status.

Figure 7.5 Male labour force participation ratios by refugee status

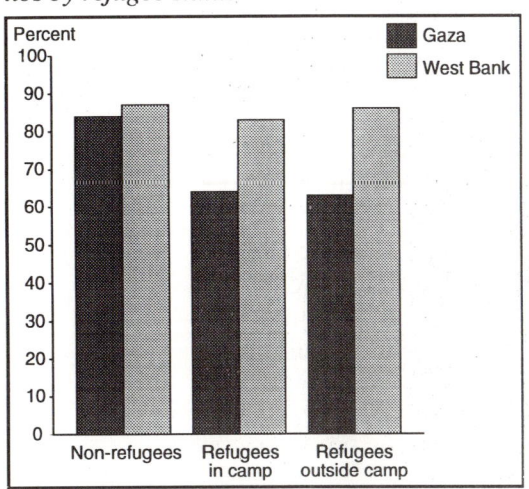

In Gaza, traditional industries like agriculture seem to have been unable to absorb the huge number of refugees[16]. The development of alternative economic activities has been checked by unfavourable conditions such as military regulations, curfews and strikes. In particular, urban refugee camps lack an independent economic base. Limited local demand for labour has led to, as will be discussed later, a high number of Gaza workers commuting to Israel for employment on a daily basis. After the outbreak of the intifada, and especially in the period since the Gulf War, employment in Israel has become less secure and tenable. Strikes, curfews, and, most importantly, new Israeli restrictions (as well as stricter enforcement of existing regulations) have seriously weakened employment opportunities in Israel as a viable alternative to local employment. The observed greater differences between Gaza and the West Bank for young and old men, rather than for the middle-aged (figure 7.4), may also be explained by the fact that the difficult economic situation in Gaza squeezes out the least attractive age groups from the labour market.

Under-utilization of Labour

The nature and evolution of under-utilization of labour do not lend themselves to easy description. Clearly, exact measurements of the occurence of this phenomenon at a given point in time is bound to be difficult. For such reasons, we have deemed it necessary to discuss the theoretical and conceptual aspects of under-utilization of labour at some length.

First it is worth noting that under-utilization of labour here refers to *involuntary* lack of work. Many persons, for example housewives, students and sick or elderly people, may not want, or seek, full-time or even part-time work. Voluntary lack of labour activity should not be considered to be a welfare loss. Thus, it is important to investigate whether or not a person's lack of labour activity is of an involuntary nature[17].

Surprisingly, to many observers, the (Israeli) CBS unemployment ratio for the occupied territories has fluctuated between 1% and 5% during the 25 years of Israeli occupation. By comparison, the unemployment ratio in Israel during the same period, has varied between 3% and 9%, on average surpassing the occupied territories by 3%. The unemployment level estimated by the CBS is roughly confirmed in the FAFO living conditions survey, which recorded a 1992 unemployment ratio in the occupied territories of 7%.

What are the reasons for the low level of recorded unemployment in the occupied territories[18]? The labour force framework described in the first part of the chapter was originally developed to record *any* labour activity, as opposed to complete non-activity, in keeping with macro-economic statistical needs. Use of such labour force definitions in a *living conditions*, however, can easily be misleading. It should be stressed that the concept of "unemployment" in the labour force framework means *total* lack of work[19]. A person classified as "employed" does not necessarily carry out a sufficient amount of labour activity to cover his or his household's economic needs. A major aim of this chapter is thus to show how under-utilization of labour can be found not only among the unemployed, but in all three main groups in the labour force framework. As a reference for the discussion, Figure 7.6 gives a schematic overview of different types of under-utilization of labour, based on the classifications in figure 7.1.

Unemployed Workers[20]

This section is concerned with "classical" unemployment, (box 1 in figure 7.6). Figure 7.7 shows regional variations in the FAFO living conditions survey unemployment ratio. The pattern of unemployment seems, perhaps, somewhat perplexing. Otherwise different regions like Gaza and Arab Jerusalem, have in fact about the same level of unemployment, which turns out to be higher than that of the West Bank.

Contrary to what may be expected, unemployment does not decrease with increasing education. A possible explanation of this result is that two different effects may be at work simultaneously:

Figure 7.6 Types of labour under-utilization

II	III	I a, b, c
Unemployed (ILO def.)	Not in labour force (ILO def.)	Employed (ILO def.)

Unemployment		Underemployment	
Visible	Invisible	Visible	Invisible
ILO definition of unemployment	Discouraged workers	Seeking additional work	Low prouctivity Difficult to measure
1	2	3	4

The first effect (which resembles mechanisms that will be described in the discussion of "discouraged workers" below), may be pinpointed as the "unemployment as luxury" phenomenon. Well educated persons from urban, wealthy households tend to be more selective as to types and places of work. Instead of accepting any low status jobs which may be available to them, these individuals may prefer to stay unemployed for some period of time while looking for an "acceptable" job. It is reasonable to believe that the relatively high unemployment ratios in Arab Jerusalem and among those most highly educated, may, in part, be attributable to the "unemployment as luxury" effect.

Figure 7.7 Unemployed persons as percentage of the labour force by gender and region

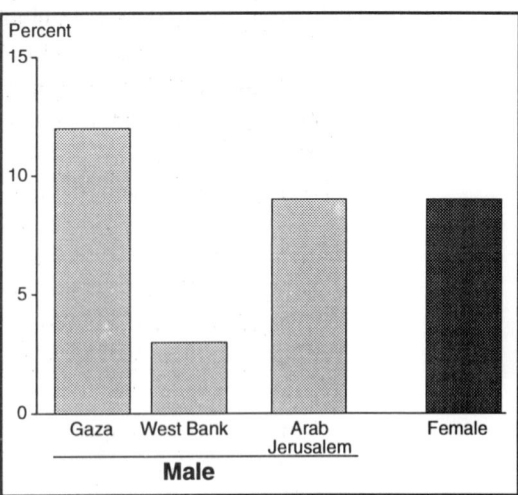

Poor persons, on the contrary, cannot afford to be unemployed. In societies without regular unemployment insurance arrangements, as is the case in the occupied territories, such persons must accept almost any kind of work offered to them in order to survive. The high unemployment in Gaza, particularly in the southern parts and among refugees, is most probably related to a high prevalence of part-time work rather than the "unemployment as luxury" effect[21]. Low job stability over time among large groups of the labour force make for relatively high unemployment ratios at specific points in time.

Unemployment in the occupied territories may to some degree be characterized as being more "evenly" distributed than in Western countries, where national unemployment insurance and other benefits may reinforce long-time unemployment among marginal workers. The low unemployment in the West Bank is probably due to the existence of a low-productivity agricultural sector as an attainable and acceptable alternative to unemployment. This hypothesis is supported by lower unemployment rates in rural than in urban West Bank localities.

"Discouraged Workers"[22]

To be classified as "unemployed" in the labour force framework, a person must not only have had no labour activity during the determinant week, but also actively have sought work. Originally developed for Western labour market conditions, application of the "seeking work" criteria is less straightforward in developing countries. A few general observations should be sufficient to illustrate this point:

The absence of good and timely information on available jobs, the seasonal nature of much work and the high proportion of self-employment all complicate the meaning of "seeking work" in the context of developing economies. Many unpaid family workers do not seek work outside the family enterprise, even though they would like to work more. "Seeking work" is often understood as seeking paid employment only. It may also be difficult to draw the line between seeking work as self-employed and the activity of actually being self-employed. To cope with these objections, ILO recommends a less strict "seeking work" criterion[23]. Persons not seeking work for reasons of lack of hope or similar, may be classified separately as "discouraged workers" in the "not in labour force" category (box 2 in figure 7.6)[24].

In our discussion of the supply of labour, variations in labour force participation ratios between regions and groups have been interpreted as indicating that involuntary non-activity is due to economic and political constraints. Keeping this hypothesis in mind, there is, however, a somewhat surprising lack of variation in the share of discouraged workers over regions and socio-economic groups. A possible explanation may be that discouragement sometimes is so great that mechanisms of retrospective rationalization come into play.

The typical discouraged worker in the FAFO survey is a young educated woman[25]. The relatively high number of discouraged workers among the highly educated is more likely to be caused by greater expectations and a more discriminating attitude with respect to place and type of job than by inability to find any kind of work at all.

Underemployment

"Underemployment" is, following ILO terminology, a phenonemon which refers to the employed category only. By contrast to the extreme situation defined as "unemployment", "underemployment" refers to situations of partial lack of work. Citing ILO, "underemployment exists when a person's employment is inadequate, in relation to specified norms or alternative employment, taking into account the occupational skills of the person"[26]. ILO distinguishes between two main types of underemployment, visible and invisible underemployment, corresponding to boxes 3 and 4 in figure 7.6 respectively. Visible underemployment refers to insufficiency in the volume of employment. Invisible underemployment refers to mis-allocation of labour resources, e.g. in the form of low productivity and under-utilization of a worker's skills[27].

Visible Underemployment[28]

Statistical measurement of visible underemployment is highly problematic in developing countries. A visibly underemployed person must both be working less than normal duration, and seeking and being available for additional work. Both normal weekly working hours in a person's usual type of activity, as well as the time actually worked during the week, have to be estimated. The tendency of self-employed and unpaid family workers to structure their work by tasks at hand rather than by fixed work hours, makes the concept of "normal working hours" ambiguous[29]. The many possible reasons for working less than normal hours also make it difficult to assess the possible involuntary nature of such labour activity.

The FAFO living conditions survey has used the distribution of employed persons by full-time and part-time work as an empirical indicator for visible underemployment[30]. Some groups, e.g. students and women, voluntarily choose to work part-time. Thus, we cannot conclude that all part-time workers are under-employed. Cultural norms in Palestinian society, however, hold that men from 25 to 59 years of age should work full-time.

Figure 7.8 Full-time/part-time employment in percent of male labour force 20-59 years of age by region

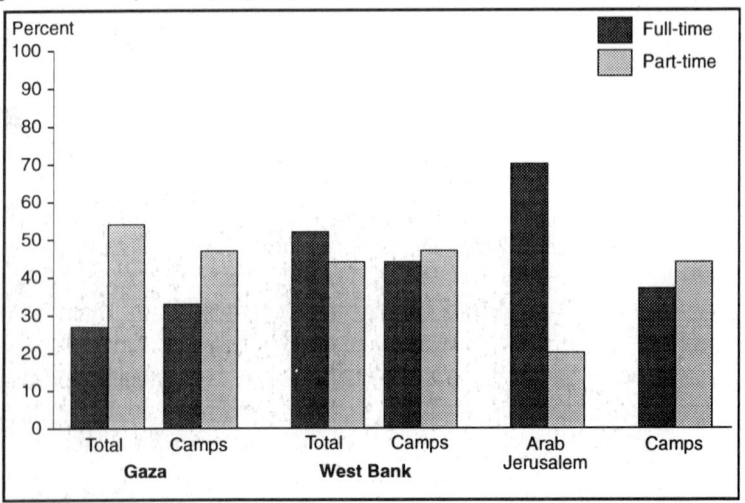

Figure 7.8 reveals great regional variations in the distribution of employed middle-aged men in respect to full-time and part-time work. Full-time work is rare in Gaza, particularly in the southern part. Within the West Bank, full-time work is much more prevalent in the central areas than elsewhere. The full-time/part-time distribution of the central West Bank resembles that of Arab Jerusalem, which has the highest prevalence of full-time work of all regions. Variations in the prevalence of full-time workers according to refugee status are small both in Gaza and the West Bank as compared to the regional differences.

It would not be reasonable to assume that the low prevalence of full-time work in Gaza is a reflection of less need for such work here than in other regions. Rather than a result of freely taken individual decisions, the low number of full-time workers is probably rooted in the generally difficult labour market situation in Gaza. When lack of full-time work is a result of structural factors outside the control of the individual, it may be deemed visible under-employment. The involuntary character of part-time work may thus validate claims that it represents a deprivation of welfare and living conditions.

The hypothesis of lack of full-time work as a living condition problem, is further supported by the fact that full-time work is more frequent among high status than among low status groups. The well educated, members of wealthy households and professionals usually

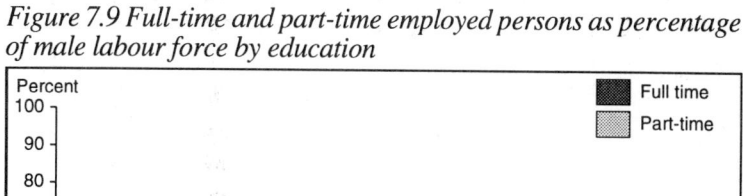

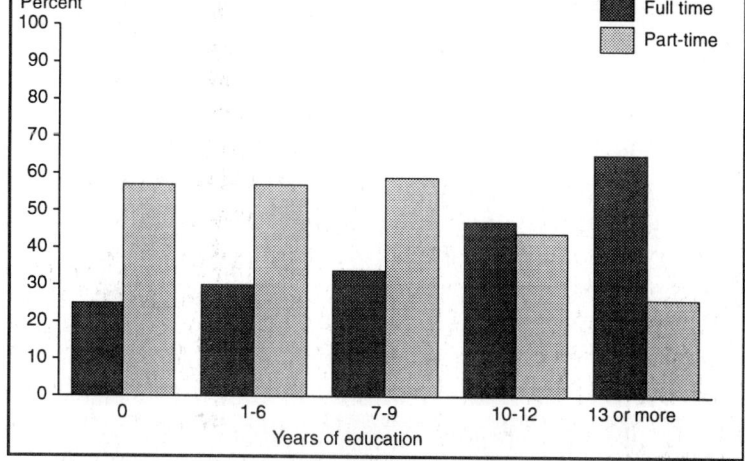

Figure 7.9 Full-time and part-time employed persons as percentage of male labour force by education

hold full-time jobs. Figure 7.9 illustrates how the prevalence of full-time employment increases with increasing education.

Individuals from poor households and persons doing unskilled or agricultural work, on the other hand, usually work part-time. Part-time workers have not been asked specifically about reasons for working less than full-time. The degree of voluntariness cannot, therefore, be determined exactly. Still, the variational pattern in full-time and part-time work shown above, is a clear indication that many part-time workers actually are under-employed.

Invisible Underemployment

Measuring invisible underemployment in developing countries is even more challenging. Invisible underemployment characterized by low productivity, is probably the most typical form of labour under-utilization found in the occupied territories. Measurement requires, however, information on the economic productivity of individual economic units. Further, such data must be augmented by information on the characteristics of individual workers[31]. Thresholds below which income is considered abnormally low, skills under-utilized, or productivity insufficient, must be established. This is generally so demanding that statisticians, even after several years of experimentation, have been forced to give up their efforts[32].

Labour Under-utilization - Concluding Remarks

By way of conclusion, it should be emphasized that unemployment ratios should be supplemented with other statistics for labour under-utilization. In spite of problems of measurement and interpretation, the number of part-time workers - and the labour force participation ratio - are useful indicators of involuntary lack of employment. Particularly variations for adult men over regions and socio-economic groups may provide useful supplementary information. The indicators used in this chapter clearly point to Gaza refugees as being the most deprived socio-economic group in terms of employment in the occupied territories[33]. Residents in Arab Jerusalem and the central parts of the West Bank, and especially the well educated, seem to be the groups which face the least severe employment problems.

Use of the Labour Force in the Occupied Territories

Whereas the first main section of this chapter has discussed underutilization of labour and its different manifestations, by contrast, the focal point of the second part of the chapter will be the labour force members and employed persons residing in the occupied territories[34]. Several questions will be raised: 1) What are the specific gender, age and educational background characteristics of labour force members residing in the occupied territories, as compared to e.g. "non-Jews" and Jews in the Israeli labour force? 2) Which labour markets are available to workers from the occupied territories? 3) What are the employment characteristics of persons residing in the occupied territories? 4) Who works in Israel, and how do working conditions in Israel compare with those in the occupied territories? 5) What are the employment and background characteristics of female labour force members residing in the occupied territories, specifically in comparison with the male majority?

Background Characteristics of Labour Force Members in the Occupied Territories[35]

This section will discuss the composition of the labour force in the occupied territories by gender, age and education. Similar characteristics of "non-Jews" and Jews in the Israeli labour force will be used as a basis for comparison.

Figures 7.10, 7.11 and 7.12 show comparative distributions between the three labour force groups by gender, age and education. There seem to be greater similarities between the composition of the labour force in the occupied territories and "non-Jews" in the Israeli labour force, than there are between the latter group and Jews in the Israeli labour force. Compared to Jews in the Israeli labour force, the labour force of the occupied territories is more male dominated, younger and less educated[36]. Both the compact majority of males as well as the young age structure can be found in most Middle Eastern countries. The labour force of the occupied territories is, however, probably better educated than it is in the neighbouring countries.

Within the occupied territories there are relatively small regional differences in the composition of the labour force by gender, age and education. The Gaza labour force is slightly more male dominated and younger than the one in the West Bank and Arab Jerusalem. The labour force in Arab Jerusalem, comprises somewhat more women, older and well educated persons than does the average total for the occupied territories.

Variations in labour force participation among different socio-economic groups have already been discussed in the first part of this

Figure 7.10 Comparative composition of labour force in the occupied territories and Israel, by gender

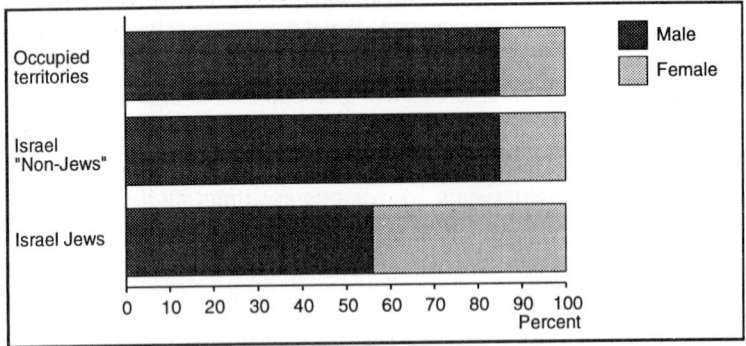

Figure 7.11 Comparative composition of labour force in the occupied territories and Israel, by age

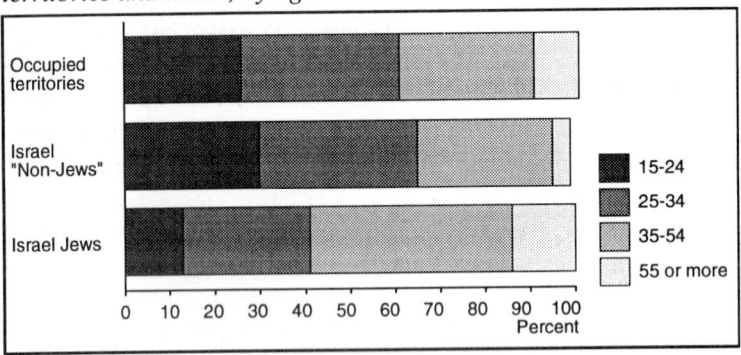

Figure 7.12 Comparative composition of labour force in the occupied territories and Israel, by education

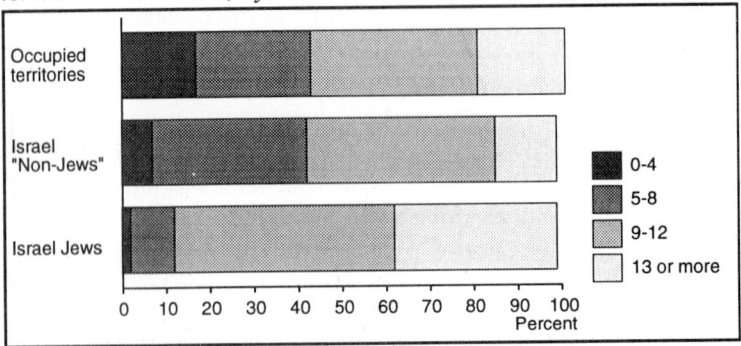

chapter. Of particular interest, in addition to the significant under-representation of women in the labour force, is the low number of workers employed in Gaza compared to Gaza's share of the total population. The relatively low number of labour force members in Gaza is caused by the existence of a younger population and a lower labour force participation ratio both for men and women in working age. The low number of persons employed in Gaza is thus a product of both a generally low labour force participation ratio and a higher share of participation in the Israeli labour market than for the other regions.

The next subsection outlines some assumptions about characteristics of different labour markets available to workers residing in the occupied territories. The section is non-empirical and is primarily intended as an introduction to the section about the distribution of employment on type of work and economic activity.

Available Labour Markets for Workers from the Occupied Territories

For analytical purposes, it may be useful to conceive of labour services as being bought and sold in markets like other goods and services. As stated above, this section about various labour markets open to residents of the occupied territories is principally meant as a non-empirical preamble to the subsequent discussions about employment.

The labour markets for workers from the occupied territories are clearly marked by segmentation: 1) Israeli authorities have introduced legal restrictions on movement inside the occupied territories and on

Figure 7.13 Graphic presentation of labour markets for men:

Occupied territories		
Rural (1)	Urban informal (2)	Urban formal (3)

Israel (inside "green line")			
Daily/seasonal (unskilled)		"Permanent" (semi or unskilled)	
Rural (4a)	Div urban (4b)	Urban (5)	

International migration

entry into Israel. 2) Cultural factors, i.e. social customs specifically pertinent to female labour activity, split up the labour market in separate male and female spheres. 3) Several types of jobs are in practice restricted to the family members of businessmen, and shop- or landowners. 4) As in other societies, many jobs require formal education or certificates. 5) Geographical distance, particularly when accompanied by restrictions on movement, sub-divide the occupied territories into regional labour markets[37]. The overall result of the strong labour market segmentation is low mobility of workers, (in theory) allowing large wage differentials to be upheld. Figure 7.13 presents an overview of assumptions about main types of labour markets available to men residing in the occupied territories, and figure 7.14 some assumptions about characteristics of these markets with regard to entry threshold, wage stipulation and job stability for workers in these markets. (Female labour activity will be further discussed at the end of this section).

Figure 7.14 Characteristics of labour markets for workers from the occupied territories

Type	Entry treshold/qualification	Wage determination	Fringe benefits	Work stability
1a Land owners	Kin relations	Share of output	Self subsistence	High
1b Agricultural workers	Few	Market (low)	Few	Low
2 Urban informal	Few/kin relations	Varying with business	Exchange of services	Medium
3 Urban formal	Formal education/connections	Market high	Health care, pensions etc.	High
4a Rural Israel	Land ownership extremly rare	Market low/medium level	Few	Low
4b Urban day laborer	Permissions	Market medium level	Few	Low
5 Semi permanent	(Skilled/academic very unusual for Palestinians) Permissions skills	Market medium level	Few	Medium

Employment Characteristics of the Labour Force from the Occupied Territories[38]

Figures 7.15 and 7.16 show the distribution of the labour force in the occupied territories by type of work and economic activity or sector according to main employment the year prior to the survey.

The distribution of the labour force by type of work and economic activity to some extent reflects the employment characteristics of Palestinian workers in Israel, e.g. the relatively high number of persons holding service and other unskilled jobs. Regional differences according to region of residence are generally small.

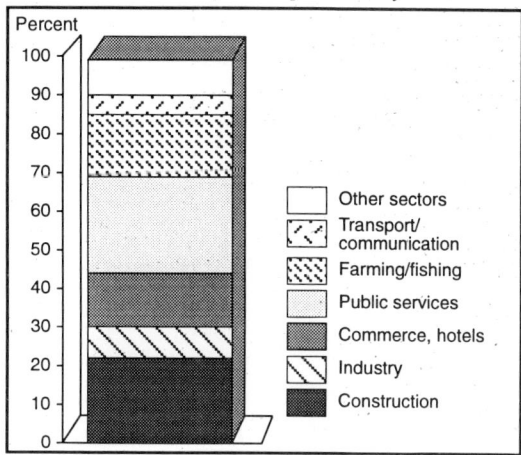

The most important lines of work are construction, public services and various commercial enterprises, (commerce, restaurants, hotels, etc.). It transpires that only 15% of the labour force in the occupied territories are employed in agriculture and fisheries. In most developing countries this share exceeds 50%[39]. The exceptionally low share of the labour force in the occupied territories engaged in primary industries is mainly an effect of the Palestinian exodus in 1948, which turned peasants into landless refugees. Since 1967 interaction with the Israeli economy has further reduced the role of agriculture.

Figure 7.15 Labour force composition by main type of work previous year

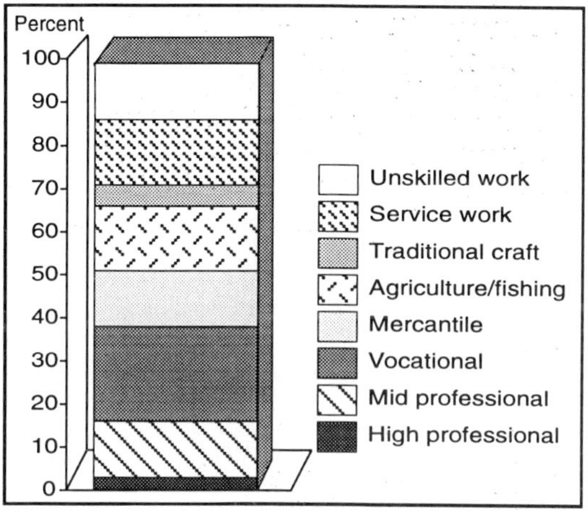

Figure 7.16 Labour force composition by main economic branch of work previous year

Work stability may be expressed both in terms of number of jobs and number of weeks worked during a fixed time period. Data analysis shows that work stability among labour force members is relatively high with regard to the number of jobs, but low with regard to intensity of work. Four out of five workers have had only one job during the last year (i.e. the last year prior to the survey). Going two years back, the share of workers having had only one job drops to three out of four. Work stability measured as intensity of work shows that one out of three workers has worked only 4 weeks or less during the last two months prior to the survey. Job stability is lower in Gaza than in other regions, particularly with respect to intensity of work[40].

A comparison of figures 7.15 and 7.17 reveals an apparent gap between education of workers, and their actual type of work.

Even if half of the labour force has 10 or more years of education, figures reveal that only 20% hold high and mid-professional jobs. We will now continue with a discussion of differences between employment in Israel and employment in the occupied territories.

Workers from the Occupied Territories Employed in Israel: A Short Historical Overview

The Israeli occupation in 1967 reduced contact between the present occupied territories' contact and its immediate Arab surroundings in Egypt and Jordan. From 1969, Israeli authorities set out on a path towards integration of the occupied territories into the Israeli economy. There was a rapid increase in the number of the Palestinian workers in Israel, from about 5.000 in 1968 to more than 100.000 in the late 1980s. The increase in employment in Israel was caused by both push and pull factors. The push factor was constituted by increasing problems in the local production of agricultural and industrial goods, caused by: 1) Lack of access to traditional Arab export markets; 2) Unrestricted competition from cheap Israeli products; 3) Israeli legal restrictions on Palestinian economic activity; and 4) Claims on land and water resources by expanding Israeli settlements (as described in chapter 1)[41]. Demand for cheap labour doing unskilled work in Israeli industry represented the pull factor. Compared to the occupied territories, wages offered for employment in Israel were relatively high, even if they are substantially below the average wage level for Jewish workers.

Figure 7.17 Male labour force members by years of education

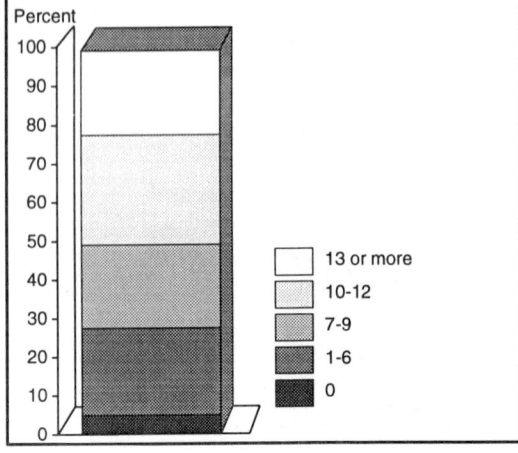

Israeli authorities maintain that there is no formal discrimination against Palestinian workers in the Israeli labour market except for reasons of state security. Palestinian workers are banned from employment in strategic Israeli industries situated both in Israel and the occupied territories[42]. A complicated system for payment and issuing permits for Palestinians workers is practised[43]. To work legally in Israel, residents of the occupied territories must hold up to four cards. The person in question must also not hold a so-called "Green Card"[44]. Permits are issued only after a considerable amount of time involving bureaucratic processing, and after taxes have been paid. No permits are usually required for women and persons below 16 years of age. Very few women from the occupied territories choose to work in Israel, however, this being due to lack of acceptance in the local Palestinian community.

Workers from the Occupied Territories Employed in Israel: Socio-economic Groups[45]

In this section we will discuss which socio-economic groups in the occupied territories that particularly supply workers to the Israeli labour market. Figure 7.18 shows that approximately 26% of the labour force members residing in the occupied territories mainly worked in Israel the year prior to the FAFO survey, wich took place in the summer of 1992 [46].

As illustrated by figure 7.19, employment in Israel is especially important in Gaza where 38% of labour force members have their main employment in Israel. In the West Bank and Arab Jerusalem the ratios of the labour force employed in Israel are 25% and 20% respectively[47].

Within the West Bank area there are small geographical variations with regard to employment in Israel. Figure 7.20 shows that the share of the labour force employed in Israel is higher in rural than in urban areas. This result illustrates the post-1967 transformation of the rural labour force from peasants to wage-labourers in Israel.

Figure 7.18 Labour force composition by main place of work previous year

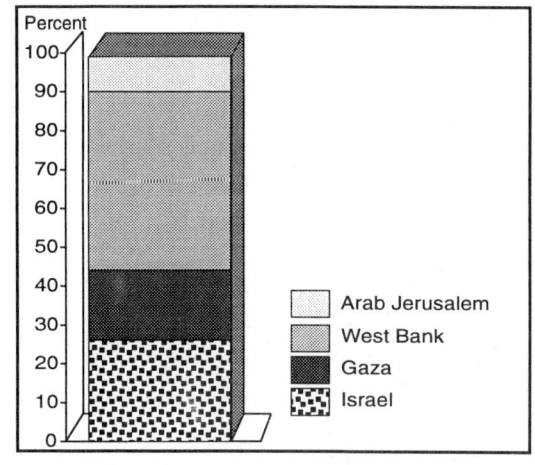

Figure 7.20 shows that the northern part of Gaza sends more workers to Israel than the southern part, which is most likely caused by the relative proximity of the former to major Israeli urban centres.

Looking at Gaza and the West Bank separately, it comes to light that camp refugees have a slightly lower ratio of employment in Israel than refugees outside camps and the non-refugee population. The effect of refugee status on employment in Israel is thus contrary to what could have been expected, taking the shortage of alternative employment in the refugee camps into consideration.

Figure 7.19 Labour force members in Gaza and the West Bank by main place of work previous year

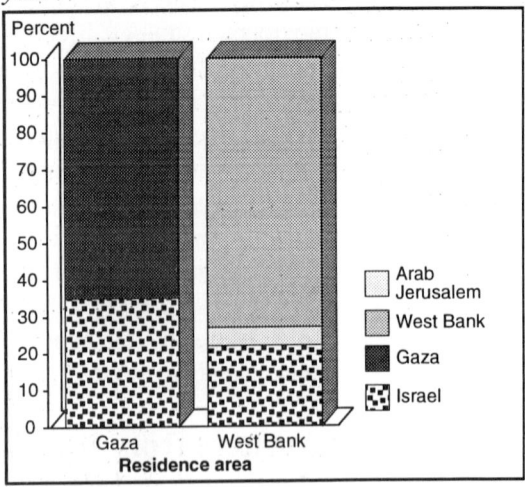

Attitudes among Palestinian workers towards work in Israel seem to be marked by ambivalence and a sense of unease. On the one hand, work in Israel may be viewed as humiliating and insecure. On the other hand, the Israeli labour market offers employment for deprived groups of landless, poor and rural residents who have few alternative means of employment[48]. Figure 7.21 show how employment in Israel increases in the group containing the poorest households.

Figure 7.20 Main place of work previous year of labour force members in Gaza and the West Bank by type of locality

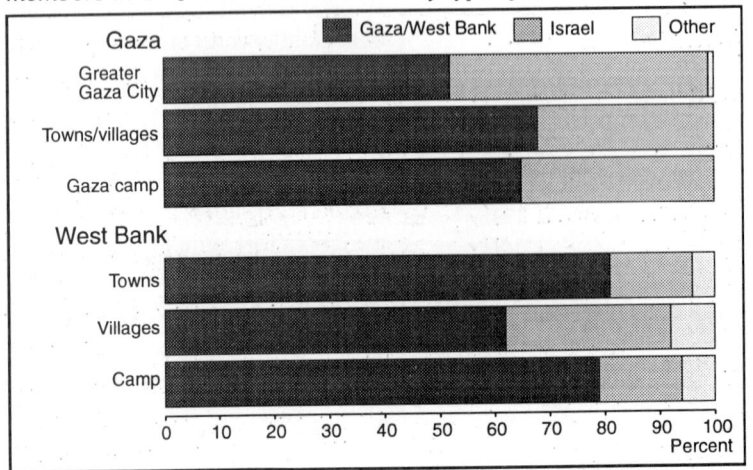

Figure 7.22 finally illustrates how employment in Israel decreases with increasing age[49]. The share of employment in Israel among the oldest age group is, as could be foreseen, very low on account of the physical strains put on workers, who usually both have to wait at the border checkpoints and endure tiresome travel to their Israeli work sites[50].

The effect of education on employment in Israel is somewhat ambiguous. In Gaza, the share of workers employed in Israel decreases with increasing education. In the West Bank, there is a weak

Figure 7.21 Main place of work previous year of labour force members in Gaza and the West Bank by household wealth

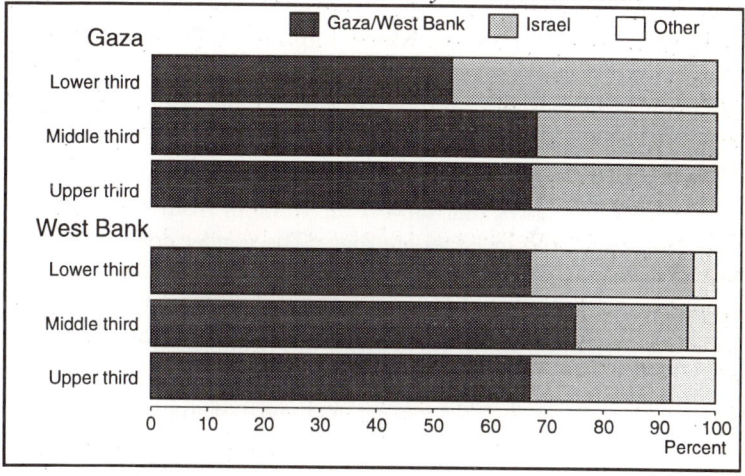

Figure 7.22 Main place of work previous year of labour force members by age

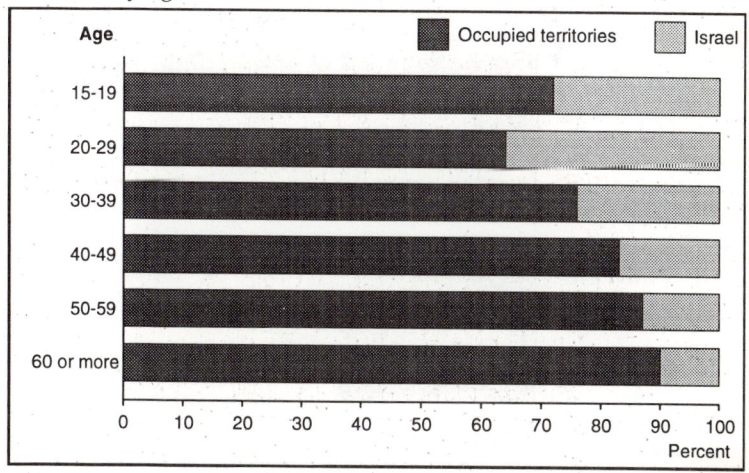

203

tendency to the opposite effect. Most likely higher education among younger than older persons plays a significant role in creating the pattern of behaviour. For the most highly educated group the share of employment in Israel is low, reflecting the status and aspirations among these persons with respect to place of work.

Workers from the Occupied Territories Employed in Israel: Characteristics of Employment[51]

This section will discuss the employment characteristics of workers from the occupied territories employed in Israel. Three other groups have been used as references for the evaluation. First, employment characteristics of workers from the occupied territories employed in Israel have been compared to those of their countrymen working in the occupied territories. Second, where comparable data is available, these two groups have also been compared to employed Jews and "Non-Jews" residing in Israel[52].

Figure 7.23 shows that almost all workers from the occupied territories employed in Israel are male. The gender composition of employed persons working in the occupied territories is almost exactly the same as that of employed "Non-Jews" residing in Israel.

The distribution of workers from the occupied territories employed in Israel with regard to type of work is very different from the one found for the other three groups. As to type of employment in the

Figure 7.23 Employed persons in the occupied territories and Israel, by gender

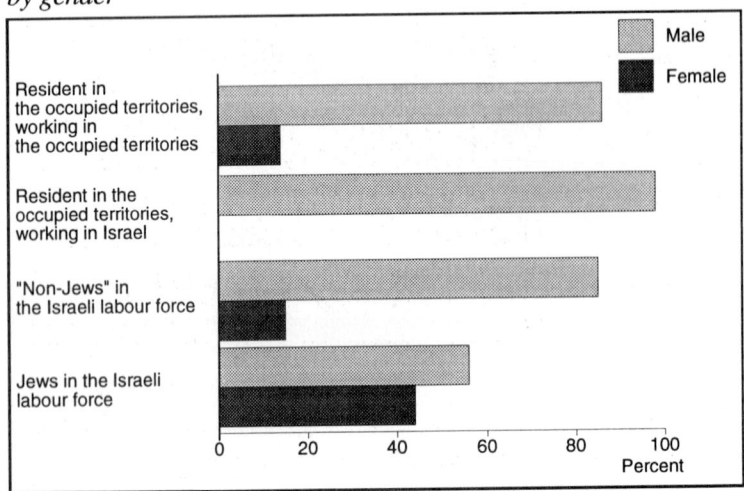

occupied territories, workers from the occupied territories employed in Israel hold more vocational, service and other unskilled jobs. The composition of types of work for workers from the occupied territories employed in Israel and for Israeli Jews respectively, are almost inverse. Figure 7.24 shows that hardly any Jews hold unskilled jobs, while the majority conduct various professional work.

Figure 7.25 illustrates the distribution of the four groups by sector of work. The dominating economic activity for workers from the

Figure 7.24 Employed persons in the occupied territories and Israel, by type of work

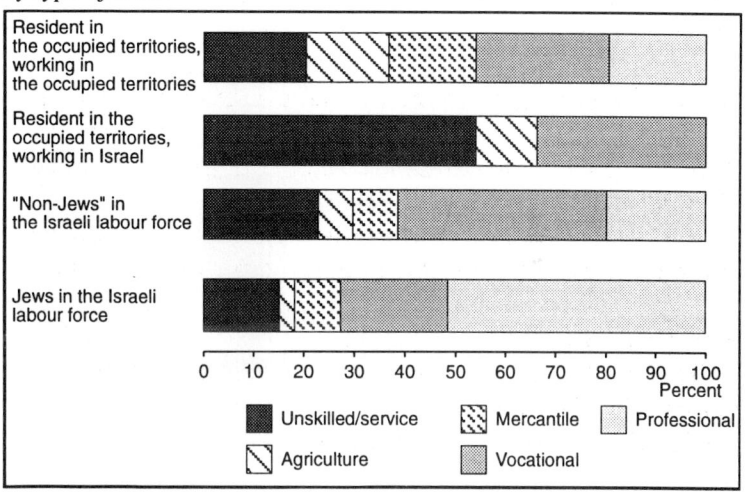

Figure 7.25 Employed persons in the occupied territories and Israel, by economic branch

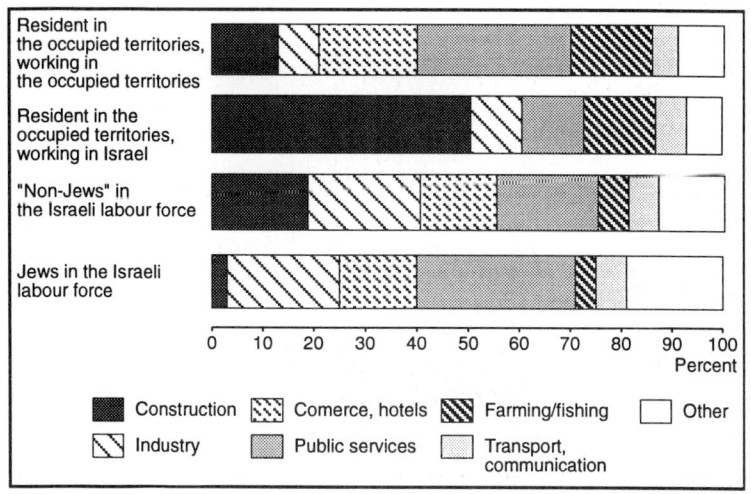

205

occupied territories employed in Israel is construction, followed by agriculture, public services and industry. While 64% of the workers are employed in construction and agriculture/ fishing, only 7% of Israeli Jews hold jobs in these branches.

With respect to job stability and daily travel time no comparable data for Israeli residents have been available. The job stability of Palestinian workers in Israel is, as noted earlier, lower than for workers employed in the occupied territories. This conclusion applies both to the number of jobs held during the last year(s) and to the number of working weeks during the last 2 months (figures 7,26 and 7.27).

As illustrated by Figure 7.28, long and burdensome daily travel constitutes the most significant difference between employment in Israel and employment in the occupied territories[53]. Transportation to work sites in Israel not only causes long working hours, but may also consume a substantial share of a worker's salary[54].

For all variables discussed in this chapter variations among labour force members from the occupied territories are seen to be larger when it comes to place of work (Israel/O.T) than area of residence (Gaza/WB/AJ). Workers from Gaza, however, exhibit less job stability and experience longer travelling time than workers from other regions do, both when employed in their area of residence and in Israel.

In total, workers from the occupied territories constitute only 7% of all persons employed in Israel[55]. As shown above, their contribution is, however, important in some econom-

Figure 7.26 Job stability of employed persons in the occupied territories measured by number of jobs over previous year and main place of work

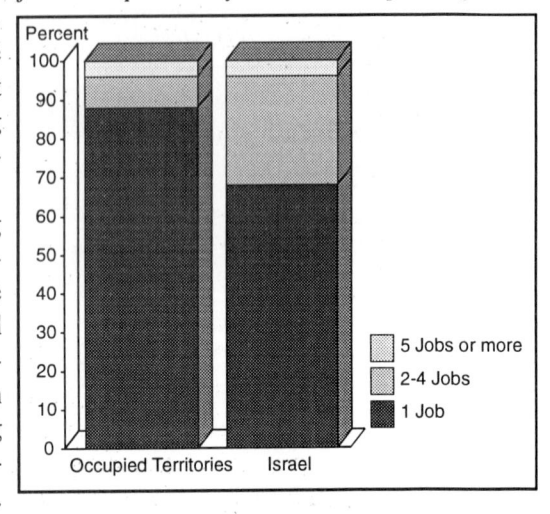

Figure 7.27 Job stability of employed persons in the occupied territories measured by number of working weeks over previous two months and main place of work

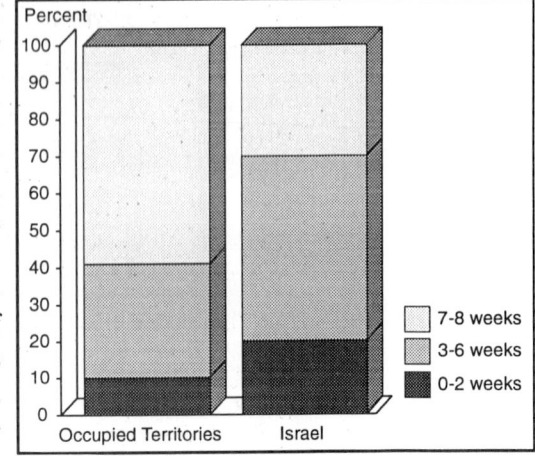

206

Figure 7.28 Daily two-way travel time to place of work of employed persons in the occupied territories measured by number of working weeks over previous two months and main place of work

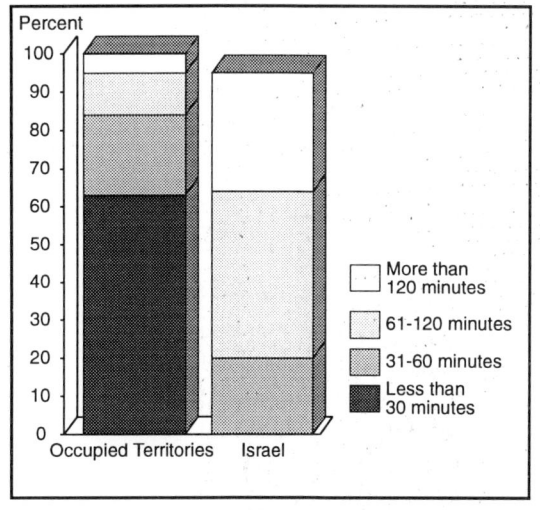

ic sectors, particularly in construction. The observed differences in employment characteristics between groups may support a hypothesis that the Israeli labour market is organized by ethnic groups. As stated by Semyonov & Lewin-Epstein: "Subordinate ethnic groups are over-represented in marginal industries and in less desirable low-status occupations"[56]. The space alloted does not, however, allow for any further discussion of this topic in the baseline report.

In conclusion, Palestinian workers in Israel are vulnerable to economic and political fluctuations, as they are the "last hired, first fired". The welfare consequences of this vulnerability are particularly serious because of the absence of a universal social security system, and the high number of dependencies for every employed person[57]. The motivation for Palestinians to seek employment in Israel appears to be relatively high wage levels compared to alternative employment in their areas of residence, even if, as we have noted earlier, wage levels in general are considerably lower than for Jewish workers holding comparable jobs[58]. There seems to be a tendency of preferring employment in the occupied territories, to the extent that workers are able to choose. Employment in Israel consequently stands out as the penultimate option, next to, but preferable to, total unemployment.

Female Labour Activity[59]

What is the essence of women's work compared to that of men? Any attempt to give a satisfactory answer to this question requires a discussion of the meaning of "work". Simon Levenhardt suggests the following definition[60]:

a) "Activities which generate income used for the survival of the family";

b) "activities which do not generate an individual income, but which serve to support the household as a unit, and which may generate part of the household unit's income";
c) "domestic labour activities which reproduce, daily, generationally or biologically the household unit".

Activities classified under (a) are clearly in accordance with the ILO definitions for work used in this survey. In most Palestinian households these activities are, however, usually considered men's responsibility. Women, on the contrary, are expected primarily to engage in activities classified under (b) and (c) above. While many non-market activities classified under (b) are included in ILO definitions for work, most activities mentioned under (c) are not.

The issue of how to view reproduction in an economic context has long been controversial. Even if reproduction of life is the material basis for the labour force, and thus constitutes the very foundation of the economy, it is usually not considered as "production". The unpaid nature of female domestic "duties" does not imply that these are of no economic interest or have no productive value. Investment in domestic labour saving devices like washing machines and modern kitchen equipment, give indications of the economic importance of house work. House work does not, however, generate direct income which can be used for acquisition of consumer goods in the market. For many women, lack of income generating employment also implies limited control of liquid economic resources. In a living conditions perspective, women may perceive this as a constraint on their ability to pursue their interests[61].

Figure 7.29 presents an overview of female labour activities. Work conducted inside the house as part of the housewife's tasks is, as could be expected, most important in terms of time[62]. Other work done in a domestic setting may be contract or piece work, particularly sewing

Figure 7.29 Graphical presentation of female employment:

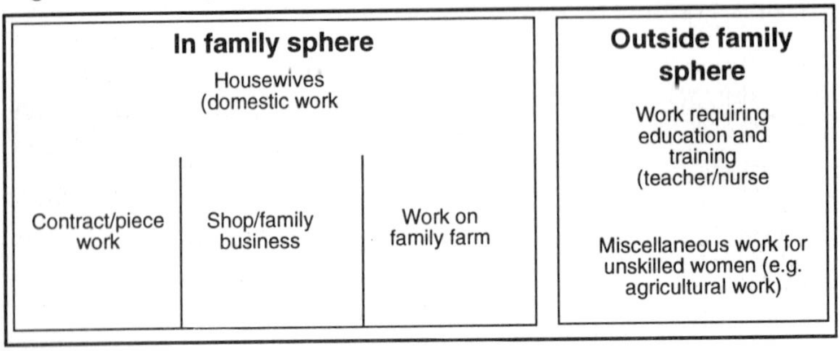

In family sphere	Outside family sphere
Housewives (domestic work)	Work requiring education and training (teacher/nurse)
Contract/piece work · Shop/family business · Work on family farm	Miscellaneous work for unskilled women (e.g. agricultural work)

clothes, work in a family shop or business, garden plot or farm, or food-processing. Out-of-house employment can be found mainly among five groups of women: The highly educated, young unmarried women, widows, divorcees and women without children.

In spite of numerous efforts undertaken when designing the FAFO survey, it proved difficult to capture women's work. A female labour force participation ratio of a mere 14% shows that most women have understood "work" as paid work, primarily conducted outside the home. Figure 7.30 illustrates the perception of "work" among women presenting labour force status of women performing various economic activities[63].

Female Labour Force Participation[64]

The fact that female labour force participation ratios above all reflect formal out-of-house work should be kept in mind. Factors influencing female labour force participation may be grouped in three main types: 1) geographical, household and individual (objective) features, 2) women's own attitudes towards work, 3) external constraints on female labour activity, i.e. influences felt outside the home.

The variations in female labour activity which emerge when linked to "objective" socio-economic background variables, are very similar to those for men.

As figure 7.31 illustrates, female labour force participation is particularly low in Gaza, and in refugee camps. These habitats thus seem to offer very weak employment possibilities for both sexes. With respect to individually related "objective" background variables, the highest female participation ratios can be found among educated women and among women from wealthy households.

Women's attitudes towards work outside the home are rather mixed. There seems to be a widespread perception among women that work outside the house is associated with low status. The very high labour force participation ratio among divorced and separated women, who are usually accorded low social sta-

Figure 7.30 Labour force participation ratios for working women by location of work

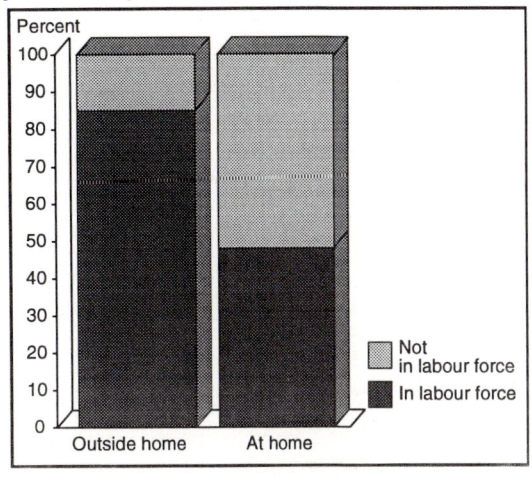

tus, and the relatively high rate of work among female Heads of Household, illustrate this point. Professional work, on the other hand, seems to be regarded as acceptable. The relatively high number of wealthy, educated working women we have observed are probably motivated for work for such reasons as desiring to make proper use of their education and to achieve "self-realization", rather than economic necessity.

It is difficult to disentangle the impact of the culturally motivated norms governing female labour activity outside the home. There is a complex interplay between the attitudes of family members, in particular Heads of Household, and the attitudes in the local community. Many employers may also harbour prejudices as to the ability of women to take part in working life. Women themselves tend to internalize scepticism to female labour activity. Most women thus avoid "non-respectable" labour activities, e.g. work which involves public contact with men[65]. The Israeli labour market is avoided in particular, irrespective of the relatively high wage levels potentially available[66].

Different labour force participation ratios for Moslem and Christian women in the West Bank and Arab Jerusalem could indicate the existence of cultural inhibitions towards women's work. The observed difference is, however, also partially caused by the Christians' higher average education and higher score on the wealth index[67]. With regard to women's freedom of movement, those "free to move at will" have a higher labour force participation than other women do[68]. The

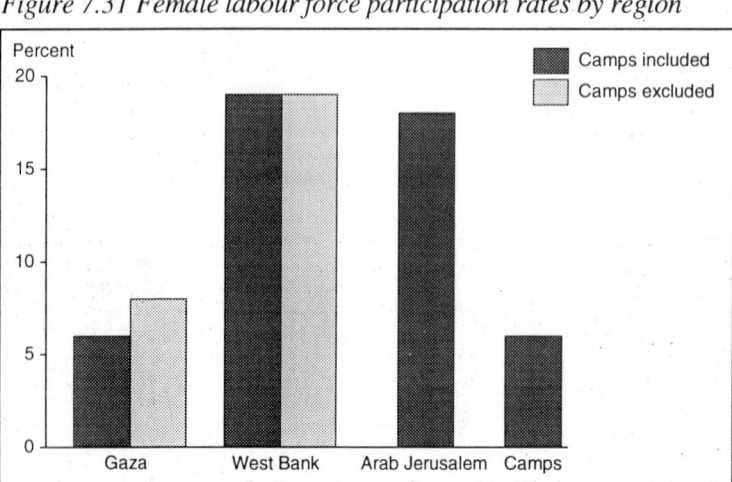

Figure 7.31 Female labour force participation rates by region

increase in labour force participation for Gaza women reaching their menopause may be an indication of cultural inhibitions towards women's work, but may also reflect the fact that less time is required for child care. The very low participation among the youngest Gaza women compared to West Bank women in the same age group, is most likely caused by the lack of employment opportunities in Gaza, although it may also comprise an element of stronger scepticism towards female employment in that region.

Female (Income Generating) Employment[69]

What are the characteristics of female employment? First, it should be remembered that "work" among women primarily tends to be understood as out-of-home employment. Second, because of higher acceptance of female work when professional rather than manual, relatively many employed women hold professional jobs. The female labour force, therefore, is small, but has an aggregate status level similar to, or above, that of the male labour force when variables such as type of work, job-stability and education are taken into account. Women are notably over-represented in mid-professional jobs in public services (nursing, teaching etc.).

Figure 7.32 illustrates how women's use of time varies with labour force participation. Labour force members do less housework than non-members, but still have "full-time" jobs discharging household obligations. Working women thus seem to have a double set of jobs, a phenomenon also observed in Western countries[70].

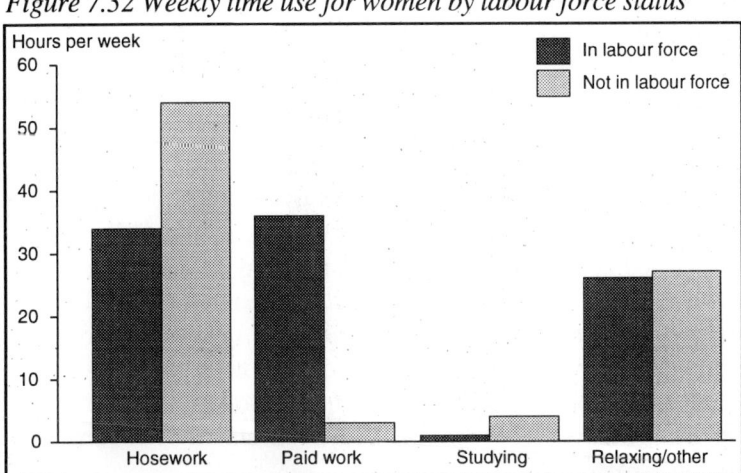

Figure 7.32 Weekly time use for women by labour force status

In conclusion, when engaging in income generating employment, women often seek job types, locations and work hours that allow a combination of home, child care and work. Ability to ensure that work does not get in the way of family obligations is an absolute requirement for women accepting conventional employment.

Conclusions

In the first part of this chapter we argued that involuntary lack of labour activity represents a significant living conditions problem. Traditionally, much emphasis has been put on unemployment ratios, which have been regarded as the most valid expression of this problem. In our opinion, the high prevalence of part-time work in the occupied territories, and the relatively low prevalence of (ILO defined) unemployment, require unemployment ratios to be supplemented by other statistics for labour under-utilization. Particularly, variations in labour force participation and part-time work among adult men between 25 to 55 years of age by regions and socio-economic groups, may provide useful complementary information.

Male labour force participation is especially low for young and old men, and among Gaza refugees. The non-activity of the the two former groups is primarily caused by education and sickness/ old age respectively. The low recorded labour activity for Gaza refugees can, however, most probably be explained by constraints on the labour market caused by political and economic circumstances.

Lack of full-time employment among adult men is prevalent in Gaza, notably in the southern part. Both in Gaza and in the West Bank the share of full-time workers decreases with decreasing household wealth and education. It is reasonable to assume that the low prevalence of full-time work in Gaza is a reflection of the generally difficult labour market situation in Gaza, rather than of a smaller need for such work here than in other regions. The involuntary character of this condition may thus validate claims that the lack of full-time work represents a deprivation of welfare and living conditions.

Results on the prevalence of "discouraged workers" must be interpreted in light of the differences that may be inferred between various socio-economic groups with regard to requirements for type of work and job location. Unemployment ratios based on ILO definitions are vulnerable to the effect of different perceptions of own status and ambitions for type and location of work, as they do not take them into account. The high unemployment ratios in Arab Jerusalem and among the well educated are probably to a large extent attributable to motivation factors, and should not necessarily be interpreted as a manifestation of deprivation.

While labour force participation is especially low for women in all three survey areas, it is hard to assess precisely to what extent this lack of recorded formalized labour activity can be ascribed to, respectively, measurement methods and definitions of "work", and the possible involuntary nature of such work. Thus, it would not be justifiable to conclude that the small prevalence of female formalized labour reflects widespread underemployment and under-utilization of labour among women. On the contrary, the results for women's use of time show that women, on average spend almost 60 hours a week on housework and income generating activities. The majority of women are thus "employed" more than full-time with productive and reproductive activities.

Investigation of Palestinian employment in Israel reveals that particularly individuals in Gaza, persons from poor households, and citizens of West Bank villages tend to work there. Employment in Israel seems to be the last expedient for groups of workers in the occupied territories unable to find employment locally. There is an obvious need for new employment opportunities, particularly in low-income Gaza. The existence of a very young population of the occupied territories - as we approach the next millennium one in two will be under 15 years of age - means that 15.000 individuals will enter the labour market annually. Taken together, Israeli unemployment and immigration from the Commonwealth of Independent States (CIS) make it unlikely that the Israeli labour market will be able to absorb surplus labour from the occupied territories. Thus, ideally, 100.000 jobs need to be created locally in the occupied territories before the turn of the century[71].

The indicators used by FAFO for under-utilization of labour have, problems of measurement and interpretation notwithstanding, clearly identified Gaza refugees, in particular refugees in camps as the group which is worst off in terms of employment.

Notes

1 Important topics like the role of the labour market as a social arena, as a place for acquiring qualifications and skills, and its consequences for worker's health, will be left for future special reports.

2 Employment is, of course, not only interesting from a perspective of living conditions, but also from that of macro-economics. In particular in Less Developed Countries, short of capital and technology, labour activity is a major determinant of

the total economy's production of goods and services. The limited reliable economic statistics available on the occupied territories has led us also to include some aspects of employment which mainly have relevance for macro-economics in the discussion.

3 The "determinant week" used in the FAFO survey varied non-systematically over geographical areas in the time period from June to August 1992. The assessment of a person's labour force status is based on what the person was actually doing during this week. Subjective perceptions of own "occupation" are not relevant for the labour force classification.

Labour activity conducted by prisoners, children or by Israeli settlers is not measured by the survey, even when taking place in the occupied territories. The omission of the widespread phenomenon of child work through imposing a 15 year age limit on the respondents was made because of the very substantial costs involved in measuring such activity with any degree of accuracy. Children's work, which mainly takes place inside family enterprises, is not likely to be reported in regular surveys, and there is a need for supplementary surveys particularly designed to cope with the characteristics of child labour. In contrast to many Western labour force surveys, no upper limit has been put on the age of the respondents because of the relatively small proportion of old people in the population.

4 For unpaid work on family farms or in businesses the time limit is 15 or more working hours in the determinant week.

5 A separate discussion of domestic work is conducted in the section on women's labour activity.

6 See Table A.7.1 in the Labour Table Appendix (A.7) for references to the discussion in this section.

7 The CBS results for "Non-Jews" in Israel include the Palestinian population in annexed Arab Jerusalem and the Druse population on the Golan Heights. The Palestinian population in Gaza and the West Bank, on the contrary, is not included. The CBS results for Jews in Israel also include Jewish settlers in the occupied territories.

In Norway, the lower and upper age limits in labour force surveys are 16 and 74 years respectively. Persons outside this age interval are not included in labour force regardless of amount of labour activity.

As can be seen from Table A.7.30 in the Labour Table Appendix, FAFO numbers are higher than CBS numbers for the occupied territories. The two sets of results are thus not directly comparable.

8 The share of the population above working age, however, is very small in the occupied territories, thus having the opposite effect when comparing with Israeli Jews and populations in Western countries.

9 See the section about women's employment at the end of the chapter for a more comprehensive discussion of this topic.

10 The close family-based economic network in the occupied territories reduces individual labour activity's value as an indicator of individual access to economic resources. The economic resources disposable for an individual household member are often more dependent on the Head of Household's labour activity than his or her own employment. Employment's direct role as indicator of income is thus mainly treated in the discussion of *Head of Household's* labour activity in the household economy chapter.

11 See Table A.7.2 and Table A.7.3, in this chapter's appendix A.7, for references to the discussion in this section.

12 See Table A.7.3 in the Labour Table Appendix (A.7) for group specific variations in (adult) male labour force participation.

13 Figure 7.4 shows that the differences between Gaza and the West Bank are much greater for the young and the old than for middle-aged men. The relatively low

participation rate for men with 0 years of education may be explained by a high number of old men in this group.

14 The 94% participation rate for males in central West Bank is the highest for any geographical region.

15 Note that the low labour force participation rate in Gaza also reflects the high share of low participation rate camp dwellers in the Gaza population.

16 The failure of agriculture to employ the increasing working age population is largely self-evident. First, Gaza has very limited land and water resources. Second, land and water resources have often been confined to expanding Israeli settlements. Third, the land remaining on Palestinian hands is unevenly distributed and partially owned by absentee landlords. Finally, competition from the modern Israeli agricultural sector has eroded Palestinian agricultural revenues by lowering prices on agricultural produce.

17 Drawing a sharp line between the possible voluntary or involuntary nature of lack of labour activity is hardly possible. These perceptions are closely tied to cultural norms governing about the relation between a person's sex, age and social status, and which places and types of work that can be considered "acceptable".

18 Low recorded levels of unemployment is a feature observed in many developing countries. Commonly, the unemployment rate, as measured according to the labour force framework, tends to increase when a country moves towards industrialization. While there is general consensus that overall under-utilization of labour probably is the greatest in very poor countries, labour force surveys in these countries often yield lower unemployment rates than for prosperous countries. (The unemployment rate measured in India is for example lower than in the US).

19 A person classified as "unemployed" according to the labour force framework must meet three criteria simultaneously. 1) He must be without work, (i.e. must not have worked even for one hour the previous week); 2) he must be seeking work; and 3) he must be available for work, if he is offered a job.

20 See Table A.7.4 in the Labour Table Appendix (A.7) for references to the discussion in this section. Note, however, the small absolute size of the unemployment group when comparing results for separate socio-economic groups.

21 See the subsequent discussion about underemployment for further discussion of part-time work.

22 See Table A.7.5 in the Labour Table Appendix (A.7) for reference to the discussion in this section. Note, however, the generally small absolute number of "discouraged workers" when comparing results for separate socio-economic groups.

23 The "relaxed" seeking work criterion in ILO terminology.

24 In the FAFO survey this classification is given to persons answering 6,7,8 or 9 on variable 244.

25 Note that the low *percentage* of discouraged workers among women is due to the high number of women outside the labour force. It is further reasonable to believe that the fairly high number of women answering "other reasons" for not seeking work on this variable, also refers to the general lack of employment opportunities for women. As will be further discussed later, female employment is frequently recognized as a sign of low status if not of a professional type.

26 See: "Surveys of economically active population, employment, unemployment and underemployment, ILO Geneva 1990, p. 121.

27 Ibid p. 143.

28 See Table A.7.6 and Table A.7.7 in the Labour Table Appendix for reference to the discussion in this section.

29 Unlike time worked, income may be transferred among reference periods, and may thus be difficult to integrate into a time-based labour force framework with a short reference period. This problem is particularly manifest in agricultural work

where income appears at the time of produce sale, even if reflecting work carried out throughout the whole agricultural season.

30 Part-time workers were defined as persons working 6 weeks or less during the last two months prior to the survey. Full-time workers as persons working 7 weeks or more during the same time period.

31 Use of low income as criterion for invisible underemployment is problematic because low income may reflect the institutional set-up rather than low labour productivity. This problem is perhaps most clearly exemplified by unpaid family labour among women and children. In family enterprises it may be particularly difficult to trace the individual income components required to measure invisible underemployment.

32 A measurement system called "labour utilization" has been used in Hong Kong, Indonesia, Malaysia, the Philippines, Singapore and Thailand. For operational reasons, ICLS (International Conference on Labour Studies) has recommended that statistical measurement of underemployment be limited to *visible* underemployment only (Ibid p. 145).

As an indicator for under-utilization of skills, the share of employed persons who have more than 13 years of education, but work in vocational or non-skilled jobs, has been estimated. These persons constitute 3% of the labour force in the occupied territories, 4% in Gaza and 2% in the West Bank. The problem of underemployment deserves more attention and research. Data requirements are such that separate surveys may be required.

33 Note that as much as 2/3 of Gaza's population are UNRWA refugees. The score for this group is thus also largely decisive in determining the regional score for Gaza.

34 In the following discussion we will use the concept "employed persons" as labour force members who, in the summer of 1992, had worked at least one month in the preceding year. See the Labour Table Appendix for a further discussion.

35 See Table A.7.8, Table A.7.9, Table A.7.10, Table A.7.11 and Table A.7.12 in the Labour Table Appendix for references to the discussion in this section.

36 See also the discussion on labour force participation in the first part of this chapter.

37 Relatively small wage differences, geographical distances and the need for permissions lead to very little labour migration between Gaza and other regions in the occupied territories. Within the main regions of the occupied territories, geographical distances should normally be a smaller obstacle than in most Less Developed Countries due to small distances and a relatively advanced communication system. Restrictions on entry into (Israeli annexed) Arab Jerusalem, however, in effect separate the northern part of the West Bank from the southern part. Frequent curfews in the central parts of the Gaza Strip similarly separate the greater Gaza City area from the southern part of the Strip.

38 See Table A.7.13 and Table A.7.14 in the Labour Table Appendix for references to the discussion in this section.

39 This low number may partially have been caused by a survey measurement system which faces problems encompassing unpaid family work, a form of production predominantly found in agriculture.

40 This result is partially due to a higher share of the labour force in Gaza employed in Israel where job stability is lower than for employment in the occupied territories. Also for persons employed in the occupied territories, however, job stability is lower for Gaza than for other regions.

41 Much agricultural land on Palestinian hands in Gaza has, in addition, been used for less labour-intensive orange plantations.

42 Since the Gulf War, new restrictions on workers from the occupied territories have been implemented but, perhaps more importantly, existing regulations have been enforced.

43 A Palestinian worker seeking legal employment in Israel, applies to the employment office in his region, which assigns a job with an Israeli employer. He is only authorized to work on the specific tasks and place assigned by the employment office, and change of work place or employer requires updating of the permission. Work permits are not considered contracts of employment, and if an employer does not longer need a worker, all he has to do is to inform the employment service. Workers employed on daily contracts are entirely dependent on their employers, who freely decide whether or not to re-engage them for the next day. Wages for (legal) employment in Israel are indirectly paid through a so-called "payment unit". Employers pay gross salaries to this unit which deducts taxes. Social benefits provided to a worker by Israeli authorities are proportional to the number of work days registered for him with the payment unit. The bureaucracy following the establishment of the payment unit has led to use of direct and indirect methods of surpassing the formal regulations imposed by Israeli authorities. Both employers and employees save taxes by by-passing the payment system. The employer also saves social costs. Because most workers have to wait two weeks for their salaries after the end of the month, there is an incentive to use directly paid, illegal "hand money". There is also a common practice among employers to register a smaller amount of days than actually worked, which has led to a de facto minimum requirement of 15 days to be declared for each worker.

Officially, the Israeli government wants to put an end to the practice of illegal and unorganized Palestinian labour activity in Israel. There has been an increase in the number of registered workers with the payment unit, from 38.500 in 1990 to 74.000 in December 1991. Today, about 70% of the workers in Israel have formal permits (source: "Communication from the Israeli Government to the ILO report on the occupied territories", 1992, page 100).

Regulations for Palestinian workers in Israel have changed frequently with fluctuations in political tension. Lately, Palestinian workers have been required to be picked up by their Israeli employers before being allowed into Israel. Not only work seekers, but also those already holding a job, have had to wait for their employers to provide authorized transport to their places of work in Israel. Such restrictions cause great difficulties for Palestinian workers who may have to wait for their employers for hours behind barbed wire, often in vain.

44 "Green Cards" are issued for periods of 6 months, and are given to persons who have been released after detention on security grounds. In December 1991, 15.000 Palestinians held a green card, 9.000 in the West Bank and 6.000 in Gaza. (Source: Haaretz June 17th, 1991).

45 See Table A.7.15 and Table A.7.16 in the Labour Table Appendix for references to the discussion in this section. The tables show the percentage of labour force members in each group that works in Israel. If the fraction for a specific group in the occupied territories in total exceeds 26%, for Gaza 38%, or for the West Bank 25%, the group is over-represented in the Israeli labour market relative to other groups of the Palestinian labour force in that area.

46 There seems to be great stability with regard to main place of work. About 99% of the workers who worked in Israel during the last year, also had their main employment in Israel during the last 2 years.

It is worth noting that a large number of Palestinian workers also are employed by Israeli institutions and enterprises inside the occupied territories. Palestinian employment in Israeli settlements number approximately 4.000 in the West Bank and 2.000 in Gaza. (Source: ILO report on the occupied territories, 1992, page 27). A further 5.000 workers from the occupied territories are employed in the Israeli "Civil Administration". None of these groups are included among "workers in Israel". The number of permits needed for employment in the settlements, has usually been lower than for employment to Israel proper.

47 Note that the West Bank still supply most workers in Israel in absolute terms.

48 There is no correlation between worker's attitudes towards a future Palestinian state and prevalence of work in Israel. This may indicate that seeking work in Israel is determined by other factors than the worker's political attitudes and opinions.

49 The relatively low share of persons in the youngest age group employed in Israel is probably caused by Israeli restrictions on work permits for the very young. Israeli authorities commonly tend to regard young men as posing the greatest "security risks".

50 See the discussion of average daily travel time in the next section.

51 See Table A.7.17, Table A.7.18, Table A.7.19, Table A.7.20, Table A.7.21 and Table A.7.22 in the Labour Table Appendix for references to the discussion in this section. Note that Table A.7.21 and Table A.7.22 partially overlap thematically with the succeeding tables, but use alternative classifications to allow for comparison with results from the CBS.

52 Note that employed persons in Arab Jerusalem are included both in the two groups residing in the occupied territories and in the group of "Non-Jews" in Israel.

53 More than 80% of Palestinian workers in Israel commute on a daily basis. Staying overnight in Israel is usually prohibited but a substantial number of workers ignore these regulations. (Sources: International Labour Conference, 79th Session 1992, Report of the Director General, page 33. Annex 2, "Communication received from the Israeli government", page 98).

54 On the other hand, daily commuting also reduces potential problems following up-rooting of workers from their homes and cultural environment, phenomena known from studies of permanent international migration.

55 In their labour force survey based on household interviews, the CBS estimated the 1990 number workers from Gaza and the West Bank in Israel to approximately 108 000. (Because only 3/4 of these workers had regularized employment it is, however, reasonable to assume a substantial degree of under-reporting in this field). The 1990 number of employed persons in Israel numbered 1.49 million out of a labour force comprising 1.65 million. (Sources: 1) International Labour Conference, 79th Session 1992, Report of the Director General, Annex 2, "Communication received from the Israeli government", page 97. 2) Statistical Abstract of Israel, 1991, tables 27.21 and 12.1).

56 See Semyonov & Lewin-Epstein, "Hewers of Wood and Drawers of Water" 1987, page 17.

57 The problem of low job security and stability has been high-lighted by the increasing number of workers seeking employment in Israel, following immigration from CIS and the consequences for Palestinian workers of the curfew during the Gulf War.

58 See Semyonov & Lewin-Epstein, "Hewers of Wood and Drawers of Water" 1987, page 89.

59 See Table A.7.23 in appendix A.7 for references to the discussion in this section.

60 "The Revaluation of Women's Work", Croom Helm, 1988, p. 15.

61 The present process of economic modernization in the occupied territories is likely to be followed by a shift in consumer preferences from services towards material goods. As an activity not directly generating income, domestic work may thus have its status further eroded in the future, compared to income generating activities.

62 See also appendix A.7.

63 Out of the 8% of all women who had a job outside the home the *year* prior to the survey, as many as 83% were members of the labour force at the time of interviewing. (The remaining 17% probably did not work during the *one-week* reference period that determined their labour force status). By contrast, only 48% of the women doing non-formalized jobs the previous year, were members of the labour force at the time

of the survey. Even if some of these women probably did not work at all in the reference week, most of them probably did not consider their labour activity as "work". Particularly such agricultural work as raising animals, was not accounted for. The overall response rate for in-house unpaid production was low compared to expectations prior to the survey. The main problem in documenting female labour activities thus seems to be how to measure work actually conducted, rather than too narrow definitions.

64 See Table A.7.3, Table A.7.24 and Table A.7.25 in the Labour Table Appendix for references to the discussion in this section.

65 See "A Study of Women and Work in Shatti Refugee Camp of the Gaza Strip", Arab Thought Forum Jerusalem (Lang/Mohanna) 1992, page 73.

To avoid criticism from male relatives and the neighbouring community, many women accept low pay work at home (e.g. embroidery or sewing). Income generating work at home is, of course, also easier to combine with child care and other domestic work. Some women even travel to another area to avoid criticism from the local community.

66 Ibid page 55.

67 Even though most Christian women live in the central West Bank region, the overall female labour force participation rate is not higher here than in the northern and the southern parts of the West Bank.

68 The small difference between working and non-working women in Gaza seems to be rooted in misperceptions of the content of the expression "free to move at will". Labour force participation in Gaza is actually much higher among women who, when presented with specific activities, answer "can go alone", than for women generally claiming they are free to move at will.

69 See Table A.7.26, Table A.7.27, Table A.7.28 and Table A.7.29 in appendix A.7 for references to the discussion in this section.

70 Information about women's weekly time use should be used with caution because of problems with reporting. Some women counted parallel activities twice, yielding more hours of weekly activity than the possible total of 168 hours. Other women, in particular older women, reported far less than 70 weekly hours, including relaxing. There is, however, a possibility that, on average, these reporting errors may offset each other.

71 In the short run, reduced Jewish immigration to Israel will also negatively affect Palestinian employment because of the high employment share in construction among workers from the occupied territories.

Chapter 8
Aspects of Social Stratification

Ole Fr. Ugland
Salim Tamari

Introduction

The purpose of this chapter is to present a general picture of Palestinian social stratification, by bringing together relevant social and economic issues investigated in the previous chapters. As in all societies the social status of any family or individual reflects realities which may appear elusive and beyond the grasp of quantitative science. This obstacle may in part be overcome by applying quantitative methods to relevant social phenomena which are in fact quantifiable. A systematic account, based on a discussion of selected characteristic features of socioeconomic differentiation in Palestinian society, may be attempted.

The analysis is divided into three parts. First, some general observations on the socioeconomic distribution are made by reference to four major head of household (HH) characteristics. Second, a description of the interrelationships between these characteristics is presented, followed by the construction of an aggregate distributive index. Third, the Palestinians' own perceptions of socioeconomic inequalities are related to the stratification pattern as it emerges from the discussion.

Research Strategy

It is common in social science to assume a more or less strong element of division or differentiation between social positions or social roles in a society. Individuals or groups of individuals are conceived of as constituting higher and lower differentiated strata or classes, in terms of some specific or generalized characteristic or set of characteristics.

There is, however, little common agreement as to which elements or aspects of a society that reflect this structure of social "layers", nor as to which explanations that are important concerning mobility between them. Likewise, some societies will be characterized by more or less clear-cut and stable differentiation between the layers, while in others the borderlines will be more blurred or changing.[1]

The concept of "class" is highly contentious in Middle Eastern societies; some would deny the salience of classes, while others would argue that although classes may exist, ownership relations are secondary to relationships of political power.[2] This latter view may partly be supported by the historic experiences from the feudal state under the Ottoman rule. It has been argued that "state monopoly, particularly over land, hindered the development of social classes, and in a sense prevented the crystallization of class conflict". Stratification has, consequently, "tended to be variegated, and unlike the Western societies to be group-based along tribal, familial, sectarian and ethnic lines, where primordial attachment rather than class consciousness typified these societies".[3]

We will not attempt to solve this problem here by superimposing absolutely consistent class divisions or by defining any kind of broadly accepted "poverty line". Nonetheless, in order to describe socioeconomic variations within contemporary Palestinian society in a coherent fashion, some indicators need to be decided upon.

Proceeding from the assumption that the family-based Palestinian household constitutes a strong network of social and economic obligations and privileges, the status of the (acknowledged) Household Head may provide us with adequate information as to the social stratification of the Palestinians.[4] First, four different indicators – education, occupation, housing conditions and economic wealth – are selected. Reflecting various aspects of the HH and his household, taken together they are assumed to have vital relevance to the identification of socioeconomic differences. Secondly, we suggest a division into four main socioeconomic status categories along each indicator – high, upper- and lower middle and low – which are assumed to reflect general levels of status differences. The latter category ("low") is crudely considered as referring to living conditions below the "deprivation line".

To avoid the difficulties in obtaining accurate information on the status of specific households within their community – i.e finding ways of measuring the deference and honour accorded the HH – the analysis instead focuses on the HHs *own* perceptions. How does he/

she rate his/her influence within the community? What are his/her attitudes to the generation – and to the prevalence – of socioeconomic inequalities?

Elements of Socioeconomic Differentiation in the West Bank, Gaza and Arab Jerusalem

Two properties are considered to be vital indicators of *social status*. First, two major *educational* shifts have occurred (see also chapter 5, on Education). In the late 1950s and -60s free and universal public education became available to camp populations and to villagers. In the mid 1970s and early -80s free university education also came within reach of more disadvantaged sections of the urban and rural population. While education in earlier times for economic reasons was confined to the higher social strata, which were in a position to send their children abroad, free and universal education now became relatively accessible to all categories of the population.

Educational status is measured here by an index combining information on level and length of education. This combination facilitates a necessary distinction between HHs with various categories of primary education (primary- preparatory-, or kuttab levels)[5], of which three in ten have had up to five years of education, while seven in ten have attended school for more than five years. All in all, one in ten HHs have acquired a higher university degree. The largest category (six in ten) have upper middle (secondary) education. One in ten have lower middle (primary) education and two in ten report no education at all.[6]

Secondly, various developments and the enhanced availability of public education has given rise to new kinds of *occupations*: professional and semi-professional employment outside the agrarian system. The dwindling number of peasant workers, who have steadily abandoned their farms under the pull of wage labour, has left the role of agriculture increasingly marginalized. With increased wage labour opportunities, the income of hitherto poor peasants has increased, redefining their status compared with the former privileged economic position of land-owners.

Different "productive" roles in a society are generally considered as being of different functional significance to society, and thus to the attainment of a higher or lower degree of prestige. The complexity of the Palestinian labour market, together with limitations on geographical mobility, complicate status ascription by reference to the present occupation of the HH. Aiming to differentiate between different occupational prestige categories, occupational training is considered a fairly valid indicator.[7] The occupations are further grouped into four categories: High-status occupations comprise high-level professionals (one in ten). Upper middle range occupations imply middle-level professionals, business management- and skilled workers (three in ten). Lower middle status occupations are understood to be sales workers, farmers and traditional craft artisans (three in ten). Low status HHs have not been trained for any specific jobs (three in ten).[8]

New types of labour have given rise to new forms of status acquisition, replacing land as the primary indicator of *economic wealth* (except where agricultural land has appreciated in terms of its real estate value). First, the increase in private disposable income, extensions of infrastructures and access to Israeli markets, have rendered "modern" *consumer durables* a prime indicator of economic well-being. The possession of certain luxury goods clearly distinguishes the better off from the rest of the population.

As previously mentioned, income has not been measured directly in this survey. Consequently, social status in terms of economic capital has to be deduced from other income-related information. This can be done by charting ownership of a set of what is commonly known as "cutting edge" consumer durables: Colour TV, washing-machine, modern oven, bathroom, video, stereo and dishwasher. When frequencies of the different items are added, the following distributive pattern emerges: HHs possessing none of the items included can be categorized as low-status (four in ten). The low middle category (two in ten) has but one of the items. The upper middle category (two in ten) possesses 2-3 items, and the high status category (two in ten) owns 4 or more.

Secondly, *housing* is of particular interest in light of the pivotal importance of the family within the Palestinian society. Housing functions as an indicator of family economic wealth and also determines or reflects the status of the family within the local community. Thus, substantial resources are pooled into housing, which is also considered a safe area of investments in an otherwise uncertain world.

The housing index provides measurement of density and internal comfort. While density indicates the number of persons per room, internal comfort reflects the availability of a set of amenities which the HH disposes of: shower, flush toilet, fitted kitchen or heating by central, electric, gas or solar energy. The best housing situation is defined as having more than three of the specified amenities and encompassing less than two persons per room (one in ten HHs). The most unfavourable position can be defined as having no or only one amenity while living in a house with more than two persons per room (three in ten, of which 70% live in households with more than three persons per room). Three out of ten occupy each of the two intermediate low- and upper middle positions of having maximum two of the specified amenities while having less than two person per room, and having three or more amenities but living with more than two persons per room.[9]

Table 8.1 summarizes the selected items, and the grouping in four categories as to whether the socioeconomic status is considered to be high, upper- or lower middle, or low. Each category is further accorded a status score ranging from 1 for the low status category to 4 for the high status category. Numbers in parentheses indicate the distribution of HHs in each category.

Although the four dimensions for theoretical reasons are treated separately, in the real world they will occur in a multitude of interdependent combinations, constituting complex life situations. Two assumptions may be made in order not to over- or underestimate good or bad situations in the following analysis:[10] First, we assume that a bad situation in one field may be compensated by a good situation in another: A person with two lower scores on the four indicators is worse off than a person with one low score. Second, as long as differences in quality or attractiveness of the four indicators (as

Table 8.1 HH stratification indicators. Percentage distribution in parentheses

Status category	High	Upper middle	Lower middle	Low
Status score	4	3	2	1
Education (index)				
No. of years	>6	>6	<5	0
Level	University (10)	Primary/secondary (58)	Primary/secondary (15)	No (17)
Occupation				
Type	High professional (6)	Mid.prof, business skilled (31)	Salesm, farmer tradcra. (33	No job qualifications (30)
Consumer durables				
No. of items	4-7 (12)	2-3 (23)	1 (23)	0 (42)
Housing (index)				
Comfort items	>3	3-2	2-1	1-0
Persons per room	<1.99 (14)	<1.99 (28)	2-2.99 (30)	3> (28)

opposed to the status categorization within them) cannot be judged, they simply are accorded equal weight: A low score according to one indicator, may be offset by a good situation in another. In other words, we allow good and bad situations to outbalance each other.

Independence, accumulation or compensation?

An important element in the analysis of social stratification is the way in which different relative rankings are connected. Which of the four present indicators are most closely related, thus contributing most significantly to differentiation among Palestinian HHs? Does high-status education translate into high status occupations, high housing standards and high material wealth? Which types of combinations of high and low status characteristics are most common?

Three general distributive effects are normally considered in this respect.[11] First, no or rather weak connections between the various indicators may be revealed, indicating a non-systematic distribution of goods and burdens. Secondly, if the distribution is systematic, good or bad situations may either accumulate (those with unfavourable conditions in one field will also experience a bad situation in the other fields) or, third, they may imply compensation (a bad situation in one field is offset by a good score in another). In the light of results in the previous chapters we may expect a pattern of accumulation of good and bad situations respectively. Table 8.2 presents the results of a statistical analysis of covariation.

The coefficients give us two valuable pieces of information that lend themselves to straightforward interpretation: First, the strength of the association between the indicators tells us to what degree there are any systematic patterns in the relation between them. The measure theoretically varies from +/- 0.0, indicating no covariation, to +/- 1.0 indicating total conformity. Further, we may observe the direction of the relation, i.e. how positive covariations indicate accumulation (status consistency), while negative correlations denote compensation (status inconsistency).

The table clearly demonstrates a systematic distribution of benefits and burdens among Palestinian HHs, although the patterns are far from totally conformal. The general trend is one of accumulation or status consistency: all four items co-vary pos-

Table 8.2 *The four socioeconomic status indicators: matrix of covariation (Pearson's r). All coefficients significant at .001 level. N=813*

	Education	Occupation	Consumer durables
Occupation	.50		
Consumer durables	.34	.25	
Housing	.21	.19	.42

itively, indicating that "privileged" and "deprived" conditions tend to accompany each other respectively.

Although all the four elements are clearly related, the most systematic covariation is the one found between education and occupation on the one hand, and between housing and consumer durables on the other.[12] Other relationships are somewhat weaker, the weakest being between occupation and housing. A distinction between on the one side "social status" (education and occupation) and on the other "economic wealth" (capital goods and housing) is indicated. This is seen from the relatively speaking weaker covariation between than within the respective social and economic categories. One might ask if this an indication of problems concerning the translation of social status into economic wealth. We will return to the question below.

The Stratification Index

So far, we have discovered clear patterns in the distribution of high and low status scores along the four socioeconomic indicators. The relationships do not, however, operate within iron laws. Some HHs break with the general pattern. To sum up, the often complex combinations of social and economic characteristics, a socioeconomic distribution index has been created. Here the status scores (from 1 to 4) along the four different indicators have been added (thus giving a score from 4 to 16) as can be seen from figure 8.1.[13]

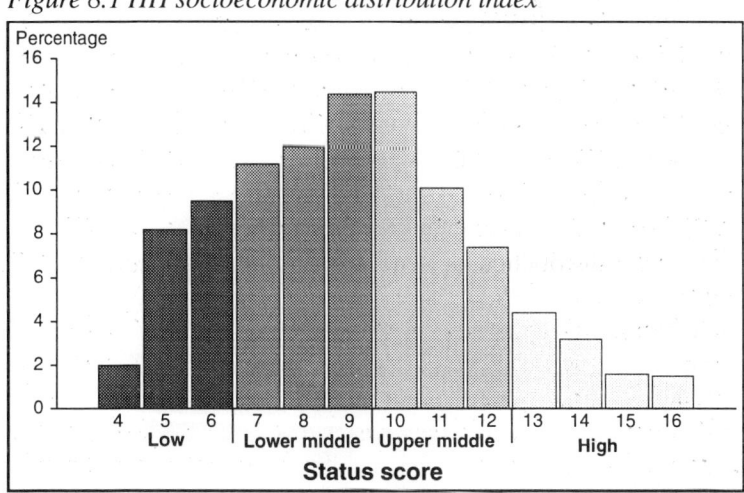

Figure 8.1 HH socioeconomic distribution index

The distribution is grouped into four status categories. Most HHs appear to experience a "middle" level situation. A peak is observed at the upper side of the upper middle category and at the lower side of the lower middle category. From this point, the status scores fall gradually. More HHs experience a relatively deprived situation than a relatively privileged one, but with very few experiencing either absolute deprivation or absolute privilege.

Comparatively speaking the distribution reflects a situation that lies somewhere between the classical "pyramidal" and "diamond" shaped structures. While the former is found in many developing societies, in which the majority of roles are ranked low, the latter is typical of many modernized societies, where there sometimes is a strong pressure toward social equality as well as a need for increasing numbers of middle-ranking officials.[14]

Although we do not have directly comparable indicators, and while it may be true that the index also reflects our own subjective evaluation of good and bad situations, it can be fairly said that the Palestinian stratification diverges from the rest of the Arab world. The deviation may be caused and reinforced by several factors: First, Palestine (as it never achieved independence) has not developed a public sector and, more specifically, a state bureaucracy, a sector that in neighboring countries accounts for enlarged strata of public officials and civil servants. Second, traditional Palestinian hierarchies were, from 1948 onwards, severely disrupted as a result of war and expulsion, leading to the loss of the landed classes and the traditional elites. Third, as a result of pressing economic hardships since 1967, a considerable segment of Palestinian professional and business elites have emigrated to the diaspora (the Gulf and the U.S.A). The observed distribution may thus reflect limited possibilities of socioeconomic mobility during the last decades, leading to the present pattern of socioeconomic homogeneity centered upon low- and lower middle status categories.

Socioeconomic Status and HH Background Characteristics

It is reasonable to assume that the socioeconomic status of any HH will be related to other background characteristics. Age, sex, refugee status and locality should be considered important in this respect.

Age and sex

In the absence of any form of social security, ability to find work becomes all the more important, and one would expect that the labour market favours the young rather than the old. Likewise the acquisition of wealth can be assumed to rise as the HH grows older. On the other hand, different historical experiences (war, the introduction of free education, etc.) may cause both variations in possibilities for acquiring skills (education) and in consumption patterns among HHs. Especially important here is perhaps the fact that most elderly Palestinian HHs have not been able to profit from the educational revolution that took place in the 1960s and 70s.

Comparing status scores across HH age groups significant variations are revealed (Figure 8.2).[15] The figure suggests a curvilinear pattern. HHs in the 20-29 years age group are over-represented in the lower status categories. In the category 30-39 years the incidence of higher scores is more frequent than in the youngest cohort. Then the level falls somewhat in the 40-49 years group – still at a somewhat higher level than for the youngest cohort – and continues to fall for the 50-59 and 60+ years cohorts. In other words, the socioeconomic status seems first to rise slightly from the young to the young middle-aged, then to fall somewhat for old middle- aged, and further to fall considerably for old HHs.

Due to the generally subordinate role of women, the social status of female headed households may be expected to be lower than that

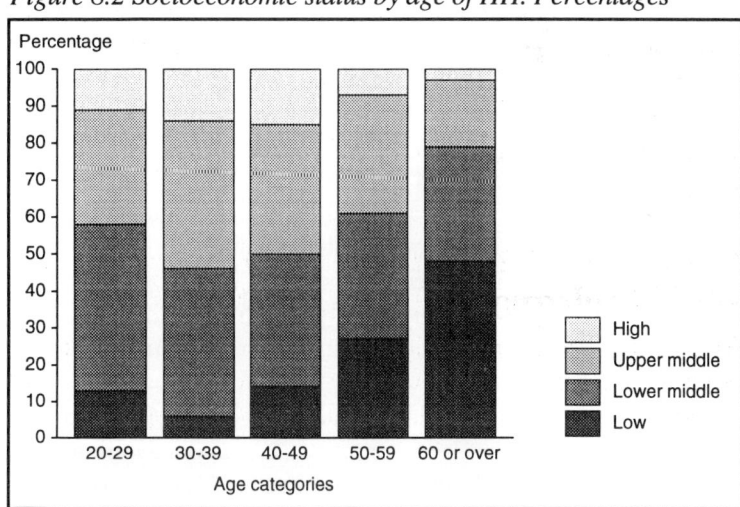

Figure 8.2 Socioeconomic status by age of HH. Percentages

of their male counterparts, and may in some cases rather be determined by the status of the (absentee) male HH. The instance of female HHs is indeed largely due to special circumstances in which the male HH is absent for a longer duration of time for reasons of work. The point is borne out by the higher amount of remittances received in this category (33% among the female as opposed to 6% among male HHs). Hence the individual female HH status may not be an exact reflection of the family socioeconomic status. Comparing the socioeconomic status of male and female headed households (figure not shown), the females appear clearly less fortunate (59% appear in the low status category and no-one in the high status category) than the male ones (15% and 12% are found in the low and high status categories respectively).

As indicated above, it is impossible to offer a conclusive interpretation of the age and gender effects. Age discrepancies may be explained in terms of both generational and life cycle factors. Further, many HHs have experienced complete lack of income in periods of curfews or as a result of changing economic regulations in the occupied territories. Such circumstances, which have been broadly felt, make it difficult to isolate the age effects on economic activities of HHs. Likewise, if the socioeconomic status of female headed households is relatively low, this may be compensated by a higher status ascribed to her absentee husband or to her sons. Suffice it to say that scores for "elderly" and female headed households are generally low, probably caused by a complicated mixture of cultural, age and gender related factors.

The general decrease in status by age, however, suggests a challenge to the traditional conception of a deferential attitude to the family elders, caused by the fact that younger family members now may be able to acquire jobs and income without their mediation.

Locality and Refugee Status

HHs in Gaza, the West Bank and Arab Jerusalem could be expected to show divergent socioeconomic patterns as these three main areas have been differently affected by the years of occupational rule. Figure 8.3 presents the distribution of the stratification index for Gaza, the West Bank and Arab Jerusalem, and is directly comparable with figure 8.1.

Although numbers are small for some categories, which increases the margins of error, the figures are tentatively applied to illuminate the regional variations. Following the curve for Gaza, we observe a quick rise at the lower end of the status index, a turn as we advance from the low to the lower middle category and a falling trend as we move towards the higher strata. Very few Gaza residents enjoy a "high" socioeconomic status. The curve for Arab Jerusalem inverts the pattern for Gaza. The curve rises more or less steadily from the low to the high status side of the index, with a peak at the upper middle level, then falls slowly for higher strata, but at a higher level than for Gaza. West Bank villages assume an intermediate position, close to that of the total distribution. The highest point is located at the left side of the upper middle category. The curve falls steadily at both extremities, but reveals a slightly greater occurrence of lower middle than upper middle scores.

Possible explanations for the differences, which may not be surprising, are dealt with extensively in the previous chapters. Here we would like to focus on some basic factors: Gaza, typically characterized by a massive refugee population, and a very high population density, is also distinguished by severe labour market problems and fewer migration possibilities. Arab Jerusalem, on the other hand, is characterized by its role as a market and service centre for the central West Bank region. It offers religious, health, travel, banking, cultural entertainment and (indeed) political services which are absent, or thinly spread, in the West Bank and Gaza. The creation of a "welfare cushion" should also be noted, by which Jerusalemites are given

Figure 8.3 Socioeconomic status by locality of HH: three main areas. Percentages

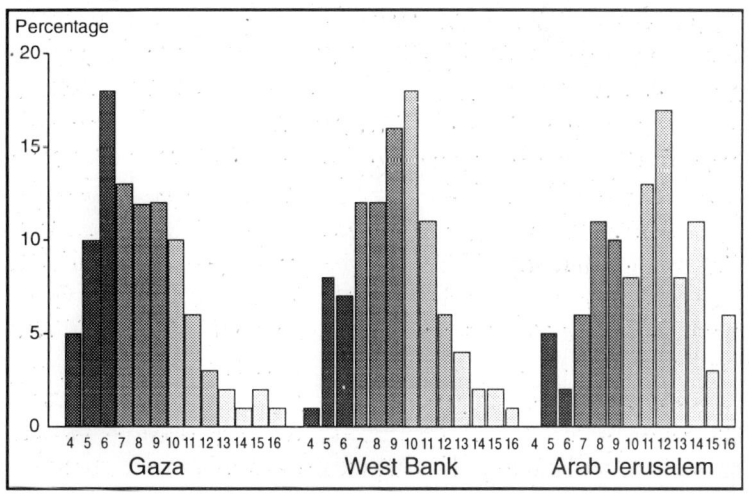

access to financial support (e.g. National Insurance, Child support, Retirement funds, etc.) not available in the other two regions.[16]

The West Bank, however, has been less affected by the disruptions of war than Gaza, having a relatively diversified economy which has allowed it to retain to a large extent its pre-war hierarchical social structure. In sum, deprivation is neither as prevalent as in Gaza nor prosperity as evident as in Arab Jerusalem. Despite major changes in agrarian social relations, as a result of increased monetization of the economy and of physical mobility, considerable degree of continuity is encountered here. The main explanation appears to be the existence of village subsistence economy and the family farm, elements which are less pronounced in the two other regions.

There are also significant socioeconomic differences along the "urban" and "rural" axes within each of the three main areas (Figure 8.4). Again focusing on the differences, Gaza camps are heavily over-represented in the lower status category. Gaza City and Gaza villages take similar positions, the occurrence of higher scores slightly more frequent in the latter category. West Bank villages and camps are relatively speaking more common in the lower middle status category. Arab Jerusalem is heavily represented in the upper middle and high status categories, accompanied by West Bank towns. The contrasts are thus striking between on the one hand HHs in Arab Jerusalem and in West Bank towns, and on the other their counterparts in Gaza camps. Six-seven out of ten HHs are found in the two upper status

Figure 8.4 Socioeconomic status by locality of HH: urban/ rural/ camp distributions. Percentages

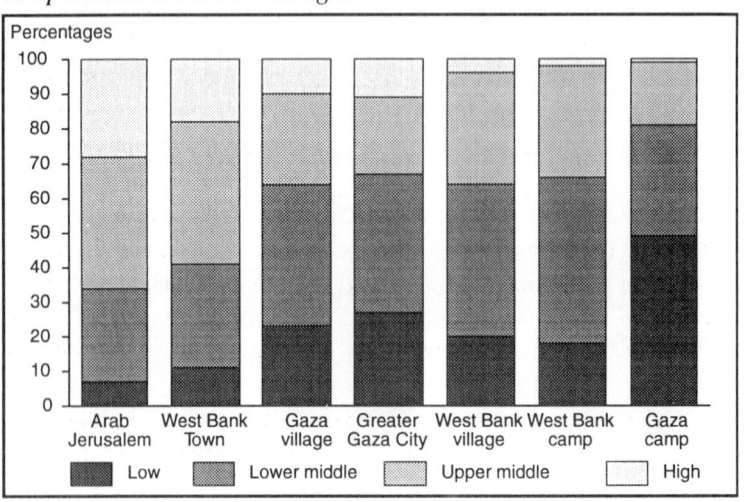

categories in the former regions while eight out of ten HHs are found in the two lower status categories in the latter.

Gaza City and Gaza villages, though, are basically on a par with West Bank villages and camps. More surprisingly, perhaps, West Bank camps show a distribution similar to that of West Bank villages. Further analysis reveals that it is the better housing standards in Gaza City, as indicated by housing amenities, that places it on the level of West Bank camps, whereas it is the lower educational attainments that bring it to the level of West Bank villages. This again may reflect differences in infrastructural provisions (piped water, sewage and electricity) and occupational possibilities in the three areas. The main differences between West Bank villages and West Bank camps, thus, are the housing and occupational standards.[17]

A comparison of the socioeconomic status of respectively non-refugees, refugees outside camps and refugees living in camps (figure not presented), suggests that camp residence, and not refugee status in itself, is the vital, determining factor. Refugees outside camps and non-refugees are generally located in the lower and upper middle strata, while more camp refugees are found in the lower middle and low categories.

So far focus has been on explaining variations between the different localities, i.e. on general differences. Yet the actual size of the differences should not be ignored. Returning briefly to figure 8.4, more than half of the HHs in the two contrasting regions of Arab Jerusalem and Gaza camps are still all within the range of the two middle status categories, thus indicating a significant element of homogeneity among the areas.

Why are the regional differences not even more frequent and clear-cut? The explanation is probably to be found at the intersection of various social and economic factors. The twin processes of "ruralization" of the cities and "urbanization" of the countryside stand out as possible explanations, as they may be expected to promote homogeneous social conditions in "rural" and "urban" areas alike.

The main factor contributing to the recent social decline in *rural* areas is the undermining in the value of non-irrigated land as a designator of traditional social status (such land has, however, retained its importance as real estate). New sources of income have emerged outside the traditional village structure and the agricultural sector.[18]

This change in the role and impact of land ownership is not only due to the upheavals of war, but to an even larger extent to long-term economic trends, invoking a greater part of young people to seek urban wage labour, who are thus freed from the control of landowners or rural notables. In addition the enhanced availability of public education has given rise to professional and semi-professional employment outside the agrarian system, leaving the role of agriculture increasingly marginalized.

Parallel to this "levelling" of the class structure of rural areas, a modification in the social composition of *urban* areas is occurring. A process of emigration of the landed elite and (more recently) professional and middle classes has been mentioned above, although the ratio of emigrating elites to emigrating lower strata is unknown. The landed elite has, nonetheless, partly been replaced by new ranks of successful businessmen and professionals moving from villages to towns.

The factors contributing to the transformation of rural areas – new possibilities of wage labour in the cities, remittances and access to education – naturally also affect life in urban areas, opening up as they do possibilities for economic (though not necessarily social) mobility for more deprived groups in urban areas.

A process of "ruralization" of townships, an exclusive West Bank phenomenon, should also be noted. This process refers to an increasing number of rural residents seeking employment and/or services in urban areas and ultimately establishing residence there. Nevertheless most Palestinians living in the West Bank today still reside in rural districts, and cannot be characterized as living in a peasant society; that is a society deriving its livelihood from agriculture and being organized socially around the family farm. West Bank townships, in themselves dominated by small trade and small workshops with a minor manufacturing sector, likewise constitute regional markets and administrative service centres for their rural hinterland.

Finally, the similarity may also reflect the strong degree of urban-rural interdependence, as is clearly demonstrated by the even, differential growth rates of towns and villages.

Social Status and Economic Wealth

So far the education and occupation of the HH have been applied as indicators to ascribe HH "aggregate" socioeconomic status. At the same time, education and occupation can also be regarded as vehicles for economic mobility. Although we cannot here in any way offer a complete analysis of social mobility among Palestinian HHs, it may be fruitful to examine in more detail the causal relationship between the socioeconomic indicators and the relevant background characteristics.

Many Palestinians subscribe to the view that education provides the main road to economic well-being. If this belief is still well-founded, one can expect that those HHs who have the highest educational scores also will have disproportionally high shares of "high-status" occupations and be in possession of more capital goods than other HHs. This assumption has, however, been questioned recently, following changes in the relative role and impact of education. The job market appears to be saturated at the time being, both locally and abroad.

In table 8.2 we observe a slightly lower covariation between occupation and economic wealth as compared to education and economic wealth. The question arises as to whether education is in fact less important than so far assumed, when taking into consideration that education needs to be transformed into an occupation to be useful as a vehicle for economic mobility.

Further, it is reasonable to assume that the transformation of education and occupation into economic wealth will be different for the various age, sex and locality categories of HH. Hence it is relevant to isolate statistically the "net" effect of each background factor, always taking into account the simultaneous effects of other factors. A multivariate analysis has been carried out to shed some light on these phenomena, with a view to explaining variations in economic status among Palestinian HHs as measured by the capital-goods indicator developed in table 8.1. Due to the confounded effects of locality and refugee status – most refugees are living in refugee camps – we have let the urban-rural indicator from figure 8.4 represent locality.[19]

The successive introduction of age, sex, locality, education and occupation into the statistical equation reveals the following complex picture:[20] The age and sex (absence of a male HH) of the HH generally only explain a small amount of the economic variation among HHs. Locality, on the other hand, turns out to have vital significance (representing 60% of totally explained variations). The effect of education and occupation is much stronger than the effect of age and sex, but again, not as strong as that of locality. In fact, it can be shown that the effect of age and sex to a large degree is attributable to educational variations between different cohorts and between men and women (age and sex differences between localities are small). Likewise, while the effect of education and occupation is quite strong taken individually, close to half of their effect can be ascribed to the other background characteristics. Educational variations are, as noted above, to a large extent due to differences in educational attainment among different cohorts. The strong covariation between education and occupation (Table 8.2) suggests that part of the effect of these background characteristics is in fact attributable to the very same phenomenon, i.e. instances of being both highly educated and having a high status job, or vice versa. The effect of locality is, however, still dominant – again with Gaza camps and Arab Jerusalem as opposite poles – and seems to be the single most important factor determining economic wealth (see also chapter 6, on Household Income and Wealth).[21]

This finding may support a general tendency of geographical mobility observed among persons who are socially upwardly mobile, tending to move to their preferred habitat: from village to urban residence, and from Gaza to the West Bank. It probably also applies to West Bank to Jerusalem movement, except that it is illegal, and to the degree that it does happen, it would be difficult to monitor.

Attitudes to Social Inequalities

Cultural factors often shape, modify and sometimes determine patterns of socioeconomic differentiation. For our purposes it is important to identify and tentatively explore the impact of norms, values and perceptions that are characteristic of Palestinian society. Important among such typical factors, it would appear, are community solidarity, deferential behaviour towards family elders, gender segregation and lineage (i.e. descendance from prominent families). For example, the cohesiveness of a traditional community, buttressed by kin solidarity at the level of extended families may serve to discourage public exhibition of wealth, especially in a village context.[22] Obviously family loyalty and tradition both have contributed to the perpetuation of household crafts and skills across the generations, an effect which is generally assumed to slow down the process (until recently) of children's individual mobility.

As mentioned initially, the social status of the HH cannot be measured directly or unequivocally. It can, however, be useful to relate the actual socioeconomic differences among HHs to their own *perceptions* of social differences in society. In the following a few attitudinal elements with a bearing on social stratification will be examined, and then related to the actual differences that have been extrapolated earlier.

HH perceived local influence

An important component of family status is the influence the HH exercises within the local community. To measure this "cultural" aspect, the HHs were posed two questions about their own perception of their influence inside the neighbourhood and village/town respectively (Table 8.3):[23]

The feeling of influence within the neighbourhood is more prominent than within the village, a result which probably reflects the egalitarianism that permeates village life, rather than actual influence. Local community decisions are seemingly made at village – not neighbourhood – level. Neighbourhood influence increases only marginally with HH socioeconomic status. (Excluding female HHs from the analysis increases the amount to 32% in the low status category, but makes no difference in the other categories). As for village influence, the difference between the status categories is more visible, as seen when comparing the opposite high and low status categories.

In figure 8.2 we observe that socioeconomic status decreases with increasing age for HHs 50 years or older. Can low scores on the socioeconomic status indicator among "elderly" HHs be compensated by elevated positions as family and/or village elders? Further investigation (table not presented) proves that village influence does not increase systematically with age of HH. Rather, it is among the age categories 40-59 that instances of high influence are most frequently invoked.[25] Such a finding is significant in that it challenges persistent assumptions of status being attributed to old age (seniority), and suggests that 'prestige' may be enhanced by age only if accompanied by other status variables.

Table 8.3 HHs perception of his/her influence in the neighborhood and village/town by socioeconomic status. Percentage reporting decisive/considerable.[24]

	Socioeconomic status				
	Low	Lower middle	Upper middle	High	All
"Neighborhood influence"	25	27	39	38	32
"Village influence"	9	15	23	28	18
N	160	306	260	87	813

The Role of the Family

Based on the initial discussion, it is fair to expect family kinship to be vital determinants of socioeconomic distribution. In Palestinian society, as in most Middle Eastern societies, the family network has always had an overriding "welfarist function". This role is reinforced by a number of considerations: The absence of a public sector that runs regular social security arrangements (in an economically and politically unstable environment) buttresses the role of children and other relatives as pillars of support for weaker and less advantaged family members.[26] This tendency is fortified by a normative system resting on a religious as well as a traditional socio-political frame of reference, which asserts the obligation of the younger generation to take care of the old and the disabled. Social ostracism and shaming are used to isolate those who do not fulfil their filial duties.[27] Table 8.4 examines the impact of kinship status and family solidarity, and relate the answers to the HH stratification index.

First, only three out of every ten Palestinians agree that the social status of the family determines one's achievements in life. Conversely, a vast majority (about nine in ten) believe that one's achievements in life depend on family solidarity. What is the explanation of the marked difference in responses to these two statements? As to the first statement, a family's social background may in fact be more important than the responses suggest. Such a reality may be ignored as it seems run counter to conventional beliefs that the constraints inherent in the old social order largely have been overcome. The relevance of family background may be rejected on the grounds that in the contemporary world it is one's *issamiyya* (personal ambition or effort) that governs, and should govern, one's position in society. On the other hand, there is widespread recognition that achievements usually are not the sole result of individual efforts, but are dependent on the collective

Table 8.4 Attitudes on the role of family background by HH socio-economic status. Percent saying "Yes". (Don't know in parenthesis)

	\multicolumn{4}{c}{Socioeconomic status}		
	Low	Lower middle	Upper middle	High	All
"Achievements in life is dependent on social background":	28	32	38	45	34
	(3)	(2)	(1)	(-)	(2)
"Achievements in life depend on family solidarity"	89	88	93	74	88
	(3)	(2)	(-)	(-)	(2)
N	160	306	260	87	813

contributions of one's kin, this being the only assured system of support in an otherwise hostile and unstable world. Hence the higher score on the family solidarity variable.

Secondly, differences between the status categories are small. Comparing the opposite categories of high and low, the most marked difference is found for the "family social background" statement. The amount of positive responses increases with increasing HH status, and is higher among the best off as compared to the worst off. The finding suggests that family social background may be felt to be particularly important for social mobility among the higher social strata. But even in this category half of the HHs disagree. With respect to family solidarity, agreement is more or less unanimous regardless of social background, although it is somewhat weaker for the high status category, and seems to cut across socioeconomic cleavages. Before attempting any further explanations, the question of perceptions of social differences will be dealt with, as expressed by attitudes to the existence of conflicts among various social strata.

Socioeconomic Status and Perceptions of Conflict

Socioeconomic differences are generally supposed to manifest themselves in social conflicts. Literature on slum neighbourhoods in the industrial countries indicates a high incidence of actual and perceived social conflicts in these communities. This is not, however, necessarily the case in poorer countries where high population densities do not exclude but rather go hand in hand with a high degree of communal solidarity.[28] By confronting the respondents with a number of statements as to the existence of social conflicts in society, the conflict potential among Palestinian HHs is revealed (Table 8.5).

As can be seen from the distributions, perceptions as to the existence of ("vertical") conflicts between management and workers and between poor and rich basically divide the population in two equally sized groups. The interpretation may seem unambiguous but does, however, call for at least a twofold interpretation. Conflicts may be real or not, and the respondent may be aware of them or not. The higher degree of "don't know" in the low-status category may indicate a general lack of awareness in this category. On the other hand, attitudinal differences between the socioeconomic status categories are small, the exception being, perhaps, the issue of relations between management and workers. Here the difference amounts to 19%

between the two extreme categories on the socioeconomic distribution index.

When it comes to ("horizontal") conflicts between employed and unemployed, and between the urban and rural populations the conflict potential is considerably weaker. Only three and two in ten respectively consider these conflicts as strong. Further, small differences in conflict attitudes between the high and low social strata are observed. Again we should note the high degree of "don't knows" in the low status category. Generally speaking a homogeneous picture emerges across the status categories, in which attitudinal similarities are more striking than the differences.

Socioeconomic Status and Attitudes to Inequalities

In social science it is generally considered that different attitudes or values interconnect in "belief-systems" or ideological groupings. Many people may take opposite stands on "objectively" speaking similar issues but may feel totally consistent. Indeed, different attitudes may co-exist as mutually dependent within the individual or society, thereby reflecting "hidden" value dimensions.[30] Do Palestinian HHs take the same stand on each question or do they have differing attitudes to the different items? And, can possible attitudinal variations be explained by differing socioeconomic backgrounds among the HHs?

A statistical analysis (factor analysis) shows fairly strong covariations between all the conflict issues, indicating a single

Table 8.5 Attitudes to social conflicts by socioeconomic status. Percentage saying very strong/strong conflict. (Don't know in parenthesis)[29]

	Socioeconomic status				
	Low	Lower middle	Upper middle	High	All
Between management and workers	44 (17)	51 (4)	59 (7)	63 (6)	54 (8)
Between poor and rich	47 (11)	53 (4)	50 (3)	43 (5)	50 (5)
Between employed and unemployed	32 (15)	36 (4)	22 (6)	25 (4)	30 (7)
Between rural and urban population	9 (15)	18 (7)	17 (9)	12 (2)	15 (9)
N	160	306	260	87	813

underlying conflict pattern. Furthermore, the issues of family background/solidarity and village/neighbourhood influence are, empirically speaking, neither associated with the conflict issues nor with each other.

To shed some light on the conflict dimension, an additive index has been constructed based on the four issues, ranging from "consensus oriented" to "conflict oriented".[31] The conflict distribution shows a bell-shaped curve, skewed towards "moderate" stands. When divided into three categories, four out of ten HHs can be classified as consensus oriented, five out of ten as moderate, and one out of ten as conflict oriented. The distribution thus reflects the division of the population observed in table 8.5, where only the "vertical" or class related issues exert a pull in the direction of radicalism.

Generally speaking, deprived socioeconomic conditions may be expected to intensify perceptions of social conflicts. A comparison of the prevailing conflict dimension for the various status categories however, brings to light only small differences.[32] Inclusion of age, sex and locality in the analysis proves that the locality of the HH is the only factor that significantly contributes to explaining differences (Figure 8.5).

The conflict potential is highest in Arab Jerusalem and lowest in Gaza, with West Bankers taking up a middle range position. This finding contradicts the hypothesis of a connection between density and occurrence of conflicts sketched above. While Gaza has the highest degree of congestion and the highest mean size of households as compared to the West Bank and Jerusalem, Gazans consistently have a weaker perception – or at least not a higher one – of conflict than the HHs in the West Bank and Arab Jerusalem have. This is an interesting finding also when compared to the parallel pattern for distress found in the chapter on Health (Chapter 4).

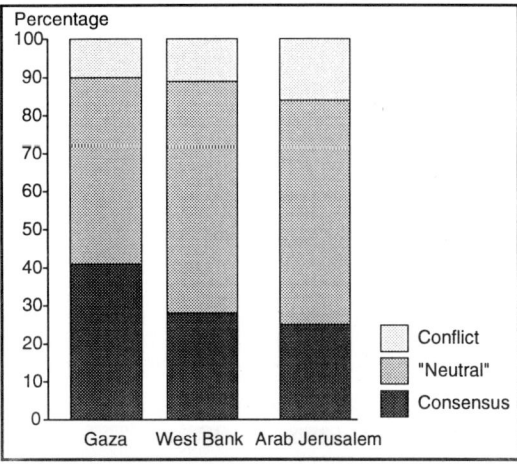

How does one explain the relatively small ideological disparities according to social background? Three tentative explanations will be put forward: First, in Western societies a process of loosening of ideological stands from social background

Figure 8.5 The conflict index by locality of HH: three main areas. Percentages

241

can be observed. With the emergence of new social and class patterns, traditions and established social groupings seem to be crumbling. Individual choices of life styles and identities become more important. What seems to count is not "where you come from", but rather "where you want to go". Applied to Palestinian society, this hypothesis suggests that locality, and the conditions of daily life, may be the critical factor that permeates perceptions of conflict, overriding other considerations of an occupational or hierarchical nature.

Secondly, potential internal conflicts between social groups may be externalized. Attitudes associated with conflict may be transferred and turned towards an external foe who is much more visible and tangible. Internal dissension can in fact be repressed, and hostility – as has happened since 1988 – can be focused on individual collaborators, or also on social outcasts (prostitutes, drug-dealers, etc). This externalization may also enforce a consensual ideology, which underplays the magnitude of conflict (real and imagined) within the society, and focuses on differences with the outsider.

As for Gaza, seemingly taking the most moderate stand, the degree of congestion and squalor, not parallelled in the other Palestinian communities, may produce a heightened feeling of being encircled or of shared destiny. This feeling, compounded by prolonged days of curfews and collective punishment of whole neighbourhoods[33], may have evoked attitudes of communal solidarity to an extent not found in West Bank or Jerusalem communities. In the City of Jerusalem a number of factors may weaken this solidarity and create an atmosphere where inherent social conflicts surface and are articulated more visibly than elsewhere: (1) Absence of Israeli military rule and the less grave confrontation with the armed forces, (2) the availability of certain social services such as health and family insurance, normally unavailable to the rest of the occupied territories, and (3) higher degree of ethnic, religious and social diversity[34]. The result is a concentration on ideology which downplays the magnitude of conflict (real and imagined) within society, and focuses on differences with the outsider.

Third, an explanation may be traced in the continued acceptance of hierarchical social structures, as is evident in many developing countries. Such acceptance, in addition to reinforcing the thesis suggested above about externalization of conflict, is rooted in a society where class and status antagonisms are modified by a system of patronage and kinship networks which modify the intensity and direction of status differences. In the context of Palestinian society under occupation these networks are likely to make themselves felt in modes of political behaviour and political mobilization. Such hypotheses cannot, however, be fully tested at the present stage.

A Homogeneous Society or Three Different Areas?

The social structure of Palestinian society has been dramatically transformed by war, migration and the emergence of new venues of mobility, such as enhanced opportunities for work and education. This is reflected today by a socioeconomic distribution in which the majority of the HHs are located in the middle level of the status hierarchy. Although time-series data are unavailable, the "reverse diamond shaped" structural pattern revealed may technically be interpreted as a trend towards homogenization and class "levelling", enforced by factors like the monetization of the village economy and the loss of land as crucial determinants of social status.

Nonetheless this general picture of socioeconomic homogeneity covers considerable regional variations. Broadly speaking, the three main areas of Gaza, the West Bank and Arab Jerusalem in fact and in many ways appear as totally different areas. Disparities are significant, however, also between urban, rural and camp sectors within the main areas. Gaza camps are generally found to be worst off, with Arab Jerusalem taking the opposite position.

Concerning socioeconomic mobility, as measured by the transformation of social status into economic wealth, education not surprisingly seems to be a major vehicle to acquire high status jobs. But the effect of education and occupation on economic wealth is overridden by the effect of the locality of the HH.

While age and sex differences are difficult to interpret (see, however, also chapter 9), the regional variations observed, in addition to reflecting more or less permanent socio-structural patterns, coincide with the assumed tendency on the part of upwardly mobile professionals and businessmen to relocate from Gaza to the West Bank, and – whenever possible – to Jerusalem. A similar tendency of horizontal movement may also contribute to socioeconomic disparities observed between rural and urban areas.

Finally, the role of cultural factors should not be underestimated, although they have not been dealt with fully. A picture of consent is revealed, supported by the fact that most Palestinian HHs take moderate stands as to the existence of socioeconomic conflicts between different social groups within their society. Further, as seen from questions on the role of the family in respect to the origin and prevalence of socioeconomic differences, values and norms are shared within the population. Thus, family bonds may cut across stratification lines, contributing to a complex pattern of socioeconomic interdependence.

Notes

1 International Encyclopedia of the Social Sciences, The Macmillan Company & The Free press, New York 1968; *Stratification, social*.

2 Richards, A. and Waterbury, J. (op.cit, p. 9): *A Political Economy of the Middle East. State, Class, and Development*. Westview Press, Boulder, San Francisco and Oxford 1990.

3 Zureik, E: Reflections on Twentieth-Century Palestinian Class Structure, in Naklieh, K and Zureik, E: *The Sociology of the Palestinians*, Croom Helm London, 1980.

4 The analysis is limited to *acknowledged* household heads. That is, the person being identified as the household head by the subjective opinion of the household members. Further the sample is confined to HHs who have also been interviewed as *"randomly selected individual"* (RSI, 38% of all HHs), the reason being that we need information on HH labour activities, *not available* in the HH questionnaire. Comparison of the randomly selected HHs (N=813) and the total sample of HHs (N=2479) reveals slight over-representation of West Bankers in the age category 30-39 years, and of Gazans in the age categories 50-60 years. As long as family size is heavily determined by age, we lose some big families in Gaza. The net effect may be the exclusion of some lower status Palestinian HHs from the analysis.

5 Kuttab level education is an Islamic kindergarten.

6 The educational categories are composed in the following way: Low (1)= No education or apprenticeship level, up to five years of duration. Lower medium (2)= Primary or secondary general level, up to five years of duration, or primary/secondary level above six years of duration. Upper middle (3)= Primary to post-secondary level, more than 6 years of duration. High (4)= BA or MA, more than six years of duration.

7 Although there are exceptions and uncertainties, the main type of occupation held by the HH last year generally corresponds to the work he/she is trained (educated) for.

8 The development of "class divisions" is generally considered a special case of composition of social layers in which the occupations of the units of analysis play a dominant role. See e.g. Treiman, D.J; *Occupational Prestige in Comparative Perspective*. Academic Press, New York, 1977. A discussion of the class structure in Gaza is found in Roy, S.M.: *The Gaza Strip: A Demographic, Economic, Social and Legal Survey*. The West Bank Data Base Project, Jerusalem, Harvard University, Cambridge, 1986. See also Zureik, E: Reflections on Twentieth-Century Palestinian Class Structure, in Nakleh, K and Zureik, E (eds.): *The Sociology of the Palestinians, Croom Helm, London 1980*.

9 This indicator is perhaps the most troublesome to construct as it implies a difficult evaluation of housing density set against the possession of housing amenities. The "main weight" is put on amenities, which is "supplied" with density. We suggest the following categorization (percentages of total, N=813):

		AMENITIES (Number of)				
		0	1	2	3	4
DENSITY		3+	3-	4-	13-	3*	1*
(Persons per room)		2-2.99	3-	5-	16*	6*	2*
		0-1.99	4>	6>	20>	10#	4#

Status categories: - = Low
                   > = Lower medium
                   * = Upper medium
                   # = High

10 Central Bureau of Statistics of Norway: *Social Survey 1989*, Oslo/Kongsvinger 1989, pp. 17-20.

11 Øyen, E 1983 (ed.); *Sosiologi og ulikhet*. Universitetsforlaget, Bergen, pp. 16-18. Norges Offentlige Utredninger 1979:51 (NOU) *Levekårsundersøkelsen*, Oslo.

12 A factor analysis demonstrates that the four elements empirically speaking constitute one single dimension. (The eigenvalue is 1.97, explaining 49% of the total variance).

13 The final distribution will thus reflect the categorization of good and bad situations presented in table 8.1. Numerous categorizations have, however, been tested during the development of the index, and it is our impression that the index is quite rugged.

14 International Encyclopedia of the Social Sciences. The Macmillan Company & the Free press, New York 1968, *Stratification, social* p. 295.

15 The socioeconomic index is here regrouped into the four status categories. The categorization is as follows, transforming old scores into new: 4-6 = Low, 7-9 = Lower middle, 10-12 = Upper middle, 13-16 = High. Please be aware of the general arbitrariness of age categorizations.

16 Se chapter 6 on household economy.

17 The distribution along each indicator over the different regions show the following mean scores (each indicator ranges from 1 to 4)

	Education	Occupation	Consumer durables	Housing	Total score
Arab Jerusalem	2,7	2,1	3,1	2,9	10,8
W.B towns	2,8	2,3	2,4	2,5	10,0
Gaza City	2,4	2,1	1,9	2,3	8,7
Gaza villages	2,7	2,1	1,8	2,2	8,7
W.B. villages	2,6	2,1	1,8	2,1	8,6
W.B camps	2,5	2,3	1,9	1,9	8,6
Gaza camps	2,3	1,9	1,4	1,6	7,3
Eta	.16	.13	.46	.32	.36

18 Migdal J, *Palestinian Society and Politics*, Princeton University Press, Princeton 1986. Glavanis 1990. Ibid.

19 The consumer durables indicator measures more or less the same phenomenon as the indicator of economic wealth, as described in chapter 6, on household economy. The covariation between them is very high (Pearson's r=.73).

20 The Multiple Classification Analysis (MCA) is a statistical technique of analysis for examining interrelationships between a set of independent (predictor) variables and a dependent variable within the context of an additive model. It provides us with three vital pieces of information. The *eta* statistic indicates the strength of covariation between the economic wealth indicator and each of the various background characteristics, considered individually. The *beta* statistic indicates the effect of each background indicator when we simultaneously take the effect of the other background characteristics into consideration. The R^2 statistic tells us to what degree variations in economic wealth are determined (explained by) the entire set of

background characteristics. All coefficients theoretically vary between 0,0 and 1,0, the bigger the size the better the explanation.

By applying a step-by-step method, introducing one background characteristic at the time, we can observe how the beta coefficients change with the inclusion of new background characteristics. We assume that the age and the sex of the HH are not influenced by the other characteristics. But age and sex may influence the educational status, which again may be vital in determining the occupational status, and, in the end, economic wealth. The size of the beta coefficient the first time a given factor is included in the analysis, indicates the "total causal effect" of this characteristic. By watching the changes in the beta coefficients at each step we have an indication of how much of the effect of the respective background characteristics is attributable to this factor itself, and how much is "transmitted" through the other characteristics. The difference between the eta coefficient and the relevant beta coefficient at the first step indicates the "spuriousness". For further reading see Andrews, F.M et al. 1973: *Multiple Classification Analysis*, The Institute for Social Research, The University of Michigan, Ann Arbor.

Economic wealth (the consumer durables index) by social background variables. Stepwise MCA-analysis. N=813

	Eta	B1	B2	B3	B4	B5
Age	.20	.20	.18	.18	.12	.12
Sex	.16		.14	.1	.10	.10
Region/refugee status	.46			.47	.43	.42
Education	.34				.26	.20
Occupation	.29					.17
R^2		.04	.06	.27	.32	.33

B1-B5=Beta at step 1 to 5.

21 Due to low numbers of respondents, complete charting of the interaction is impossible.

22 Lutfiyyeh, A: *Baytin: A Jordan Village*. Mouton, 1964.

23 That is, we do not know the actual status of any HH as measured by the opinion of his own *community*.

24 The questions were posed as follows: 1. "Do you feel that you can affect important decisions inside your neighborhood?" 2. "Do you feel that you can affect important decisions inside your village/town?"

25 The perception of influence varies among localities where West Bank HHs score higher than Gazans and Arab Jerusalemites -also when comparing urban-rural-camp differences. The perception of influence may be interpreted as a reflection of Israeli presence, rather than a result of the cultural status of the HH.

26 Farsoun, S.K: Family Structure in Modern Lebanon (p 292), in Sweet L.E (ed.) *Peoples and Cultures of the Middle East*, New York 1970.

27 L. Ammons (op.cit., 1978) notes that emigration has resulted in the strengthening of the extended family. While emigrants have tended to leave their wives and children in the care of their parents (i.e. the wife's in-laws) for extended periods, remittances have contributed to the preservation and strengthening of the patriarchal household.

28 For a discussion of assumptions by Western social scientists about "urban decay" in the developing countries, see Elizabeth Wilson, *The Sphinx in the City: Urban Life, the Control of Disorder, and Women* (University of California Press, 1991) pp. 121-135.

29 The question reads: "In all countries there are contradictions or conflicts between different social groups. In your opinion, in our country, how much conflict is there between: ......(the different groups)?"

30 Converse, P.E: The Nature of Belief Systems, in Apter, D.: *Ideology and Discontent*, New York Free Press 1964.

31 The index is constructed by giving a score of 1 for "There are no conflicts" and a score of 5 for "Very strong conflict". Likewise "strong" and "not very strong conflicts" are rated as 2 and 4. Those who "cannot choose" are given the medium value of 3. The final score thus ranges from 4 to 20. The distribution is further divided into three categories: consensus oriented = scores 4-8, moderate = scores 9-14 and conflict oriented = scores 15-20.

32 This picture also holds true when relating the different conflict issues to relevant background characteristics individually (conflict between rich and poor along the stratification index, urban-rural conflict between HHs in urban and rural areas, conflict between managers and workers between different occupational categories etc.).

33 See chapter 1, section of conditions of daily life, for a discussion of this factor.

34 The fact that Jerusalem has an active and legal trade union movement, especially in the service sector which dominates the city's employment facilities, reinforces the hypothesis that social inequalities and social tensions are not only felt, but also disclosed.

Finally we should add a methodological observation. It is quite possible that the higher security experienced by Jerusalemites in their daily life, allow them to express feelings of hostility more freely than Gazans and West bankers, in which case the higher scores on conflict noted here would be spurious rather than real.

Chapter 9
Opinions and Attitudes
Marianne Heiberg

The Attitudinal Framework

That man does not live by bread alone is an adage that gains particular saliency in level of living conditions studies. Living conditions are not determined solely by objective evaluations of living standards. They also have to be assessed in conjunction with the individual's own evaluation of his or her life situation. Again the critical distinction is the degree to which individuals feel they have access to the resources required to gain influence over their own life and future. To what extent do they see themselves as full and purposeful human beings? The determinants of the dignity and integrity of the human being differ from society to society and, of course, have changed radically over time. However, in the contemporary world certain dimensions seem generally applicable. They involve the ability of the individual to participate and exercise choice within political, social and religious life. Among the many questions raised are the following: Can the individual participate in the formation of decisions and practice that directly impact on the quality of his or her life? Does the life situation provide the individual with a sense of personal purpose and fulfilment? To what extent is the nature of daily life a product of choice or of coercion? Is there some correspondence between individual aspirations and real opportunities for their achievement? Does the individual view the course of his past and the potential for his future with optimism and hope or apprehension and despair?

A serious methodological problem in level of living conditions studies is, however, that while the exact measurement of, say, quantities of bread and calorific intakes may be relatively simple, measurements of empowerment and a sense of individual dignity are more problematic. Attitude surveys could be flawed on many levels. Frequently respondents do not wish to or simply cannot reveal their real views in a formally constructed interview situation which is of short duration and in which answer categories are fixed beforehand. Moreover, people are contradictory. Their expressed attitudes often do not form a coherent whole and may not correspond to or predict their actual behaviour in any case. In addition, unlike the more structurally embedded social norms and values which they in part reflect, attitudes tend to be elusive and changeable. They are shaped by a range of different forces, some transient and some enduring, some implicit and some explicit, some which operate in tandem and some which tear the individual in opposing directions.

Difficulties in measuring and interpreting attitudes are intensified in societies undergoing rapid change and social disruption. (This comes in addition to the general statistical difficulties inherent in sample survey data, as discussed in Appendix A, on sampling strategy.) In Palestinian society a sense of social dislocation, instability and uncertainty is pervasive. Although all Middle Eastern- societies have undergone profound transformations during the last 40 years, Palestinians have experienced sharper, more dramatic and more violent change than most.

In relation to this survey, another critical factor is decisive. A central parameter affecting Palestinian perceptions and attitudes is that imposed by the occupation regime. For numerous reasons described elsewhere, the survey does not attempt to explore Palestinians' reactions to this regime nor the impact of the regime upon their attitudes. Nonetheless, the fact of occupation forms an integral, conspicuous framework which impacts directly on Palestinian dispositions, attitudes and consequent behaviour.

Attitudes on the Status of Women

Conflict and disagreement are inherent in all societies. However, pervasive strong conflict and disagreement can also be signs of relative social instability. They can signal that the norms and structure of a society are being challenged and, through challenge, are under stress and potentially a process of transformation. The survey attempts to examine some of the specific conflicts and tensions internal to Palestinian society. (See also Chapter 8 on social stratification).

As discussed in previous chapters, gender is a fundamental organising principle in Palestinian society as it is throughout the Middle East. To what extent is there consensus on this pivotal pillar of social organisation? Do men and women subscribe roughly to the same attitudes concerning the roles and symbolic behaviour deemed appropriate for women?

Figure 9.1 indicates that on the level of Palestinian society as a whole there is a certain consensus among men and women concerning appropriate dress for women. While men are more restrictive than women, differences in attitudes are not strongly marked. However, the figure also indicates that there is conspicuously less consensus concerning women's ability to participate in paid employment, exercise choice in relation to marriage and in the restrictions implied by motherhood. However, both women's and men's attitudes are subject to major regional variations.

Figure 9.2 suggests that whatever consensus might exist between men and women with regard to notions of proper dress on the level of Palestinian society generally is shattered at the regional level. With regard to dress codes, attitudes in Gaza are much more restrictive than those in Arab Jerusalem, with the West Bank in an intermediatory position. Reversely, with regard to women's roles regional variations are less significant. The degree of consensus among men and the opposing degree of consensus among women tend to transcend regional boundaries. With regard to conflicting attitudes in general, Gaza represents the region which is most dissimilar in attitudes and the region in which discrepancies between men and women are most striking. In part this could reflect the relative social isolation of Gaza and its longer, more acute experience with the Islamic movement.

Figure 9.1 Comparison between men's and women's attitudes concerning women

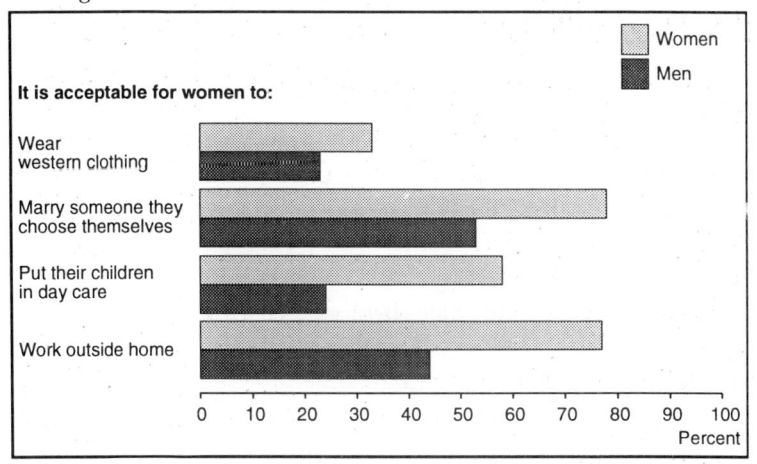

These points are further illustrated in table 9.1 and figure 9.3 which attempt to give a more detailed picture of attitudes concerning the boundaries of what is considered acceptable behaviour for women. Notably, with reference to married women working, the disagreement seems to centre on whether women should be allowed to work at all. Almost all Palestinians, men and women, seem to agree that child care is a woman's first priority. Responses are broken down by region and gender.

Although there are regional variations between genders, table 9.1 suggests that with respect to notions concerning proper behaviour for married women, women in Gaza tend to be more similar to women in Arab Jerusalem than to their male counterparts in Gaza. In other words, disagreements on women's roles reside mainly on the level of gender. The situation is very different if attitudes concerning women's dress are examined where region, rather than gender, seems to be decisive in conditioning attitudes.

Although there are clear differentials between men and women concerning appropriate dress for women, these differentials are

Figure 9.2 Comparison between men's and women's attitudes concerning women by region

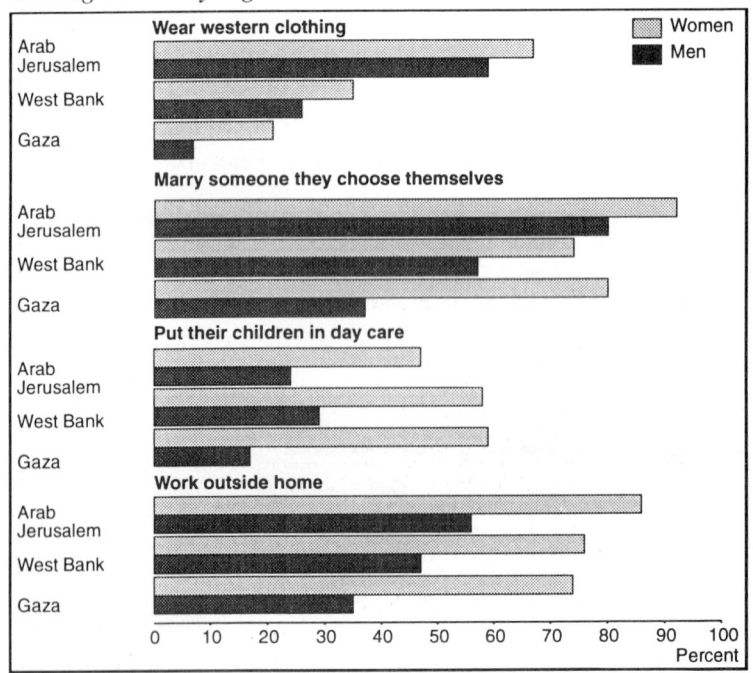

greater between the regions than between men and women within any single region.

The significance of the strictures placed on women's dress in Palestinian society relates not so much to definitions of appropriate roles for women, as to concerns relating to control over women in whatever roles they fulfil. At the core of this concern lies the notion of honour and shame defined in terms of family control over the sexuality, or reproductive capacity, of female members. Western dress symbolises a loss of family control. It connotes an implied sexual complacency and reproductive disorder and, as such, signifies a potential threat to family honour. Clothing which fully covers a women's body and hair operates to reinforce an image of family control. As illustrated by the growing use of head scarfs among young

Table 9.1 Appropriate roles for married women by region and gender

	Stay home and care for children	Give priority child-care, but can work	Can work outside house	Can study outside house	Don't know
Male Gaza	67	26	5	1	1
Female Gaza	37	57	5	0	1
Male West Bank	51	46	1	1	1
Female West Bank	35	61	2	0	3
Male Arab Jerusalem	48	49	2	0	0
Female Arab Jerusalem	21	77	2	0	1
Total	45	50	3	1	2

Figure 9.3 Reaction to female household members appearing in public without a head scarf by region and gender

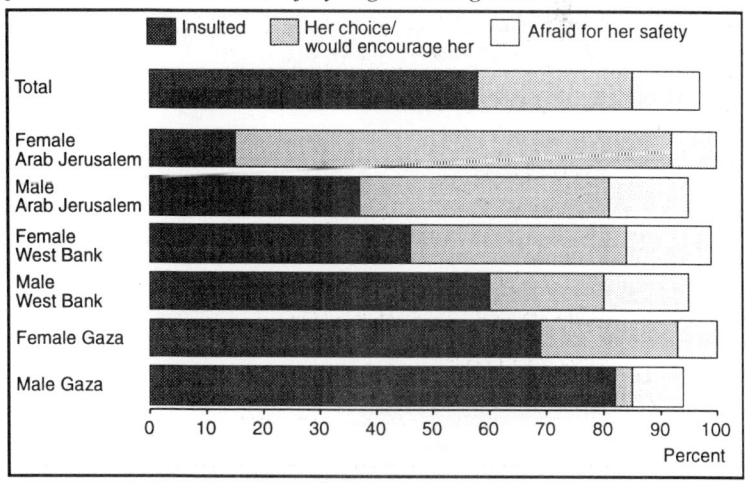

girls far below the age of puberty, however, dress codes are also becoming linked to specific political messages relating to activist Islamic doctrines.

Both men's and women's attitudes concerning the status of women seem to be affected by age, but in a particular manner. Broadly speaking, the middle-aged have more liberal attitudes towards women than either the very old or the relatively young. The drop in tolerance is particularly marked for those currently between 15 and 19 years of

Figure 9.4 Percentage of women who approve of day care, women working outside house and western dress by age

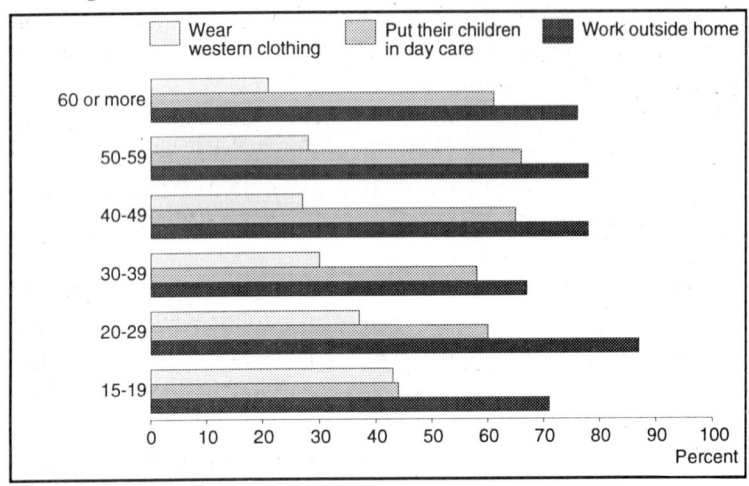

Figure 9.5 Percentage of men who approve of day care, women working outside home and western dress by age

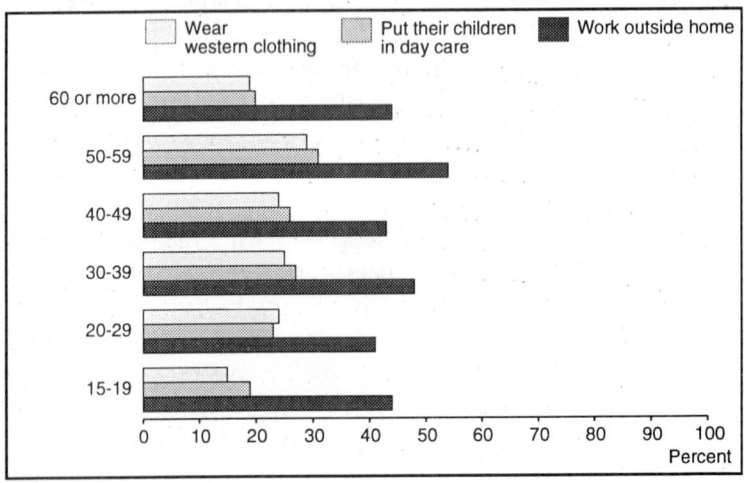

age. The survey data shows two exceptions to this trend. Men's attitudes concerning the acceptability of women working outside the house is unaffected by age. Women's acceptance of Western dress declines steadily with increasing age although a majority of all women regardless of age disapprove of Western dress styles for women. However, although young Palestinian men and women seem to be increasingly restrictive in their attitudes to women, they are restrictive about different things. Young men are notably less tolerant of Western female attire, young women of behaviour linked to women's roles, such as placing children in child care or working outside of the home. These findings seem to hold in all three regions.

When broken down regionally, on both the issue of day care and women working outside the home, the decline in acceptability is most marked among the youngest age group of Gazan women who currently hold attitudes that are more restrictive than either those of their mothers or grandmothers. For instance, while 68% of Gazan women between 20 and 29 report that it is acceptable for women to place their children in child care, only 43% of those in the youngest age group appear to hold this opinion.

The decline in tolerance for Western dress for women is especially striking among the youngest age group of West Bank Palestinians. Whereas 31% of men in the West Bank between 20 and 29 years regard Western dress as acceptable, only 17% of those between 15 and 19 share this view.

With regard to dress codes, a critical issue is whether women are able to translate their own attitudes concerning dress into choice over what they actually wear despite the opposition of men. The data suggests that such choice is at best restricted. Women who approve of Western dress are twice as likely to actually wear some form of Islamic dress than Western attire and equally likely to wear full Islamic attire.

If what women wear is factored for age, in all age groups, the percentage of women who wear Western dress is less than one half of the women who approve of such dress.

Table 9.2 Women's attitudes on the acceptability of western dress by what they actually wear

	Acceptable	Not acceptable
Thobe	11	34
Strict Islamic	28	48
Islamic headscarf	29	16
Western	29	1
Other	3	2

Table 9.3 suggests that the traditional Palestinian thobe is being replaced by two new, modern forms of dress, neither of which is customary in the region. For a minority of women the new form is Western. For a much larger segment it is strict Islamic, an imported form of new "traditionalism". These new dress forms are not only in opposition

to each other, but the social messages they carry concerning the status of women are antagonistic.

The differences shown here between men and women regarding women's status in society indicate that the underlying norms are under considerable pressure particularly from women themselves. Notably in terms of roles the discrepancy is most pronounced in Gaza. However, the data also suggests that particularly among the youngest age group of Palestinians the gender divisions in society seem under a process of redefinition and reinforcement.

Attitudes to Social Divisions in Palestinian Society

However, Palestinian society also contains other divisions, for instance, between the poor and rich, the old and young, management and employees. (See also Chapter 8). What are Palestinian perceptions concerning the conflict potential of these divisions and do they vary according to region? In table 9.4 the regional index separates refugee camps (both in Gaza and the West Bank) into a distinct category.

Table 9.3 Forms of dress worn by women outside home by age groups

	Thobe	Strict Islamic	Islamic headscarf	Western
15-19	3	44	36	17
20-29	8	50	31	11
30-39	29	53	12	6
40-49	50	34	9	7
50-59	61	23	7	9
60 or more	70	19	3	9
Total women	27	42	21	11

Table 9.4 Percentage of Palestinians who perceive the degree of conflict as strong or very strong: by region

Between	Gaza	West Bank	Arab Jerusalem	Camps
Rich and poor	32	49	55	38
Old and young	31	49	54	42
Employed and unemployed	34	32	43	32
Management and workers	35	57	64	44
Urban and rural	14	17	22	16
Men and women	28	33	48	33

In comparison to the results of an international survey of several different countries, the degree of perceived conflict in Palestinian society is high[1]. Notably, it is highest in Arab Jerusalem, the region which also enjoys the best physical living conditions. This is also the region in which the process of change has been most profound, the competition between contending political and social ideas most enunciated and the degree of interaction with Israel most intense. Gaza as well as the camps are located on the opposing end of the spectrum. For many in Gaza, life has been characterised not so much by rapid change as by prolonged stagnation. Moreover, except in the sphere of wage labour in Israel, Gaza is in many ways sealed off from daily contact with Israeli society. The contact that does occur often takes the form of violent confrontation. It could well be that the intensity of this confrontation generates a special feeling of solidarity which mutes Gazan perceptions of conflicts that are more internal to the Palestinian situation, a point also commented on in Chapter 4 and Chapter 8. Interestingly, Arab Jerusalem where the discrepancy between men and women concerning the status of women is least is also the region in which conflict between men and women is viewed as most acute. Reversely, in Gaza where these discrepancies are most marked, the degree of reported conflict is lowest.

Do the patterns of perceived conflict vary between men and women?

In general women perceive more conflict than men. When the data is analyzed on a regional level, women resident in Arab Jerusalem seem markedly more inclined to perceive conflict than any other segment of the population. The discrepancy between men and women among Palestinians generally is particularly evident in their views concerning the degree of conflict between men and women. The gap is also notable in their varying perceptions of the conflict between unemployed and employed, a conflict that women experience directly through the loss of income of household members. The only dimension in which the pattern is broken is the conflict between management and workers, the conflict which Palestinians as a whole regard as most intense. This is a conflict which is largely

Table 9.5 Percentage of Palestinians who perceive the degree of conflict as strong or very strong by gender

Between	Men	Women
Rich and poor	44	45
Old and young	41	49
Employed and unemployed	29	37
Management and workers	57	43
Urban and rural	15	18
Men and women	26	42

257

played out in the work place, an arena in which women's participation is minimal.

Age and education also affects perception of conflict, but again these variables have very different impacts for men and women.

For men perceptions of conflict in general are not significantly altered by increased education. More than any other factor, they seem to be determined by age – the old reporting more intense degrees of conflict than the young. In fact the very stability of men's perception of conflict, despite different educational and age levels, is unexpected. For women the picture is very different. Their perception of conflict seems much more influenced by differentials in age and education. While older women are much more prone to report conflict, the impact of education greatly intensifies the perceived pattern of conflict among younger women. Partly this is explained by the fact that educated women are more certain in their attitudes. They make specific choices rather than stating that they simply cannot choose. But their choices go overwhelming in the direction of observing the world with a more acute sense of severe conflict. The combined impact of age and education can also partly explain the conflictive profiles of women in Arab Jerusalem, in which older, well educated women are over-represented in relation to the Palestinian population generally.

Significantly, economic position seems to have little, if any, impact on perceptions of conflict, a result quite different from that characteristic of Western class based societies. This would seem to indicate that class based attitudes and identifications remain relatively

Table 9.6 Impact of background variables on perception of conflict

	Men			Women		
Between	Wealth	Age	Education	Wealth	Age	Education
Rich and poor	0	++	-	0	++	++
Old and young	0	+	+	0	++	++
Employed and unemployed	0	0	0	0	++	++
Management and workers	0	+++	++	0	++	+++
Urban and rural	0	0	0	0	++	0
Men and women	0	+	0	0	+	++

+++	=	very strong positive correlation (more conflictive)
++	=	strong positive correlation
+	=	weak positive correlation
0	=	no correlation
-	=	weak negative correlation (less conflictive)

undeveloped in Palestinian society partly due, perhaps, to the continued primacy of family links and vertical clientele relationships.

Religious Attitudes

Because of the small sample of Christians surveyed, survey results cannot be reliably used to analyze attitudinal variations among Palestinian Christians and, indeed, only certain comparisons between Muslims and Christians as a whole can be made. Analysis of religious attitudes in this report will focus, therefore, only on the Muslim part of the population.

Based on survey variables, a three point indicator of religiosity was constructed. The variables included weekly (or more) attendance at a mosque and/or religious study circle, visits to religious sites, Islam as an important political attribute in a future Palestinian state and Islam as the primary focus of personal loyalty. Some of these variables imply mainly religious belief and practice, others have more political connotations. A score of 0, "secular", indicates that the individual is neither religiously observant nor expresses any sort of religious political values. A score of 1, "observant", indicates religious belief and observance and a score of 2, "activist", indicates religious observance combined with political religious identity. Thus the index attempts to measure the range of religiosity from the secular to the religiously activist. Because the index is constructed in a manner that is only applicable to the Muslim sector of the Palestinian population, in the following analysis the Christian population has been removed from the sample.

Following this index, the distribution of religiosity for the Palestinian Muslim population, broken down by region and type of locality, is as illustrated in figures 9.6 and 9.7.

These results seem to challenge some of the more common notions concerning Islamic activism in the occupied territories. They indicate that Islamicism is not particularly associated with Gaza refugee camps, nor indeed with Gaza at all, despite the long historical connection between Gaza and the Egyptian based Muslim Brotherhood. Of the various types of localities surveyed, Gaza camps, along with Arab Jerusalem, seem to be the most secular. To the extent there is a regional concentration of Islamicist activism, it appears to be more associated with the towns and camps of the West Bank. Moreover, the general percentage of Palestinians who are secular, observant or activist does not vary with their refugee status. Non-refugees and refugees, regardless of whether they live inside camps or outside of them, appear to have broadly the same religious profiles.

The survey results do indicate a certain correlation between religiosity and economic position. Table 9.7 presents the economic background of the secular, observant and activist inside the occupied territories.

The table shows that secular as well as observant Palestinians are drawn more or less evenly from all economic levels inside Palestinian society. The activists, however, tend to come more from the middle economic sectors.

Figure 9.6 Religious index by region

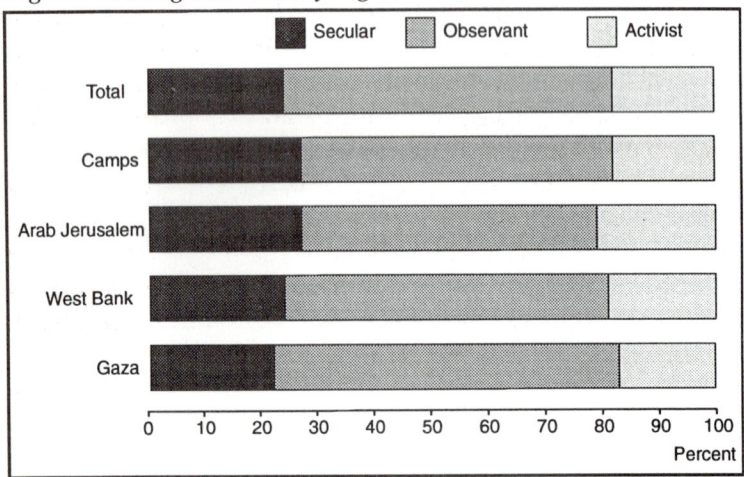

Figure 9.7 Religious index by type of locality

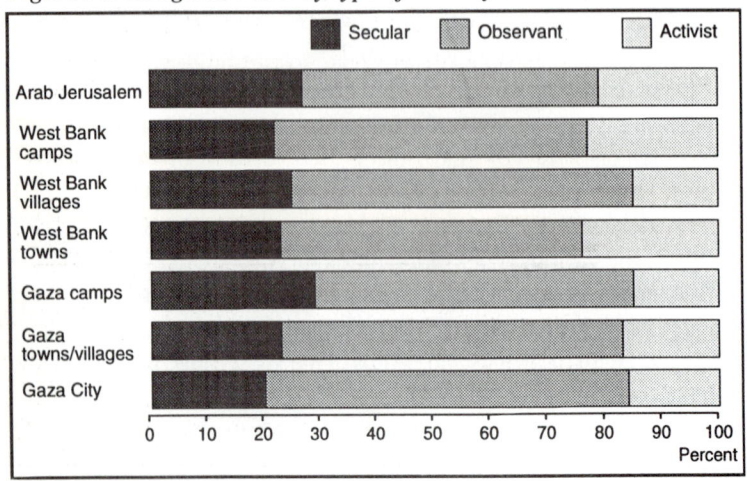

Table 9.7 Religiosity index by economic strata

	Secular	Observant	Activist
Lower third	29	35	36
Middle third	35	37	46
Upper third	36	29	34

There are also gender differences. Women tend to be more secular than men (29% for women versus 20% for men) and men more religiously activist than women (24% versus 12%).

In addition, age seems to affect the degree of religiosity and the impact of age is somewhat different for men and women.

The trend among the youngest age groups of men is very similar to the trend observed in relation to their attitudes to women. Among those aged 15 to 19, the group most affected by the street activism of the intifada, the trend toward secularisation has suddenly reversed and there is a very sharp jump in the portion who are observant Muslims or militants in relation to the preceding age group. Also notable is the concentration of Islamicists among those aged 50 to 59, the age group who experienced the 1948 war and the subsequent massive dislocation of Palestinians at a young, impressionable age.

Among women there is a slight decrease in the number of observant Muslims and a corresponding increase in the degree of secularisation among those under 50 years of age. However, the proportion of women who profess sentiments linked to political Islam seems fairly steady over the generations. The only exception is, again, women currently in the age group of 50 to 59.

Figure 9.8 Religious index by age, for men

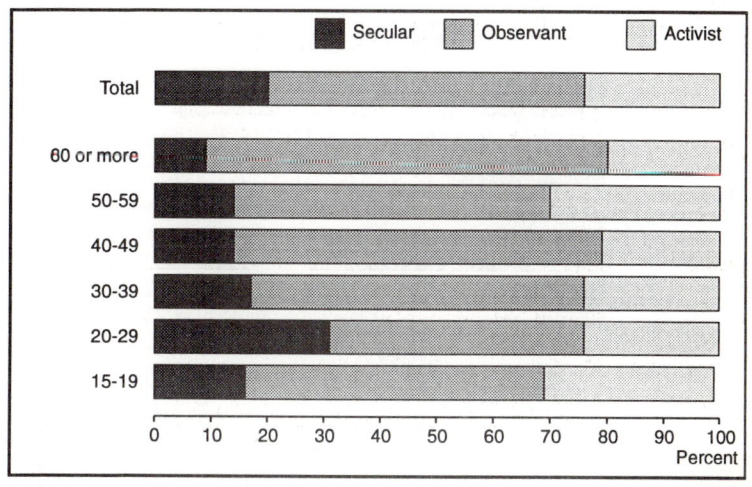

Education also seems to impact on the degree of religiosity and once more the impact differs among men and women although the trends appear the same.

Figure 9.10 indicates that while education seems to produce a decline in religious observance, the most educated male sectors of Palestinian society are being to some extent polarised. On the one hand increased education produces a steady drive toward secularization. On the other, among the most educated a certain shift toward militancy is also noticeable.

Figure 9.9 Religious index by age, for women

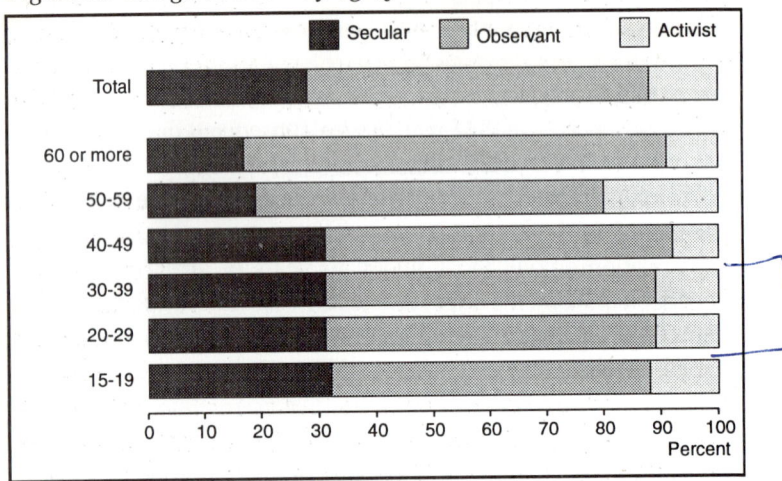

Figure 9.10 Religiosity index by educational level, for men

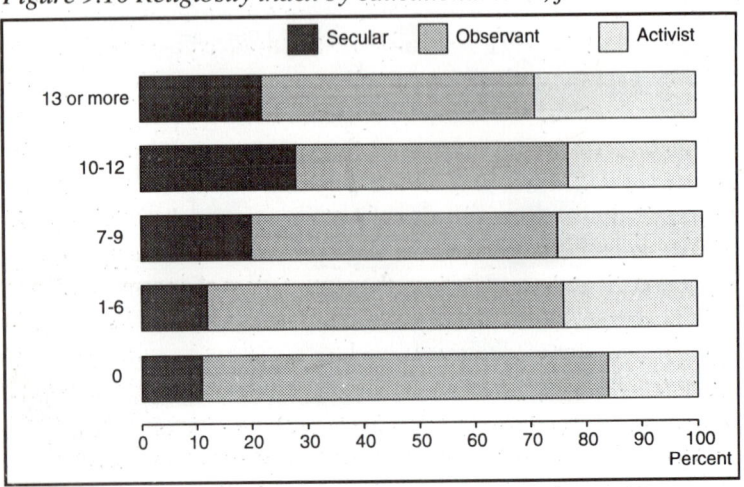

Among women education is associated with the same drive towards secularization and away from Islamic practice. It is only among those women who have post-secondary education that an increase in the percentage of Islamic activists can be observed. Among this group some 18% score highest on the index. However, this group must be compared to the 41% of Palestinian women with post-secondary educations who are secular.

In a society in which hierarchical gender relations are an important organising principle with both social and religious legitimation, it can be assumed that religious beliefs help to shape attitudes toward women. If men's attitudes to women's roles are examined, there appears a clear correlation between increased religiosity and an attitude that women should be largely confined to the domestic sphere. While 50% of secular men feel that it is acceptable for women to work outside the home, only 42% of observant Muslims and 37% of activist Muslims share this view. This pattern is repeated when men are asked about the most appropriate behaviour for married women. While 48% of non-religious men feel that women should stay at home, take care of their children and not indulge in money generating activities of any sort, 59% of religious activists express this view. In short, for men religious radicalism seems to reinforce social conservatism.

Among women, however, the attitudes of secular women and activists concerning women's roles share somewhat the same profile. The trend is weak, but consistent. For instance, while 64% of non-religious women expressed the attitude that women should give priority to child care, but could otherwise work outside the home, 66% of activist women stated the same view. In contrast, only 57% of religiously observant, but not activist, women gave this reply. Activist women seem to be marginally more accepting of day care facilities for children than either their secular or observant counterparts.

Religious beliefs also appear to have an impact on the degree of parental authority that is deemed fitting for women. For instance, concerning the choice of a woman's husband, 60% of non-religious men stated it was the woman's, rather than the father's, choice, while only 48 – 49% of observant and activist men shared this opinion.

Among women on this issue, the same pattern of a correspondence of views between secular and activist women seems to emerge. Both these groups have slightly more liberal attitudes with regard to women's roles and prerogatives than observant women. However, the vast majority regardless of religious persuasion (range 79% to 85%) felt that it was mainly the daughter's, rather than parents', choice.

While disparities in religious attitudes among men also translate into conflicting notions concerning appropriate roles for women, first and foremost, these differing religious attitudes impact on notions as to how women should dress. In this case the pattern is equally clear for both men and women.

Table 9.8 Percentage who feel western dress acceptable by religiosity index

	Secular	Observant	Activist
Men	42	16	13
Women	45	26	19

Opinions are also clear with regard to head scarfs for women and the trend is the same. Among men, 37% of non-religious men state they would be insulted if a female member of their household appeared in public without a head scarf, but 83% of activist men share this view. Among women, the figures are 35% for secular women, 61% for observant women and 56% for activist women.

However, in the more detailed replies that were possible in relation to the survey question on head scarfs, another factor emerges. This is what could be termed the "fear factor". Among activist men only 8% state that they are concerned with what other people might say or do to a women who appeared publicly without a head scarf, but almost a full quarter, 24%, of secular men have this primary anxiety.[2]

Among women, it appears to be the activists who are most fearful. For instance, 21% of activist women in the West Bank compared to 9% of secular West Bank women seem to fear the consequences of appearing in public without a head scarf. Telling, a full 33% of West Bank women who actually wear head scarfs seem to fear the consequences of not doing so. This trend is present in all three regions.

The previous chapter on education indicates that a sense of influence within Palestinian society is critically affected by age, gender and household position. A crucial issue concerning religious attitudes is whether or not strong religious conviction also enhances the individual's sense of influence. Does a sense of certainty that frequently accompanies intense religious belief and purpose, translate into a sense of power within the household, neighbourhood, country or in respect to the Arab-Israeli conflict? Does religiosity affect the individual's self-assessment of the importance of his or her place within society? Certain, somewhat unexpected, trends seem to exist.

For men religious militancy does not seem to provide a greater sense of control or dominance. Indeed, to the extent a relation exists, it seems slightly negative. For instance, with regard to influence within their village or on the Arab-Israeli conflict somewhat more religious activists than non-religious men express complete powerlessness.

However, with regard to women, the pattern is reversed and the trend is stronger and consistent. In every sphere militantly religious women express a greater sense of influence and empowerment than their non-religious or observant counterparts.

The impression of female empowerment through religious involvement is reinforced when attitudes to the force of destiny, as determinant of the individual's future, are examined. While 33% of activist men and about the same percentage of the observant believe in the determining power of fate, only 21% of the non-religious men agree. For women, however, the equations seem reversed. Increased religious identity tends to correlate with a decreased belief in the control of fate. While 18% of secular women give credit to the force of fate, only 13% of women religious activists concur.

The explanation of the different impact religious militancy has on men and women's sense of empowerment could relate to the different aims they pursue through religion. Within the constraints of their social environment, by taking on the ideology and attributes of piety, women can gain leverage and manoeuvrability. Their ability to move in public, for instance, is much less threatening to their families because they are "protected" by their dress. Moreover, many women activists are currently attending religious study groups which represents a major break with former practice. Historically women have been denied the right to participate actively in the discussion and reading of religious texts.[3] In short, for women religious activism can assist them in entering into the spheres of life dominated by men.

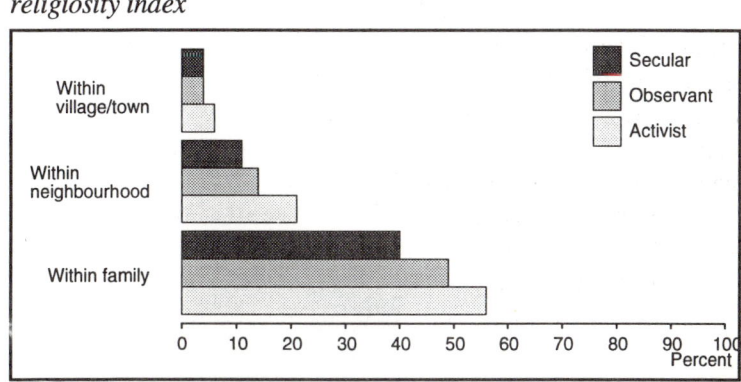

Figure 9.11 Degree of women's perceived influence in percent by religiosity index

265

Political Attitudes

Because political attitudes are exceedingly sensitive in the occupied territories, the survey did not attempt to poll Palestinian political affiliations. It was thought that any endeavour to do so would prejudice the survey as a whole by suggesting a political motivation behind the study. However, because of the political complexity of the region, Palestinians have been subject to a range of disparate, at times conflicting, ideologies and claims to loyalty, some of which have long historical precedents, others which are of more recent origins and all of which are competing for a constituency in order to help shape the future contours of Palestinian society. Therefore, the survey did try to assess the effects of the political forces that are contending in the region to gain individual political sympathies and shape identities.

The survey contained three explicitly political questions. The first tried to determine broad political preferences. The question posed a range of alternative attributes – Arabism, Islam, democracy and socialism – and asked the respondent to select the one attribute he or she though most important in a future Palestinian state. The second question listed a range of countries representing different political systems and asked the respondent to choose the model he or she felt best suited for Palestine. The question aimed not only at determining political sympathies, but also at examining the familiarity that Palestinians had of the outside world and the political options it contained. The final question tried to explore the boundaries of ultimate political

Figure 9.12 What is the main attribute you wish to see in a future palestinian state political preferences by gender

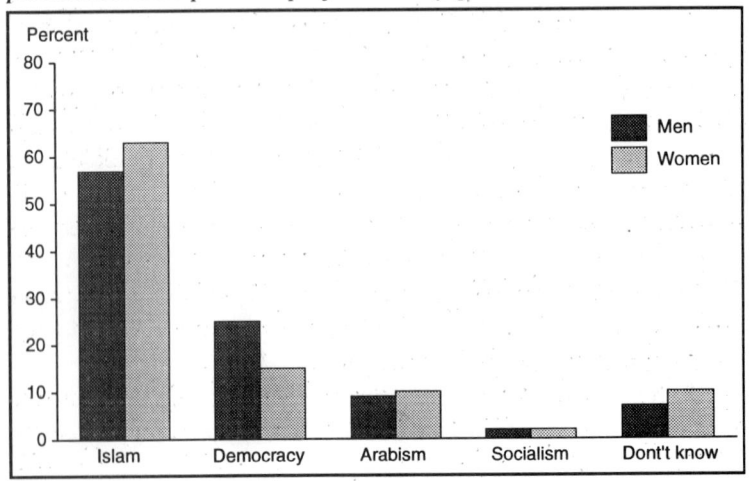

loyalty and the primary determinant of identity. Here the respondent was requested to choose one cause for which he or she was willing to make the ultimate sacrifice. The choices ranged from the family, the Palestinian people, the Arab nation to the Islamic nation.

In assessing Palestinian political values the data suggests that Islam is by far the single most important attribute valued by Palestinians. Islam is the majority response of all Palestinians regardless of age, gender, education, locality of residence, refugee status and socio-economic position.

Support for the more traditional ideology of Arab nationalism is relatively weak among Palestinians although it enjoys the support of 9% of the population. However, support for notions of socialism, a current of thought which during the late 1960s and early 70s had a certain constituency in the Middle East, is almost non-existent. Most notable is the finding that support for Islam is some three times stronger than support for democracy, with Islam more strongly represented among women and democracy more strongly represented among men.

With regard to Islam's support among women, two aspects need to be mentioned. First, Islam can be understood in at least two different ways. It can be understood as a religious belief and practice, primarily a matter of scripture. It can also be understood as a political framework, primarily a matter of law, government and society. Survey results suggest that women tend to see Islam more in terms of religious orthodoxy than of political activism. Second, in comparison to men, women seem less politicised and consequently their understanding of various political options tends to be more restricted. Therefore, there are indications that to some extent women overwhelmingly have chosen Islam because this is the attribute with which they are most familiar.

When political preferences are broken down by age groups, the data indicates that majority preference for Islam goes through all age categories, but that there is a very marked resurgence of Islamic sentiment among the youngest age group of men. Reversely, for both men and women in this age group, there has been a sharp decline in democratic attachments.

When the impact of education on political preferences are examined, the data suggests that education serves more than any thing else to strengthen democratic preferences.

Two trends are noticeable. First, with increased education, the value placed on Islam seems to decrease. However, while support for

Islam might be less, survey results also indicate that it is probable that the definition of Islam shifts under the educational process from primarily a religious belief to more of an activist political creed. Second, support for democracy is three times more frequent among those with the highest education than among those with the least, confirming the trend not only toward secularisation, but also toward acceptance of plurality and tolerance as mentioned in a previous chapter.

Figure 9.13 Men's political preferences by age groups

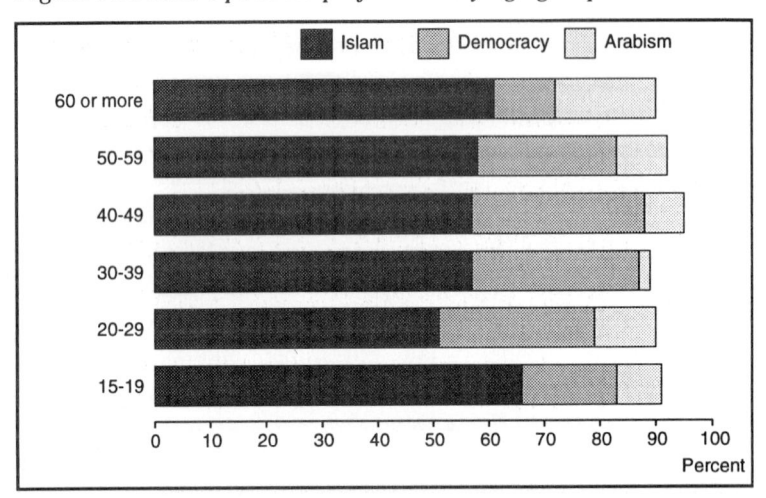

Figure 9.14 Women's political preferences by age groups

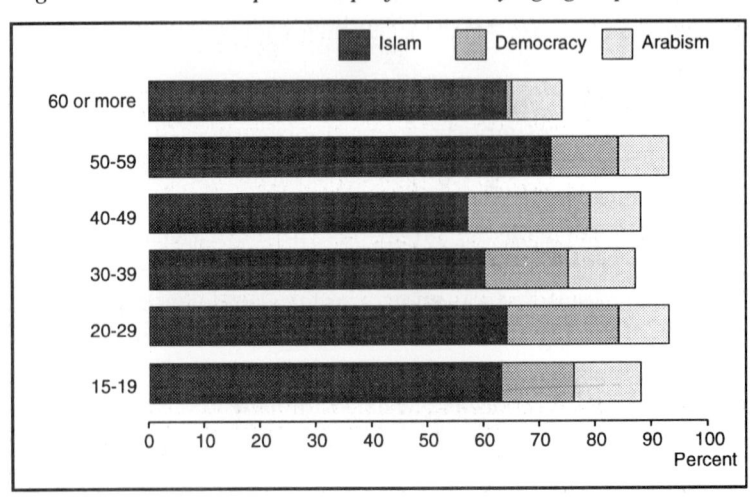

If examined together, the data indicates that education is a strong promoter of democratic values. The steep decline in such values among the youngest age group of Palestinian men and the abrupt shift to Islamic preferences could be one effect of the prolonged disruption of education for this age group during the intifada.

Socio-economic position also seems to affect political values. The upper one third of Palestinian society express more sympathy for Arabism (12% versus 6% for the bottom third), relatively less for Islam and relatively more for democracy. Particularly among women,

Figure 9.15 Political preferences by educational level, for men

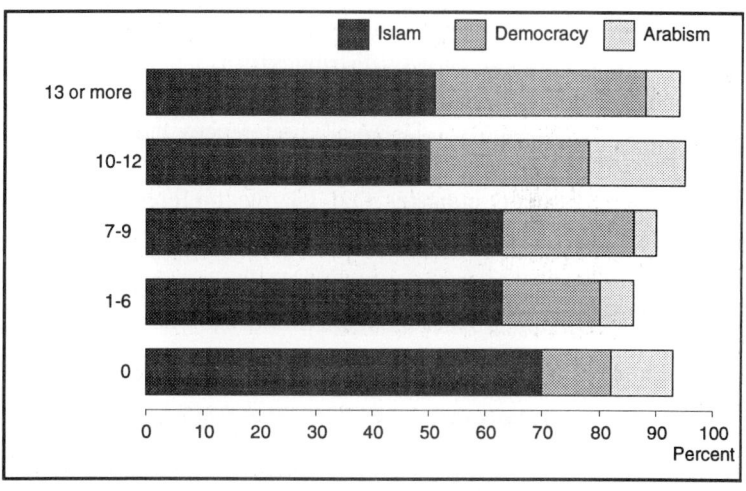

Figure 9.16 Political preferences by educational level, for women

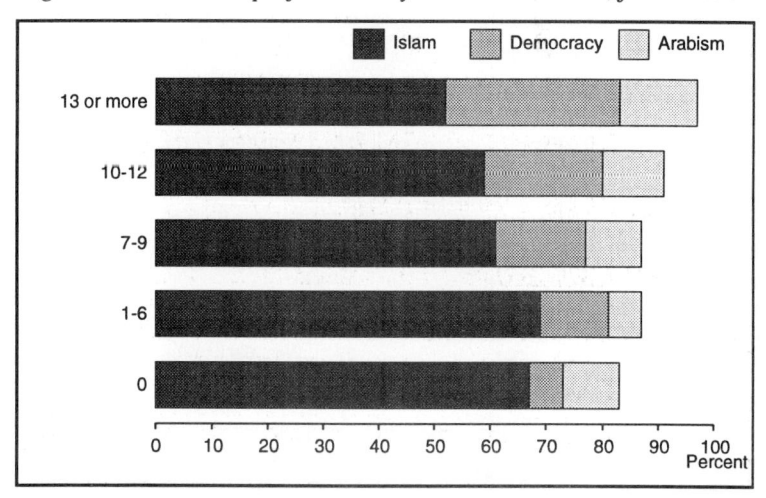

the trend toward increasing preference for democracy with increasing prosperity is marked. Islamic preferences are again more associated with the middle economic strata of Palestinian society, a point which will be returned to shortly.

Whether or not the household has refugee or non-refugee status seems to have no effect on political values except that non-refugees lean somewhat more toward Arabism (11% of non-refugee versus 7% of UNRWA refugees).

The distribution of political values between different types of localities presents a very intricate picture although in every locality gender differentials are apparent. Figure 9.17 lists the types of localities that are most associated and those that are least associated with the various political preferences examined. Within the localities not listed, preferences are broadly distributed in a manner more or less representative of the Palestinian population generally. Because of the disparities between men's and women's preferences, the list has been broken down by gender.

Figure 9.17 again indicates that Islamic preferences are not particularly associated with Gaza, but more with the West Bank.

Figure 9.17 Localities most associated and least associated with specific political preferences

Men				
	Most associated		**Least associated**	
Arabism	West Bank villages	14	Gaza camps	4
	Gaza towns/villages	12		
Islam	West Bank camps	70	Gaza towns/villages	48
	West Bank towns	63	Gaza camps	53
Democracy	Gaza camps	31	Gaza towns	20
	West Bank camps	21		
Socialism	Gaza camps	5		
Don't know	Gaza town	17	West Bank towns	2
	Arab Jerusalem	12		

Women				
	Most associated		**Least associated**	
Arabism	Gaza camps	16	Gaza camps	5
	West Bank villages	12		
Islam	Greater Gaza City	70	Arab Jerusalem	51
Democracy	Gaza camps	23	West Bank towns	10
	Arab Jerusalem	22		
Socialism	West Bank towns	3		
Don't know	Gaza towns	14	Gaza camps	4
	Arab Jerusalem	14		

Surprisingly perhaps, Gaza male camp residents appear more similar in political values to men in Arab Jerusalem than to men in the West Bank.

A previous study has suggested a relationship between arrest records of household members, used as an indirect measurement of political activism, and the political attitudes of household members.[4] This survey found no such correlation with reference to political values.

Do Palestinians find inspiration in the political systems of other countries and do their political values lead them to look to other countries for confirmation of these values? The survey provided respondents with seven different models together with the optional category of "none of the above".

With this sort of question the expectation is usually that "none of the above" will score very high. Political reality can rarely compete with the idealized. For the vast majority of Palestinians no country seems to provide a model. The preference of those who have any seem more based on familiarity than on ideological propensities. However, when specific choices are made, they mirror to some extent the political affinities of Palestinians as measured by political values. Of the men who stated Islam as the most important attribute in a future Palestinian state, 74% claim "none of the above" as model, 13% Jordan, and 7% Iran. Among women, 17% choose Jordan, 7% Saudi Arabia and 2% Iran. For respondents who state democracy, their preferences in declining order are 61% "none of the above", 14% France, 11% Jordan, 6% USA, and 5% Cuba. The wealthiest top third of the Palestinian population has a slightly higher preference for France (7% versus 3% of lowest third). The only variations in the general pattern seem to relate to educational levels. While 15% of the most educated group prefer France (compared to 5% of the general population), only 5% prefer Jordan (compared with 13% of the general population). Nonetheless, even among this group a full 67% answer "none of the above".

The final question relates to a more fundamental pillar of political life. It involves the boundaries of ultimate loyalty and the definition of political identity. Nationalism is premised on the imperative that cultural (national) boundaries and political boundaries should coincide. A corollary of this

Table 9.9 Which of the following countries is the most suitable model for a future Palestinian state by gender

	Men	Women
France	6	3
Cuba	4	1
Iran	4	2
USA	3	4
Saudi Arabia	1	5
Jordan	12	15
Libya	1	2
None of these	68	68

271

premise is that the individual owes his strongest loyalty to the nation and that his political identity is principally shaped by his nationality. The nationalist doctrine insists that both local loyalties and those that transcend national boundaries should be subordinated to the nationalist imperative.

In the Middle East the ethnic nationalist message has never had the precision as it has had in its western home of origins where for at least the last 150 years it has operated to replace empires with states claiming to be nationally based. In the Middle East local and family loyalties have remained strong and, partly because of a shared language and religion which transcend state and even regional borders, the definition of a common identity has had to deal with many contending meanings. The Arabic language reserves the word for nation – *umma* – for the Arabic and Islamic nation solely. Syrians, Palestinians, Lebanese and so forth refer to themselves generically as peoples – *sha'b* – rather than nations. Thus the question aimed at mapping the levels of ultimate loyalty among Palestinians and relating this map to the pattern of political values described previously.

The answers reveal that family loyalties, particularly among women, are still an exceedingly vigorous source of identification. Not unexpectedly perhaps in light of Palestinian history, attachment to the concept of Arab nationalism which has been a prime mover, especially in the Fertile Crescent, for most of the century and is still ardently advocated by key Arab leaders, is conspicuously weak among Pales-

Figure 9.18 For whom would you be willing to make the ultimate sacrifice? Political loyalties by gender

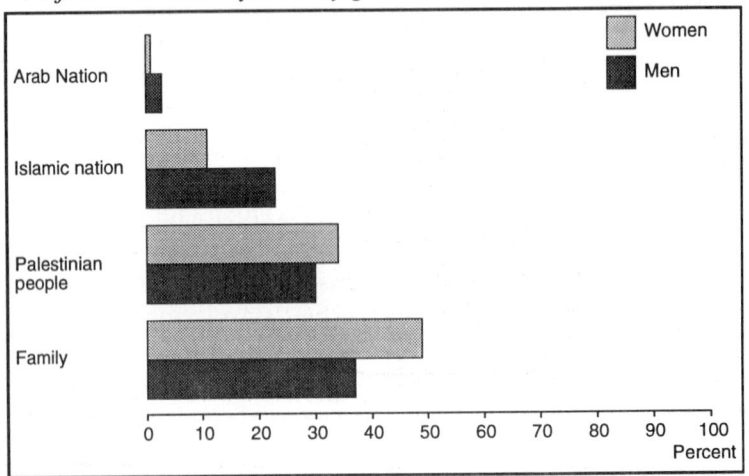

tinians. The 9% support of Arabism as a prime political preference does not translate into a political constituency for Arab nationalism. Instead, adherence to this allegiance seems to have been replaced, first and foremost, by loyalty to the Palestinian cause. Especially among men, attachment to emerging forms of Islamic identity is very notable. The distribution of family loyalties and loyalties to Palestine and Islam for men are examined by type of locality, and presented in Figure 9.19.

The figures indicate that local family loyalties remain strongest in Arab Jerusalem and Gaza Town and weakest in the Gaza refugee camps. The low correlation with the Gaza camps may reflect the extent to which wider family units have been splintered and the subsequent penetration of more explicitly politically defined sentiments, especially Palestinian nationalism. However, again the figures show that Islamic militancy is not particularly associated with Gaza. The figure would suggest that such militancy is more developed in the refugee camps of the West Bank.

If these loyalties are examined in relation to age, the picture that emerges confirms trends seen elsewhere in this chapter (Figure 9.20).

The young express less attachment than the middle-aged to family bonds and more attachment to bonds that are ideologically delineated. The increase in identification among young women with Palestinian nationalism is particularly marked. 43% of women in the age group 15 to 19 name the Palestinian people as their ultimate attachment compared to 34% of women in general. Loyalty to Islam among

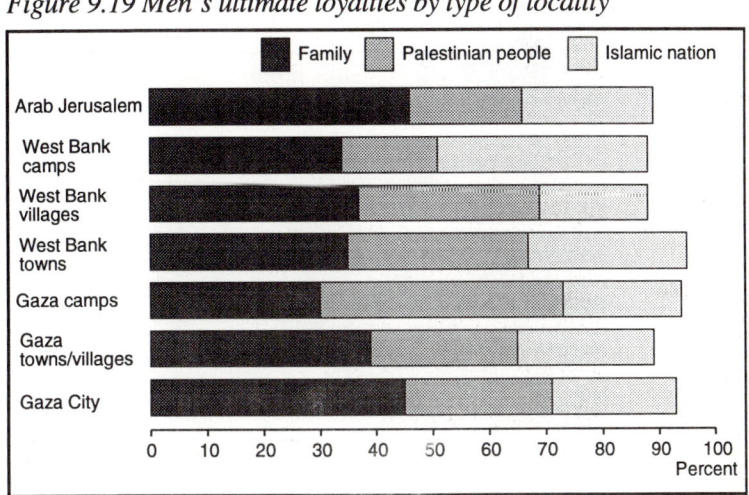

Figure 9.19 Men's ultimate loyalties by type of locality

273

women seems not to be affected by age, but has broadly the same size of constituency in all age groups.

The picture that emerges from men's responses indicates different trends. The data suggests that among younger men loyalties are shifting from the family to Islam with the inroads of Islamic militancy most marked in the youngest age group. A comparison between the answers of young women and men suggests almost a feminisation of the Palestinian national movement. Currently, Palestinian nationalism seems to be recruiting many more of its most devoted adherents from the ranks of young women, rather than young men.

In relation to the inroads of Islamic militancy, again age, more than education, seems to have the greater impact. Except for men with no education, educational levels do not seem to affect political loyalties. For instance, whereas 32% of the best educated men defined their primary loyalty as Palestine and 27% as Islam, among those with only 1 to 6 years of education, 27% state Palestine and 23% Islam. The

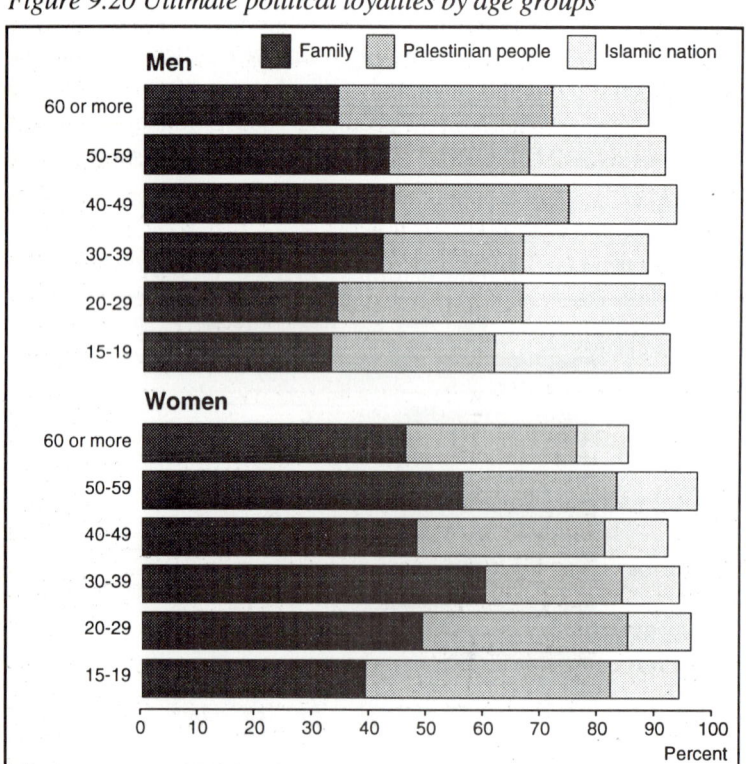

Figure 9.20 Ultimate political loyalties by age groups

274

Table 9.10 Ultimate loyalty by arrest record of household members

	Household member arrested	Household member not arrested
Family	38	46
Palestinian people	38	29
Arab nation	4	2
Islamic nation	17	17
None	1	1
Don't know	3	5
Total	36	64

picture is similar for women. Ultimate political identities and loyalties seem to remain largely unaltered by the educational process.

Unlike political preferences, ultimate political loyalties have a clear association with economic status. The relationship can be seen by looking at the economic background of individuals with different political loyalties (Figure 9.21).

This figure demonstrates that those whose primary loyalty is focused on the family or the Palestinian national movement come more or less equally from all economic strata. Contrary to commonly accepted views, however, this table would suggest that Islamic militancy is not primarily generated by economic deprivation and distress. Islamic militants are more commonly drawn from the upper, but especially the middle, economic echelons of the Palestinian population. In this respect Islamic activists are very similar to ethnic nationalist activists to whom they are structurally and ideologically akin. Like ethnic nationalism, the data suggests that the Islamic movement is not so much fuelled by despair as it is fed by the frustrations of the middle sections of society, especially the frustrations of young, reasonably educated individuals whose upward mobility in society is blocked. The inability of many Palestinians to translate their education into white collar employment is one such block. But the most important one is the occupation regime itself.

It has frequently been noted that the Israeli policy of mass detention has functioned to transform Israeli detention centres and prisons in the

Figure 9.21 Political loyalties by economic strata

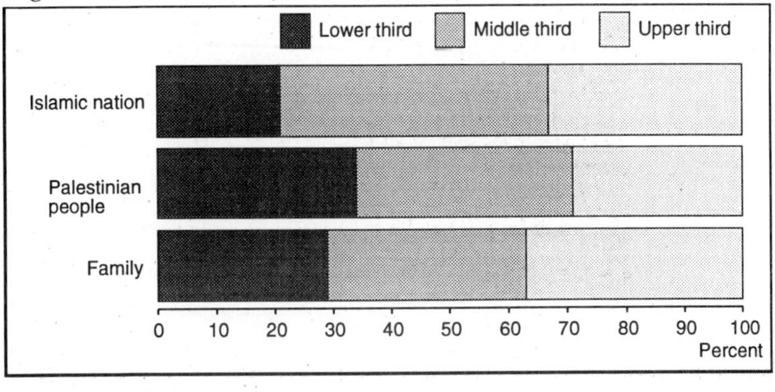

occupied territories into advanced training centres for political activists. A comparison of the responses of those individuals who had at least one of the members of their household arrested during the period of the intifada could suggest tentatively that the experience has had a politicising effect and the effect is uniformly in one direction, a reinforcement of Palestinian loyalties. Islamic sentiments appear to remain unaffected.[5]

Evaluation of the Past

A central assumption of social planning and development is that over time the quality of individual lives should improve. In the contemporary world this assumption also constitutes a fundamental expectation of most people in relation to the future of themselves and their children and a key measure by which people judge the success or failure of their own lives. The belief – or lack of it – that the course of one's life has in general been better than the lives of one's parents and that one's children are destined to experience still further improvements is a central, albeit indirect, indicator of an individual's evaluation of his or her life situation. How individuals view their lives in retrospect and the optimism or pessimism with which they gauge the future of their children are pivotal psychological aspects of total living conditions.

In order to assess Palestinian attitudes to the course of their lives in retrospect, the survey posed the question in figure 9.22.

Broadly speaking more Palestinians assess their lives in positive terms than in negative ones. However, the responses reveal a clear gender difference. Women tend to assess their lives as either positive, almost a majority, or stagnant. Men are much more negative in their appraisal. It should be noted that the "no answer" category in this

Figure 9.22 "When you look back at your life with all its ups and downs, do you think that your life has been better or worse than that of your parents?" (Appraisal of life condition)

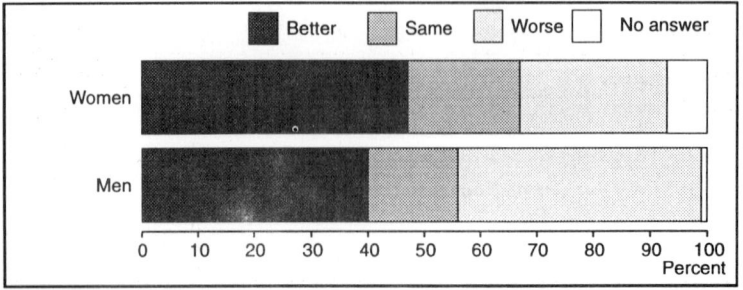

Table 9.11 Appraisal of life condition by age group

	Better	Same	Worse	No answer
15-19	41	19	26	14
20-29	40	24	33	3
30-39	47	17	34	2
40-49	51	12	36	1
50-59	41	12	44	2
60 or more	45	9	46	0

question corresponds to those respondents who answer the question with a statement such as, "Only God knows!", or a determined shrug of the shoulders.

Does self-appraisal vary with age? Except for Palestinians 50 years or more, in all age groups Palestinians assess their lives as better rather than worse than that of their parents. The highest levels of discontent are found among those aged 50 years or over. This is the generation that experienced the upheavals of 1948 war and the creation of the first massive wave of Palestinian refugees. Interestingly, the generation that experienced the 1967 war and the beginning of Israeli occupation sees their lives in more positive terms. But among those aged 40 years or less there is an increasing feeling that the quality of life has been stagnant. This sense of stagnation is particular strong among women regardless of age.

While attitudes among refugees and non-refugees as a whole show similar profiles, the differences in appraisal among men and women refugees resident in camps are striking.

The bitterness and discontent of men living in refugee camps is well illustrated in table 9.13. In this table camp residents have been divided into three generations; those from 15 to 30 who have most directly experienced the intifada, those from 31 to 49, the "War of 1967" generation, and those currently 50 or above, the "War of 1948" generation.

Table 9.12 Appraisal of life condition by refugee status

	Better	The same	Worse
Non-refugees			
Men	43	16	41
Women	45	20	26
Camp refugees			
Men	33	10	53
Women	55	20	22
Refugees resident outside camp			
Men	39	15	45
Women	47	20	26

The single most embittered sector of the population is the first generation of male Palestinian refugees resident in camps, individuals who are now 50 years or more. The contrast between these men and their female counterparts is remarkable (table 9.14). The third generation of female camp residents is simultaneously the group that is most approving of its general life situation and the individuals who see the course of their lives as most stagnant.

Table 9.13 Male camp refugees appraisal of life condition by generation

	Better	The same	Worse	No answer
Intifada generation (15-30 years)	36	11	50	3
'67 War generation (31-49 years)	42	5	52	
'48 War generation (50+ years)	14	16	63	7

Table 9.14 Female camp refugees appraisal of life condition by generation

	Better	The same	Worse	No answer
Intifada generation (15-30 years)	60	27	10	3
'67 War generation (31-49 years)	49	16	33	2
'48 War generation (50+ years)	51	10	39	

Table 9.15 Appraisal of life condition by gender and region

	Better	The same	Worse	No answer
Male Gaza	30	17	51	2
Female Gaza	45	24	23	8
Male West Bank	45	14	41	
Female West Bank	49	16	29	7
Male Arab Jerusalem	47	21	29	3
Female Arab Jerusalem	50	30	18	2

Table 9.16 Men's appraisal of their own lives by type of locality

	Better	The same	Worse	No answer
Greater Gaza City	34	23	40	3
Gaza Towns/villages	32	18	50	1
Gaza camps	26	11	60	3
West Bank towns	38	15	47	
West Bank villages	48	12	40	
West Bank camps	48	20	32	
Arab Jerusalem	47	21	29	3

Despite the vast expansion of education over the past several decades, educational levels do not seem to affect significantly the relative assessment of the individual life situation. However, the most educated Palestinian men do seem to judge their lives somewhat more positively than those with little or no education.

Expectedly, a strong correlation exists between an individual's economic position in Palestinian society and a positive assessment of life so far. While 36% of those in the bottom economic third of Palestinian society feel their own lives have been better than that of their parents, 51% of those in the top third seem relatively satisfied with the course of their lives.

It could be argued that individuals who hold activist religious or political beliefs would tend to assess their life situation more negatively – because of the wide gap between their beliefs and the world they live in – or, alternatively, more positively – because these beliefs give life a special, enriched value. The survey would indicate that neither proposition is valid. Religious and political attitudes seem to have no impact whatsoever.

Using the various regional indexes constructed, the survey can identify the types of localities within the occupied territories in which relative resentment is most intense. If the three regions, broken down by gender, are examined, the pattern is demonstrated in table 9.15.

The sector of the population that stands out in this table is men in Gaza. Fully 50% describe their lives as worse than that of their parents. In contrast only one of five women in Gaza seem to view their lives as less satisfactory than that of the previous generation although about the same number view their lives as static. Other indexes confirm that resentment, especially among men, is at its most intense in the Gaza camps, but is also commonplace in the towns and villages of Gaza. They indicate that bitterness is also widespread in the towns of the West Bank. Men in West Bank villages and West bank camps as well as men in Arab Jerusalem are generally more cheerful in the assessment of their lives.

Attitudes to the Future

Having examined briefly how Palestinians assess the course of their lives so far, how do the various sectors of the Palestinian population see the future? Have the experiences of the past made Palestinians basically pessimistic or optimistic in outlook? Do they feel the lives of their children will be better or worse than their own? Here the "no answer" category is higher since many respondents insist that the fate of their children is in God's hands.

The picture is one of a relative confidence and belief in the future. As women are more positive in the assessment of their own lives, they are also more hopeful concerning the lives of their children.

How does refugee status combined with generational differences impact on this general image of confidence? Taken as entire groups, the profiles of refugees and non-refugees are again broadly similar. But generational differences among men within the two groups, especially those refugees who live in camps, reveals a more complex picture.

Among the non-refugee population the young are more or less as optimistic as their parents and grandparents. Moreover, very few non-refugees seem to believe that the future will remain more or less like today. Among refugees, however, the contrasts are more marked. The youngest generation of male camp refugees are significantly more optimistic than their grandfathers. However, the general optimism of the older generations seems curbed by the some 22% who seem to believe, in resignation, that the future will be mostly a replay of the present. 25% of the generation which is most negative in the appraisal of their own lives seem also the most pessimistic regarding the future.

While education has only marginal effect on the assessment of ones own life, it does affect faith in the future. The most pessimistic sectors of the population are also the best educated. While 67% of the

Table 9.17 Do you think the lives of your children will be better than your own? (Assessment of the future)

	Men	Women
Better	61	72
The same	5	5
Worse	18	10
No answer	16	13

Table 9.18 Male non-refugees' assessment of the future by generations

	Better	The same	Worse	No answer
Intifada generation (15-30 years)	59	4	20	17
67 War generation (31-49 years)	62	2	15	21
48 War generation (50+ years)	61	4	19	17

Table 9.19 Male camp refugees' assessment of the future by generations

	Better	The same	Worse	No answer
Intifada generation (15-30 years)	64	4	20	12
67 War generation (31-49 years	57	22	15	6
48 War generation (50+ years	47	23	25	5

population in general believe in a better future, only 59% of those with advanced education shared this view.

The data indicates that this general sense of hope and belief that Palestinians have in the future is independent of the family's wealth or the individual's political or religious convictions. A general sense of encouragement also seems evenly distributed through all regions of the occupied territories. The refugee camps taken as a whole are only distinct in that their residents have a slightly stronger expectation that the status quo will continue (9% for the camps versus 5% in general). The only marked distinctions found relate to the differing attitudes of men and women in the three regions.

Again the disparity in attitudes between men and women in Gaza is notable. In general table 9.20 suggests that the least optimistic portion of the Palestinian population are the men of Gaza and the West Bank, the most optimistic, Gazan women and the rather conflict prone women resident in Arab Jerusalem.

Conclusions

The findings presented in this chapter represent only an initial analysis of the survey data. A fuller analysis could well uncover a different and certainly more detailed picture than that described here. Again, the reader should be reminded about the possibility of statistical variations due to sampling error, as discussed in Appendix A. However, even a cursory look at the data suggests that Palestinian society is undergoing deep change and that some of its fundamental norms and assumptions are under rigorous challenge. The data depicts a society that could be moving in two directions simultaneously. On one hand, it is moving toward more liberal attitudes concerning the status of women in society, toward a greater degree of secularisation and an enhanced emphasis on the value of democracy. On the other, spearheaded especially by disaffected and frustrated sectors of the younger

Table 9.20 Assessment of the future by gender and region

	Better	The same	Worse	No answer
Male Gaza	61	6	16	17
Female Gaza	77	7	6	9
Male West Bank	60	4	20	16
Female West Bank	68	3	13	16
Male Arab Jerusalem	64	7	11	18
Female Arab Jerusalem	81	6	4	10

generation, Palestinian society also appears to be drifting toward a reinstatement of social conservatism and patriarchal values, a reinforcement of religiously defined identities and social codes and a drifting away from the acceptance of plurality. Particularly when the westernising impact of education on Palestinian attitudes is examined, the question emerges as to whether this drift toward social and political rigidity is not at least partially due to the fact that for over five years Palestinian schools have often been closed, whereas the turbulence of the streets have been wide open.

Some of the stresses to which Palestinian society are subject are indicated by the very different views men and women seem to hold concerning the critical organising function of gender. The social roles prescribed by society for women appear to be under strong attack by women themselves, especially in Gaza, the region in which social conservatism has most hold. Women's strategies for dealing with this adversarial encounter are probably many, but the data indicates that, paradoxically, one such strategy seems to involve adopting the symbols and ideology of religious activism. The data suggests that such activism has a liberating effect on women, providing them with more manoeuvrability and influence, not less.

The opposing directions of change in society combined with Palestinian perceptions of conflict suggest that some of its internal tensions might be growing. These tensions in part are caused by the workings of the structuring conflict into which Palestinians are caught and, as indicated by the data from Gaza, tensions which in part are also suppressed by the overwhelming supremacy of that conflict. Under the circumstances, it is probably unrealistic to expect Palestinians to turn their attentions abundantly and productively to the internal issues that divide them before the external circumstances that so powerfully bring them together are successfully addressed.

Notes

1 As compared to results from ISSP, the International Social Survey Programme.

2 The "fear factor" is especially pronounced among secular men in Gaza. In Gaza 35% of secular men versus only 2% of religious activists state that they are concerned what people might do to a women who appears without a head scarf.

3 Rema Hammami, personal communication.

4 M. Shadid and R. Seltzer, "Political attitudes of Palestinians in the West Bank and Gaza Strip", *The Middle East Journal*, vol.42 no.1, 1988.

5 The results could also suggest that Israeli authorities have arrested a disproportionate number of Palestinian nationalists.

Chapter 10
Women in Palestinian Society

Rema Hammami

The author would like to thank Kristine Nergaard, Tone Fløtten, Marianne Heiberg and Helge Brunborg for valuable suggestions and comments to this chapter.

Introduction

In order to capture the totality of women's lives in a given society, level of living studies usually involve several conceptual levels. These different levels of conceptualization enable both comparison between genders, on the one hand, and discussion of aspects of life that are unique to the situation of women.

In any study of living conditions, a comparison between male and female responses to the basic issues and phenomena serves as a fundamental level of analysis. This provides an understanding of the extent of gender asymmetry in a society; the extent to which there is differential access to material resources and mechanisms of social and economic mobility between men and women. Stated more simply, the aims would be to generate information as to whether women, as a whole, share in the ownership of wealth, the attainment of education, and participate in the work force in the same way and to the same extent as men.

In addressing more subjective aspects of life, this level of analysis raises questions about whether women perceive the differences and conflicts in their society like men do, and whether they have a different set of social and political aspirations for the future of their society.

This comparison across gender lines is generally prepared for in a study during the sampling period, when it normally must be assured that there is equal representation of men and women in the sample frame. Within the questionnaire, men and women should answer the same questions, posed in the same way, if one is to be able to do a gender comparison in the analysis.

But what about issues that are specific to women's experience? While health studies always have treated women's health issues as having their own specificity, incomparable to those of men, social and feminist research over the past few decades has shown that in other areas of life, gender is a decisive factor, not only in how individuals relate to objective social and economic phenomena, but also in shaping those phenomena themselves. Thus, while a basic analysis based on gender division has its uses, it cannot fully account for various phenomena that are gender specific from the outset.

This means that a host of issues relating to women's childbearing role (marriage, marriage age, daycare, work patterns, housework, etc...) should be addressed separately and specifically to women. Moreover, a cognizance of how a society elaborates and encodes gender must inform the analysis of both the objective conditions of women and how women perceive them.

Finally, if one aim of living conditions studies is to delineate social and economic divisions within a given society, then women cannot be viewed solely as gendered individuals but must also be studied as members of other social categories. While being women may entail certain shared experiences based on the elaboration of gender roles within a specific social context, other factors such as education, age, economic status, or regional difference also carry their own unity of experience. Therefore, it becomes necessary to analyze the circumstances and issues in which gender takes primacy over other identities, and when the latter plays a more determinant role.

A number of chapters in this study assess various aspects of gender division in Palestinian society through the overall analysis of various issues such as education, health, labour, and social and political attitudes. Some of them also analyze issues specific to women, e.g. fertility, specifically female forms of economic production, and women's (as well as men's) attitudes towards 'women's issues' such as day care, dress forms, etc. This chapter more strongly focuses on differences between groups of women. On the one level it analyzes material differences between women and the conditions that shape them; differing ownership of property and access to economic resources and support networks. On the other, it looks at how factors such as age, marital status, education or regional residence may mould women's perceptions of their world; their attitudes towards various women's issues; and their sense of feeling constrained or supported by their society.

While some of the themes in this chapter would be addressed in any study of women's living conditions, the way in which these wider themes are addressed here attempts to highlight the distinctive character of living conditions of women in the occupied territories. Thus, the issues of marital status and women's marital age, while important in any context, take on added importance for the study of women's living conditions in the occupied territories since they determine so much of the social and economic context in which women's lives are lived. Women's access to property and support networks also takes on a more profound importance in the context of women's low participation in the labour force and in the absence of a state with its requisite social welfare systems. Freedom of movement is an issue that has its own specific importance for men and women in the occupied territories. For both sexes this issue is significant in order to understand the political constraints on their lives and it may help explicate attitudes to a variety of social and political issues. For women, perceptions of their freedom of movement have an additional importance, as they are relevant to an understanding of the possible social constraints on their lives. Finally, because women's participation in formal labour activities is so often seen as a means to empowerment in other areas of their lives, it is important to assess their attitudes towards this issue so as to understand where there is room for change.

Marriage and Attitudes Towards Marriage Age

While some form of marriage organization exists in all societies, the social rules for ordering those relations vary dramatically from context to context and they change historically alongside transformations in the larger socio-economic structure of a society. In the West Bank and Gaza, these larger determinants of 'who marries whom and why' have undergone some profound transformations since the late 19th century.

Prior to the rise of wage labour, when social relations were predominantly peasant-based, the need to organize production through land within and between extended families, was the primary determinant of marriage relations. Lineage solidarity, property and family labour maintenance or distribution were thus primary determinants, not only of who married whom, but also at what age. While a social ideology that refuses to recognize individuals as adults outside of the structure of marriage persists, the logic of contemporary marriage arrangements in the West Bank and Gaza are both diverse and different from those in the past.

Since the beginning of the century, with growing education levels for women and hence social mobility, marriage arrangements based on individual relationships outside the context of family have developed. Local universities have represented an important site for this development, as have the rise of student movements. Where access to higher education and social mobility does not exist (in many villages and some refugee camps), the family continues to play an important role in organizing marital relations, and the exigencies of the entire family unit play a determinant role in the logic of marriage relationships. In villages where women's mobility is constrained, and issues of land inheritance are sometimes involved, marriage relations can remain determined by the property or solidarity arrangements of the extended family group. In refugee camps, however, where property is usually not a factor, issues of household density and scarce family resources are often the crucial determinants of marriage. Marriage arrangements based on a need to preserve kinship bonds persist in some sectors of society, although their original role as a way to preserve property or power arrangements has disappeared. Instead, kinship-based marriage arrangements now exist as a way to preserve the continued identity of dispersed communities. Although this pattern has disappeared among refugees in the West Bank and Gaza, who continued to organize marriage in the framework of their village or place of origin up through the 1970s, it remains strong among migrant workers and exiles living outside of the occupied territories. The latter phenomenon is typified in the (almost) annual summer months of 'bride-shopping' that takes place when overseas Palestinians visit the occupied territories.

Marital status is a factor of profound importance in assessing women's living conditions in any social context. But in social contexts in which women do not participate heavily in the labour force, and do not have independent sources of income, marriage becomes the mechanism through which much of their economic life is decided. This also has implications for women's ability to make independent decisions about their lives; if women are dependents does this also imply constraints on their ability to act as individuals and to seek ways to improve their own future as women? Alternatively, are women empowered through the mechanism of marriage? Are there other forms of support for married women that affect their ability to make more active decisions about their lives and future?

Some basic data on marital status is presented in table 10.1. The table presents the basic frequencies of marital status of women in the sample population and then breaks marital status down by age sets.

While the overall number of women who are or have been married in the sample population seems quite low (69%), this is primarily due to the age range of the sample. The largest number of unmarried women in the sample are in the pre-marriage ages of 15 to 19; they constitute 55% of all unmarried women in the sample population. Women in their twenties also comprise a sizable part of the unmarried women in the population (26%): there is a high likelihood that these women could be categorized as pre-marriage as opposed to permanently unmarried. However, once a single woman reaches beyond her twenties in Palestinian society, marriage is less likely. It is interesting to note the distribution of unmarried women within each age category of 30 years upward. In each of the top three age categories (40 years and up), less than ten per cent of the women have been unmarried all their lives. But for women in the 30 to 39 age category, a full 17% are still unmarried. This may mean that the upper limits of socially acceptable marriage age are higher than expected, or it may imply that for certain reasons a number of women in this age range either choose not to marry or do not have the opportunity. An analysis of their educational achievement shows that they have a higher educational achievement level than married women in the same age group, and that a higher percentage of them work outside the home. These factors may be a cause or an effect of their being unmarried.

Exemplifying the strong stigma attached to divorce in Palestinian society, and the lack of social and economic support available to divorced women, only about 1% of the female sample population is

Table 10.1 Marital status by age. Percentage.

Age	Unmarried	Married	Married but spouse working abroad	Divorced	Widowed	Separated	N
15-19	81	19	0	0	0	0	258
20-29	27	70	2	1	1	0	364
30-39	17	76	2	4	1	0	219
40-49	8	86	0	2	3	0	155
50-59	9	77	0	0	15	0	94
60+	7	38	0	1	50	3	130
All	31	59	1	1	7	1	1220

divorced. On the other hand, 7% of women in the population are widows, the majority of them are in the 60+ age category, thus their status seems to be the result of natural life cycle processes added to age differentials that exist between women and their spouses among the older generations.

Marriage Age

While marital status is important as such, marriage age may have a stronger impact on women's living conditions taken as the quantitative and qualitative aspects of life. If women are marrying at ages which undermine their ability to complete their formal education, also implying that the ability to reach experiential maturity is denied, there is a much greater difficulty for them to acquire the skills (and not just the resources) that will enable them to take an active role in shaping their lives according to their own priorities.

The formal legal standards of marriage age are set in the occupied territories by the legal system that was in place at the time of the occupation in 1967. Thus the West Bank Islamic courts, following Jordanian law, set the marriage age at 15 for women and 16 for men. In the Gaza Strip, which follows Egyptian codes, marriage age for girls is legally set at 17 and 18 for boys. While these are the legal minimums, in practice the courts are much more flexible. In Gaza the Shari'a court claims that its practical minimum age is based on a girl's physical maturity and consent to be married, since Shari'a law itself sets these as the only conditions rather than stipulating a minimum age. In the West Bank, although the minimum age is low, the law is easily circumvented by the reliance on witnesses to a girl's age rather than documentation. Thus, although the legal minimums (especially for Gaza) are comparable to those in Western countries, there is a profound problem of enforcement due to the absence of a state institution for regulating proper execution of the law.

While the recognized trend in the occupied territories over the last two decades has been that education and urbanization have led to a relative rise in marriage age, there has been much concern that the first period of the Intifada reversed this trend somewhat. One study documented a rise in early marriage in the years 1988/1989 in the Bethlehem and Tulkarim districts[1]. (Early marriage is locally defined as marriage below age 18). The suggested reasons for this were the long term school closures, which have de-motivated parents to extend their daughters' adolescence until they have finished school. This was coupled with the deteriorating economic situation, which has meant that for many families an adolescent girl is simply another mouth to feed. From the point of view of parents of sons, the motivation to marry them to young women during this period was based on a number of factors. First of all, the Unified Leadership banned wedding parties (which used to take up a large part of the cost of getting married) – thus marriage was cheaper. Secondly, extended school and university closures meant that many young men began to enter the work force earlier, and thus families felt is was their right to 'settle down'. Thirdly, there was a psychological dimension at play in which death is considered even more tragic for a young man if he leaves no male heir behind. Real fear for the lives of especially young men often was a main force in parents' decisions to marry young sons during this period.

Table 10.2 expresses the distribution of marriage age across the female sample population and for the different regions

More than a third (37%) of the entire female population got married under the age of 17 – the legal minimum marriage age for women in Gaza.

A sample survey can only give some clues about the changes that have taken place in marriage age in the occupied territories. In addition to problems caused by small sample size, a disadvantage of a sample survey is that a large proportion of the women in the FAFO sample are too young to be married. For example, 15.3 per cent of the women in the sample are below the age of 18. Moreover, because of high fertility, there are many more young women than old women in the Palestinian population – and in the sample. There are, for example, 187 women at ages 13-17 and only 101 women at ages 33-37, and only

Table 10.2 Age at marriage by region. Percentage.

	Gaza	West Bank	Arab Jerusalem	All
10-14 years	12	11	8	11
15-16 years	25	26	30	26
17-18 years	27	26	28	26
19-21 years	22	22	16	21
22-24 years	7	9	11	8
25+ years	8	7	8	7
Total	100	100	100	100
N	307	457	68	832

64 women at ages 43-47. These factors may make the mean age at marriage, etc., for the full sample misleading. If calculated, much caution must be taken in the interpretation of the results.

We may, however, get a better picture of the development over time if we look at the *median* age at marriage, which is the age at which "half the women are married".[2] The advantage of this measure is that it can be calculated as soon as half the group of women have married, whereas the commonly used *mean* age at marriage for a birth cohort in principle cannot be calculated until all women have passed the upper "age limit" for marriage -if such a limit exists in practice. However, this varies from culture to culture, and may also change over time. It is difficult to say that women will not marry beyond a certain age within a given context.

We have calculated the median age at marriage for different five-year birth cohorts, i.e. women born in the same five years (table 10.3).[3] The median age of marriage has increased strongly: among women born before 1935, half of them had married at age 17, whereas the median age was 19 years for women born in the 1950s. For younger women, born in 1970-74 and who got married around 1990, the median age at marriage is fully 19.9 years. Among the youngest women in the sample, who were born in 1975-79, only 10 per cent were married, which is not surprising since they were only 13-17 years when they were interviewed. Consequently, their median age at marriage cannot be calculated yet.

Table 10.3 Median age at marriage by year of birth.

Year of birth (cohort)	Age at interview	N	Median age at marriage
All women		1218	19,5
1975-79	13-17	187	-
1970-74	18-22	197	19,9
1965-69	23-27	182	19,4
1960-64	28-32	149	18,4
1955-59	33-37	101	19,3
1950-54	38-42	89	19,2
1945-49	43-47	64	17,8
1940-44	48-52	70	17,3
1935-39	53-57	40	18,2
1930-34	58-62	57	17,3
1929 and before	63+	84	16,3

The increase in age at marriage is not monotonical, that is, every cohort does not marry at a higher age than the previous cohort. For example, the median age for the 1960-64 cohort is 0.9 years *lower* than for the previous five-year cohort. These irregularities *may* have been caused by social, economic or political factors, for example the occupation in 1967 and the Intifada, but they may also be due to sample uncertainty.

The increase in age at marriage is probably related to several structural changes in the Palestinian society, described in other chapters of this book, in particular the increasing education among women. (See, e.g., chapter 5, on Education).

The actual distribution of marriage age within age groups, organized in ten year age sets, is shown in table 10.4. This gives a clearer idea of the number of women who married early across age sets.

The table shows that there was a large decrease in early marriage among women in therir twenties compared to women in their thirties and above. While only 17% of the women aged 20 to 29 at the time of the study had married below age of 17, 31% of women aged 30-39 at the time of the study had married below age 17. Again, because of the large number of unmarried women in the 15-19 age cohort, we are unable to compare the instance of early marriage among their group to the older cohorts.

Are there differences in marriage age between the different regions? Table 10.5 presents median marriage age according to year of birth by region[4].

The table shows that in recent years women in Gaza have married at a substantially younger age than their age cohorts in the West Bank.

Table 10.4 Marriage age by current age. Percentage.

Age	10-16	17-18	19-24	25+	Unmarried	Total	N
15-19	12	5	-	-	83	100	258
20-29	17	20	31	3	29	100	364
30-39	31	21	26	5	18	101	307
40-49	35	17	25	16	8	101	155
50-59	31	35	17	9	9	101	94
60+	48	22	17	6	7	100	128
All	25	18	20	5	32	100	1220

Preferred Marriage Age

As mentioned in the introduction to this section there is a variety of factors and actors that play a role in deciding the marriage age and partner of women in Palestinian society (the West Bank, Gaza, and Arab Jerusalem). While the survey did not ask whether women chose to marry at the age they did, or ask whether they themselves chose their spouse, they were asked about who in their opinion should decide on a woman's marriage partner. From table 10.6 it would appear that there are few substantial disagreements between men and women on who should decide on a girl's spouse. However, men are slightly more supportive of women's participation in choosing a spouse than women are themselves. Responses to a different question, however, indicate that a considerably greater share of women than men hold the belief that a woman should be allowed to choose on her own.

While the table does not tell us about the realities of whether girls actually choose their marriage partners themselves, general knowledge of the society tells us that decisions about marriage partners tend to be taken more collectively depending on the education, economic status and social outlook of the parents and their daughter.

Similar processes are at work in deciding women's marriage age. While we cannot assess the role women in the survey sample have taken in deciding on their marriage age, we can gauge the degree of satisfaction they have with respect to the age at which they themselves married.

Tables 10.7 and 10.8 represent assessments of women's preferred marriage age when related to a set of questions of what age they think it is right to have their daughter married.

Regardless of age, education or marriage age, there is a strong general rejection of marrying before 15, this being considered an

Table 10.5 Median marriage age by year of birth

Year of birth (cohort)	Age at interview	Gaza	N	West Bank	N
1975-5	13-17	-	81	-	92
1965-74	18-27	18.5	122	20.9	221
1950-64	28-42	19.4	119	18.7	191
1935-49	43-57	18.7	58	17.7	101
Pre 1935	58+	17.2	46	16.2	83
All		19.1	426	19.8	688

Table 10.6 In the choice of a girls husband, which statement do you agree with most. By sex. Percentage.

	Men	Women
Daughter's choice alone	11	7
Mainly daughter's choice	80	76
Parents should have decisive influence	5	11
Father's choice only	4	5
Do not know	0	1
Total	100	100
N	1243	1198

inappropriate age for women to marry. While 15 to 18 years are considered comparatively more acceptable, only about 40% of women support this marriage age. Clearly, most women are in favour of marriage at ages 19 to 25 (79%).

Is there a relationship between women's own age at marriage and their preferred marriage age for women generally?

From table 10.8 a clear pattern emerges, implying that the older a woman's own marriage age, the more supportive she is of older marriage ages. However, what is probably most surprising is the general lack of support, especially among women married at 16 years and above, for a marriage age close to the mean for the whole society.

While a general pattern exists in which women married at later ages prefer a later marriage age for women in general, another pattern can be seen in table 10.9, showing responses to the question of whether women would like a real or imagined daughter to marry later than they did themselves.

Table 10.7 Do you think it is right to have your daughter married at age.... ? Percentage.

	Below 15	15 to 18	19 to 25	More than 25
Yes	3	39	79	27
No	97	61	21	75
Total	100	100	100	100
N	1218	1218	1218	1218

Table 10.8 Percentage who answers yes to the questions "Do you think it is right to have your daughter married at age...". By marriage age. Percentage.

	\multicolumn{4}{c}{Daughters marriage age}	
Actual marriage age	Below 15	15-18	19-25	More than 25	N
10-15	11	59	61	22	197
16-19	1	40	78	26	411
20 hi	2	34	90	29	224
ALL	4	43	77	26	832

293

Here it becomes clear that almost 70% of women who married between ages 10 to 19 apparently felt that their own marriage age was too young for their daughters. Even among women married well beyond the mean marriage age (20+), a full 22% prefer that their daughters marry at even later ages. In sum, there seems to be a contradiction between the actual ages at which women are getting married in Palestinian society, and women's perceptions of what are the appropriate or preferable ages at which to do so.

Table 10.9 Would you like your daughter to marry later than you did. By actual marriage age. Percentage.

	Actual marriage age			
	10-15	16-19	20+	All
Yes	77	65	22	56
No	18	26	9	36
Do not know	5	9	7	7
Total	100	100	100	99
N	197	411	224	832

Women, Property and Access to Economic Resources

In the Palestinian context, in which so few women directly participate in the labour force, it becomes extremely important to assess other means through which they get access, as individuals, to economic resources. Historically, the main mechanism the society used to ensure women some form of independent economic resources was through the payment of dowry at marriage. While the form, amount and women's actual control over their dowry payment have varied historically – between social levels and among individuals - some overall patterns can be delineated. Moors (1990) has shown that prior to the predominance of wage labour, many peasant women received their dowry in the form of land or fruit trees, or exchanged their monetary dowry for productive property (such as livestock)[6]. In Shari'a law a woman's dowry is solely her property. According to Palestinian peasant social custom a division of the dowry usually took place with some of it going to the woman's father and to cover the costs of the wedding. But the part that was given to her as jewelry or property was recognized as solely hers, as was any income she could generate from it. With the rise of wage labour, the associated rise of women's economic dependence solely on the spouse, and the breakdown of the extended family as a productive unit, Moors has argued that women began to use their dowry more for the economic well-being of the nuclear family. Thus women invested their dowry either in the building of home, productive property for the husband, or for children's education.

Historically, inheritance does not seem to have been a generalized means for women to get access to economic resources in Palestinian society, even though it is their right to inherit family property in Shari'a law. The historical problem with women's inheritance rights to land in Palestine was primarily due to the problem of land fragmentation. No rule of primogeniture existed in Palestinian society, thus inheritance among a number of sons over generations led to land being broken down into ever smaller, economically unviable units. In this context, women's inheritance rights were viewed not only as a luxury, but more so as a threat to their brothers' ability to inherit enough land to form an economic base for a whole family. The generalized social compromise that took place on this issue was that peasant women exchanged their rightful share of land inheritance for the guarantee of economic and social support from their brothers.

Despite major transformations in Palestinian society and economy over the past century, dowry payment (although now in the form of money) continues as an important social practice, although it may no longer provide a sustainable source of economic support for women, given its amount in relation to ongoing costs of living even for village women. Simultaneously, an increase in women's ability to inherit does not seem to have occurred.

In order to try to obtain information about women's property as individuals (rather than family property), women have been asked about what property they could sell as individuals if they needed money in an emergency.

Table 10.10 gives an overview of the responses to this set of questions. While jewelry constitutes the major form of women's independent property ownership in the West Bank, Gaza Strip and Arab Jerusalem, women do own other forms of property although to a much lesser degree.

About 40 percent of the women in the sample claimed that they had nothing to sell or mortgage in case they needed money badly, whereas 24 per cent had two or more forms of property which were theirs to sell.

Only 8% of women claimed they owned land which was theirs

Table 10.10 Do you have anything that is your own that you could sell or mortgage to raise money? N=1218 Percentage

	Yes	No	Total
Jewelry	48	53	101
Land	8	92	100
House	9	91	100
Tools of the trade	12	88	100
Livestock	7	93	100
Thobe	15	85	100
Banksavings	8	92	100
Money, women's savings group	7	93	100
Other	9	91	100

to sell. Because of a low sample size indeed, it is only possible to make some general statements about who these women are. They are overwhelmingly from the West Bank (77%), probably due to the availability and price of land there, compared to either Gaza or Arab Jerusalem. This factor is also supported by the fact that most of them are rural women (59%). They tend to be in the upper wealth category (66%), although this may be a cause or determinant of their owning land. Their age as well as the area in which most of the women who own land live, suggest that it is predominantly women in the West Bank villages who succeed in inheriting and keeping land inherited from their father. This assumption is supported by the findings of a recent, unpublished study on women and inheritance in the West Bank village of Beit Furik. The author found that land inheritance is still problematic for women, and found only five married women in the village with the support of their husbands who took relatives to court in order to wrest their property rights over inherited agricultural land[7].

Women who claim to own houses which are theirs to sell are similar in background, age and residence to those women claiming to own land. Again, the sample size is extremely low (9%), and thus only some general remarks can be made. Again, the vast majority of them live in the West Bank (84%). They tend to be predominantly rural women (57%). Older women and widows were somewhat over-represented in the group that have a house that is theirs to sell. This may mean that some of the issues and processes that affect women's inheritance of land are also factors in women's ability to inherit homes.

By far, the most widespread independent economic resource women claim to have is jewelry, with a full 47% claiming they have jewelry they could sell if they need to raise money. Although the data does not give us the actual amount, it can be inferred that women consider it economically meaningful if it is mentioned as a possible source of money.

Owning saleable jewelry is very much tied to marital status, since it is the form in which women usually receive a good part of their dowry, and in amounts that are economically meaningful. After marriage, the other occasion in which women usually receive jewelry is upon the birth of a child. The type of jewelry sold locally (usually 20 carat gold), and the way it is sold (by weight), attests to its recognized significance as capital. Married women, who constitute 59% of the female population, are 78% of those claiming to possess saleable jewelry. Table 10.11 represents married women by age owning jewelry.

A possible reading of the above table is that, over time, women's dowry jewelry is gradually dissipated as various investments for the family, husband or children. This process seems to begin when women are in their thirties when costs accrue due to children. Judging by the extent of jewelry ownership among women in their sixties, repayment on women's investment does not take place in kind.

In terms of regional difference among married women, 71% of Jerusalem married women claim to own saleable jewelry, compared to 55% of West Bank women and a comparatively lower percentage (37%) of women living in Gaza. However, this may be a product of the wealth differences between the three regions. When crossed by wealth categories, logically women in the wealthiest category exhibit greater ownership of saleable jewelry.

Table 10.12 represents women's ownership of jewelry in relation to urban/rural residence:

The table shows that among married women in Gaza villages and towns (other than Gaza City) there is substantially less ownership of jewelry than in the other areas, which show a fairly even distribution[8]. This is surprising, given the fact that in terms of age distribution, this area has higher numbers of young married women in the sample - women of the age and marital status that are most likely to have saleable jewelry. Moreover, this does not seem to be related to wealth

Table 10.11 Married women owning jewelry. By age. Percentage

	15-19	20-29	30-39	40-49	50-59	60+	All
Yes	76	75	58	60	54	27	63
No	24	26	42	40	46	74	47
Total	100	100	100	100	100	100	100
N	49	253	166	134	72	50	725

Table 10.12 Married women's ownership of saleable jewelry by urban-rural dimension. Percentage

	Gaza			West Bank			Arab Jerusalem
	City	Town	Camps	Town	Village	Camps	
Yes	62	33	62	70	69	(43)	75
No	38	67	38	30	31	(57)	25
Total	100	100	100	100	100	(100)	100
N	91	84	96	139	229	27	58

differences: the differences in jewelry ownership between Gaza town and village residents and other Gaza residents are consistent when controlled for different wealth categories.

Commenting on the overall distribution in table 10.10, it is clear that women are more likely to own property in the form that the society traditionally reserves for them (dowry jewelry and thobe). Simultaneously, the other traditional form of women's property ownership (livestock; usually poultry and rabbits) that was part of women's domestic economy, seems to have dwindled in comparison to the other two. Tools of the trade (capital machinery such as sewing and knitting machine) might be understood as a modern means of domestic production - thus playing the same role that livestock once did in the family economy. Finally, women's ownership of more modern forms of property (banksavings, group savings) as well as of more substantive property (land or house) is also very low.

Women's Informal Support Networks

In any society, individuals have networks of friends, colleagues and relatives who they can rely upon for various types of support: monetary, emotional, physical. These support networks, an important dimension of human existence, take on added importance in contexts where institutions of civil society are underdeveloped. Whereas the state usually takes over the provision of many of these services (daycare, welfare payments, social security, etc...) in welfare states, in many third world contexts, the family or larger kinship networks continue to provide these numerous forms of support. The West Bank, Gaza and, to a lesser degree, Arab Jerusalem, seem to represent some transitional form between these two extremes.

The FAFO questionnaire only dealt with monetary support networks, since other forms of support are more difficult to quantify. Sources of monetary support for men were treated in the debt and loans section; for women, the issue was treated separately in a series of questions that tried to get women to conceive of themselves as needing money on an individual basis rather than as part of the family. The questionnaire posed various sources of support grouped conceptually in growing concentric circles - beginning with husbands, then in-house relatives, followed by relatives living outside of the house, and finally, non-relatives. The resultant data suggests that this conceptual organization fits a real pattern that exists in the society; women's ability to get monetary support increasingly diminishes the further they get away from the household. While this might seem to suggest the persistence of kinship ties as economically significant, the data also shows that it is the degree of relatedness which is most important; for instance, women can depend much more on husbands than on other kin.

The ultimate importance of these questions lies in their ability to show the degree to which women are reliant on the family for economic support rather than on their own income or networks of colleagues, friends or institutions.

A full 85% of married women claim they can get money from their husbands if they are in need of money as individuals. The degree to which women cite husbands as the prime source of economic support may suggest that not only does the nuclear family have much greater economic significance than the extended family, but that, perhaps more negatively, women see themselves as extremely dependent on the spouse for economic support. This is a relationship that cuts across socio-economic, age and educational levels, and does not vary significantly between the various urban and rural categories. For age, a slight decrease in the ability of wives to get financial help from their husbands can be seen as women get older; the range being 90% of 30 to 39 year old, compared to 76% of 50 to 59 year old, and only 57% of married women over 60. Because of age differentials between women and their spouses, older women are perhaps either taking a more active role in the family's finances; or their economic dependence becomes transferred onto their sons who often replace the former role of their father as head of household.

Little variation exists among women in the different wealth categories, although only 80% of women in the poorest economic category claim they can get economic help from their husbands, compared to 85% and 90% of mid-range and high range respectively.

The issue of married women depending almost solely on their spouse is strengthened when asked about their ability to get financial support from in-house relatives (table 10.13); only 36% of married women claim they can get economic support from relatives within the household. Alternately, since most married women are able to get economic help from their husbands, the ability to get money from the father and other in-house relatives becomes more important for unmarried women; 85% of whom claim to be able to acquire financial support within the household. This difference between unmarried and married women's ability to get in-house support is logically due to the high numbers of young married women, living alone with husbands, who do not have children old enough to constitute a source of financial support. Wealth status differences seem to have little influence on women's ability to get support from in-house relatives.

Table 10.13 Can you get economic help from in-house relatives? By marital status. Percentage

	Unmarried	Married	Other9	All
Yes	85	36	44	52
No	15	64	66	48
Total	100	100	100	100
N	376	725	118	1218

Irrespective of marital status, women have much less ability to get financial support from relatives outside of the household (table 10.14). A mere 20% of all women claim to be able to get economic assistance from relatives outside of the household. This perhaps expresses the breakdown of wider extended family structures. Married women's ability to get help appears to be slightly higher (22%) than for unmarried women's (15%), since the former potentially have either parents, brothers or sons living outside the household, while the latter would only have brothers living outside the household who could be depended upon financially. This ability seems to have no relationship to wealth. The low numbers of women able to count on support from relatives outside the immediate household may also be due to women's lack of mobility.

Table 10.14 Can you get economic help from relatives outside house? By marital status. Percentage

	Unmarried	Married	Other10	All
Yes	15	22	25	20
No	85	78	75	80
Total	100	100	100	100
N	376	725	118	1218

While the wider extended family support networks seem to have weakened, non-kin relationships do not seem to have replaced them (table 10.15). Only 18% of women claim to be able to get support from friends.

In conclusion, it seems that married women have a relatively higher ability to get economic support than unmarried women do; and they also have a wider variety of sources of support than unmarried women.

Table 10.15 Can you get economic help from a friend? By marital status. Percentage

	Unmarried	Married	Other11	All
Yes	14	19	21	18
No	86	81	79	82
Total	100	100	100	100
N	376	725	118	1218

More important perhaps, is the nature of the support networks themselves: women regardless of age, wealth and status differences almost consistently cite family members living in the household as not only the most important sources of support, but as almost their only sources of support.

Freedom of Movement

What are the constraints on women's ability to move freely in the West Bank and Gaza Strip? The immediate assumption deriving from the academic literature on Middle Eastern women might suggest that 'traditional' cultural norms of 'public' and 'private' space are the main determinants of women's freedom of movement. While this 'privatization' may have been a norm for upper class women during the Ottoman period, few other classes of women during that period had this luxury, since they were needed for family labour in agricultural and other production. While it could be argued that, historically, peasant women were 'privatized' in their villages, in fact the mobility of all sectors of the population was highly circumscribed before the advent of modern transportation systems. What does seem to have been a constraint on women's movement was the notion of 'mixing' - i.e. women should not be alone with non-family males. This has historically been the main problem with mixed schooling in the local context. The problem of 'mixing' to a large extent disappeared with women's entry into universities, the work place, and political activism - either need or changing notions of what was prestigious for women overrode fears of potential for scandal.

In recent years Islamicist groups have spearheaded a reversal of this trend. Although these ideas had been promoted since the 1970s, they only began to find resonance among the population in the context of the latter years of the intifada, when fears for women's security became generalized because of army violence and rumors of collaborators' and security services' sexual entrapment of women.

While these social and cultural factors are important when analyzing women's ability to move freely, there are also important practical and political considerations, specific to the Palestinian context, which must be taken into account. Freedom of movement is severely constrained on a daily legalized basis for the whole population living in the West Bank and Gaza. In Gaza people are restricted to their homes every evening at 9:00 p.m. curfew. Women experience in the same way that men do severe restrictions on their ability to move within, between and outside of their communities. Thus, in analyzing women's perceptions of their freedom of movement, this context of an overall real denial of this right to the whole population must be taken into account.

Besides cultural and political factors, relative perceptions are also important when analyzing women's freedom of movement. For certain women 'freedom of movement' may mean simply the fact that they can visit their neighbours in the neighbourhood, for others, lack of freedom may mean they are unable (for a variety of reasons) to travel overseas.

In the survey, women have been asked two series of direct questions about their ability to move. The first part is about their ability to move in general and at will. Women answering no to this first question, are subsequently asked about their ability to go to more specified destinations (other town, overseas, etc.) and whether this ability is contingent on being escorted or not.

Table 10.16 presents women's ability to move freely by age.

While 50% of all women claim they are free to move at will, table 10.16 makes clear that there is a very strong relationship between age and women's perceived or real ability to move freely; with young women aged 15 to 19 feeling dramatically constrained in their movement, and women in the oldest age groups feeling an almost opposite degree of personal mobility. While the reasons for this may simply be understood as cultural (i.e. post-menopausal women are considered beyond the age of sexual activity), it must also be understood that teenagers in any context are supervised in their movement and schedule by parents.

The majority of women claiming they were free to move at will are married or formerly married women (table 10.17); 54% of married women and 90% of widows compared to only 32% of unmarried women. Again, this is very likely related to age factors (with the majority of unmarried women being in the 15 to 19 age category).

Table 10.16 Are you free to move at will. By age. Percentage.

	Age						All
	15-19	20-29	30-39	40-49	50-59	60+	
Yes	22	42	59	65	77	76	50
No	78	58	41	35	23	24	50
Total	100	100	100	100	100	100	100
N	258	364	219	155	94	128	1218

Table 10.18 shows perceptions of personal freedom of movement by marital status and area of the country.

Overall, women in Gaza feel significantly less free to move than their West Bank or Jerusalem counterparts. While this may partly be due to the assumed social and cultural importance of some Islamicist groups in Gaza, it probably also expresses a general sense of restriction felt by all Gazans in their movement due to both the nightly curfew and their inability to move in and out of the Strip without requisite passes. In all three areas, unmarried women constitute the marital status group feeling least free to move, with unmarried women in Gaza exhibiting a much greater sense of restriction. For all three groups there is a significant increase in actual or perceived mobility among married women, with more than twice as many married Gazan women than single women claiming they are free to move. In fact, there are no significant differences between married women in Gaza and the West Bank, while unmarried women in Gaza feel significantly more restricted than unmarried women in the West Bank.

Table 10.19 illustrates perceived freedom of movement of women 20 years and older by urban-rural residence in the three areas.

Camp women in Gaza above the age of 19 claim to be free to move to a much greater degree than Gaza village, town or City women. In the West Bank there are no significant differences between town, village and camp residents.

Table 10.17 Are you free to move at will. By marital status. Percentage

	Unmarried	Married	Other12	All
Yes	32	54	87	50
No	68	47	13	50
Total	100	101	100	100
N	376	725	118	1218

Table 10.18 Percentage of women who feel free to move at will. By marital status and area.

	Gaza	West Bank	Arab Jerusalem
Unmarried	19 (n=117)	37 (n=230)	(44) (n= 39)
Married13	54 (n=307)	61 (n=457)	66 (n= 68)
All women	44 (n=424)	53 (n=687)	57 (n=107)

Table 10.19 Are you free to move at will. By urban-rural dimension. Women age 20 years or more. Percentage

	Gaza			West Bank			
	City	Town/ Villlage	Camps	Town	Village	Camps	Arab Jerusalem
Yes	47	45	70	62	57	54	67
No	53	55	30	38	43	46	33
Total	100	100	100	100	100	100	100
N	105	100	108	179	332	52	84

Another interesting point in this connection is that only 71% of women working outside the home feel free to move - this implies that almost 30% of women who travel daily between their home and work place feel restricted in their movement.

Table 10.20 Are you free to move at will. By dress forms. Percentage

	Thobe	Strict Islamic	Semi Islamic	Modern
Yes	63	45	34	65
No	37	55	66	35
Total	100	100	100	100
N	322	497	245	127

Table 10.20 presents perceptions of freedom of movement by forms of dress. Here again the issue of perception seems to arise. Women wearing 'modern dress' (no headscarf) feel least restricted in their movement, while women wearing 'modified Islamic' feel most restricted. These are women who would have been wearing modern forms of dress a few years ago. Their response might be interpreted as an indication of a larger feeling of coercion at work in their lives. However, there is also an effect of age and marital status. Young unmarried women are more likely to wear 'modified Islamic' than married women are, and this is the age group which feels the least free to move at will.

Of the 50% of women who claimed they are not free to move at will, table 10.21 describes their ability to go to various destinations and their dependence on being escorted or not.

When breaking the above table down by marital status, a fairly regular pattern arises; married and unmarried women are almost equally unable to go any place, but unmarried women are less able to go to the various destinations alone. This pattern remains regular with respect to going to the market, the doctor and in-town relatives. However, unmarried women's ability to go to more distant destinations (relatives out of town or abroad), alone or escorted, is somewhat more restricted than that of married women. Still, if one excludes women under the age of 20, the differences between married and

Table 10.21 Are you free to go to the following destinations? N=608. Percentage

	Cannot go	Can go escorted	Can go alone	Total
Market	11	56	33	100
Doctor	-	80	20	100
Relatives in town	2	56	42	100
Relatives outside town	17	78	5	100
Abroad	32	63	5	100

unmarried women are significantly reduced. Women between the ages of 15 and 19 form the group which is most restricted in their movement to all destinations.

In conclusion, younger and unmarried women have a greater sense of restriction of movement than older and married women. While this relationship cuts across socio-economic, regional and educational levels, there is evidence that overall, women in Gaza (with some variation) feel more restricted than their West Bank counterparts.

Attitudes Towards Women's Appropriate Work Roles

According to the analysis in chapter 7 on women in the labour force, one tenth of the women surveyed claim to work outside the home, while little over another tenth claim to do some type of income generating work within the home. Thus, not only is women's overall formal labour force participation low, but so is their involvement in home-based income generating activities. While chapter 9 analyzes the difference of opinion that exists between men and women towards women's roles in Palestinian society, this section attempts to look at attitudes among women towards the very important issue of women's right to participate in the labour force.

As has become apparent in other areas of analysis in this chapter, the larger context of political and economic structures and processes delimit the boundaries of action and experience in the occupied territories. Simultaneously, for women, their ability to make decisions and to act within this context tend to be mediated by the social factors of especially age and marital status.

Thus, when analyzing women's attitudes towards a wide variety of social and political issues, it is time and diversity of life experience that most clearly seems to shape women's vision of themselves.

Tables 10.22 – 10.25 depict women's perceptions of the appropriate working roles for women and other work-related issues by age.

In looking at the totals for the four questions raised, it is clear that a great majority of women (77%) support the general right or appropriateness of women to work outside the home. But what seems to be more important is the actual type of work; while only 53% of women support the idea of women working in business, 86% would like their daughters to hold a professional job. This apparent ambivalence towards women working in business is probably rooted in its association with the tradition of indigenous mercantilism which has historically been viewed as a male domain.

The contradictory nature of women's feelings towards their primary identity (wife and mother versus working women) becomes

Table 10.22 Is it acceptable for women to work outside the house? By age. Percentage

	15-19	20-29	30-39	40-49	50-59	60+	All
Yes	71	87	66	78	77	76	77
No	28	12	31	21	21	18	21
Do not know	1	1	3	1	2	6	2
Total	100	100	100	100	100	100	100
N	258	364	219	155	94	128	1218

Table 10.23 Is it acceptable for women to run a business? By age. Percentage

	15-19	20-29	30-39	40-49	50-59	60+	All
Yes	50	62	48	54	52	43	53
No	50	36	50	45	46	45	44
Do not know	0	2	2	1	2	12	3
Total	100	100	100	100	100	100	100
N	258	364	219	155	94	128	1218

Table 10.24 Would you like your daughter to work in a professional job[14]? By age. Percentage

	15-19	20-29	30-39	40-49	50-59	60+	All
Yes	82	91	84	88	85	78	86
No	9	7	12	11	15	8	10
Do not know	9	2	4	1	1	13	5
Total	100	100	100	100	101	101	101
N	229	350	208	154	92	121	1154

Table 10.25 Is it acceptable for women to put their children in daycare? By age. Percentage

	15-19	20-29	30-39	40-49	50-59	60+	All
Yes	46	59	58	64	67	60	57
No	52	39	41	31	31	31	40
Do not know	2	2	1	5	2	10	3
Total	100	100	100	100	100	100	100
N	258	364	219	155	94	128	1218

most clear when looking at their responses to the issues of daycare. Out of all the issues raised, women's right to put their children in daycare (a prerequisite for many women to work) is supported by 57% of all women. When broken down by marital status it becomes clear that married women (63%) are more supportive of this right than unmarried women (46%); and women with children are much more supportive (62%) than women without children (20%). Thus, when daycare is an actual need rather than an abstract idea, women are much less reticent about it.

In general, when looking at attitudes across age categories, the usual assumption is that the older individuals are, the more 'conservative' they are on social issues. This is especially true when dealing with the issue of women and work in the Middle East, which usually assumes that a 'traditional' ideology about women's privatization and modesty slowly became superseded by 'modern' ideologies about women's right to education and work - suggesting that younger women tend to be 'modern' while older women are 'traditional'. However, the above tables make clear that such a conceptualization is too simplistic. On both the issues of the acceptability of women working outside the home and putting their children in daycare, women in the oldest age category seem more 'modern' than women in their teens. Women in the 60+ age category display dispositions similar to those of women in their forties and fifties.

Perhaps the most interesting comparison is the regular difference in attitudes between the age groups 15 to 19 and 20 to 29. On every issue, the youngest age group of women is consistently more conservative than women in their twenties. The important point lies not so much in the degree of difference on the attitudes between these first two age groups, but in the regularity of the differences. This suggests that there might be a larger set of interrelated ideas about women's correct role in society that has had an impact on the young women who came of age during the past few years of the intifada. Stated more directly, the data seems to vindicate observations that there has been a general social retrenchment during the intifada, with women in their teens being most affected by new conservative ideologies.

Tables 10.26 and 10.27 provide an estimate of two of these attitudes, according to age and region.

When comparing age categories and women in West Bank and Gaza respectively, the two points which stand out are: in Gaza, the strong difference between teenagers and women in their twenties;

and, in the West Bank, the strong difference between women in their twenties and thirties.

In the West Bank educational achievement explains some of the difference between these two age categories, with women in their twenties being substantially better educated than women in their thirties. Even when controlled for education, a higher percentage of West Bank women in their twenties find it acceptable that married women work outside the house.

Overall, there are no differences between women living in Gaza and the West Bank when it comes to the question of daycare.

Daycare centers on a large and affordable level (run by women's committees and charitable societies) have only come into general usage over the past 15 years in the occupied territories. Thus, their usage and acceptance would be expected to be greater among women in the first three age groups, who would have had children of preschool ages during this same period. While in Gaza, women in these younger age groups are somewhat more supportive, in the West Bank there is a surprisingly higher support among women in the upper age categories. In both regions, women in the teen years are the least supportive of daycare.

In conclusion, in both West Bank and especially in Gaza, there is evidence that women in their teen years are more conservative than are women in their twenties towards the range of issues pertaining to

Table 10.26 Percentage who answers "yes" to the question: Is it acceptable for women to work outside the house? By age and region.

	15-19	20-29	30-39	40-49	50-59	60+	All
Gaza	64	84	74	78	(71)	75	74
N	111	108	84	55	24	42	424
West Bank	76	87	58	78	80	75	77
N	124	222	116	88	59	79	687

Table 10.27 Percentage who answers "yes" to the question: Is it acceptable for women to put their children in daycare? By age and region

	15-19	20-29	30-39	40-49	50-59	60+	All
Gaza	45	65	70	63	(58)	52	59
N	111	108	84	55	24	42	424
West Bank	50	58	52	65	71	64	58
N	124	222	116	88	59	79	687

women's appropriate working role in society. Despite this, the majority of women support the notion of women working outside the home, but their support increases when the type of work specified is 'respectable', i.e. professional work.

Conclusions

This chapter has addressed only a small part of the data on Palestinian women generated by the FAFO survey. Nevertheless, a few overall conclusions may tentatively be drawn from some of the issues treated.

The issues covered provide different types of clues for building an overall picture of women's living conditions in the occupied territories. On the one hand, there are various economic indicators that suggest the degree of women's access to and control over economic resources. There are also women's assessments of their economic roles. On the other hand, there is a range of indicators of the various social dimensions of women's lives: marriage as a mechanism of empowerment and/or constraint, and the differing degrees of social regulation of women based on age and marital status. There are also women's assessments of the various social constraints and values assigned to them by the larger social context.

In terms of the economic indicators, it is quite clear that women have relatively few independent economic resources. Further, their access to such resources is overwhelmingly tied to the mechanism of marriage. In light of the low participation of women in the labour force, the overall economic picture for women is bleak if analyzed as separate from spouses or families. What this means is that women's standard of living seems largely to be determined by either the spouse or the family - they are, in other words, overwhelmingly economic dependents. However, because divorce is very uncommon, this dependence is mitigated by the apparent strong social rejection of divorce. Thus, despite economic dependence, there is a strong degree of security for women within the structure of marriage, based on social taboos against divorce. However, this overall structure means that women rarely have the financial independence that allows for independence in decision making.

The data suggests that women on the whole do not have a radical critique of this connection of marriage and economic resources, but would like a certain degree of change. Women would like to get married later (perhaps so as to finish various levels of higher education), and would also like greater access for women to particular, professional work. In other words, they would like more access to some of the resources (higher education and professional work) that would empower them within the context of marriage.

On the social level, it is apparent that there is a range of constraints on women's lives. Although there has been an overall steady growth in women's age at marriage, women would still prefer to marry at ages later than what seems to be the current social norm. The vast majority of women do not find their own marriage ages acceptable, but would prefer their daughters to marry at ages substantially higher than the current mean. Simultaneously, the majority of women feel constrained in their ability to move freely in their community. It is clear that young unmarried women are the most constrained in their mobility.

While there is a lot of unity in the overall social and economic dimensions of women's lives, factors such as age, regional residence, education and marital status show that there are often differences in how these dimensions are experienced and assessed. Perhaps the greatest differences between women's experiences and perceptions seem to be a product of age difference. In general, older women (post menopause) are allowed more social freedom than are younger (especially teenaged women) and, perhaps as a consequence, older women are more free to criticise the present and desirous of change when compared to women in their thirties and forties. Women in the youngest age categories seem to have suffered the most serious social constraints. This young age group seems to have a generally more conservative stance to a range of issues related to women's freedom and choice. Women in their twenties have had relatively better access to education and relatively less experience of social constraints than any other age group of women. They seem to make up the age group with the most liberal social views towards the range of women's issues addressed.

Married women fare better in terms of independent economic resources, and in their ability to be mobile, than unmarried women of all ages.

There is no systematic evidence that women living in urban environments enjoy higher degrees of social freedom or access to resources than women living in rural or camp environments. The data suggests, however, that while women living in Arab Jerusalem and West Bank towns may fare better, in Gaza women living in Gaza City and other Gaza towns tend to fare worse, especially on the social indicators, than their counterparts living in camps.

Notes

1 Manasrah, Najah. *Early Marriage: Temporary Retreat in the March of Palestinian Women*. Al Kateb Journal. August 1989, pp. 24-31.

2 This definition of the median age at first marriage is unusual in that it considers the median age for the *total* birth cohort, and not only women who marry. The reason for this is, as mentioned below, that we for "young" cohorts do not know the number of women cohort who will not marry at all.

3 The median age has been calculated by linear interpolation, assuming that marriages are evenly distributed over the year. This implies, for example, that women who said they were 19 when they married, on average were 19.5 years old as measured by exact age.

4 The table does not present any estimates for Arab Jerusalem due to the low number of respondents in this group.

5 Half of the women are not married yet.

6 Moors, Annaleis. *Countrywomen in the West Bank: A Study of the Gender and Economic Division of Labor*. Afaq Filastiniyya (Summer 1990), pp. 130-145.

7 Hamdan, Nadia. *Women and Inheritance in a West Bank Village: the Case of Beit Furik*. Unpublished Research Paper Women's Affairs Research Center, Nablus (June 1991).

8 Due to the low number of respondents, the results for West Bank camp residents are left uncommented.

9 'Other' includes divorced, widowed, and separated women, as well as women whose husbands are working abroad.

10 See endnote 9.

11 See endnote 9.

12 See endnote 9.

13 In this table "married" includes divorced, widowed, and separated women, as well as women whose husbands are working abroad.

14 Those who answer "not applicable" are excluded from the table.

Appendix A
Sampling Strategy

Steinar Tamsfoss

1 Introduction

The purpose of this paper is to describe the principal guidelines for sample selection in the FAFO International survey on living conditions in the Gaza Strip, West Bank and Arab Jerusalem. The account is both textual and mathematical. The intention is to document sample design(s) and estimators in fairly general terms. Details as to the outcome of numerical calculations or of random selections involved are – with a few exceptions – not included.

As a matter of course, sample designing to a large extent relies on what kind of information about the survey population is actually available at the time of planning. Existing information can be utilized both for improving the sample design in terms of statistical reliability and for reducing field work costs. Except for the Gaza Strip, the only relevant information available was population numbers for subdistricts and localities. The corresponding figures for Gaza proved to be too outdated and unreliable for our purposes, implying a separate strategy had to be designed for Gaza. However, as preparations proceeded we became aware of unpublished population data for Gaza Strip localities, which was of great benefit in the final stages of the design.

The total sample size is, in accordance with the survey budget, approximately 2,500 units. It should be kept in mind that the survey in fact comprises three separate surveys – each using a specific questionnaire:

1. A survey of households
2. A survey of individuals of age 15 years or older
3. A survey of females of age 15 years or older

Ideally, one might have designed separate sampling strategies for each of the surveys. On practical grounds, not least the high costs that

313

would be involved, this was considered unrealistic. Moreover, the additional advantages that could be expected were clearly marginal from the point of view of representativity. A combined design for all three surveys was chosen, adopting the following conceptual approach:

1. Selection of a sample of 2,500 households.
2. Selection of a sample of individuals by random subsampling of one individual from each of the 2,500 households included in sample 1.
3. All women in sample 2 were to comprise the female sample 3, the expected sample size of which would be approximately 1,250.

According to Benvenisti[1], the Arab population totals for individuals of all ages for the three areas are shown in table A.1.

Although these figures are estimates for the 1987 populations, and not very reliable ones at that, they should be able to give an indication of the relative distribution of the "permanent" population (including residents abroad for less than a year). No census has been taken in the occupied territories since 1967, and all population statistics are estimates. According to Benvenisti, an Israeli Central Bureau of Statistics estimate of the West Bank population amounted to 858,000 as of December 31, 1987. The Interior Ministry figure for the West Bank as of November 1987 was 1,252,000. A critical discussion of the three sets of figures are found in the cited Benvenisti publication. When comparing with other Israeli official statistics, no equivalent estimates are found. However, for the adult population the estimates in table A.2 can be extracted from these.[2,3]

Obviously, it is difficult to compare the absolute magnitude of the two sets of population figures as the latter one is logically as well as numerically a subset of the former. Assuming that the proportions of adults within each area are about the same in the three areas, it is seen that the relative proportions in the tables above are not very different. For the purpose of the present survey – aiming at providing relative distributions rather than absolute numbers – the

Table A.1 Estimates of the permanent population (non-Jewish) in the Gaza Strip, West Bank and Arab Jerusalem

Region	Individuals	Percent
Gaza Strip	633.000	35
West Bank	1.067.000	58
Arab Jerusalem	136.000	7
Total	1,836.000	100

Table A.2 Estimates of the adult non-Jewish population in the Gaza Strip, West Bank and Jerusalem

Region	Individuals	Percent
Gaza Strip (15+ years, 1987)	283,000	34
West Bank (15+ years, 1987)	456,000	56
Jerusalem (All Jerusalem, non-Jews, 15+ years, 1988)	83,000	10
Total	822,000	100

accuracy of the Benvenisti proportions is assumed to be fairly satisfactory, taking into account that estimates of relative distributions are more robust against distortions of the population proportions than are estimates of absolute magnitudes. The particular issue of "illegal" immigration to Arab Jerusalem (Palestinians living without proper permits) may serve as an illustration of some of the problems involved in evaluating the reliability of the various population estimates. According to official figures compiled by the Israeli security services, illegal immigration amounts to 10,000[4]. Another estimate (probably originating from the Interior Ministry) was conveyed by Jerusalem City Councilman Shmuel Meir in an interview[5]: "Some 100,000 Arabs from Judea and Samaria have moved to East Jerusalem since 1967, many illegally". A third estimate, reported by the Jerusalem Post the same winter, stated that "nearly 2,000 illegally built homes were discovered in East Jerusalem in a recent Interior Ministry survey which also showed tens of thousands of Arabs from the territories were living illegally in the capital."

The evaluation problem does not merely lie in the difficulties in assessing which estimate is the most accurate one, but also in the uncertainty with regard to whether the illegal residents are included in the estimates or not. However confusing this unclear state of statistics may be, it should be made clear that this survey comprises the *present* population in the three areas – illegal residents included.

One of the inherent survey objectives has been to analyze data for the three regions separately. For such analyses to be reliable a certain minimum number of observations has to be collected in each of the regions. For surveys comprising a wide range of variables a proportionate regional sample allocation is normally recommended as a compromise yielding fairly reliable all-over estimates. However, for Arab Jerusalem a proportionate allocation would imply a sample size of only 175 observations (approximately 90 females), which is too small to support the reliability standards required. These standards were set to the equivalence of 500 (female sample 250) as the minimum number of observations for one single area. This measure obviously implied that the regional sample allocation would have to be disproportionate, and that considerations of optimality would make little sense. The regional sample allocation finally arrived at is shown in table A.3.

The sample designs for each of the regions are described in detail in the subsequent sections. A general, self-explanatory overview of the various sampling stages and the corresponding sampling units involved at each stage, is shown in Figure A.1.

The question of inclusion probabilities also needs to be considered (inclusion probability is the probability of an arbitrary unit of the population being included in the sample). As will be seen, inclusion probabilities for the various sampling units involved differ for more reasons than the fact that the regional sample allocation would have to vary. One major implication of variations in inclusion probabilities is that proper weights must be assigned to each of the observations in order to achieve unbiased survey results. In most cases the inversed inclusion probabilities or variates derived from these are chosen as the individual weights. Estimators (computational methods) are discussed in a separate section.

Table A.3 Regional sample allocation.

Region	Households	Individuals	Females	Percent
Gaza Strip	960	960	480	38
West Bank	1,040	1,040	520	42
Arab Jerusalem	500	500	250	20
Total	2,500	2,500	1,250	100

Figure A.1 Overview of the Sampling Stages and the corresponding Sampling Units at each Stage

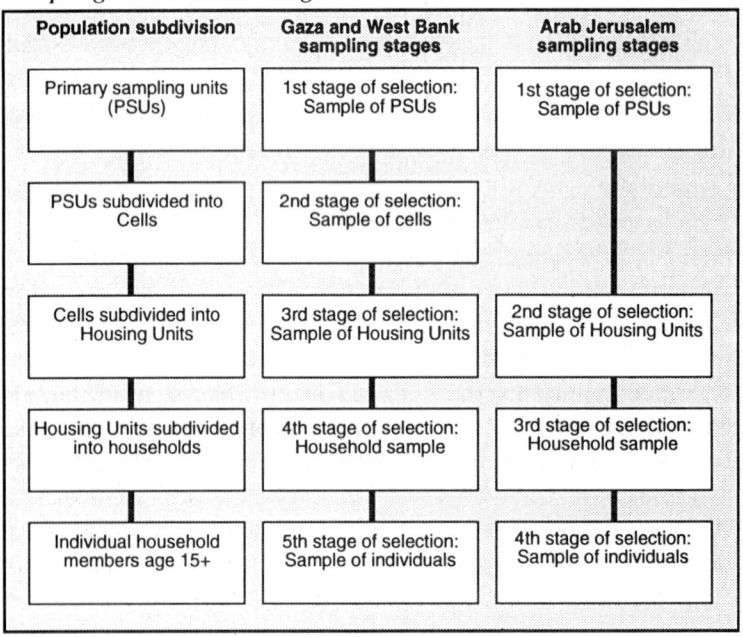

Population subdivision	Gaza and West Bank sampling stages	Arab Jerusalem sampling stages
Primary sampling units (PSUs)	1st stage of selection: Sample of PSUs	1st stage of selection: Sample of PSUs
PSUs subdivided into Cells	2nd stage of selection: Sample of cells	
Cells subdivided into Housing Units	3rd stage of selection: Sample of Housing Units	2nd stage of selection: Sample of Housing Units
Housing Units subdivided into households	4th stage of selection: Household sample	3rd stage of selection: Household sample
Individual household members age 15+	5th stage of selection: Sample of individuals	4th stage of selection: Sample of individuals

2 Gaza Strip Sample Design

The design adopted has been a stratified, 4-5 stages procedure involving simple random sampling at each stage. Information about the survey population was initially quite scarce. It seemed that the reliable, basic statistics necessary for proper sampling would have to be produced during the process of sampling itself. Fortunately, by the conclusion of the planning process some of the information most needed for sample allocation, emerged in the form of unpublished material provided by the Gaza statistical office. Thus population figures which otherwise had to be estimated by enumeration of some 100 neighbourhoods, became accessible.

Relevant sampling frames (directory, register of the household population) for selection of households were not available. The final stages of the sampling procedure therefore were carried out through "on-the-spot sampling", involving map preparations prior to the data collection stage.

Sampling Details

The complete sample design comprises the following steps:

1 Definition/construction of Primary Sampling Units (PSUs). The PSUs are areas or localities which are easily identified on maps. In most cases a PSU coincides with the administrative concept of a "locality", for which more detailed maps were available.

2 The PSUs were stratified by type of locality (see table A.4). Strata are labeled **s** ($= 1,...,8$), and PSUs are labeled **k** ($= 1,2,...$). The total number of PSUs in stratum s is denoted **K(s)**. We will use the notation "PSU (s,k)" to denote the k'th PSU of the s'th stratum.

3 A 1st stage sample of PSUs to be surveyed were selected by simple random sampling within each stratum. The sample number of PSUs in stratum s is denoted **k(s)**. The 1st stage sampling fraction for the s'th stratum is

$$(2.1) \quad P_1(s, k) = \frac{k(s)}{K(s)}$$

which in this case (simple random sampling) is the inclusion probability of PSU (s,k) as well. (2.1) implies that all PSUs of the same stratum have an equal chance of being included in the sample.

It may be seen from table A.4 that stratum 8, "Outside localities", was not included in the sample. The character of these areas is somewhat different from that of other localities, as there is no municipal authority. On strict scientific grounds it could be argued that this particular feature might require separate investigation in the present survey. However, the estimated size of the population in these areas amounts to just 1% of the Gaza Strip total, i.e. approximately 10 sample observations. Furthermore, inclusion of the areas in the sample would require special measures as to the sample design, and field work costs would be significantly higher than elsewhere. Thus, exclusion of these few observations from the sample would have negligible impact on aggregate survey results, while making practical sense.

Table A.4 Stratification of primary sampling units (PSUs), 1st stage sample. Gaza Strip

Stratum		Number of PSUs	
No.	Type of locality	Population	Sample
s		K(s)	k(s)
1	Gaza City EAST	3	2
2	Gaza City WEST	3	1
3	Towns	4	2
4	Northern Camps	2	1
5	Middle Camps	4	1
6	Southern Camps	2	1
7	Villages	9	3
8	Outside localities	1	0
	TOTAL	28	11

4 Each of the (sample) PSUs were subdivided into *cells* by using maps provided by the local statistical office. For the 2nd stage selection of cells within each of the sample PSUs, simple random sampling was applied.

Denote by **B(s,k)** the total number of population cells within PSU (s,k), and by **b(s,k)** the number of cells included in the sample. Thus, the 2nd stage sampling fraction (conditional inclusion probability) for the cells (labeled **c**) of PSU (s,k) is:

$$(2.2) \quad P_2(s, k, c) = \frac{b(s, k)}{B(s,k)}$$

The B(s,k)s were counted by inspection of the maps of the sample PSUs. The inclusion probability is independent of c, i.e. all cells of the same PSU have an equal probability of being selected. The numbers of population and sample cells for each of the PSUs selected at the 1st stage, are shown in table A.5.

5 Due to the absence of satisfactory sampling frames for the cells, households to be visited for the purpose of interview(s) had to be selected in the field. We denote the total number of households of the cell **D(s,k,c)**, and the number to be included in the sample **d(s,k,c)**. Rough estimates of the (sample) D(s,k,c)s were provided by the Gaza statistical office.

However, prior to the selection of households an additional sampling stage had to be imputed by the sampling of *housing units*. A "housing unit" is a set of one or more households sharing a common *main entrance* (front door) of a building or compound. In cases where there were several main entrances, presumably leading to different groups of households, each would be regarded as a separate housing unit.

During the process of sample preparations a procedure for direct selection of sample households was considered. However, inspection of some cells showed that such a procedure would generally be very difficult to implement, due to complex housing structures, inadequate detailing and updating of maps, non-display of road names and house numbers, absence of doorbells or other hints to help identify pre-selected households. As opposed to the problems of enumerating households, housing units (front doors) proved to be more easily identifiable even in complex areas.

For each sample cell an enumeration system was developed for identifying and selecting housing units. Briefly stated, it included random selection of spots defining the starting points from which uniquely specified "enumeration walks" (instructions for the directions of the walk and how to count housing units) were to be initiated. During these walks every 3rd housing unit was to be selected until a full subsample was obtained. For each "enumeration walk" 4-6 housing units were normally selected. To help the data collectors identify sample housing units, the field work supervisors were thoroughly instructed – theoretically as well as through training in the field – in the selection of housing units and preparation of map sketches of every "enumeration walk".

In order to ease the practical identification, the starting points normally were designated at corners of road crossings within the cells.

Denote by **H(s,k,c)** the total number of *housing units* within cell (s,k,c) – a number which was not available prior to the field work. As mentioned previously, estimates of the total number of *households* within the sample cells, D(s,k,c), were available, providing an opportunity to estimate H(s,k,c) upon completion of the field work.

The number of households included in housing unit (s,k,c,h) is denoted **D(s,k,c,h)**. The average number of households per housing unit of cell (s,k,c) can be estimated from the sample data:

(2.3) $\overline{D}(s, k, c, .) = \frac{1}{d(s, k, c)} \sum_{h=1}^{d(s, k, c)} D(s, k, c, h)$

An estimate for the total number of cell housing units is thus:

(2.4) $\hat{H}(s, k, c) = \frac{D(s, k, c)}{\overline{D}(s, k, c, .)}$

Multi-household housing units frequently, though not always, comprise households which are closely linked through family ties, and are thus likely to be more homogeneous than are households from different housing units. Therefore, selecting more than one household from the same housing unit can be seen as a waste of resources as observations may be highly correlated. The selection of one household per sample housing unit implies more housing units – mutually less homogeneous – to be included in the sample, which may cause smaller sampling error.

When selecting just one household from each unit, the number of housing units to be selected of course equals the number of households – i.e. d(s,k,c). Thus, the sampling fractions for the two stages involved are:

Housing units (3rd stage):

$$(2.5) \quad P_3(s, k, c, h) = \frac{d(s, k, c)}{H(s, k, c)}$$

Households (4th stage):

$$(2.6) \quad P_4(s, k, c, h, d) = \frac{1}{D(s, k, c, h)}$$

A special form carrying random numbers was prepared for the selection of one household from a housing unit. The form used comprised separate columns for every relevant total number of households within a housing unit (column headings). Each column thus contained a sequence of random numbers less than or equal to the total in the heading. Each random number was to be used only once, and the questionnaire number entered into the form adjacent to the number used in each particular case for control reasons.

Before selecting a household, all households of the housing unit were enumerated. Standard rules for enumeration were:
* Enumeration should start from the top floor or top level and proceed downwards.
* Households on the same floor/level should be enumerated in clockwise order, starting at the spot of entrance.

6 The respondent to the main questionnaire was to be the Head of Household. In case the Head of Household was not available for interview, he/she might be substituted by another household member likely to provide the same questionnaire information as the Head of Household.

7 Sample of Individuals and Females

The gender of the RSI was decided prior to the field work. By doing this, one could allocate more efficiently female enumerators to interview women, which was considered paramount in order to ensure trust and confidentiality. For the same reason, enumerators worked in pairs of the same sex.

The sample of individuals ("Randomly Selected Individual's (RSI) questionnaire") as well as the sample of women ("Women's questionnaire") to be interviewed were both derived from the sample of households.

The following procedure was adopted, based on the premise that the proportion of women among the Gaza population of age 15 years or older is close to 50%.

a After the household (main) sample had been selected, a subsample of size 50% was drawn from the main sample. The subsample was selected separately for each of the cells by simple random sampling. (If the number of cell interviews was uneven, the "majority sex" of each cell was altered successively so that the accumulated sex proportions for all cells approximated the correct ones). Thus there were *two* subsamples – one female and one male. The data collectors had particular instructions for deciding who was to interview the various types of respondents.

b The members (15+) of each sex were to be enumerated for each sample household, and the numbers, denoted **W(s,k,c,h,d)** for females and **M(s,k,c,h,d)** for males.

c The members (15+) of the pre-decided sex were then listed by descending age.

d One of the individuals thus listed was selected by simple random sampling, applying a random numbers form especially prepared for the random selection of individuals (similar to the household selection form). The 5th stage sampling fractions (selection probability for individual (s,k,c,h,d,i)) are thus:

$$(2.7) \quad P_5(s, k, c, h, d, i) = \begin{cases} \dfrac{0.5}{W(s, k, c, h, d)} & \text{for females} \\ \dfrac{0.5}{M(s, k, c, h, d)} & \text{for males} \end{cases}$$

Sample Allocation

In this section the calculations needed for allocating the Gaza household sample among the various sample units are described. The aggregate overall inclusion probability for an arbitrary *household* (s,k,c,h,d) is obtained by multiplying the various selection probabilities at each of the first four sampling stages:

$$(2.8) \quad P(s, k, c, h, d) = \frac{k(s)}{K(s)} \frac{b(s, k)}{B(s, k)} \frac{d(s, k, c)}{H(s, k, c)} \frac{1}{D(s, k, c, h)}$$

As can be seen on the right hand side of (2.8), this probability is independent of the household index d, implying all households within the same housing unit have equal inclusion probabilities. For the samples of males and females, which are derived directly from the household sample, the probabilities of inclusion are obtained by multiplying the household probabilities by the 5th stage sampling fractions.

In (2.8) the statistics K(s), k(s) and B(s,k) are known. The statistic D(s,k,c,h) is observed from the sample, and H(s,k,c) is estimated from sample data by (2.4). Thus it remains to determine the b(s,k)s and the d(s,k,c)s.

Allocation of Sample of Cells – b(s,k)

The number of cells to be selected from the various sample PSUs, the b(s,k)'s, are determined as follows: The 1st stage sampling fractions, $P_1(s, k)$, are already fixed (Table A.4). The 2nd stage fractions, $P_2(s, k, c)$, are determined so that:

$$(2.9) \quad P_1(s, k) P_2(s, k, c) = \frac{k(s)}{K(s)} \frac{b(s, k)}{B(s, k)} = C1$$

C1 is a constant for all PSU (s,k)s. Formula (2.9) implies the design for sampling of cells be an **epsem** one (equal probability selection method for all strata and PSUs).

On the average per sample cell 10 households were to be selected. Having a total Gaza sample size of 960 households, the number of cells to be selected at the 2nd stage was thus 96, i.e. the sum of the b(s,k)s over all sample PSUs amounts to 96. (Due to numerical approximations the actual calculations implied 97 cells to be selected and the total household sample size to be 964).

The expression (2.9) can be rearranged:

$$(2.10) \quad b(s, k) = C1 \frac{K(s)}{k(s)} B(s, k)$$

Except for the constant C1, all the statistics on the right hand side of (2.10) are known. C1 is determined by taking the sum of all (sample) (s,k) of both sides of (2.10):

$$\sum_s \sum_{k=1}^{k(s)} b(s, k) = C1 \sum_s \frac{K(s)}{k(s)} \sum_{k=1}^{k(s)} B(s, k)$$

On the left hand side the sum is 96, while the sum on the right hand side amounts to C1 multiplied by some (known) factor. Hence, C1 is fixed, and the number of sample cells within each of the sample PSUs, the b(s,k)s, is determined from (2.10) by insertion of the respective numbers.

Allocation of Sample of Housing units and Households -d(s,k,c)

As the cell total number of housing units, H(s,k,c), was unknown at the stage of sample allocation, the housing unit sample size for each of the cells had to be determined indirectly by using the information on the cell total number of *households*, D(s,k,c). Thus a distinction has to be made between the allocation task and the calculation of inclusion probabilities.

In order to determine the number of housing units to be selected from each sample cell, d(s,k,c), we would require the sample size to be *proportionate* to the total number of households, D(s,k,c), i.e.

(2.11) $\quad \dfrac{d(s, k, c)}{D(s, k, c)} = C2$

Here, C2 would be constant. By rearranging (2.11) we would get:

(2.12) $\quad d(s, k, c) = C2 \cdot D(s, k, c)$

Taking the sum of all sample cells (s,k,c) of both sides of (2.12), the left hand side adds up to 960, while the right hand side adds up to some known multiple of C2:

$$\sum_s \sum_{k=1}^{k(s)} \sum_{c=1}^{b(s,k)} d(s, k, c) = C2 \sum_s \sum_{k=1}^{k(s)} \sum_{c=1}^{b(s,k)} D(s, k, c)$$

Thus, C2 is determined, and the cell sample size of households is finally calculated by formula (2.12). This way of allocating is what would have been done if households could be selected directly without the intermediate stage of housing unit selection. In this case the household sample would have been an epsem one. However, the introduction of the housing unit stage makes application of an epsem design for household selection practically impossible.

Table A.5 shows the number of population and sample cells for each of the sample PSUs. The aggregate PSU household sample size, i.e. the sum of sample households over all sample cells within each sample PSU, is also displayed.

Table A.5 Population and sample number of cells, and aggregate household sample size (d(s,k)) for each of the sample PSUs. Gaza Strip

Nos	Name of sample PSU (s,k)	Number of cells Population B (s,k)	Number of cells Sample b (s,k)	PSU household sample size d (s,k)
1	Zaitoun	25	4	29
	Shajaeya	49	9	114
2	Rimal	20	7	44
3	West Khan Yunis	17	4	52
	Rafah Town	31	7	97
4	Shati Camp	73	17	120
5	Bureij Camp	25	12	122
6	Rafah Camp	68	16	154
7	Jabalia Village	40	14	157
	Beit Lahia	11	4	40
	Qararah	8	3	35
	TOTAL	367	97	964

3 West Bank Sample Design

The design for the West Bank is a multistage stratified one. As compared to Gaza, more prior information was available on the West Bank localities, providing opportunities for improving the sample design – at least concerning the practical preparatory work involved. The main features of the design are outlined in the following sections.

Stratification of Primary Sampling Units (PSUs)

The localities as defined by Benvenisti (adjusted for Camp Areas included in other types of localities) are the PSUs. The PSUs were stratified according to *location* (7 sub-districts) and *status* (5 categories, i.e. District Capitals (DC), Other Towns (OT), Developed Villages (DV), Underdeveloped Villages (UV) and Refugee Camps (RC)). The number of strata are thus 32 (3 of the theoretical 35 combinations of sub-district and status are empty). Table A.6 shows estimates of the strata populations:

Table A.6 Population estimates for West Bank strata. (Individuals all ages. Benvenisti/ estimates for 1987. "Permanent" population)

Sub-district	Status				
	DC	OT	DV	UV	RC
Bethlehem	32,800	18,300	23,100	30,000	10,200
Hebron	79,100	44,000	68,600	24,100	8,300
Jenin	16,800	36,000	36,900	56,700	14,600
Jericho	12,500	.	.	4,100	3,400
Nablus	80,800	.	42,600	41,800	26,200
Ramallah	24,800	35,100	25,200	87,100	15,500
Tulkarem	19,600	29,600	67,500	35,800	15,300

Although these estimates may be somewhat inaccurate, they cannot be dispensed with for want of more reliable alternatives. We assume they give a reasonably fair representation of the relative proportions of localities and strata, which for sampling purposes is the most relevant information.

Allocation of Household Sample on Strata

The sample size for the West Bank is 1,040 households (from which both the sample of 1,040 individuals and 520 women also are derived). The allocation of the household sample among strata is proportionate to the estimated population size. The allocation is shown in Table A.7.

Table A.7 Allocation of West Bank household sample on strata (proportionate allocation)

Sub-district	Status					Total
	DC	OT	DV	UV	RC	
Bethlehem	32	18	23	31	9	113
Hebron	77	42	67	24	8	218
Jenin	17	35	35	56	14	157
Jericho	13	.	.	5	4	22
Nablus	78	.	40	42	26	186
Ramallah	23	34	25	85	15	182
Tulkarem	18	29	65	36	14	162
Total	258	158	255	279	90	1,040

Selection of Sample PSUs (1st stage)

Sample PSUs were selected from each stratum with a probability proportionate to population size. In order to determine the 1st stage inclusion probability, we need the following variables (all referring to individuals, Benvenisti estimates):

- $N(s,k)$ = Population total for PSU (s,k)
- $N(s)$ = Population total s-th stratum (table A.6)
- N = Population total (West Bank)

The first stage inclusion probability for PSU (s,k) is approximately:

$$(3.1) \quad P_1(s, k) = \frac{k(s) N(s, k)}{N(s)}$$

in which **k(s)** is the number of PSUs selected from the s-th stratum. In case k(s)=1, the equality above is exact. The approximation occurs for k(s)>1, as 2nd order (and higher) probabilities are assumed negligible. The number of PSUs to be selected, the k(s)'s, has been decided like this in order to avoid situations where the number of sample households of a PSU exceeds the total number of PSU households. Thus, for each stratum both the household sample size, the total number of PSUs and the size of the various PSUs have been considered.

In our design the household, not the single individual, is the ultimate unit of selection. If the average size of households is equal for all PSUs, which is a fairly realistic assumption, (3.1) can be expressed thus:

$$(3.2) \quad P_1(s, k) = \frac{k(s) D(s, k)}{D(s)}$$

in which **D(s,k)** is the total number of *households* in PSU (s,k), and **D(s)** the corresponding total for the s-th stratum.

The number of sample PSUs selected from each of the strata are shown in table A.8. The total number of sample PSUs is 45.

Selection of Cells, Housing Units and Households

As in Gaza, there were no sampling frames available for the selection of households in the West Bank PSUs. Thus it was convenient to introduce two further sampling stages. At the 2nd stage sample PSUs were subdivided into cells, and samples of cells were selected by simple random sampling from the respective PSUs. Housing units were selected at the 3rd stage, and, finally, the samples of households (4th stage) were selected from the sample of housing units. The procedures operate exactly as for Gaza and are thus not repeated. However, the mathematics for sample allocation are not the same. This will be dealt with in the next section.

Inclusion Probabilities

Adopting the same notations as for the Gaza design, the overall inclusion probability for an arbitrary West Bank household (s,k,c,h,d) is:

$$(3.3) \quad P(s, k, c, h,) = \frac{k(s) D(s, k)}{D(s)} \frac{b(s, k)}{B(s, k)} \frac{d(s, k, c)}{H(s, k, c,)} \frac{1}{D(s, k, c, h)}$$

In (3.3) it remains to determine the b(s,k)'s and the d(s,k,c)'s. For the same reasons as for Gaza, it is practically impossible to have an overall epsem design. For the purpose of allocating each stratum sample of households (or housing units) among PSUs, let us temporarily disregard the cell and housing unit stages of selection, assuming that households can be selected directly within PSUs. In this case the household inclusion probability can be written thus:

$$(3.4) \quad Q(s, k) = \frac{k(s) D(s, k)}{D(s)} \frac{d(s, k)}{D(s, k)} = \frac{k(s) d(s, k)}{D(s)}$$

where d(s,k) is the household sample size of PSU (s,k). In order to have an epsem design, it is required that Q(s,k) be a constant, independent of which PSUs (k) are selected at the 1st stage. For this to be true it can be seen from (3.4) that *the d(s,k)s have to be equal for all selected PSUs within the stratum*, i.e. the stratum sample of households, denoted d(s), has to be equally divided among the sample PSUs:

$$(3.5) \quad d(s,k) = \frac{d(s)}{k(s)}$$

Table A.8 Total (K(s)) and sample (k(s)) number of PSUs in the West Bank strata

	Status									
	DC		OT		DV		UV		RC	
Sub-district	K(s)	k(s)	K(s)	k(s)	K(s)	k(s)	K(s)	k(s)	K(s)	k(s)
Bethlehem	1	1	2	1	5	1	24	2	3	1
Hebron	1	1	3	1	14	3	47	2	2	1
Jenin	1	1	4	1	9	1	44	3	2	1
Jericho	1	1	.	.	.	.	9	1	2	1
Nablus	1	1	.	.	15	1	34	2	3	1
Ramallah	1	1	6	1	14	1	69	4	4	1
Tulkarem	1	1	3	1	28	3	45	2	2	1

Having thus determined the household sample allocation among PSUs within the strata, the next step is to allocate the various PSU subsamples among PSU cells. The housing unit selection stage is still disregarded. The (conditional) inclusion probability for an arbitrary household (s,k,c,d) within PSU (s,k) is:

$$(3.6) \quad R(s, k, c) = \frac{b(s, k)}{B(s, k)} \frac{d(s, k, c)}{D(s, k, c)}$$

In order to have a local (within PSU) epsem design, the R(s,k,c) must be a constant, i.e. independent of c. However, having two unspecified variables – b(s,k) and d(s,k,c) – and only one equation for determining them, we are free to specify any of them independently. To make a proper choice one should, however, appraise both cost and sampling error components. While budgetary constraints might suggest that the number of cells to be selected should be "small", considerations of sampling error induce no obvious choice. The sampling error can be split into two components reflecting *within* cell variations and variations *between* cells, respectively (variations refer to the survey variables). In general, preference should be given to the dominating component of variation. Thus, great between cell variations imply a large number of cells (and few households per cell) to be included, while great within cell variations suggest a smaller number of cells (and more households per cell).

As no prior information about the magnitude of the components of variation was available, further elaboration of sampling error considerations would obviously have been both speculative and questionable. We thus leave this discussion in order to address a more practical approach.

It was decided above that 45 PSUs be included in the 1st stage sample, implying on average approximately 23 households to be selected within each of the PSUs. To avoid concentration of all PSU interviews to one single area it was also decided to include at least 2 sample cells in every PSU. An average sample size per cell of 5-10 households was convenient for practical reasons as well. Thus the number of cells selected in each of the sample PSUs was for the majority of PSUs 2-5. There are, however, a few exceptions where only 1 or more than 5 cells were selected, depending on both the total number of cells and the household sample size for the PSU. In practice the b(s,k)s are roughly proportionate to the PSU total number of cells, B(s,k). The allocation of sample cells among PSUs is shown in table A.9.

Having thus decided the number of sample cells in each of the PSUs it remains to determine the allocation of the PSU household sample among cells. According to (3.6) this allocation obviously has to be proportionate in order to have a local (within PSU) epsem design. As stated previously, the latter requires $R(s,k,c)$ to be a constant independent of the cell (c) under consideration. Thus, in $R(s,k,c)$ we may omit the index c and reformulate (3.6):

$$(3.7) \quad d(s, k, c) = R(s, k) \frac{B(s, k)}{b(s, k)} D(s, k, c)$$

In order to calculate $R(s,k)$ for each of the sample PSUs we take the sum for every (s,k) of both sides of (3.7):

$$(3.8) \quad \sum_{c=1}^{b(s,k)} d(s, k, c) = R(s, k) \frac{B(s, k)}{b(s, k)} \sum_{c=1}^{b(s,k)} D(s, k, c)$$

The left hand side adds to the PSU sample size, $d(s)/k(s)$. On the right hand side all statistics are known except for the constant $R(s,k)$. Hence $R(s,k)$ is determined, and the individual $d(s,k,c)$s can be calculated from (3.7), concluding the sample allocation calculations. The $d(s,k,c)$s arrived at also determine the number of housing units selected from each cell.

The final household and cell sample allocation is displayed in table A.9 for the selected PSUs.

Before concluding this section, we return to the overall inclusion probability (3.3), to see how this can be calculated.

$$(3.3) \quad P(s, k, c, h,) = \frac{k(s) D(s, k)}{D(s)} \frac{b(s, k)}{B(s, k)} \frac{d(s, k, c)}{H(s, k, c,)} \frac{1}{D(s, k, c, h)}$$

The first fraction on the right hand side is the 1st stage inclusion probability. At the planning stage the numbers of PSU and stratum households, the $D(s,k)$s and $D(s)$s, were not available. Instead, the Benvenisti estimates[6] of the total population figures were used (equation (3.1)). The second fraction is the 2nd stage inclusion probability which can be calculated from the figures in table A.9. To calculate the third fraction, the $d(s,k,c)$s are taken from the finally observed (net) sample, and the $H(s,k,c)$s are estimated by formula (2.4) in the Gaza design section. The last fraction – the 4th stage inclusion probability – is determined by the sample observations of the $D(s,k,c,h)$s.

4 Arab Jerusalem Sample Design

The sample design for Arab Jerusalem (AJ) is a stratified three stage design similar to that of the West Bank, except for the omittance of the subselection of cells. In order to keep the mathematical notations unchanged, we will, however, assume there is an imaginary subsampling of cells by the subselection of one out of a total of one cell per PSU.

Table A.9 Total and sample number of cells, and household sample size in the West Bank sample PSUs

Stratum District/ Status	PSU name (Locality) (s,k)	Number of cells Total B(s,k)	Sample b(s,k)	Household sample size d(s,k)
	Bethlehem			
DC	Bethlehem	42	6	32
OT	Beit Sahour	22	3	18
DV	Beit Fajjar	8	3	23
UV	Artas	4	4	16
	Husan	4	2	15
RC	El Daheisha	13	2	9
	Hebron			
DC	Hebron	107	10	77
OT	Yatta	21	5	42
DV	Beit Ummar	7	4	23
	El Dhahiriya	8	6	22
	Kharass+Nuba	7+3	3+1	14+8
UV	El Rihiya	2	2	12
	Sair	8	2	12
RC	El Fawar	7	2	8
	Jenin			
DC	Jenin	21	3	17
OT	Ya'abad	12	5	35
DV	Jalame	3	3	35
UV	A'qabe	5	3	18
	Jaba'a	6	3	19
	Kfar Dan	4	3	19
RC	Mukayam Fara'a	8	3	14
	Jericho			
DC	Jericho	21	3	13
UV	Nue'ima	5	1	5
RC	Jericho RC	6	1	4

The procedures for selecting housing units, households and individuals are exactly like the ones applied elsewhere in the survey.

Stratification of PSUs

AJ is subdivided into 28 "statistical areas" having Arabs (non-Israelis) as the majority population. Israelis living within the PSUs are not considered part of the survey population. The 28 areas constitute our PSUs. The areas are those displayed in the Statistical Yearbook of Jerusalem 1990[7], with a map dated 1983. Cell contours have, however, been transferred to up-dated maps (1990) to make in-field identification of the areas more easy. Cell numbers refer to the numbers on the

Table A.9 (continued) Total and sample number of cells, and household sample size in the West Bank sample PSUs

Stratum District/ Status	PSU name (Locality)	Number of cells Total	Number of cells Sample	Household sample size
(s,k)		B(s,k)	b(s,k)	d(s,k)
	Nablus			
DC	Nablus	106	10	78
DV	A'sira Shimaliya	8	5	40
UV	Beit Dajan	5	4	22
	Salem	3	3	20
RC	Balata RC	19	4	26
	Ramallah			
DC	Ramallah			
OT	Silwad	8	5	34
DV	Singel	5	5	25
UV	A'nata	6	4	22
	Deir Jerir	4	4	21
	Kafr Malek	4	4	22
	Qibya	3	3	20
RC	Am'ari	10	3	15
	Tulkarem			
DC	Tulkarem	43	3	18
OT	Qalqilya	37	5	29
DV	Allar	6	4	21
	Habla	5	5	22
	Kafr Qadum	4	4	22
UV	Dannabe	5	3	18
	Shufa	2	2	18
RC	Nur el Shams	5	2	14

1983 map (other statistical maps have different numbers). The PSUs were grouped into 3 strata. The choice of location (North, Middle, South) as the stratification variable is somewhat arbitrary, and is not expected to yield reliability gains. However, it was considered safe to make sure that all main districts of AJ were represented in the sample. Table A.10 shows the stratification and the estimated population 1990 of each stratum (source: Statistical Yearbook of Jerusalem 1990).

Table A.10 Stratification of Arab Jerusalem PSUs

Stratum (s)	Number of PSUs K(s)	PSUs (cell numbers) (s,k)	Population 1990 N(s)
North	7	711, 712, 713, 714, 715, 716, 717	39,100
Middle	16	611, 621, 641, 642, 643, 751, 752, 753, 754, 761, 762, 763, 811, 812, 813, 814	82,900
South	5	545, 821, 822, 823, 824	19,200

First Stage Sample of PSUs

A sample of k(s) PSUs was selected within each stratum. The PSUs were selected with probabilities proportionate to estimated population size:

$$(4.1) \quad P_1(s,k) = \frac{k(s) N(s,k)}{N(s)}$$

where N(s,k) and N(s) have the same meaning as earlier, namely the population totals (individuals) for PSU (s,k) and stratum s, respectively. The number of PSUs to be selected from each stratum has been decided this way as a "compromise" between theoretical, statistical considerations and cost/implementation effectiveness. The household sample (total 500) was proportionately allocated among strata. The 1st stage inclusion probabilities imply the stratum sample of households to be equally divided among sample PSUs to have an (approximate) epsem allocation. The sample PSUs are listed in table A.11 along with the corresponding household sample size and the 1990 population estimates as compiled from Statistical Yearbook of Jerusalem 1990.

Table A.11 Arab Jerusalem sample of PSUs, and PSU sample size (households)

Stratum (s)	Sample PSUs (s,k)	Sample size (households) d(s,k)	Population 1990 (individuals) N(s,k)
North	713	70	8,100
"	716	70	5,600
Middle	611	50	4,600
"	752	50	7,600
"	753	50	4,900
"	754	50	5,900
"	813	50	9,100
"	814	50	9,300
South	821	30	4,500
"	823	30	6,900

Inclusion Probabilities

According to the details described above, the overall (household) inclusion probability (household (s,k,c,h,d) – the d'th household of the h'th housing unit (of imaginary cell c) within PSU (s,k)) is:

$$(4.2) \quad P(s, k, c, h, d) = \frac{k(s) N(s, k)}{N(s)} \cdot \frac{d(s, k, c)}{H(s, k, c,)} \cdot \frac{1}{D(s, k, c, h)}$$

where H(s,k,c) is the total number of housing units of PSU (s,k), and D(s,k,c,h) the total number of households within housing unit (s,k,c,h). The various H(s,k,c)s have to be estimated from sample observations and population figures:

$$(4.3) \quad \hat{H}(s, k, c) = \frac{N(s, k)}{e(\bar{N}(s, k, .))}$$

where the N(s,k)s are referred in table A.11 and the e ($\bar{N}$ (s, k, .)) is an estimate for the average number of individuals per PSU (s,k) housing unit:

$$(4.4) \quad e(\bar{N}(s, k, .)) = \frac{1}{d(s, k, c)} \sum_{h=1}^{d(s, k, c)} N(s, k, c, h) D(s, k, c, h)$$

In (4.4) N(s,k,c,h) is the number of individuals in sample household (s,k,c,h). (Strictly, h is the housing unit label. For the sample, however, it also works as a household label as long as only one household is selected from each sample housing unit.)

The overall inclusion probabilities for the individual samples are calculated by multiplying (4.2) with the individual probabilities of selection at the "5th" stage:

$$(4.5) \quad P_5(s, k, c, h, d) = \begin{cases} \dfrac{0{,}5}{W(s, k, c, h, d)} & \text{for females} \\[1em] \dfrac{0{,}5}{M(s, k, c, h, d)} & \text{for males} \end{cases}$$

where W(s,k,c,h,d) and M(s,k,c,h,d) are the numbers of females and males of age 15 years or more of household (s,k,c,h,d), respectively. These statistics are deducted from the sample.

5 Estimators

In this section the estimator used for computing averages or *proportions*, is described. The estimates may be proportions of the total survey population as well as of any sub-population, including those of the three main regions. As the issue of discussion is of a highly technical character, mathematical formulas have to be used extensively.

The variable of interest is denoted x. Given that x is a variable defined on the individual level (examples: level of education, age etc.), $x(s,k,c,h,d,i)$ is the x-value of population unit (individual) (s,k,c,h,d,i). The sum of x-values for all (population) members of a household (s,k,c,h,d) is denoted $x(s,k,c,h,d)$. We will use the latter notation also in cases where x is a variable defined on the basis of households.

We introduce a random variable $Y(s,k,c,h,d,i)$ taking the value 1 if individual (s,k,c,h,d,i) is included in the sample, and 0 otherwise. For the sample of households the variable is denoted $Y(s,k,c,h,d)$. The variable Y is a *sample indicator* in which all the information about the sample design is incorporated. In fact, Y is the only random element involved in the survey design, aiming at separating the sample units (having Y=1) from the non-sample units (Y=0). The probability of Y being 1 is of course the overall inclusion probability P. The sample indicator may be extended by attaching a subscript T indicating a subset of the population. Thus $Y_T(s, k, c, h, d, i)=1$ if unit (s,k,c,h,d,i) both is included in the sample and belongs to the sub-population T, and 0 otherwise (and similarly for the sample of households). T may also be the total survey population itself.

The survey observations may be expressed through the composite variable

$$X_T(s,k,c,h,d,i) = x(s,k,c,h,d,i) Y_T(s,k,c,h,d,i)$$

defined on the basis of individuals, or

$$X_T(s,k,c,h,d) = x(s,k,c,h,d) Y_T(s,k,c,h,d)$$

in case x is defined on the basis of households.

For variables on individuals the sum of x-values for all members of the household is estimated by:

$$\hat{X}_T(s,k,c,h,d) = \sum_i \frac{X_T(s,k,c,h,d,i)}{P_5(s,k,c,h,d,i)}$$

where the summation runs through all population members of the household, and the denominator is the conditional inclusion probability of the i-th member of the household (provided the household has been selected at the previous stage). In the present design, only one individual has been selected from each sample household, all members (15 years or more) of the household having the same probability of being included.

If the variable is defined according to households, the "x-aggregate" of the household is of course the observation itself:

$$\hat{x}_T(s, k, c, h, d) = X_T(s, k, c, h, d)$$

By aggregating step by step through the various sampling stages, we obtain estimates for the respective sampling unit sums by summation of weighted observations, the weights being the inverse of the inclusion probabilities at each stage (Horvitz-Thompson estimator[8]):

Estimated x-total for housing unit (s,k,c,h):

$$\hat{x}_T(s, k, c, h) = \sum_d \frac{\hat{x}_T(s, k, c, h, d)}{P_4(s, k, c, h, d)}$$

where the 4th stage inclusion probability is

$$P_4(s, k, c, h, d) = \frac{1}{D(s, k, c, h)}$$

for all households, d, of the housing unit, d=1,..., D(s,k,c,h). Estimate of cell (s,k,c) x-total:

$$\hat{x}_T(s, k, c) = \sum_h \frac{\hat{x}_T(s, k, c, h)}{P_3(s, k, c, h)}$$

where the 3rd stage inclusion probability is

$$P_3(s, k, c, h) = \frac{d(s, k, c)}{H(s, k, c)}$$

for all housing units of the cell, h=1,...,H(s,k,c).

Estimated PSU (s,k) x-total:

$$\hat{x}_T(s, k) = \sum_c \frac{\hat{x}_T(s, k, c)}{P_2(s, k, c)}$$

where the 2nd stage inclusion probability is

$$P_2(s, k, c) = \frac{b(s, k)}{B(s, k)}$$

for all cells of the PSU, c=1,...,B(s,k).

For the s-th stratum the x-total estimate is:

$$\hat{x}_T(s) = \sum_k \frac{\hat{x}_T(s, k)}{P_1(s, k)}$$

where the 1st stage inclusion probabilities have been defined in previous sections, and k=1,...,K(s).

Finally we have the estimate for the aggregate total for all strata:

$$(5.1) \quad \hat{x}_T = \sum_s \hat{x}_T(s)$$

This estimator is unbiased.

By successively inserting the various components it is easily seen that the estimator (5.1) may be written thus:

$$(5.1) \quad \hat{x}_T = \sum_s \sum_k \sum_c \sum_h \sum_d \sum_i \frac{X_T(s, k, c, h, d, i)}{P(s, k, c, h, d, i)}$$

where the denominator is the overall inclusion probability of the unit (in this case individual (s,k,c,h,d,i)). The inverse of this probability may thus be regarded as an individual weight to be attached to the respective observations in order to obtain unbiased estimates.

The very size of sub-population T is estimated similarly by putting x(s,k,c,h,d,i) or x(s,k,c,h,d) equal to 1 for all units of the population. For the sake of clarity we will use the following notations for these estimates:

$\hat{N}_T(s, k, c)$ T-units total within cell (s, k, c)

$\hat{N}_T(s, k)$ T-units total within PSUs (s, k)

$\hat{N}_T(s)$ T-units total within stratum s

$\hat{N}_T$ T-units total

Our estimator for the x-mean of sub-population T (or proportion if x is an attribute variable) is:

$$(5.2) \quad e(\bar{x}_T) = \frac{\hat{x}_T}{\hat{N}_T} = \frac{\sum_s \hat{x}_T(s)}{\sum_s \hat{N}_T(s)}$$

6 Sampling and Non-sampling Errors

The statistical quality or reliability of a survey may obviously be influenced by the errors that for various reasons affect the observations. Error components are commonly divided into two major categories: Sampling and non-sampling errors. In sampling literature the terms "variable errors" and "bias" are also frequently used, though having a precise meaning which is slightly different from the former concepts. The total error of a survey statistic is labeled *the mean square error*, being the sum of variable errors and all biases. In this section we will give a fairly general and brief description of the most common error components related to household sample surveys, and discuss their presence in and impacts on this particular survey.

Secondly, we will go into more detail as to those components which can be assessed numerically.

Error Components and their Presence in the Survey

(1) *Sampling errors* are related to the sample design itself and the estimators used, and may be seen as a consequence of surveying only a random sample of, and not the complete, population. Within the family of probability sample designs – that is designs enabling the establishment of inclusion probabilities (random samples) – sampling errors can be estimated. The most common measure for the sampling error is the *variance* of an estimate, or derivatives thereof. The derivative mostly used is the *standard error*, which is simply the square root of the variance.

The variance or the standard error does not tell us exactly how great the error is in each particular case. It should rather be interpreted as a measure of *uncertainty*, i.e. how much the estimate is likely to vary if repeatedly selected samples (with the same design and of the same size) had been surveyed. The variance is discussed in more detail in section 6.2.

(2) *Non-sampling errors* is a "basket" comprising all errors which are not sampling errors. These type of errors may induce *systematic bias* in the estimates, as opposed to *random* errors caused by sampling errors. The category may be further divided into subgroups according to the various origins of the error components:

* Imperfections in the sampling frame, i.e. when the population frame from which the sample is selected does not comprise the complete population under study, or include foreign elements. Exclusion of certain groups of the population from the sampling frame is one example. As described in the Gaza section, it was decided to exclude "outside localities" from being surveyed for cost reasons. It was maintained that the exclusion would have negligible effects on survey results.
* Errors imposed by implementary deviations from the theoretical sample design and field work procedures. Examples: non-response, "wrong" households selected or visited, "wrong" persons interviewed, etc. Except for non-response, which will be further discussed subsequently, there were some cases in the present survey in which the standard instructions for "enumeration walks" had to be modified in order to make sampling feasible. Any departure from the standard rules has been particularly considered

within the context of inclusion probabilities. None of the practical solutions adopted imply substantial alterations of the theoretical probabilities described in the previous sections.
* The field work procedures themselves may imply unforeseen systematic biases in the sample selection. In the present survey one procedure has been given particular consideration as a potential source of error: the practical modification of choosing road crossing corners – instead of any randomly selected spot – as starting points for the enumeration walks. This choice might impose systematic biases as to the kind of households being sampled. However, numerous inspection trials in the field proved it highly unlikely that such bias would occur. According to the field work instructions, the starting points themselves were never to be included in the sample. Such inclusion would have implied a systematic over-representation of road corner households, and thus may have caused biases for certain variables. (Instead, road corner households may now be slightly under-represented in so far as they as starting points are excluded from the sample. Possible bias induced by this under-representation is, however, negligible compared to the potential bias accompanying the former alternative.)
* Improper wording of questions, misquotations by the interviewer, misinterpretations and other factors that may cause failure in obtaining the intended response. "Fake response" (questions being answered by the interviewer himself/herself) may also be included in this group of possible errors. Irregularities of this kind are generally difficult to detect. The best ways of preventing them is to have well trained data collectors, to apply various verification measures, and to introduce the internal control mechanisms by letting data collectors work in pairs – possibly supplemented by the presence of the supervisor. A substantial part of the training of supervisors and data collectors was devoted to such measures. Verification interviews were carried out by the supervisors among a 10% randomly selected subsample. No fake interviews were detected. However, a few additional re-interviews were carried out, on suspicion of misunderstandings and incorrect responses.
* Data processing errors include errors arising incidentally during the stages of response recording, data entry and programming. In this survey the data entry programme used included consistency controls wherever possible, aiming at correcting any logical contradictions in the data. Furthermore, verification punch work

was applied in order to correct mis-entries not detected by the consistency control, implying that each and all questionnaires have been punched twice.

Sampling Error – Variance of an Estimate

Generally, the prime objective of sample designing is to keep sampling error at the lowest level possible (within a given budget). There is thus a unique theoretical correspondence between the sampling strategy and the sampling error, which can be expressed mathematically by the *variance* of the estimator applied. Unfortunately, design complexity very soon implies variance expressions to be mathematically uncomfortable and sometimes practically "impossible" to handle. Therefore, approximations are frequently applied in order to achieve interpretable expressions of the theoretical variance itself, and even more to estimate it.

In real life practical shortcomings frequently challenge mathematical comfort. Absence of sampling frames or other prior information forces one to use mathematically complex strategies in order to find feasible solutions. The design of the present survey – stratified, 4-5 stage sampling with varying inclusion probabilities – is probably among the extremes in this respect, implying that the variance of the estimator (5.2) will be of the utmost complexity – as will be seen subsequently.

The (approximate) variance of the estimator (5.2) is in its simplest form:

$$(6.1) \quad \text{Var}[e(\bar{x}_T)] = \bar{x}_T^2 \left(\frac{\text{Var}\hat{x}_T}{x_T^2} + \frac{\text{Var}\hat{N}_T}{N_T^2} - 2 \frac{\text{Cov}(\hat{x}_T, \hat{N}_T)}{x_T N_T} \right)$$

The variances and covariances on the right hand side of (6.1) may be expressed in terms of the stratum variances and covariances:

$$\text{Var } \hat{x}_T = \sum_s \text{Var } \hat{x}_T(s)$$

$$\text{Var } \hat{N}_T = \sum_s \text{Var } \hat{N}_T(s)$$

$$\text{Cov}(\hat{x}_T, \hat{N}_T) = \sum_s \text{Cov}[\hat{x}_T(s), \hat{N}_T(s)]$$

Proceeding one step further the stratum variance may be expressed as follows[9]:

$$\text{Var}\,\hat{x}_T(s) = \frac{1}{2}\sum_k\sum_{l\neq k}[\pi_s(k)\pi_s(l) - \pi_s(k,l)]\left[\frac{x_T(s,k)}{\pi_s(k)} - \frac{x_T(s,l)}{\pi_s(l)}\right]^2 + \sum_k \frac{\sigma^2_{x_T}(s,k)}{\pi_s(k)}$$

where we have introduced the notation $\pi_s(k) = P_1(s,k)$. The $\pi_s(k,l)$ is the joint probability of inclusion for PSU (s,k) and PSU (s,l), and $\sigma^2_{x_T}(s,k)$ the variance of the PSU (s,k) unbiased estimate $\hat{x}_T(s,k)$.

The variance of $\hat{N}_T(s)$ is obtained similarly by substituting x with N in the above formula. The stratum covariance formula is somewhat more complicated and is not expressed here.

The PSU (s,k) variance components in the latter formula have a structure similar to the stratum one, as is realized by regarding the PSUs as separate "strata" and the cells as "PSUs". Again, another variance component emerges for each of the cells, the structure of which is similar to the preceding one. In order to arrive at the "ultimate" variance expression yet another two or three similar stages have to be passed. It should be realized that the final variance formula is extremely complicated, even if simplifying modifications and approximations may reduce the complexities stemming from the 2nd – 5th sampling stages.

It should also be understood that attempts to estimate this variance properly and exhaustively (unbiased or close to unbiased) would be beyond any realistic effort. Furthermore, for such estimation to be accomplished certain preconditions have to be met. Some of these conditions cannot, however, be satisfied (for instance: at least two PSUs have to be selected from each stratum comprising more than one PSU). We thus have to apply a more simple method for appraising the uncertainty of our estimates.

Any sampling strategy (sample selection approach and estimator) may be characterized by its performance relative to a simple random sampling (SRS) design, applying the sample average as the estimator for proportions. The *design factor* of a strategy is thus defined as the fraction between the variances of the two estimators. If the design factor is, for instance, less than 1, the strategy under consideration would be better than SRS. Usually, multi-stage strategies are inferior to SRS, implying the design factor being greater than 1.

The design factor is usually determined empirically. Although there is no overwhelming evidence in its favour, a factor of 1.5 is frequently used for stratified, multi-stage designs. (The design factor may vary among survey variables). The rough approximate variance estimator is thus:

$$(6.2) \quad s^2(\bar{x}_T) = 1.5 \frac{p(1-p)}{n_T}$$

where p is the estimate produced by (5.2) and n_T is the number of observations underlying the estimate (the "100%"). Although this formula oversimplifies the variance, it still takes care of some of the basic features of the real variance; the variance decreases by increasing sample size (n), and tends to be larger for proportions around 50% than at the tails (0% or 100%).

The square root of the variance, i.e. $s(\bar{x}_T)$ or briefly s, is called the standard error, and is tabulated in table A.12 for various values of p and n.

Confidence Intervals

The sample which has been surveyed is one specific outcome of an "infinite" number of random selections which might have been done within the sample design. Other sample selections would most certainly have yielded survey results slightly different from the present ones. The survey estimates should thus not be interpreted as accurately as the figures themselves indicate.

A *confidence interval* is a formal measure for assessing the variability of survey estimates from such hypothetically repeated sample selections. The confidence interval is usually derived from the survey estimate itself and its standard error:

Confidence interval: [p−cs, p+cs] where the c is a constant which must be determined by the choice of a *confidence coefficient*, fixing the probability of the interval including the true, but unknown, population proportion for which p is an estimate. For instance, c=1 corresponds to a confidence probability of 67%, i.e. one will expect that 67 out of 100 intervals will include the true proportion if repeated surveys are carried out. In most situations, however, a chance of one out of three to arrive at a wrong conclusion is not considered satisfactory. Usually, confidence coefficients of 90% or 95% are preferred, 95% corresponding to approximately c=2. Although our assessment as to the location of the true population proportion thus becomes less uncertain, the assessment itself, however, becomes less precise as the length of the interval increases.

Comparisons between groups

Comparing the occurrence of an attribute between different sub-groups of the population is probably the most frequently used method for making inference from survey data. For illustration of the problems involved in such comparisons, let us consider two separate sub-groups for which the estimated proportions sharing the attribute are $\hat{p}_1$ and $\hat{p}_2$, respectively, while the unknown true proportions are denoted p_1 and p_2. The corresponding standard error estimates are s_1 and s_2. The problem of inference is thus to evaluate the significance of the difference between the two sub-group estimates: Can the observed difference be caused by sampling error alone, or is it so great that there must be more substantive reasons for it?

Table A.12 Standard error estimates for proportions (s and p are specified as percentages).

Number of obs. (n)	\multicolumn{6}{c	}{Estimated proportion (p %)}
	5/95	10/90	20/80	30/70	40/60	50
10	8.4	11.6	15.5	17.7	19.0	19.4
20	6.0	8.2	11.0	12.5	13.4	13.7
50	3.8	5.2	6.9	7.9	8.5	8.7
75	3.1	4.2	5.7	6.5	6.9	7.1
100	2.7	3.7	4.9	5.6	6.0	6.1
150	2.2	3.0	4.0	4.6	4.9	5.0
200	1.9	2.6	3.5	4.0	4.2	4.3
250	1.7	2.3	3.1	3.5	3.8	3.9
300	1.5	2.1	2.8	3.2	3.5	3.5
350	1.4	2.0	2.6	3.0	3.2	3.3
400	1.3	1.8	2.5	2.8	3.0	3.1
500	1.2	1.6	2.2	2.5	2.7	2.7
700	1.0	1.4	1.9	2.1	2.3	2.3
1000	0.8	1.2	1.5	1.8	1.9	1.9
1500	0.7	0.9	1.3	1.4	1.5	1.6
2000	0.6	0.8	1.1	1.3	1.3	1.4
2500	0.5	0.7	1.0	1.2	1.2	1.2

We will assume that the estimate $\hat{p}_1$ is the larger of the two proportions observed. Our problem of judgement will thus be equivalent to testing the following hypothesis:

Hypothesis: $p_1 = p_2$
Alternative: $p_1 > p_2$

In case the test rejects the hypothesis we will accept the alternative as a "significant" statement, and thus conclude that the observed difference between the two estimates is too great to be caused by randomness alone. However, as is the true nature of statistical inference, one can (almost) never draw absolutely certain conclusions. The uncertainty of the test is indicated by the choice of a "significance level", which is the probability of making a wrong decision by rejecting a *true* hypothesis. This probability should obviously be as small as possible. Usually it is set at 2.5% or 5% – depending on the risk or loss involved in drawing wrong conclusions.

The test implies that the hypothesis is rejected if

$$\hat{p}_1 - \hat{p}_2 > c \sqrt{s_1^2 + s_2^2}$$

where the constant c depends on the choice of significance level:

Significance level	c-value
2.5%	2.0
5.0%	1.6
10.0%	1.3

As is seen, the test criteria comprise the two standard error estimates and thus imply some calculation. It is also seen that smaller significance levels imply the requirement of larger observed differences between sub-groups in order to arrive at significant conclusions. One should be aware that the non-rejection of a hypothesis leaves one with no conclusions at all, rather than the acceptance of the hypothesis itself.

Non-response

Non-response occurs when one fails to obtain an interview with a properly pre-selected individual (unit non-response). The most frequent reasons for this kind of non-response are refusals and absence ("not-at-homes"). Item non-response occurs when a single question is left unanswered.

Non-response is generally the most important single source of bias in surveys. Most exposed to non-response bias are variables related to the very phenomenon of being a (frequent) "not-at-homer" or not (example: cinema attendance). In Western societies non-response rates of 15-30% are normal.

Various measures have been undertaken to keep non-response at the lowest level possible. Most of all confidence-building has been of concern, implying contacts with local community representatives have been made in order to enlist their support and approval. Furthermore, many hours have been spent explaining the scope of the survey to respondents and anyone else wanting to know, assuring that the survey makers neither would impose taxes on people nor demolish their homes, or – equally important for the reliability of the survey – bring direct material aid.

Furthermore, up to 4 call-backs were applied if selected respondents were not at home. Usually the data collectors were able to get an appointment for a subsequent visit at the first attempt, so that only one revisit was required in most cases. Unit non-response thus comprises refusals and those not being at home at all after four attempts.

Table A.13 shows the net number of respondents and non-responses in each of the three parts of the survey. The initial sizes of the various samples are deduced from the table by adding responses and non-responses. For the household and RSI samples, the total size was 2,518 units, while the female sample size was 1,247. It is seen from the bottom line that the non-response rates are outstandingly small compared to the "normal" magnitudes of 10 – 20% in similar surveys. Consequently, there should be fairly good evidence for maintaining that the effects of non-response in this survey are insignificant.

Table A.13 Number of (net) respondents and non-respondents in the tree parts of the survey

Region	Households Resp.	Households Non-resp.	RSIs Resp.	RSIs Non-resp.	Women Resp.	Women Non-resp
Gaza	970	8	968	10	482	4
West Bank	1,023	16	1,004	35	502	14
Arab Jerusalem	486	15	478	23	240	5
Total	2,479	39	2,450	68	1,224	23
Non-response rate	1.5%		2.7%		1.8%	

Notes

1 Benvenisti, M. & Khayat, S.: *The West Bank and Gaza Atlas*. The West Bank Data Base Project. Jerusalem 1988.

2 Central Bureau of Statistics, Israel: *Statistical Abstracts of Israel*, 1989.

3 Central Bureau of Statistics, Israel: *Judea, Samaria and Gaza Area Statistics*, 1988.

4 Jerusalem Post, 29.04.1992.

5 Jerusalem Post, 03.02.1992.

6 See endnote 1.

7 Choshen, M. & Greenbaum, S.: *Statistical Yearbook of Jerusalem*, 1990. The Jerusalem Institute for Israel Studies. Jerusalem 1992.

8 Chaudhuri, A. & Vos, J.W.E.: *Unified Theory and Strategies of Survey Sampling*. North-Holland Series in Statistics and Probability, Vol. 4, Amsterdam 1988.

9 See, e.g., Chaudhuri, A. & Vos, J. W. E.: *Unified Theory and Strategies of Survey Sampling*. North-Holland Series in Statistics and Probability, Vol. 4. Amsterdam 1988.

Appendix B
Recruitment, Training and Organisation of the Field Work

Neil Hawkins

Introduction

The best planned survey will fail in its aims if the field work is not adequately organised or controlled. This is particularly true of the occupied territories where the special conditions prevailing combine to erect a host of obstacles and challenges not ordinarily found when conducting a survey.

FAFO are not the first to experience these problems. Writing at the time of the British Mandate Sir Henry Gurney, then Chief Secretary of Palestine, made the following observation:

> "Palestine as you know is full of uncertainties. The first thing you have to do here in Jerusalem is to find out which particular century anyone else is living in. There are people who still think it's the Middle Ages and claim to have been living in the same house for 1700 years. To us it is 1947, but the Jews are in 5707 and the Arabs have it that it's 1366... On the other hand there are several people living in the next century or two and much ahead of the facts, such as some politicians and press correspondents. So we have given up bothering very much about what year it is, and anyway many of the things that happen in Palestine would be unusual at any time"[1].

It was under similar uncommon circumstances that FAFO had to develop a pragmatic structure and organisation for the implementation of the survey, with all its theoretical and technical demands. These demands were not always practical but the emphasis on the quality of the data was uppermost and had to be translated into a workable system. This system also had to take into account the natural limitations of time, money and human resources that exist in any field survey. Finding a compromise that did not sacrifice quality was essential.

The various components of the field work will be dealt with in turn, highlighting the problems faced and the ways in which they were overcome or avoided. The field work proceeded in two stages. Firstly a pilot project was carried out in Gaza in August 1991 to test the questionnaire, the sampling methods, the training course and the control procedures. The valuable experiences gained from this exercise helped FAFO to plan and carry out the second stage, the main survey. The collection of data of the main survey took place from mid-May to mid-July 1992 in both fields. It was important to collect the data in both Gaza and the West Bank at the same time in order to ensure that accurate comparisons could be made. One incident could have altered opinions and answers drastically, thus impairing the desired uniform quality of the data.

Recruitment

The number of field workers that were hired was determined by the time-frame for the field work and its budget. To ensure accuracy and quality FAFO insisted that each questionnaire be filled in by two data collectors. At least one in each team had to be female. This was necessary because half the respondents were to be women and only female data collectors could ask them questions on such sensitive subjects as contraception. FAFO estimated it would need sixty data collectors in the West Bank and Jerusalem and forty in Gaza, and it was decided that field work would be carried out in the course of two months.

As in the pilot project, one of FAFO's concerns was to avoid being linked to and identified with any one organisation or institution. This would have lessened FAFO's effectiveness in the field since it was essential for the success of the enterprise to have as wide a base of support and involvement as possible. An open and pragmatic approach could also be a practical and desirable way to avoid any problems arising out of factionalism.

A further requirement was to hire competent, keen, sensible and, if possible, experienced data collectors. Unfortunately, there are very few trained and experienced data collectors in the occupied territories, and FAFO therefore had to concentrate on hiring people who showed the basic qualities needed.

In November and December 1991 applications were distributed throughout local universities and research institutions. Local leaders were approached and the purpose and implications of the project explained to them. They gave advice on how best to proceed, and their support proved extremely valuable in that it helped pave the way for the acceptance of the project by the local community.

Early on, FAFO considered it important that local institutions should be given an opportunity to use the data gathered for planning and further analysis. Therefore six institutions and universities around the occupied territories were contacted, and in January 1992 FAFO ran an introductory course on SPSS (Statistical Package for Social Science) for two representatives from each institution. FAFO also shared in the purchase of a computer equipped with the SPSS programme for each of the institutions. The aim was not only that these institutions would receive a copy of the data base at the end of the project, but also that they should have the capacity and training to use it. A welcome result of this course was the increased cooperation received from the institutions at all stages of the project, especially the recruiting stage.

FAFO received a total of over six hundred applications. Each application was checked and graded by FAFO and a short-list of 350 names was prepared for interviewing. In December and January each of these applicants was interviewed by two FAFO members in Arabic. The aim of having two interviewers was to avoid accusations of bias.

Each interviewee was graded and FAFO then chose the best in each area, bearing in mind the requirement that at least fifty per cent of each of the teams be female. In Gaza fifty per cent of the field workers were women, while in the West Bank and Arab Jerusalem the female proportion was around seventy five per cent. The candidates who scored highest in the interviews were marked down as potential supervisors and assistant supervisors.

Some candidates who were qualified were found to be working as social workers, and FAFO decided not to employ these. Social workers assess families and recommend aid, and FAFO did not feel it would be in the surveys' interests to employ people who would be known in their areas as social workers. This could easily have led to biased answers if families exaggerated their needs and the severity of their conditions in the belief that the survey might qualify them for aid.

Training

This stage of a project is one of the most essential, yet one that is, sadly, often overlooked. If the field workers are to be effective, motivated, informed and confident, they must have a thorough practical and theoretical training course to prepare them. The pilot project in Gaza enabled FAFO to design a course which went a long way to meeting these requirements.

FAFO staff and consultants firstly produced a booklet covering the main aspects of field work, namely: The role and importance of the data collector; the aim of the project; technical aspects and definitions of terms used; confidence-building steps, and an explanation of each section in the questionnaire.

In February 1992, a twenty-hour course was held for the supervisors in the West Bank. The aims were to give the candidates the background to the project, and to provide an in-depth knowledge of the questionnaire, instructions on sampling, group management, confidence building steps in the local community, practical approaches to problem solving and office procedures.

It must be emphasized that all these courses were a two way exchange, as FAFO relied on brief lectures followed by group discussions. This way local knowledge and experience shaped the final outcome of the course and the questionnaire. Contributions and comments from the candidates on all the courses were invaluable, and helped give the participants a feeling of involvement in the project.

Employment was not guaranteed until the candidates had successfully completed the course, which was treated as part of the interview. This led to increased commitment and participation in the course.

Following the supervisors' course FAFO held two courses for data collectors in the West Bank, and one in Gaza. The latter course also acted as a refresher course for the original data collectors from the pilot survey. The field workers were required to complete seven test questionnaires at addresses selected by their supervisors. These addresses were obtained using the maps generated from the supervisors' training course. Only when these questionnaires were accepted by the supervisors and the FAFO-coordinator were the field workers employed. Those who did not achieve the minimum standard were not employed.

The aims of the data collectors' courses were similar to those of the supervisors' course. However, the emphasis was more on the solving of practical problems and learning how to deal with reluctant and suspicious respondents, in addition to gaining an understanding of the ideas behind the questions. The method of role playing possible situations was used to train the data collectors in how to deal with all sorts of respondents and to encourage them to anticipate problems. Time was spent teaching the candidates how to explain questions dealing with opinions without subconsciously influencing an answer, in other words keeping them as neutral and objective as possible at all times.

The data collectors course also provided the supervisors with the opportunity to establish their authority and become the focal point of the group. They were assigned minor administrative tasks and also led the discussions, putting into practice what they had learnt in their course, such as giving everyone a chance to speak, being encouraging and being firm but fair.

FAFO's hope was that an increased understanding of the project and the questionnaire would lead to increased motivation, which in turn would produce dedicated and skilled field workers.

Organisation

If the survey were to both deliver the results within a certain time frame and conform to rigorous scientific standards, then the organisation and structure of the field work needed to be efficient and flexible, without sacrificing control and quality.

As the areas that were to be covered by the survey are geographically separated it was decided to have two field operations, one in Gaza and one in the West Bank and Jerusalem. FAFO's Middle East Coordinator had overall responsibility for the field operation and was also West Bank and Arab Jerusalem Coordinator, with Gaza having its own Coordinator.

FAFO engaged several local consultants to assist in various stages of the project, in particular recruitment, developing the questionnaire and running the training courses. Due to the difficulty of travel between areas as a result of distance, security restrictions and strikes, it was decided to form six groups of data collectors in the West Bank and four groups in Gaza, each covering a particular area close to where they lived. The problem of travel was somewhat eased by the authorities providing travel permits to data collectors who required them.

The advantage of this structure was that they knew the area, and their proximity not only kept transport costs down but also meant they were able to do more interviews in one day, which increased efficiency.

Each group had between ten and twelve data collectors, and each team had a supervisor and an assistant supervisor. In the West Bank FAFO rented or loaned offices in Jenin, Nablus, Jerusalem, Bethlehem and Hebron to provide venues for each group to meet, in addition to the main office in Ramallah. The supervisors distributed, received and checked the questionnaires in their offices before returning them to Ramallah for entry into the computer. In Gaza, FAFO's centre was based in the YMCA and due to the short distances involved there, was not supplemented by any other offices.

During the sampling stage supervisors went to each survey area and drew maps (see Appendix A). This process served to act as a confidence-building measure in itself because the supervisors, especially in villages and refugee camps, needed to explain the project and its aims before being accepted by the local population.

The initial reaction of many people was that the data collectors and supervisors were from the tax department or were undercover Israeli units. In order to convince people of the data collectors' identity and intentions careful persuasion was needed.

In one instance the local population closed their shops, staged a demonstration and burnt tires as the data collectors approached, believing the data collectors to be tax officials and hoping to scare them off. The data collectors managed to talk to the youths involved and were allowed to continue after delicate negotiations.

Local sensitivities also proved problematic. A particularly religious man refused to let his wife be interviewed so the data collectors approached a person in the local Chamber of Commerce they knew to be a colleague of the man who objected. When the project was explained by the colleague, he consented to his wife being interviewed.

The field workers were assisted by the provision of a FAFO ID card with a photo and with a letter in Arabic clarifying the purpose of the project. The data collectors were carefully trained in how to present themselves, emphasizing FAFO's contact with local institutions and local leaders but being cautious not to promise or imply that any material benefit would follow. This would not only have been unfair, but it would also have encouraged false answers in the misguided hope that by highlighting their condition the respondents may receive aid.

Controls

A strict system of checks and controls was instituted by FAFO at each stage of the field work. Data collectors had to keep records of their transport expenses, and forms were completed recording the date a questionnaire was issued, with information on each stage. FAFO could check how many times a data collector had to visit a certain house, which household they chose, how many people lived in it, which person was chosen as the randomly selected individual, and whether anyone refused and why.

As everyone had to follow the same system using random number tables for any selection, it was possible for each selection stage to be checked. This made it very difficult for anyone to select a respondent out of convenience, not using the designated system, because it could be checked by the supervisors. Any respondents who refused to be interviewed were visited by the supervisor, who would attempt to convince them to answer. This also acted to encourage the data collectors to spend time persuading reluctant respondents.

Supervisors were required to check at least 25% of all interviews. In fact the supervisors controlled almost 30% of all interviews. There were three main types of control. At the beginning, it was emphasized that they should be sitting in with the data collectors during interviews to ensure there were no problems, and to encourage and advise them on how to improve work. The second method involved the supervisors checking the returned questionnaires for mistakes and ambiguities. Finally, supervisors used a short re-interview questionnaire, choosing at random households that had been interviewed and returning to them to check the veracity of the data collectors' observations and the accuracy of the answers provided by the respondent. These measures ensured that interviews were made correctly and that the selection steps were properly adhered to.

A further check was made once the questionnaire had been entered on computer, the details of which can be found in Appendix C of this book.

If an inconsistency was found, the questionnaire was returned to the data collectors for clarification(which may have involved a return visit). Once the questionnaire was returned to the office, any necessary correction were made on the computer. Questionnaires were entered in one centre in Gaza and one in Ramallah almost as soon as they were handed in.

A final check was to re-enter all the questionnaires a second time. The rationale for this was that a value could have been entered wrongly but being "logical" might not have been picked up by the cleaning pass.

Incentives

Incentives are an integral part of motivation and as such were important in contributing to the apparently high quality of the data collected. Supervisors in all areas received a fixed salary per month.

As FAFO wished to create a climate of cooperation, it was felt that any other system could have been unproductive. In Gaza, payment was made on a fixed scale per questionnaire to data collectors, with females earning slightly more due to the fact that they had to cover three sections as opposed to two for the males. In the West Bank, payment was made on a sliding scale, which was also more generous for females. Increases were made after the first 15, 30 and 45 completed questionnaires only if the data collectors had reasonable transport costs. FAFO covered all such costs approved by the supervisors. Due to high transport expenses in the West Bank it was important to provide incentives to save on transport.

Data collectors were restricted to two questionnaires a day unless they were of a very good quality; then they were given three a day to complete. This rewarded accuracy and efficiency, for the better the standard, the more questionnaires they had, and thus the more money they earned.

In order to discourage poor work, a system of penalties or disincentives was made. If, after a cleaning pass by the computer, a filled questionnaire had to be returned to the data collectors due to their mistake, they would receive a warning. If this happened again, they were paid only half the amount for the questionnaire, and if it happened a third time, they received no payment at all.

As well as encouraging accuracy, this system also supported the supervisors' authority. When they checked the questionnaires (before being entered into the computer) and found mistakes, they would return them to the data collectors for correction. As there was no penalty attached to questionnaires returned by the supervisors to the data collectors, they did not resent the supervisors doing this, as in practice they were saving the data collectors a warning or a fine.

The motivation of the field workers and supervisors and the system of incentives and controls made an important contribution to the achievement of an extremely low non-response rate and to data of a seemingly high quality.

Summary

The field work was faced with a variety of problems, in addition to the ones mentioned. These included the worst winter in eighty years with heavy snows, long curfews in Gaza and Ramallah, constant strikes and, strangely enough, the peace talks, which acted to deprive FAFO of a number of consultants for long periods. Despite these obstacles, the field work was completed successfully, maintaining the highest standards. A workable compromise was established which satisfied both the requirements of the theoreticians and the limitations imposed by a survey of this nature in this area.

The dedication and professionalism of the field staff was remarkable. This vindicated the approach adopted by FAFO from the outset, which was to gather and encourage a broad base of support and involvement in the project, and to keep to the highest standards. The system used for recruitment provided FAFO with a competent core of people who were willing and able to be trained into skilled and confident field workers. By placing emphasis on the importance of a thorough and practical training, and coupling this with a system that applied stringent controls and encouraged accurate work, FAFO could be confident the quality of the data.

It is hoped that the data will make a valuable contribution to information on the occupied territories, and not suffer the same fate as statistics in the 1940s:

> "Nearly all problems have answers, but no one has yet discovered an answer to the Palestine one, and that is why there are more facts and statistics about Palestine than any other place its size....You can tell from them exactly how many Jewish boys with blue eyes whose parents exported grapefruit to Syria in 1946 now attend Arab schools and vice versa. It seems a pity that from all these figures and graphs and diagrams no one has yet been able to discover what they prove"[2]

Notes

1 Hopwood, D. *Tales of Empire*, Tauris, 1989.
2 Ibid.

Appendix C
Processing of Data
Geir Øvensen

Cleaning a data set implies identification of individual entries or combinations of entries which might seem dubious, and to make decisions about what to do with them. In many projects based on information from household interviews this process has been initiated only after the completion of field work. Using SPSS-DE in the local field offices in Gaza and Ramallah, the FAFO living conditions survey managed to integrate the processes of collecting and cleaning data respectively. This approach had several advantages: First, data quality was improved by allowing for corrections of errors while still working in the field. Second, the integration of data cleaning into the field work procedures reduced the time span from the end of the field work until completion of the report.

SPSS-DE offered two main possibilities for identifying questionable entries. The simplest method was to check if values entered for individual variables were within the legal ranges. A more elaborate cleaning procedure was to check if combinations of variable values were consistent.

Valid (Individual) Entries

For each individual variable valid entry, specifications (or "ranges", for short) were defined. Most variables had standard answer alternatives which defined the acceptable ranges. For some variables without standard responses, these ranges had to be determined on the basis of experiences from the FAFO Gaza Pilot Survey (e.g., which would provide guidelines for determining the maximum credible number of persons living in a household, etc.[1]).

During data punching an audio-visual warning would appear if the puncher entered "illegal" values outside the specified ranges. Following a "beep", the screen message "Value out of range" would tell the puncher that a mistake had been made. (The programme did not, however, technically force the puncher to correct errors). Violations of the legal ranges were checked both automatically when data was entered or changed, and on specific instructions from the office staff (see reference to use of "cleaning passes" below).

Cleaning Rules

As indicated above, cleaning data also implied checking if *combinations of values* for several variables were credible and consistent. For this purpose FAFO developed a data entry programme containing more than 500 logical rules about acceptable relations between two or more variable values in each interview.

Some rules were logical in the strict sense, i.e. always to be observed (like "a son must be younger than his father"). Other rules were of a kind that would hold true in 95% of the cases, based on evaluation of behavioural patterns in Palestinian society (e.g. a husband who encourages his wife to appear in public without a head scarf is also likely to accept that women are allowed to vote).

In contrast to checking legal ranges of variable values, cleaning rules could not be controlled continuously. (Rules involving two or more variables in different parts of the questionnaire could not be checked until values for all involved variables had been entered). Instead, cleaning specifications were checked by the office staff through so-called "cleaning passes". By using a cleaning pass, all entries in a file would be checked against all ranges and rules concerning the variables in that file. The results could be reproduced by the field office staff in several ways, by exposing either the ranges and rules that had been violated in each case or the cases that had violated ranges and rules. By using the possibility of consistency checks between entries offered by the data entry programme, computerized data quality checks, equalling hours of manual control, could be performed in a few seconds.

Correction of Wrong or Questionable Entries

While SPSS-DE offered comprehensive and effective procedures for identifying entries transgressing legal ranges or logical rules, it did not provide detailed instructions about what to do with improbable or problematic entries. The task of the computer programme was thus confined to facilitating the task of identifying problematic entries, leaving the office staff time and energy to concentrate on finding a fair and honest solution.

Most violations of the legal ranges turned out to be "straightforward" writing or punching errors, which could easily be explained and corrected. Violations of logical rules, however, usually posed greater challenges. For each violation of a logical rule, judgements had to be made about its cause and substance. Some rules which were violated in a substantial number of the initial interviews had to be reformulated. Most violations of rules, however, were caused by various types of non-sampling errors.

Notes

[1] The FAFO Gaza Strip Pilot Survey interviewed 300 households in August 1991, employing a questionnaire 90% similar to the one used in the present survey.

Appendix A.2 Tables

A2.1 Distribution of population by sub-region and type of locality

	Occupied territories	Gaza	West Bank	Arab Jerusalem
Total (HO)	100	31(21)	59(54)	10
Total (RSI)	100	34(22)	57(52)	9
Total (TOT)	100	37(25)	55(50)	8
Sub-region				
North (HO)			53	
Central (HO)			28	
South (HO)			19	
North (RSI)			52	
Central (RSI)			28	
South (RSI)			19	
North (TOT)		52	51	
Central (TOT)		15	28	
South (TOT)		33	22	
N (UNW)	2439	958	1004	477

Type of locality			
Gaza		**West Bank**	
Gr. Gaza City (HO)	33	WB towns (HO)	37
Gaza towns/villages (HO)	35	West Bank villages (HO)	56
Gaza camps (HO)	32	WB camps (HO)	8
Gr. Gaza City (RSI)	29	WB towns (RSI)	33
Gaza towns/villages (RSI)	36	West Bank villages (RSI)	59
Gaza camps (RSI)	35	WB camps (RSI)	8
Gr. Gaza City (TOT)	31	WB towns (TOT)	34
Gaza towns/villages (TOT)	37	West Bank villages (TOT)	58
Gaza camps (TOT)	32	WB camps (TOT)	8
N (UNW)	958		1004

Symbols:
HO = households
RSI = individuals 15 years or older
TOT = all individuals
UNW = unweighted number of respondents
( )   = without camps

A2.2 Distribution of population by refugee status, religion and marital status

	Occupied territories	Gaza	West Bank	Arab Jerusalem
Refugee status				
Non-refugees (HO)	59	36	73	60
Refugees outside camps (HO)	23	31	18	
Urban camps (HO)	13	28	5	
Rural camps (HO)	4	5	4	
Non-refugees (RSI)	59	36	73	60
Refugees outside camps (RSI)	23	31	18	
Urban camps (RSI)	13	28	5	
Rural camps (RSI)	4	5	4	
Non-refugees (TOT)	58	38	74	59
Refugees outside camps (TOT)	24	32	17	
Urban camps (TOT)	14	25	5	
Rural camps (TOT)	4	5	4	
Religion				
Moslem (HO)	95	99.7	96	79
Christian (HO)	5	0.3	4	21
Moslem (RSI)	96	99.8	96	82
Christian (RSI)	4	0.2	4	18
Moslem (TOT)	97	99.8	96	85
Christian (TOT)	3	0.2	4	15
Marital status				
Unmarried (RSI)	30	27	31	33
Married (RSI)	65	67	64	60
Widowed (RSI)	4	3	4	5
Other (RSI)	1	2	1	2
N (UNW)	2439	958	1004	477

Symbols:
HO   =   households
RSI =   individuals 15 years or older
TOT =   all individuals

A2.3 Age distribution by region and type of locality

	Occupied territories	Gaza	West Bank	Arab Jerusalem	Gaza camps	West Bank camps
M 0-4	9,23	10,52	8,80	6,61	10,70	8,72
M 5-9	6,94	7,81	6,51	5,73	8,16	6,48
M 10-14	6,67	6,96	6,58	6,00	7,49	6,70
M 15-19	5,39	5,32	5,29	6,53	5,41	5,33
M 20-24	5,12	4,41	5,44	6,35	4,28	5,33
M 25-29	4,18	3,73	4,29	5,11	3,38	4,32
M 30-34	2,83	2,60	3,00	2,65	2,25	3,03
M 35-39	1,89	1,92	1,72	2,12	2,03	1,73
M 40-44	1,48	1,70	1,43	1,59	1,69	1,44
M 45-49	1,08	0,90	1,14	1,76	1,01	1,30
M 50-54	0,94	0,68	1,00	1,23	0,68	1,01
M 55-59	0,94	0,90	1,00	1,41	0,90	0,86
M 60-64	1,08	1,02	1,14	1,41	0,90	1,15
M 65-69	0,81	0,68	0,86	0,88	0,68	0,86
M 70 +	1,35	0,90	1,57	1,41	0,68	1,73
F 0-4	9,23	10,52	8,80	6,61	10,70	8,72
F 5-9	6,94	7,81	6,51	5,73	8,16	6,48
F 10-14	6,67	6,96	6,58	6,00	7,49	6,70
F 15-19	5,53	5,20	5,44	6,17	4,73	5,62
F 20-24	4,85	4,41	5,01	5,11	3,94	4,76
F 25-29	3,77	2,94	4,29	3,88	2,82	4,32
F 30-34	2,43	2,49	2,43	2,47	2,48	2,45
F 35-39	1,89	1,81	2,00	2,12	2,03	2,02
F 40-44	1,75	1,58	1,72	2,47	1,69	1,73
F 45-49	1,35	1,24	1,43	1,76	1,35	1,30
F 50-54	1,21	1,24	1,14	1,50	1,13	1,15
F 55-59	1,21	0,90	1,29	1,94	0,79	1,30
F 60-64	1,35	1,36	1,43	1,23	1,24	1,44
F 65-69	0,67	0,45	0,86	0,88	0,45	0,72
F 70 +	1,21	1,02	1,29	1,23	0,79	1,30
N (UNW)	2439	958	646	1004	919	477

A2.4 Age distribution by religion and refugee status

	Moslems	Christians	Non refugees	Refugees otside camps	Refugees in camps
M 0-4	8,98	9,37	4,72	9,82	9,83
M 5-9	6,72	6,93	5,58	6,89	6,59
M 10-14	6,93	6,66	6,12	5,57	5,64
M 15-19	5,49	5,41	4,51	5,15	5,28
M 20-24	5,21	5,15	3,86	5,15	5,16
M 25-29	4,39	4,09	5,79	4,67	4,68
M 30-34	2,61	2,77	4,72	3,23	3,36
M 35-39	1,78	1,85	2,15	1,68	1,68
M 40-44	1,65	1,58	1,29	1,44	1,32
M 45-49	1,23	1,06	2,36	0,72	0,60
M 50-54	1,23	0,92	1,72	0,96	0,96
M 55-59	0,82	0,92	2,36	1,08	1,20
M 60-64	0,96	1,06	1,93	1,20	1,08
M 65-69	0,82	0,79	1,29	0,72	0,72
M 70 +	1,23	1,32	1,50	1,20	1,32
F 0-4	8,98	9,37	4,72	9,82	9,83
F 5-9	6,72	6,93	5,58	6,89	6,59
F 10-14	6,93	6,66	6,12	5,57	5,64
F 15-19	5,76	5,54	2,58	5,75	6,00
F 20-24	4,53	4,88	4,08	6,11	6,12
F 25-29	3,43	3,83	4,72	3,47	3,60
F 30-34	2,19	2,51	3,00	2,63	2,52
F 35-39	2,47	1,98	2,58	1,44	1,44
F 40-44	1,92	1,72	3,65	1,44	1,32
F 45-49	1,65	1,32	1,93	1,44	1,44
F 50-54	1,37	1,19	2,36	1,32	1,32
F 55-59	1,10	1,19	2,36	1,08	1,08
F 60-64	1,10	1,32	2,79	1,68	1,80
F 65-69	0,69	0,66	1,29	0,72	0,60
F 70 +	1,10	1,06	2,36	1,20	1,32
N (UNW)	2321	117	1365	644	399

A2.5 Age distribution in Gaza and the West Bank by refugee status

	Gaza			West Bank		
	Non-refugees	Refugees outside camps	Refugees in camps	Non-refugees	Refugees outside camps	Refugees in camps
M 0-4	10,11	10,16	10,65	9,20	8,57	7,84
M 5-9	6,97	6,79	7,92	6,63	5,83	5,67
M 10-14	5,83	5,81	7,40	4,94	5,01	6,60
M 15-19	5,03	5,11	5,35	5,41	6,04	5,59
M 20-24	4,69	4,65	4,56	6,50	7,68	5,75
M 25-29	4,57	4,53	3,42	5,14	4,94	5,12
M 30-34	3,20	3,14	2,16	3,11	3,98	3,26
M 35-39	1,83	1,86	2,28	1,35	0,55	1,40
M 40-44	1,49	1,51	1,71	1,08	0,69	1,40
M 45-49	0,57	0,58	0,91	1,08	0,69	1,40
M 50-54	0,69	0,58	0,80	1,49	2,19	1,71
M 55-59	1,03	1,05	0,91	1,49	1,78	0,62
M 60-64	1,26	1,16	0,68	0,95	0,82	1,40
M 65-69	0,69	0,81	0,68	0,81	0,41	0,78
M 70 +	1,37	1,51	0,91	0,68	0,69	1,71
F 0-4	10,11	10,16	10,65	9,20	8,57	7,84
F 5-9	6,97	6,79	7,92	6,63	5,83	5,67
F 10-14	5,83	5,81	7,40	4,94	5,01	6,60
F 15-19	6,29	6,39	5,13	4,33	4,12	6,21
F 20-24	5,37	5,46	3,64	7,98	8,78	5,28
F 25-29	3,31	3,25	3,08	3,92	4,53	3,73
F 30-34	2,63	2,79	2,39	2,44	1,65	2,02
F 35-39	1,49	1,39	2,28	1,62	1,37	2,80
F 40-44	1,37	1,28	1,59	1,49	1,51	2,02
F 45-49	1,14	1,05	1,48	2,17	3,57	1,71
F 50-54	1,49	1,51	1,37	0,68	0,69	1,24
F 55-59	1,14	1,05	0,68	1,08	0,82	1,24
F 60-64	1,60	1,74	0,80	1,76	2,33	1,24
F 65-69	0,46	0,58	0,46	1,22	0,82	0,93
F 70 +	1,49	1,51	0,80	0,68	0,55	1,24
N (UNW)	342	299	313	737	177	87

A2.6 Household composition by region and type of locality

	Occupied territories	Gaza	Gaza Without camps	West Bank	West Bank Without camps	Arab Jerusalem	Camps
Total	7.5	8.9	9.0	7.0	7.0	5.7	8.3
Adult males	2.0	2.2	2.1	2.0	1.9	1.8	2.3
Adult females	2.0	2.2	2.1	2.0	2.0	1.8	2.4
Children	3.4	4.5	4.7	3.0	3.0	2.1	3.7
Children per adult	0.84	1.02	1.11	0.77	0.78	0.58	0.81
N (UNW)	2439	958	646	1004	919	477	399

	Gaza north	Gaza central	Gaza south	Greater Gaza City	Gaza towns/villages	Gaza camps
Total	8.6	9.6	9.1	8.4	9.5	8.8
Adult males	2.1	2.6	2.3	2.0	2.3	2.3
Adult females	2.1	2.5	2.3	1.9	2.3	2.4
Children	4.4	4.5	4.5	4.4	5.0	4.0
Children per adult	1.06	0.91	0.99	1.12	1.09	0.85
N (UNW)	501	41	416	313	332	313

	West Bank north	West Bank central	West Bank south	West Bank towns	West Bank villages	West Bank camps
Total	6.5	7.0	8.4	6.5	7.2	7.4
Adult males	1.9	1.9	2.3	1.8	2.0	2.1
Adult females	2.0	2.1	2.0	1.8	2.1	2.2
Children	2.7	3.0	4.2	2.9	3.1	3.1
Children per adult	0.70	0.74	0.99	0.81	0.76	0.71
N (UNW)	506	284	213	399	517	89

A2.7 Household composition by refugee status. Average number of:

	Non-refugees	UNRWA refugees	Refugees otside camps	Camps
Occupied territories				
Total	7.3	7.7	7.3	8.3
Adult males	2.0	2.1	2.0	2.3
Adult females	2.0	2.1	2.0	2.4
Children	3.3	3.5	3.3	3.7
Children per adult	0.84	0.82	0.83	0.81
N (UNW)	1365	1033	644	399
Gaza				
Total	9.1	8.8	8.8	8.8
Adult males	2.2	2.2	2.1	2.3
Adult females	2.2	2.3	2.1	2.4
Children	4.8	4.3	4.6	4.0
Children per adult	1.10	0.95	1.08	0.85
N (UNW)	342	609	299	313
West Bank				
Total	7.1	6.7	6.5	7.4
Adult males	2.0	2.0	2.0	2.1
Adult females	2.0	2.0	1.9	2.2
Children	3.1	2.7	2.6	3.1
Children per adult	0.80	0.68	0.67	0.71
N (UNW)	737	257	177	87

A2.8 Household composition in occupied territories by religion.
Average number of:

	Moslem	Christian
Occupied territories		
Total	7.6	4.7
Adult males	2.1	1.6
Adult females	2.1	1.6
Children	3.5	1.5
Children per adult	0.85	0.48
N (UNW)	2321	117
West Bank		
Total	7.0	5.5
Adult males	2.0	1.6
Adult females	2.0	1.7
Children	3.1	2.1
Children per adult	0.78	0.64
N (UNW)	958	46
Arab Jerusalem		
Total	6.2	3.8
Adult males	1.9	1.5
Adult females	1.8	1.5
Children	2.4	0.8
Children per adult	0.64	0.27
N (UNW)	409	68

A2.9 Household composition by age of head of household. Average number of:

	15-30	31-40	41-50	51-60	61-70	70 or more
Occupied territories						
Total	5.2	7.5	9.3	8.7	7.4	5.4
Adult males	1.4	1.3	2.3	3.1	2.6	2.0
Adult females	1.5	1.5	2.3	2.7	2.5	2.0
Children	2.4	4.6	4.7	2.9	2.3	1.3
Children per adult	0.84	1.62	1.01	0.49	0.45	0.34
N (UNW)	395	594	496	433	315	138
Gaza						
Total	6.3	8.5	10.8	10.7	8.9	6.3
Adult males	1.7	1.5	2.5	3.3	2.7	2.2
Adult females	1.8	1.6	2.5	2.9	2.8	2.1
Children	2.8	5.5	5.8	4.5	3.4	2.0
Children per adult	0.81	1.79	1.15	0.73	0.61	0.47
N (UNW)	151	247	199	175	102	49
West Bank						
Total	4.8	7.1	8.7	8.1	7.3	5.2
Adult males	1.2	1.3	2.2	3.1	2.7	2.1
Adult females	1.4	1.5	2.2	2.7	2.5	2.0
Children	2.3	4.3	4.3	2.2	2.2	1.2
Children per adult	0.87	1.58	0.97	0.39	0.42	0.28
N (UNW)	177	236	198	166	148	61
Arab Jerusalem						
Total	4.4	6.2	7.3	5.9	4.7	3.9
Adult males	1.3	1.2	2.2	2.6	2.0	1.3
Adult females	1.2	1.4	2.0	2.2	1.9	1.7
Children	1.9	3.5	3.0	1.1	0.8	1.0
Children per adult	0.74	1.34	0.71	0.23	0.21	0.33
N (UNW)	67	111	99	92	65	28

A2.10 Percent of households in which the head is not the oldest male or oldest person

	Not oldest male in household	Not oldest person in household	N (UNW)
Total	4	20	2439
Main region			
Gaza	3	22	958
West Bank	4	20	1004
Arab Jerusalem	4	13	477
Age of head of household			
15-30	10	39	395
31-40	5	27	594
41-50	4	22	496
51-60	-	9	433
61-70	-	4	315
70 or more	-	-	138

Appendix A.6 Tables

(UNW = Unweighted number of respondents)

A6.1 Household wealth by region, refugee status and religion

	\multicolumn{4}{c}{Occupied territories}	\multicolumn{4}{c}{Arab Jerusalem}
	Lower third	Middle third	Upper third	N UNW	Lower third	Middle third	Upper third	N UNW
Total	30	37	33	2439	5	29	66	477
Region								
Gaza without camps	37	40	23	646				
WB without camps	23	39	37	916				
Refugee status								
Non-refugees	22	39	39	1365	(4)	25	71	287
UNRWA-refugees	42	35	23	1033				
-in camps	61	32	8	399				
-outside camps	31	37	32	644	(7)	39	55	170
Religion								
Moslems	31	38	31	2321	(4)	27	70	409
Christians	(7)	27	67	117	(12)	36	52	68

369

A6.2 Household wealth by household composition and Head of Household characteristics

	\multicolumn{4}{c	}{Occupied territories}	\multicolumn{4}{c}{Arab Jerusalem}
	Lower third	Middle third	Upper third	N UNW	Lower third	Middle third	Upper third	N UNW
Persons per household								
1-5	29	37	34	808	(7)	33	60	218
6-10	29	37	34	1155	-	23	74	219
11 or more	33	39	28	474	-	-	70	41
Adult males per household								
0-1	32	37	31	1172	7	31	62	240
2-3	28	38	34	870	-	24	72	177
4 or more	24	37	39	397	-	(30)	69	61
Female adults per household								
0-1	31	36	33	1058	(7)	34	59	229
2-3	30	38	33	1049	-	21	76	203
4 or more	25	42	33	332	-	-	69	46
Children per household								
0	32	33	34	499	(9)	29	62	138
1-2	23	38	40	527	-	30	67	129
3-4	29	40	32	617	-	25	71	132
5 or more	34	38	28	796	-	33	65	79
Relation to other households in housing unit								
Family	27	36	37	496	-	28	71	142
No relations	19	30	50	177	-	26	67	98
Only 1 household	33	39	29	1770	-	33	59	238
Sex of Head of Household								
Male	29	38	33	2216	(3)	29	68	409
Female	45	25	30	151	(19)	31	50	53
Age of Head of Household								
15-30	33	42	26	395	-	32	64	67
31-40	31	36	33	594	-	36	62	111
41-50	27	35	37	496	-	30	65	99
51-60	26	36	39	433	-	23	74	92
61-70	28	38	34	315	-	23	69	65
70 or more	33	39	28	138	-	-	52	28
Years of education for Head of Household								
0	46	36	19	391	(23)	(34)	42	48
1-6	27	43	30	779	-	34	61	147
7-9	33	39	28	466	-	42	57	108
10-12	25	31	44	449	-	(19)	77	96
13 or more	22	30	48	354	-	(16)	82	79

A6.3 Household wealth in Gaza and the West Bank by sub-region, type of locality, refugee status and religion

	Gaza				West Bank			
	Lower third	Middle third	Upper third	N UNW	Lower third	Middle third	Upper third	N UNW
Total	48	35	17	958	25	40	36	1004
Region								
Gaza without camps	37	40	23	646				
WB without camps					23	39	37	916
Sub-region								
North	41	34	26	501	29	41	30	506
Central	(48)	(40)	-	41	13	36	51	284
South	56	36	8	416	30	42	28	213
Type of locality								
Greater Gaza City	32	34	34	313				
Gaza towns and villages	42	45	13	332				
Gaza camps	69	25	6	313				
WB towns					19	35	47	399
WB villages					26	42	31	517
WB camps					41	46	13	87
Refugee status								
Non-refugees	28	43	29	342	23	40	37	737
UNRWA-refugees	59	31	10	609	28	40	32	257
-in camps	69	25	6	313	41	46	13	87
-outside camps	48	36	16	299	23	38	39	177
Religion								
Moslem	48	35	17	958	26	41	34	958
Christian	-	-	-	3	-	(18)	80	46

A6.4 Household wealth in Gaza and the West Bank by household composition and Head of Household characteristics

	Gaza Lower third	Gaza Middle third	Gaza Upper third	N UNW	West Bank Lower third	West Bank Middle third	West Bank Upper third	N UNW
Persons per household								
1-5	54	27	19	221	27	41	33	370
6-10	46	37	17	460	23	39	38	478
11 or more	44	40	16	280	24	39	37	154
Adult males per household								
0-1	53	30	17	412	29	41	30	529
2-3	45	38	17	378	21	40	39	316
4 or more	41	42	17	178	18	35	47	159
Female adults per household								
0-1	51	29	20	378	27	39	34	460
2-3	46	38	17	433	25	40	35	415
4 or more	44	43	13	157	15	43	42	129
Children per household								
0	59	27	14	137	29	38	35	224
1-2	43	35	22	157	19	41	40	242
3-4	45	40	16	224	25	42	34	261
5 or more	47	35	18	443	26	40	34	277
Relation to other households in housing unit								
Family	37	38	25	209	25	35	40	145
No relations	46	26	28	35	21	36	43	44
Only 1 household	54	34	13	717	25	42	34	815
Sex of Head of Household								
Male	46	36	18	892	23	41	36	919
Female	74	-	-	31	46	24	30	67
Age of Head of Household								
15-30	50	31	19	151	29	48	23	177
31-40	47	35	18	247	26	37	37	236
41-50	47	35	18	199	22	35	43	198
51-60	43	38	19	175	20	38	42	166
61-70	47	39	14	102	24	41	35	148
70 or more	55	32	13	49	27	43	30	61
Years of education for Head of Household								
0	56	34	11	181	42	36	22	162
1-6	51	34	16	280	21	48	31	353
7-9	48	40	13	154	31	39	30	204
10-12	45	36	20	191	18	32	50	164
13 or more	37	34	29	155	15	31	55	121

A6.5 Household weekly meat consumption by region and selected background variables

	Less than 1 kg	1-2 kg	3 kg or more	N UNW
Total	36	43	21	2439
Main region				
Gaza	42	44	14	958
Gaza excl. camps	39	44	17	646
West Bank	36	41	24	1004
West Bank excl. camps	34	41	25	916
Arab Jerusalem	43	56	31	477
Sub-region				
Gaza north	31	52	17	501
Gaza south	52	36	12	416
WB north	41	44	15	506
WB central	14	49	37	284
WB south	54	19	27	213
Type of locality				
Greater Gaza City	31	49	20	313
Gaza towns and villages	46	40	15	332
Gaza camps	47	45	9	313
WB towns	32	42	26	399
WB villages	36	40	25	517
WB camps	51	41	7	87
Refugee status				
Non-refugees	31	44	25	1365
UNRWA refugees	44	41	15	1033
-in camps	48	44	9	399
-outside camps	41	39	20	644
Religion				
Moslem	37	43	21	2321
Christian	(8)	59	33	117
Household wealth				
Lower third	55	33	12	739
Middle third	37	46	17	872
Upper third	18	48	34	827
Sex of head of household				
Male	35	44	22	2216
Female	48	38	14	151

A6.6 Household weekly meat consumption by household composition and Head of Household characteristics

	Less than 1 kg	1-2 kg	3 kg or more	N UNW
Persons per household				
1-5	40	48	11	808
6-10	33	46	22	1155
11 or more	37	35	28	474
Adult males per household				
0-1	41	46	13	1172
2-3	36	43	21	870
4 or more	26	27	29	397
Adult females per household				
0-1	38	49	13	1058
2-3	37	43	20	1049
4 or more	26	27	29	332
Children per household				
0	42	41	17	499
1-2	34	48	19	527
3-4	30	49	22	617
5 or more	38	37	25	796
Years of education for Head of Household				
0	43	32	25	391
1-6	35	44	21	779
7-9	41	43	16	466
10-12	33	46	21	449
13 or more	23	53	24	354

A6.7 Change in household income since the Gulf War in percent of households by selected background variables

	Much less	Somewhat less	Same	Somewhat more	Much more	N UNW
Total	41	22	31	5	-	2439
Main region						
Gaza	47	22	28	2	-	958
West Bank	40	23	30	6	1	1004
Arab Jerusalem	25	17	48	9	-	477
Gaza excl. camps	46	22	29	2	-	646
WB excl. camps	40	24	30	6	1	916
Camps	50	19	28	3	1	399
Sub-region						
Gaza north	46	22	30	-	-	501
Gaza south	49	22	26	-	-	416
WB north	42	26	24	7	-	506
WB central	32	20	41	6	-	284
WB south	49	22	28	-	-	213
Type of locality						
Greater Gaza City	46	20	31	-	-	313
Gaza towns/villages	46	24	27	-	-	332
Gaza camps	49	21	27	-	-	313
WB towns	41	24	28	7	-	399
WB villages	37	24	31	6	-	517
WB camps	51	16	47	9	-	87
Refugee status						
Non-refugees	39	22	33	5	1	1365
UNRWA refugees	44	22	28	4	-	1033
-in camps	50	19	28	(3)	-	399
-outside camps	41	24	28	5	-	644
Religion						
Moslem	41	23	30	5	-	2321
Christian	34	13	43	6	-	117
Adult males per household						
0-1	37	24	33	6	-	1172
2-3	42	21	32	5	-	870
4 or more	52	21	23	4	-	397
Sex of head of household						
Male	41	23	30	5	1	2216
Female	29	20	50	-	-	151

A6.8 Percent of households earning labour income from

	Wages	Salary UNRWA	Other salary	Business	Land cultivation	Animal husbandry	N UNW
Total	59	5	9	23	21	7	2439
Main region							
Gaza	48	10	14	19	9	2	958
West Bank	64	3	4	26	31	10	1004
Arab Jerusalem	66	-	16	17	-	-	477
Gaza excl. camps	48	6	14	19	13	3	646
WB excl. camps	63	2	4	27	34	10	916
Sub-region							
Gaza north	49	7	13	22	8	(3)	501
Gaza south	48	13	15	15	12	-	416
WB north	58	4	5	28	34	10	506
WB central	63	-	5	29	28	14	284
WB south	80	-	-	18	30	(4)	213
Type of locality							
Greater Gaza City	46	6	15	23	10	-	313
Gaza towns/villages	50	7	14	16	17	-	332
Gaza camps	49	18	13	18	-	-	313
WB towns	59	-	5	36	15	4	399
WB villages	68	-	4	21	46	15	517
WB camps	65	(10)	-	25	-	-	87
Refugee status							
Non-refugees	62	-	-	28	29	8	1365
UNRWA refugees	55	12	10	22	10	4	1033
-in camps	54	15	11	20	-	-	399
-outside camps	56	9	9	24	15	5	644
Religion							
Moslem	60	5	8	23	22	7	2321
Christian	48	-	15	27	-	-	117
Adult males per household							
0-1	56	5	9	21	17	4	1172
2-3	58	4	9	26	24	9	870
4 or more	70	5	6	25	31	8	397
Sex of head of household							
Male	60	5	8	24	22	6	2216
Female	42	-	10	8	19	7	151

A6.9 Head of Household labour income index by selected background variables, Occupied territories

	Non-working	N UNW	Working Household Heads Labour income index Lower	Middle	Upper	N UNW
Total	29	2439	24	25	22	1710
Main region						
Gaza	32	958	31	22	15	650
West Bank	26	1004	23	28	23	741
Arab Jerusalem	34	477	10	15	41	319
Gaza excl. camps	27	646	31	24	18	469
WB excl. camps	26	916	23	28	23	678
Refugee status						
Non-refugees	25	1365	24	27	24	1014
UNRWA refugees	35	1033	25	22	18	662
-in camps	37	399	29	22	12	244
-outside camps	33	644	23	22	22	427
Religion						
Moslem	28	2321	25	25	22	1634
Christian	39	117	-	30	27	75
Household wealth						
Lower third	37	739	34	18	11	456
Middle third	27	872	25	28	19	616
Upper third	23	827	14	28	35	637
Sex						
Male	25	2216	25	27	23	1649
Female	76	151	12	8	-	32
Age						
15-30	14	395	38	27	20	340
31-40	9	594	31	30	31	519
41-50	19	496	23	28	30	399
51-60	39	433	18	26	18	267
61-70	59	315	13	18	11	130
70 or more	77	138	(6)	9	8	26
Years of education						
1-3	60	391	19	16	5	152
4-6	33	779	27	27	14	512
7-9	18	466	34	30	19	374
10-12	19	449	25	27	29	360
12 or more	11	354	10	24	55	312

A6.10 Head of Household labour income index in Gaza and the West Bank by selected background variables

	Non-working	N UNW	Working Household Heads Labour income index Lower	Middle	Upper	N UNW
Gaza	32	958	31	22	15	650
Sub-region						
Gaza north	28	501	35	22	15	364
Gaza central	(53)	41	-	-	-	18
Gaza south	35	416	28	23	14	268
Type of locality						
Greater Gaza City	26	313	33	23	18	236
Gaza towns/villages	29	332	29	25	17	233
Gaza camps	41	313	32	19	8	181
Refugee status						
Non-refugees	27	342	30	25	19	258
UNRWA refugees	35	609	32	21	12	383
-in camps	41	313	32	19	8	181
-outside camps	28	299	33	23	16	205
Household wealth						
Lower third	40	462	37	15	9	273
Middle third	29	336	26	30	16	241
Upper third	16	163	28	29	28	136
West Bank	26	1004	23	28	23	741
Sub-region						
WB north	26	506	22	27	25	376
WB central	28	284	20	30	22	205
WB south	26	213	29	29	16	160
Type of locality						
WB towns	22	399	20	32	26	306
WB villages	29	517	25	26	20	372
WB camps	27	87	22	30	22	63
Refugee status						
Non-refugees	24	737	24	30	22	560
UNRWA refugees	33	257	20	25	20	173
-in camps	27	87	22	30	22	63
-outside camps	35	177	18	22	25	116
Household wealth						
Lower third	32	252	33	23	13	172
Middle third	25	397	27	29	19	290
Upper third	24	354	12	31	33	278

A6.11 Household income types by Head of Household labour activity

	Occupied territories			Arab Jerusalem		
	All	HH=0	HH>0	All	HH=0	HH>0
Labour income						
Wages	59	42	66	66	40	8
Salary UNRWA	5	6	4	-	-	-
Other salaries	9	12	7	16	15	1
Business	23	8	29	17	-	2
Sub-contracting	2	(1)	2	-	-	-
Land cultivation	21	21	22	-	-	-
Animal husbandry	7	7	6	-	-	-
Fishing	1	-	-	-	-	-
Non-labour income						
Rent revenues	3	3	3	5	(7)	-
Remittances	8	19	3	7	15	-
Pensions	3	6	1	5	11	-
Sale of land	1	-	-	-	-	-
Social benefits	9	18	5	39	57	3
Other income	9	19	5	7	(9)	?
Change in household income since the Gulf war						
Much less	41	44	40	25	27	2
Somewhat less	22	20	23	17	13	2
The same	31	33	30	48	55	4
Somewhat more	5	3	6	9	-	1
Much more	1	-	1	-	-	-
N (UNW)	2433	723	1710	476	157	319

HH=0: Head of Household worked less than 1 month last year
HH>0: Head of Household worked more than 1 month last year

A6.12 Household income types in Gaza and the West Bank by Head of Household labour activity

	Gaza			West Bank		
	All	HH=0	HH>0	All	HH=0	HH>0
Labour income						
Wages	48	31	56	64	49	70
Salary UNRWA	10	12	9	3	3	2
Other salaries	14	15	14	4	9	3
Business	19	8	23	26	10	33
Sub-contracting	2	-	2	2	-	3
Land cultivation	9	(4)	12	31	36	30
Animal husbandry	2	(3)	(2)	10	11	10
Fishing	2	-	-	-	-	-
Non-labour income						
Rent revenues	3	-	3	3	3	3
Remittances	7	16	2	9	23	4
Pensions	2	(3)	-	3	7	1
Sale of land	(1)	-	-	-	-	-
Social benefits	8	19	3	4	9	3
Other income	11	22	5	8	19	5
Change in household income since the Gulf war						
Much less	47	53	45	40	42	40
Somewhat less	22	18	23	23	22	24
The same	28	27	29	30	32	29
Somewhat more	2	-	3	6	4	7
Much more	-	-	-	1	-	1
N (UNW)	956	306	650	1001	260	741

HH=0: Head of Household worked less than 1 month last year
HH>0: Head of Household worked more than 1 month last year

A6.13 Percent of households receiving various non-labour income types by selected background variables

	Remittances	Pensions	Social benefits	Other income	N UNW
Total	8	3	9	9	2439
Main region					
Gaza	7	2	8	11	958
West Bank	9	3	4	8	1004
Arab Jerusalem	7	5	39	7	477
Gaza excl. camps	6	(2)	6	10	616
WB excl. camps	9	3	4	8	916
Sub-region					
Gaza north	9	-	6	14	501
Gaza south	3	-	8	7	416
WB north	11	3	6	8	506
WB central	12	4	-	9	284
WB south	-	-	-	10	213
Type of locality					
Greater Gaza City	8	-	5	13	313
Gaza towns/villages	(4)	-	7	8	332
Gaza camps	8	-	13	12	313
WB towns	8	3	2	10	399
WB villages	11	3	5	7	517
WB camps	5	-	11	13	87
Refugee status					
Non-refugees	8	3	6	8	1365
UNRWA refugees	8	3	13	11	1033
-in camps	7	(3)	12	12	399
-outside camps	9	3	14	10	644
Religion					
Moslem	8	3	8	9	2321
Christian	9	-	23	10	117
Adult males per household					
0-1	9	2	11	10	1172
2-3	7	5	7	7	870
4 or more	6	(3)	5	8	397
Sex of head of household					
Male	7	3	7	9	2216
Female	31	-	31	13	151

A6.14 Distribution of household income sources by household wealth group

	Lower third	Middle third	Upper third	N UNW
Wages	30	37	33	1448
UNRWA salary	41	41	18	137
Other salary	40	26	34	251
Business income	16	35	50	525
Sub-contracting	19	35	46	58
Rent revenues	-	22	74	83
Remittances	26	39	35	198
Pensions	17	34	49	80
Land cultivation	15	44	41	410
Animal husbandry	18	45	37	116
Social benefits	42	29	29	329
Other income	41	32	27	211
Change in income since the gulf war				
Much less	35	41	24	1005
Somewhat less	26	39	35	519
The same	29	31	40	803
Somewhat more	15	38	48	125
Much more	-	-	60	19

Appendix A.7
Labour Table Appendix

Comparison with Israeli CBS Labour Force Survey for "Judaea, Samaria, and the Gaza Area".

Because of the widespread reference to the Israeli Labour Force survey in discussions about employment in the occupied territories, it may be of interest to discuss the compatibility of concepts and definitions between this survey and the FAFO Living Conditions survey. Even if both surveys are based on the ILO endorsed "labour force framework", they have some differences that are of relevance for comparison of results. This appendix will provide some guidelines for comparison of the two surveys. The discussion will be conducted along comparison of results for the three main labour force groups; "not in the labour force", "employed" and "unemployed".

At this stage it may be useful to point to the different purposes of the two surveys to be compared. As a standard "labour force survey",

Figure A.7.34; Construction of labour force categories in the FAFO 1992 living conditions survey for the occupied territories

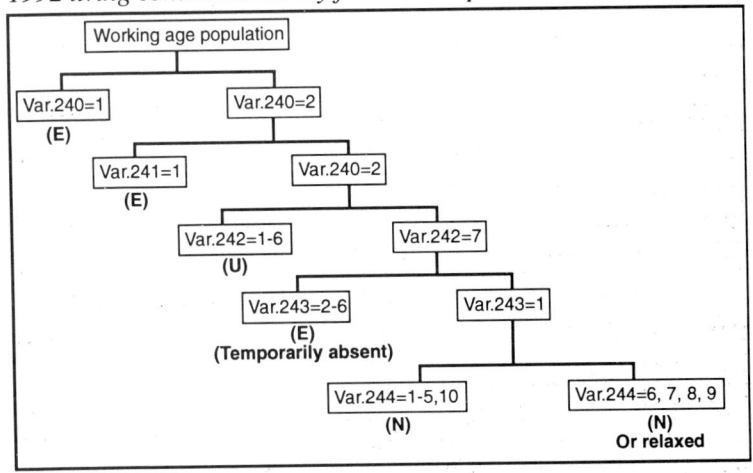

```
              Working age population
              /                    \
       Var.240=1              Var.240=2
         (E)                  /        \
                       Var.241=1      Var.240=2
                         (E)          /        \
                               Var.242=1-6    Var.242=7
                                  (U)         /        \
                                       Var.243=2-6    Var.243=1
                                          (E)         /        \
                                    (Temporarily absent)
                                                Var.244=1-5,10   Var.244=6, 7, 8, 9
                                                   (N)               (N)
                                                                   Or relaxed
```

Symbols:
E = Employed
U = Unemployed
N = Not in labour force
Numbers refer to variable numbers in part two of the questionnaire.
Note: Full-time employed persons are defined as employed persons answering 7 weeks or more on variable Employed persons answering 6 weeks or less were considered as part time employed.

the CBS survey is primarily concerned with measuring labour activity conducted by the Palestinian population in the occupied territories. The FAFO living conditions survey, on the contrary, is at least as interested in documenting *non*-activity, and the possible reasons for this lack of labour activity. Figure A.7.34 presents how the respondents are ascribed their labour force status in the FAFO survey according to their answers in the employment section of the questionnaire.

Not in Labour Force/ Labour Force Participation

Table A.7.30 presents labour force participation ratios for the occupied territories of the FAFO 1992 living conditions survey and the 1990 CBS labour force survey. (In percent of "working age population", 15 years or older):

After the war in 1948, Beit Safafa South remained the only area in West-jerusalem with compact Arab settlement. Except for this small area, almost all "Non-Jews" in Jerusalem still live in the eastern part of the city, i.e. in areas covered by the FAFO survey. The Jerusalem Institute for Israel Studies' results for "Non-Jews" in Jerusalem has thus been weighted into the CBS labour statistics for "Judaea, Samaria and Gaza" to construct a CBS estimate parallel to the area covered by the FAFO survey.

Labour force membership in the FAFO living conditions survey required, as in the CBS labour force surveys, either at least one hour paid work, or at least 15 hours work in family farm or business, or both in the preceding (determinant) week. All FAFO results concerning under-utilization of labour are based on these definitions. Even if both surveys thus use the same basic defini-

Table A.7.30 Comparative labour force participation rates FAFO 1992 and CBS 1990

	Occupied territories		Gaza		West Bank		Arab Jerusalem	
	FAFO (1992)	CBS (1990)	FAFO (1992)	CBS (1990)	FAFO (1992)	CBS (1990)	FAFO (1992)	CBS (1990)
Total	48	38	39	34	53	41	50	36
Men	80	71	72	69	86	72	77	67
Women	14	7	7	2	18	10	19	7

Note: The CBS results for the "Occupied Territories" have been taken from two separate sources. The results for Gaza and the West Bank are taken from the CBS "Statistical Abstract of Israel 1991", Table 27.17. The results for "Arab Jerusalem", also presented separately in Table A.7.30, are calculated from The Jerusalem Institute for Israel Studies' "Statistical yearbook of Jerusalem no. 9 - 1990", Tables VII/1 and VII/2.

tions from the labour force framework, FAFO numbers systematically exceeds those of the CBS. The 1990 CBS data are based on quarterly interviews, and are thus adjusted for seasonal variations in labour force participation. In the FAFO survey on the contrary, interviewing took place in June, July and August 1992 only. Seasonal variation in labour force participation may thus explain some of the differences between the two surveys.

1990 was deliberately selected as CBS reference year instead of 1991, to reduce the influence of the Gulf war on employment. Still, differences in the political situation, like the reduction of the intensity of the intifada from 1990 to 1992, may have led to increased labour force participation in this time span.

Finally, the observed differences between FAFO and CBS labour force participation ratios may also be rooted in the interviewing situation itself: To gain confidence with female respondents, FAFO used female interviewer pairs to interview women. The fact that the relative differences in labour force participation ratios between the two surveys are greater for women than for men, could be an indication of greater confidence among respondents with FAFO enumerators. Even if the FAFO survey was carefully designed to obtain more accurate statistics on women's activities, we still feel the coverage of unpaid female economic activities can be further improved. Thus, there is, no doubt, scope for future innovative research to be conducted in this field.

Unemployed Persons

Table A.7.31 presents unemployment ratios of CBS and FAFO, using slightly different versions of the labour force measurement framework. Note that unemployment is measured in relation to the labour force, *not* in relation to the population at working age, (15 years or older). The registered unemployment rate is thus depend-

Table A.7.31 Comparison of unemployment rates in the FAFO 1992 and CBS 1990 surveys

	Occupied Territories		Gaza		West Bank	
	FAFO (1992)	CBS (1990)	FAFO (1992)	CBS (1990)	FAFO (1992)	CBS (1990)
All labour force	7	4	12	4	3	4
Men	6	4	12	4	3	4
Women	6	3	-	7	-	3

ent *both* on the definition of "unemployed" and the definition of "labour force".

The FAFO survey measures higher unemployment ratios among women, and for Gaza than CBS. The higher unemployment ratio for women in the FAFO survey may be due to the inclusion of Arab Jerusalem in this survey. A possible explanation for the difference for male unemployment in Gaza is differences in the political situation between 1989 and 1992. At the time of interviewing in the FAFO survey, new restrictions on employment in Israel (age limits on entry, new permissions, e.t.c.) had recently been introduced, obstructing several Gaza workers from access to their usual employment in Israel.

Employed Persons

The last part of the employment chapter in the FAFO living conditions survey mainly deals with the distribution of the labour force by type, place and economic branch of work. Because interviewing in the FAFO survey was made over a few months only, two adaptations of the labour force concept were made to reduce the effect of seasonal variations:

1. Persons who were not members of the labour force at the time of the survey, but had still worked one month during the last year were included in the tables for distribution of the labour force. (Approximately 95% of the persons who had worked for one month or more during the preceding year were also labour force members).
2. Labour force members who had not worked one month or more during the preceding year on the contrary, were not included in the results for distribution of employment over type, place and economic branch of work. This group comprised 84% of the labour force, referred to in the first part of the employment chapter.

All results presented in this part thus comprise persons who were *both* labour force members, and had worked at least one

Figure A.7.35 Distribution of employed persons in the FAFO and CBS surveys

	Employed Full time	Employed Part time	Temporarily absent	Unemployed	Not in labour force
Worked less than one month last year	1	2	3	4	5
Worked more than one month last year	6	7	8	9	10

month during the preceding year. Figure A.7.35 illustrates the difference between the CBS labour force survey and the FAFO living condition survey on this point:

The distribution of employed persons over type, place and economic branch of work in the FAFO living condition survey comprise persons classified in boxes 6,7,8 and 9 above. In the CBS survey the corresponding distribution of employment over type, place and economic branch of work refers to persons in boxes 1,2,3,6,7 and 8. In a living condition perspective the main attribute of persons in grouped in boxes 1,2 and 3 above is their small amount of labour activity (less than one month the preceding year), and not e.g. the economic branch of this small amount of work. The lack of labour activity is thus covered by the estimates of full-time / part-time work.

Tables
(UNW = Unweighted number of respondents)

Table A.7.1 International comparison of labour force participation rates

	Occupied territories	Israel "non-jews"	Israel jews	Norway
Percentage of total population in labour force	26	23	38	55
Percentage of population 15 years or older in labour force	48	40	54	64
Percentage of male population 15 years or older in labour force	80	68	61	76
Percentage of female population 15 years or older in labour force	14	12	46	60
Percentage of population below 15 years	45	42	31	19

Table A.7.2 Regional comparison of labour force participation rates

	Arab Jerusalem	Occupied territories	Gaza	West Bank
Percentage of total population in labour force	26	20	30	31
Percentage of population 15 years or older in labour force	48	39	53	50
Percentage of male population 15 years or older in labour force	80	72	86	77
Percentage of female population 15 years or older in labour force	14	7	18	19
Percentage of population below 15 years	45	50	43	37

Table A.7.3 Labour force participation rates by region, gender and selected background variables

	Male						Female	
	Gaza	N UNW	West Bank	N UNW	Arab Jerusalem	N UNW	Occupied territories	N UNW
Region								
Gaza	71	477					6	481
Gaza excl. camps	76	319					6	326
West Bank			86	501			19	503
WB excl. camps			86	458			19	458
Arab Jerusalem					76	234	18	242
Sub-region								
Gaza North	80	247					8	254
Gaza South	63	210					4	206
WB North			86	248			19	258
WB Central			94	146			18	138
WB South			74	106			20	107
Type of locality								
Greater Gaza City	81	154					8	159
Gaza towns/villages	72	164					7	167
Gaza camps	64	158					3	155
WB towns			82	201			19	198
WB villages			89	257			19	260
WB camps			76	42			14	45
Refugee status								
Non-refugees	84	169	87	361	(79)	147	18	686
UNRWA refugees	64	305	83	133			8	519
-in camps	64	158	76	42	-	-	6	200
-outside camps	63	147	86	94	(67)	77	10	326
Religion								
Moslems	71	475	85	480	(75)	204	14	1161
Christians	-	2	89	21	-	29	23	65

	Male						Female	
	Gaza	N UNW	West Bank	N UNW	Arab Jerusalem	N UNW	Occupied territories	N UNW
Household wealth								
Lower third	64	227	81	124	-	4	7	385
Middle third	78	175	87	185	(68)	54	16	456
Upper third	73	74	87	192	(79)	176	20	384
Male adults per household								
0-1	85	174	91	247	(86)	109	16	642
2-3	67	202	87	170	(63)	98	16	399
4 or more	68	101	75	84	-	27	8	185
RSI is head of household								
Yes	75	264	90	349	(82)	155	17	106
No	69	213	79	152	(66)	79	14	1119
Age								
15-20	34	90	67	66	(41)	34	12	182
20-29	83	142	90	126	-	58	14	359
30-39	96	107	97	128	-	50	15	273
40-49	86	63	95	81	-	34	20	169
50-59	71	26	92	40	-	17	14	96
60 or more	34	49	59	60	(49)	41	9	147
Marital status								
Unmarried	50	140	73	129	(69)	73	22	249
Married	80	333	92	366	(81)	158	10	845
Years of education								
0	38	48	70	31	-	9	13	273
1-6	84	100	86	124	(67)	39	12	251
7-9	76	82	88	134	-	66	12	294
10-12	67	160	87	129	(76)	74	11	299
13 or more	82	87	84	83	-	46	40	109

Table A.7.4 Unemployed persons as percentage of the labour force by gender, region and selected background variables

	Total	N UNW	Men	N UNW	Men Gaza	N UNW	Men West Bank	N UNW
Total	6	1123	6	955	12	341	3	436
Main region								
Gaza	12	373	12	341				
Camps excluded	11	266	(11)	242				
West Bank	(3)	532	(3)	436				
Camps excluded	(2)	492	(3)	403				
Arab Jerusalem	(12)	219	(9)	179				
Campss	(11)	146	(11)	131				
Sub-region								
Gaza North	(8)	213	(9)	194				
Gaza South	(15)	149	(14)	136				
WB North	(4)	262	(4)	214				
WB Central		158		131				
WB South		111		90				
Type of locality								
Greater Gaza City	(9)	134	(9)	122				
Gaza towns/villages	(13)	131	(13)	119				
Gaza camps	(14)	107	(15)	99				
WB towns	(5)	213	6	175				
WB villages	(1)	279		228				
WB camps		39		32				
Refugee status								
Non-refugees	(3)	691	(3)	576	(4)	141	(4)	317
UNRWA refugees	11	411	12	363	19	197	(4)	111
Refugees in camps	12	146	(11)	131	(15)	98		32
Refugees outside camps	12	270	(11)	235	(24)	99		82

390

	Total	N UNW	Men	N UNW	Men Gaza	N UNW	Men West Bank	N UNW
Household wealth								
Lower third	12	287	12	259	(20)	152	(5)	105
Middle third	(5)	395	(5)	333	(8)	134	(3)	162
Upper third	(4)	441	(4)	363		55		169
Adult males per household								
0-1	(5)	560	(5)	461	(12)	146	(3)	225
2-3	6	396	(6)	344	(15)	133		146
4 or more	(7)	167	(8)	150	(10)	62	(6)	65
Age								
15-19	(6)	102		87		30		44
20-29	8	344	(8)	292	(15)	120		119
30-39	(6)	317	(6)	273	(9)	102		125
40-49	(4)	188	(5)	156	(14)	52		75
50-59		81		69		17		36
60 or more		91		78		20		37
Years of education								
0		78		49		23		22
1-6	(7)	244	(7)	216	(15)	81		109
7-9	(5)	262	(5)	237		62		121
10-12	(6)	294	(6)	263	(14)	101		110
13 or more	(8)	245	(7)	190	(11)	74	(5)	74
Occupation								
Mid professional	(6)	169		112	(13)	52		42
Skilled worker, vocational	(7)	216	8	207	(20)	59		106
Other	(8)	170	(7)	153	(16)	54		75
Haven't been trained/ housewife/student	(9)	318	(10)	261	(14)	112	(7)	94

Table A.7.5 "Discouraged" workers as percent of persons not in labour force by selected background variables

		N (UNW)			N (UNW)
Total	4	1315	**Household wealth**		
Main region			Lower third	(4)	453
Gaza	(4)	585	Middle third	6	476
Gaza excl. camps	3	379	Upper third	(3)	385
West Bank	5	472	**Sex**		
WB excl. camps	4	424	Male	(7)	257
Arab Jerusalem	(4)		Female	4	1058
Type of locality			**Age**		
Greater Gaza City	4	179	15-19	(4)	270
Gaza towns/villages	7	200	20-29	9	341
Gaza camps	4	206	30-39	(4)	241
WB towns	(4)	186	40-49	-	159
WB villages	(4)	238	50-59	-	98
WB camps	(14)	48	60 or more	-	206
Refugee status			**Years of education**		
Non-refugees	4	672	0	-	283
UNRWA refugees	6	623	1-6	(4)	270
-in camps	(7)	254	7-9	(5)	314
-outside camps	(5)	374	10-12	(5)	368
			13 or more	(15)	80

Table A.7.6 Full-time and part-time employed persons as a percentage of labour force members by selected background variables. Full time/part-time

	Total	N UNW	Men total	N UNW	Women total	N UNW
Total	43/48	1123	42/48	955	44/47	168
Main region						
Gaza	27/52	373	25/54	341	(42)/(39)	32
Gaza excl. camps	25/57	266	23/58	242	(40)/(45)	24
West Bank	46/49	532	47/48	436	44/53	96
WB excl. camps	46/49	492	47/49	403	45/54	89
Arab Jerusalem	65/21	219	70/(20)	179	(43)/-	40
Camps	35/44	146	34/45	131	(43)/-	15
Sub-region						
Gaza North	30/53	213	30/53	194	(30)/(51)	19
Gaza South	22/56	149	(18)/59	136	(72)/-	13
WB North	42/51	262	41/52	214	46/48	48
WB Central	59/39	158	61/37	131	(48)/(52)	27
WB South	39/58	111	40/56	90	(34)/(66)	21
Type of locality						
Greater Gaza City	35/47	131	33/47	122	(49)/-	12
Gaza towns/villages	15/66	131	(14)/68	119	-/-	12
Gaza camps	31/44	107	30/46	99	-/-	8
WB towns	49/44	213	46/46	175	65/(34)	38
WB villages	46/52	279	48/50	228	35/64	51
WB camps	42/44	39	(43)/(45)	32	-/-	7
Refugee status						
Non-refugees	45/50	691	45/50	576	47/49	115
UNRWA refugees	38/43	411	38/43	363	(37)/(47)	48
-in camps	35/44	146	34/45	131	-/-	15
-outside camps	41/42	270	42/40	235	(33)/(51)	35
Religion						
Moslem	41/49	1065	41/49	913	42/49	152
Christian	75/20	57	76/(16)	41	(70)/-	16
Household wealth						
Lower third	28/54	287	29/53	259	-/(64)	28
Middle third	36/55	395	35/55	333	41/55	62
Upper third	59/36	441	60/36	363	56/35	78

Table A.7.6 (Continued) Full-time and part-time employed persons as a percentage of labour force members by selected background variables. Full time/part-time

	Total	N UNW	Men total	N UNW	Women total	N UNW
Adult males per household						
0-1	51/41	560	51/41	461	52/39	99
2-3	40/49	396	40/48	344	39/51	52
4 or more	34/57	167	34/56	150	(35)/(63)	17
Age						
15-19	23/68	102	(15)/74	87	(47)/(50)	15
20-29	38/50	344	37/51	292	(45)/(42)	52
30-39	51/38	317	51/40	273	(52)/(31)	44
40-49	49/44	188	49/43	156	(47)/(51)	32
50-59	55/41	81	61/35	69	-/(72)	12
60 or more	38/47	91	40/43	78	-/(77)	13
Years of education						
0	19/65	78	(25)/57	49	(16)/81	29
1-6	31/56	244	30/57	216	(51)/(43)	28
7-9	35/57	262	34/59	237	(38)/(49)	25
10-12	45/45	294	47/44	263	(48)/(46)	31
13 or more	60/27	245	65/26	190	69/(18)	55
Occupation						
High professional	72/(27)	55	72/(28)	48	-/-	7
Mid professional	66/(26)	169	62/28	112	75/(19)	57
Business/Administration	92/-	19	91/-	18	-/-	1
Skilled worker	41/48	216	39/50	207	(66)/-	9
Sales worker	65/27	47	65/(27)	47	/-	5
Farmer/fisher	21/75	79	22/74	74	-/-	15
Traditional craft	45/46	50	(49)/(47)	35	-/-	17
Other	36/47	170	30/54	153	(76)/-	
Haven't been trained/ housewife/student	33/56	318	38/49		261	(11)/8

Table A.7.7 Full-time and part-time employed persons as a percentage of male labour force members in Gaza and the West Bank by selected background variables. Full time/part-time

	Men Gaza	N UNW	Men West Bank	N UNW
Total				
Refugee status				
Non-refugees	22/68	141	48/49	317
UNRWA refugees	29/43	197	45/46	111
-in camps	30/47	98	(43)/(45)	32
-outside camps	(25)/38	99	47/45	82
Religion				
Moslem	25/54	339	45/50	420
Christian		2	89/-	16
Household wealth				
Lower third	(19)/50	152	38/55	105
Middle third	24/60	134	38/55	162
Upper third	(47)/(46)	55	60/38	169
Adult males per household				
0-1	34/46	146	52/44	225
2-3	27/47	133	44/52	146
4 or more	(14)/72	62	43/51	65
Age				
15-19	-/(73)	30	(14)/79	44
20-29	21/56	120	46/51	119
30-39	(29)/57	102	58/35	125
40-49	(37)/(43)	52	51/46	75
50-59	(54)/(46)	17	57/(36)	36
60 or more	-/-	20	(40)/53	37
Years of education				
0	-/(57)	23	(25)/(59)	22
1-6	(15)/58	81	35/60	109
7-9	(24)/59	62	33/64	121
10-12	(18)/58	101	59/38	110
13 or more	53/(36)	74	68/24	74
Occupation				
High professional		14	(75)/(25)	18
Mid professional	(52)/(35)	52	68/24	42
Business/Administration		3	(90)/-	9
Skilled worker	(20)/50	59	46/52	106
Sales worker		10	73/(25)	30
Farmer/fisher	(10)/90	31	(30)/66	42
Traditional craft	-	6	(35)/(65)	20
Other	(18)/(41)	54	30/65	75
Haven't been trained/ housewife/student	(20)/61	112	43/48	94

Table A.7.8 Labour force members by region, sub-region, type of locality, refugee status, religion, sex and age

	Labour force in the occupied territories	Labour force in Gaza	Labour force in West Bank	Labour force in Arab Jerusalem
Main region				
Gaza	28			
Gaza excl. camps	19			
West Bank	64			
West Bank excl. camps	59			
Arab Jerusalem	9			
Refugee camps	14			
Sub-region				
North		55	52	
Central		(4)	30	
South		41	18	
Type of locality				
Greater Gaza WB towns		32	32	
Gaza town/villages/WB villages		35	61	
Gaza/WB camps		33	7	
Refugee status				
Non-refugees	66	43	76	65
UNRWA refugees	33	57	23	
-in camps	14	33	7	
-outside camps	20	25	17	(29)
Religion				
Moslem	96	100	97	81
Christian	4	-	(3)	(19)
Sex				
Male	85	92	83	82
Female	15	(8)	17	(18)
Age				
15-19	11	(8)	13	-
20-29	34	43	30	35
30-39	24	24	25	(22)
40-49	15	15	16	(14)
50-59	8	(5)	8	(12)
60 or more	8	(5)	8	(10)
N (UNW)	1123	373	532	218
N (NIW)	1165	322	742	101

Table A.7.9 Labour force members by region, education and occupation

	Labour force in the occupied territories	Labour force in Gaza	Labour force in West Bank	Labour force in Arab Jerusalem
Years of education				
0	7	(8)	7	-
1-6	23	24	24	(15)
7-9	23	15	25	(28)
10-12	28	31	26	30
13 or more	20	23	17	(25)
Type of education				
Apprenticeship	(1)	-	-	-
Primary/kuttab/preparatory	45	38	48	39
Secondary general	20	20	20	(18)
Secondary vocational/agricultural	(1)	-	-	-
Post-secondary course/nursing/teaching/labo etcetera	10	12	9	-
Bachelors Academic University	5	(7)	(3)	(11)
Academic B.A. for engineering/medicine	(2)	-	(2)	-
Academic University degree above B.A.	(1)	-	(2)	-
Non-specified education	(2)	(4)	(1)	-
No education	7	10	7	-
Still studying	6	(4)	7	-
Occupation				
High professional	4	-	4	-
Mid professional	13	17	12	(14)
Business Administration/ related professional work/ 4 years at University	(2)	-	(2)	-
Skilled worker/vocational	19	16	20	(21)
Sales worker	5	-	6	-
Farmer/fisher	11	14	11	-
Traditional	5	-	6	-
Other	15	15	15	(16)
No training	27	30	25	30
N (UNW)	1123	373	532	218
N (NIW)	1165	322	742	101

Table A.7.10 Male labour force members by main region, sub-region, type of locality, refugee status, religion, gender and age

	Male labour force in the occupied territories	Male labour force in Gaza	Male labour force in West Bank	Male labour force in Arab Jerusalem
Main region				
Gaza	30			
Gaza excl. camps	20			
West Bank	62			
West Bank excl. camps	57			
Arab Jerusalem	8			
Refugee camps	15			
Sub-region				
North		54	53	
Central		(4)	30	
South		42	18	
Type of locality				
Greater Gaza/WB towns		31	32	
Gaza town/villages/WB villages		35	60	
Gaza/ WB camps		34	8	
Refugee status				
Non-refugees	64	43	74	69
UNRWA refugees	35	57	25	
-in camps	15	34	8	
-outside camps	20	23	18	(27)
Religion				
Moslem	96	99	97	82
Christian	4	-	(3)	(18)
Age				
15-19	9	(8)	11	-
20-29	35	45	31	(34)
30-39	25	24	27	(20)
40-49	15	14	16	(14)
50-59	8	(5)	8	(14)
60 or more	8	(5)	8	(14)
N (UNW)	955	341	436	178
N (NIW)	994	297	615	82

Table A.7.11 Male labour force members by region, education and occupation

	Male labour force in the occupied territories	Male labour force in Gaza	Male labour force in West Bank	Male labour force in Arab Jerusalem
Years of education				
0	4	(6)	4	-
1-6	24	26	25	(16)
7-9	23	16	25	(31)
10-12	30	34	28	(30)
13 or more	19	20	19	(21)
Type of education				
Apprenticeship	(1)	-	-	-
Primary/kuttab/preparatory	46	41	48	44
Secondary general	21	21	21	(18)
Secondary vocational/agricultural	(2)	-	-	-
Post-secondary course/nursing/teaching/labo etcetera	9	(10)	10	-
Bachelors Academic University	5	(7)	(3)	-
Academic B.A. for engineering/medicine	(2)	-	(2)	-
Academic University degree above B.A.	(1)	-	(1)	-
Non-specified education	(2)	(4)	-	-
No education	5	(9)	4	-
Still studying	6	(4)	7	-
Occupation				
High professional	5	-	5	-
Mid professional	12	14	11	-
Business Administration/related professional work/4 years at University	(2)	-	(2)	-
Skilled worker/vocational	20	18	21	(24)
Sales worker	5	-	7	-
Farmer/fisher	12	15	12	-
Traditional	4	-	5	-
Other	15	16	15	(13)
No training	25	29	23	(32)
N (UNW)	955	341	436	178
N (NIW)	994	297	615	82

Table A.7.12 Comparative composition of labour force in the occupied territories and in Israel by gender, age and education (CBS classification of education and age)

	Labour force in the occupied territories (FAFO) (1992)	"Non-Jews" in the Israeli labour force (CBS) (1990)	Jews in the Israeli labour force (CBS) (1990)
Sex			
Male	85	85	56
Female	15	15	44
Age			
15-17	7	3	2
18-24	19	27	11
25-34	35	35	28
35-44	17	19	29
45-54	13	11	16
55-64	5	4	10
65 or more	5	(0)	4
Years of education			
0	7	2	1
1-4	10	5	1
5-8	26	35	10
9-10	14	18	12
11-12	24	25	38
13 or more	20	14	37
N (UNW)	1123	*	*
N (NIW)	1165	*	*

Sources CBS data: "Statistical abstract of Israel 1991", tables 12.1, 12.4, 12.5 and 12.8

Table A.7.13 Main employment of labour force members who worked at least 1 month the previous year by region of residence, type and economic branch of work, employment stability and average daily two-way travel time

	Resident in the occupied territories	Resident in Gaza	Resident in the West Bank	Resident in Arab Jerusalem
Type of work				
High professional	3	-	(3)	-
Mid professional	12	14	12	(15)
Vocational	22	19	24	(20)
Mercantile	13	(10)	15	(11)
Agriculture/fishing	15	19	16	-
Traditional craft	5	-	7	-
Service work	16	19	12	(29)
Unskilled work	13	15	12	(11)
Economic branch				
Construction	22	23	23	-
Industry	8	(8)	7	(18)
Commerce, hotels, restaurants etc.	14	10	17	(12)
Public Services	25	25	23	43
Farming/fishing	16	20	16	-
Transport and communication	5	-	6	(11)
Other sectors	9	(10)	8	-
Main place of work				
Arab Jerusalem	9	-	(5)	74
West Bank	46	-	72	-
Gaza	18	64	-	-
Israel	25	35	22	19
Number of jobs last year				
1 job	83	78	85	83
2-4 jobs	13	16	11	13
5 jobs or more	4	(5)	(4)	-

Table A.7.13 (Continued) Main employment of labour force members who worked at least 1 month the previous year by region of residence, type and economic branch of work, employment stability and average daily two-way travel time

	Resident in the occupied territories	Resident in Gaza	Resident in the West Bank	Resident in Arab Jerusalem
Number of jobs last 2 years				
1 job	75	72	76	78
2-4 jobs	17	18	16	15
5 jobs or more	7	(9)	(6)	-
Number of working weeks last 2 months				
0 weeks	5	(5)	5	-
1-2 weeks	8	13	7	-
3-4 weeks	18	30	13	-
5-6 weeks	18	20	19	-
7-8 weeks	51	31	56	79
Daily two-way travel time to place of work				
Less than 15 min	21	18	24	(17)
16-30 min	27	28	26	(32)
31-60 min	21	16	22	(30)
61-120 min	19	19	19	(20)
More than 120 min	11	19	9	-
N (UNW)	934	314	435	185
N (NIW)	960	274	604	82

Table A.7.14 Main employment of labour force members who worked at least 1 month the previous year by region of residence, place of work, education and occupation

	Resident in the occupied territories	Resident in Gaza	Resident in the West Bank	Resident in Arab Jerusalem
Years of education				
0	5	(5)	5	-
1-6	23	25	23	(16)
7-9	22	16	24	(26)
10-12	29	31	28	(31)
13 or more	22	23	20	(27)
Type of education				
Apprenticeship	(1)	-	-	-
Primary/kuttab/preparatory	46	41	49	40
Secondary general	21	20	22	(18)
Secondary vocational/agricultural	(2)	-	-	-
Post-secondary course/nursing/teaching/laboratory etcetera	12	13	11	-
Bachelors Academic University	5	(7)	(4)	(11)
Academic B.A. for engineering/medicine	(2)	-	(2)	-
Academic University degree above B.A.	(2)	-	(2)	-
Non-specified education	(2)	(4)	-	-
No education	6	(8)	5	-
Still studying	(2)	-	(2)	-
Occupation				
High professional	5	-	(5)	-
Mid professional	15	18	13	(13)
Business Administration/related professional work/4 years at University	(2)	-	(2)	-
Skilled worker/vocational	22	18	23	(21)
Sales worker	5	-	7	-
Farmer/fisher	11	16	10	-
Traditional	5	-	7	-
Other	15	15	15	(14)
No training	21	25	19	(29)
N (UNW)	934	314	435	185
N (NIW)	960	274	604	82

Table A.7.15 Distribution of labour force members by region of residence, place of work and selected background variables

	Total labour force						Men Gaza			Men West Bank		
	(1) OT	(2) Isr	(3) Gaza	(4) WB	(5) AJ	NUW	Gaza	Isr	NUW	WB	Isr	NUW
			(1)=(3)+(4)+(5)									
Total	73	26	18	46	9	1123	62	38	341	70	24	436
Region												
Gaza	64	38	64	-	-	373	62	38	341			
Camps excl.	63	37	63	-	-	266	60	39				
West Bank	72	22	-	72	5	532			242	70	24	436
Camps excl.	76	23	-	72	5	492				69	25	403
Arab Jerus.	80	20	-	6	74	218						
Camps	72	27	45	27	-	146	65	35	99	79	(15)	32
Sub-region												
Gaza North	63	37	62	-	-	213	60	39	194			
Gaza South	67	33	67	-	-	149	65	35	136			
WB North	78	21	-	78	-	262				77	22	214
WB Central	79	21	-	67	12	158				63	24	131
WB South	72	27	-	65	7	111				63	30	90
Type of locality												
Gr. Gaza City	56	44	56	-	-	134	52	47	122			
Gaza towns/villages	70	30	69	-	-	131	68	32	119			
Gaza camps	67	33	67	-	-	107	65	35	99			
WB towns	86	13	-	83	(3)	213				81	15	175
WB villages	72	28	-	65	(6)	279				62	30	228
WB camps	85	13	-	82	-	39				79	(15)	32
Refugee status												
Non-refugees	74	25	11	53	10	691	61	39	141	67	26	320
UNRWA refugees	74	26	33	33	(7)	411	63	37	197	76	20	111
-in camps	72	27	45	27	-	146	65	35	99	79	(15)	32
-outs camps	75	24	25	40	(11)	270	60	40	270	75	22	82
Religion												
Moslem	74	26	19	47	8	1065	62	38	339	70	24	420
Christian	84	(16)	-	(37)	(44)	57	-	-	2	(63)	(30)	16
Household wealth												
Lower third	64	36	27	35	(3)	287	53	47	152	67	29	105
Middle third	75	24	23	48	(5)	395	68	31	134	75	20	162
Upper third	80	21	9	52	18	441	67	32	55	67	25	169
Number of adult males per household												
0-1	76	23	15	50	12	560	65	34	146	69	23	225
2-3	74	26	18	49	7	396	58	42	133	75	22	146
4 or more	70	30	26	35	(9)	167	64	36	62	61	29	65

Table A.7.16 Distribution of labour force members by region of residence, place of work, age and education

	\multicolumn{6}{c}{Total labour force}	\multicolumn{3}{c}{Men Gaza}	\multicolumn{3}{c}{Men West Bank}
	(1) OT	(2) Isr	(3) Gaza	(4) WB	(5) AJ	NUW	Gaza	Isr	NUW	WB	Isr	NUW
			(1)=(3)+(4)+(5)									
Total	73	26	18	46	9	1123	62	38	341	69	25	436
Age												
15-19	72	(28)	(14)	55	-	102	(72)	-	30	61	(39)	44
20-29	64	36	21	35	8	344	57	43	120	56	37	119
30-39	75	24	18	51	(6)	317	59	40	102	76	20	125
40-49	82	17	19	49	(15)	188	(71)	(29)	52	73	(14)	75
50-59	87	(13)	(12)	58	(17)	81	(62)	(38)	17	85	-	36
60 or more	90	(10)	(18)	58	(15)	91	(96)	-	20	99	-	37
Years of education												
0	56	(40)	(13)	(44)	-	78	-	(65)	23	(69)	23	22
1-6	76	25	(18)	50	(7)	244	58	42	81	75	21	109
7-9	71	29	(11)	50	(9)	262	(53)	48	62	67	28	121
10-12	67	31	19	39	10	294	(63)	36	101	61	33	110
13 or more	86	12	26	49	11	245	80	(20)	74	80	(12)	74
Main desired attribute of future palestinian state												
Arabism	72	30	(18)	44	(8)	80	(80)	-	15	58	39	33
Islam	74	26	15	50	9	639	58	42	172	72	21	275
Democracy	72	25	20	46	10	304	61	38	104	67	29	110

Table A.7.17 Main employment of labour force members who worked at least 1 month the previous year by place, type, and economic branch of work, employment stability and average daily two-way travel time

	Labour force working in occupied territories	Labour force working in Israel		Labour force working in occupied territories	Labour force working in Israel
Type of work			**Number of jobs last year**		
High professional	(3)	-	1 job	88	68
Mid professional	16	-	2-4 jobs	8	28
Vocational	19	32	5 jobs or more	4	(4)
Mercantile	17	-	**Number of jobs last 2 years**		
Agriculture/fishing	17	12	1 job	82	57
Traditional craft	7	-	2-4 jobs	11	34
Service work	13	23	5 jobs or more	6	(9)
Unskilled work	7	30	**Number of working weeks last 2 months**		
Economic branch			0 weeks	(3)	(8)
Construction	13	50	1-2 weeks	7	(12)
Industry	8	(10)	3-4 weeks	15	26
Commerce, hotels, restaurants etc.	19	-	5-6 weeks	16	24
Public Services	30	(12)	7-8 weeks	59	30
Farming/fishing	16	14	**Daily two-way travel time to place of work**		
Transport and communication	5	(6)	Less than 15 min	28	-
Other sectors	9	(7)	16-30 min	35	-
Main place of work			31-60 min	21	20
Arab Jerusalem	13		61-120 min	11	44
West Bank	63		More than 120 min	5	31
Gaza	25		N (UNW)	676	244
Israel		100	N (NIW)	707	244

Table A.7.18 Labour force members who worked at least 1 month the previous year by main place of work, education and occupation

	Labour force working in occupied territories	Labour force working in Israel		Labour force working in occupied territories	Labour force working in Israel
Years of education			**Type of education**		
0	(4)	(8)	Apprenticeship	-	-
1-6	23	23	Primary/kuttab/preparatory	46	47
7-9	21	25	Secondary general	20	25
10-12	27	35	Secondary vocational/agricultural	(2)	-
13 or more	25	(10)	Post-secondary course/nursing/teachi etcetera	13	(8)
Occupation			Bachelors Academic University	6	-
High professional	5	-	Academic B.A. for engineering/medicine	(2)	-
Mid professional	16	(9)	Academic University degree above B.A.	(2)	-
Business Administration/related professional work/ 4 years at University	(2)	-	Non-specified education	(2)	-
Skilled worker/vocational	20	27	No education	5	8
Sales worker	7	-	Still studying	(2)	-
Farmer/fisher	12	(7)	N (UNW)	676	244
Traditional	7	-	N (NIW)	707	244
Other	12	22			
No training	18	32			

Table A.7.19 Main employment of labour force members resident in Gaza and the West Bank who worked at least 1 month the previous year by place, type, and economic branch of work, employment stability and average daily two-way travel time

	Res. Gaza working in the occupied territories	Res. Gaza working in Israel	Res. WB working in the occupied territories	Res. WB working in Israel
Type of work				
High professional	-	-	(3)	-
Mid professional	21	-	14	-
Vocational	(11)	36	22	29
Mercantile	(16)	-	18	-
Agriculture/fishing	25	-	15	(18)
Traditional craft	-	-	9	-
Service work	(13)	(30)	11	(16)
unskilled work	(9)	(27)	6	33
Economic branch				
Construction	(-)	56	16	50
Industry	(8)	-	7	(9)
Commerce, hotels, restaurants etc.	16	-	21	-
Public Services	33	(12)	27	(7)
Farming/fishing	27	-	15	(20)
Transport and communication	-	-	(5)	(11)
Other sectors	(7)	(16)	10	-
Main place of work				
Arab Jerusalem	-		(6)	
West Bank	-		94	
Gaza	99		-	
Israel		100		100

	Res. Gaza working in the occupied territories	Res. Gaza working in Israel	Res. WB working in the occupied territories	Res. WB working in Israel
Number of jobs last year				
1 job	86	64	89	71
2-4 jobs	(8)	32	7	25
5 jobs or more	(7)	-	(4)	-
Number of jobs last 2 years				
1 job	83	52	81	60
2-4 jobs	(7)	39	12	30
5 jobs or more	(10)	-	(5)	(10)
Number of working weeks last 2 months				
0 weeks	-	(11)	(4)	-
1-2 weeks	(10)	(18)	(6)	(9)
3-4 weeks	25	40	12	(18)
5-6 weeks	21	(20)	16	29
7-8 weeks	42	(12)	62	40
Daily two-way travel time to place of work				
Less than 15 min	27	-	30	-
16-30 min	43	-	32	-
31-60 min	20	-	21	25
61-120 min	(6)	42	12	48
More than 120 min	-	48	(5)	(21)
N (UNW)	196	113	336	93
N (NIW)	175	97	466	132

Table A.7.20 Main employment of labour force members resident in Gaza and the West Bank who worked for at least 1 month the previous year by place of work, education and occupation

	Res. Gaza working in the occupied territories	Res. Gaza working in Israel	Res. WB working in the occupied territories	Res. WB working in Israel
Years of education				
0	-	(9)	(5)	(8)
1-6	23	(29)	24	(20)
7-9	13	(20)	24	26
10-12	31	32	25	37
13 or more	30	(10)	22	(10)
Type of education				
Apprenticeship	-	-	-	-
Primary/kuttab/preparatory	38	46	50	47
Secondary general	21	(19)	20	31
Secondary vocational/agricultural	-	-	-	-
Post-secondary course/nursing/teaching/labo etcetera	(14)	(10)	12	-
Bachelors Academic University	(9)	-	(4)	-
Academic B.A. for engineering/medicine	-	-	(3)	-
Academic University degree above B.A.	-	-	(2)	-
Non-specified education	-	-	-	-
No education	(8)	-	(5)	(8)
Still studying	-	-	(2)	-
Occupation				
High professional	-	-	(6)	-
Mid professional	22	(12)	12	-
Business Administration/ related professional work/ 4 years at University	-	-	(3)	-
Skilled worker/vocational	(12)	(28)	23	25
Sales worker	-	-	11	-
Farmer/fisher	21	-	13	(9)
Traditional	-	-	7	-
Other	(10)	(25)	11	23
No training	23	(30)	15	33
N (UNW)	196	113	336	93
N (NIW)	175	97	466	132

Table A.7.21 Comparative composition of persons residing in the occupied territories who worked one month or more the previous year and "non-Jewish" and Jewish labour force members in Israel by gender, age and education. CBS classification of education and age

	Resident in the occupied territories working in the occupied territories (FAFO 1992)	Resident in the occupied territories working in Israel (FAFO 1992)	"Non-Jews" in the Israeli labour force (CBS 1990)	Jews in the Israeli labour force (CBS 1990)l
Sex				
Male	86	98	85	56
Female	14	-	15	44
Age				
15-17	(4)	-	3	2
18-24	16	27	27	11
25-34	37	41	35	28
35-44	19	18	19	29
45-54	15	(6)	11	16
55-64	7	-	4	10
65 or more	(3)	-	(0)	4
Years of education				
0	(4)	(8)	2	1
1-4	9	(8)	5	1
5-8	26	29	35	10
9-10	12	14	18	12
11-12	23	31	25	38
13 or more	25	(10)	14	37
N (UNW)	676	244	*	*
N (NIW)	707	244	*	*

Sources CBS data: "Statistical abstract of Israel 1991", tables 12.4, 12.5 and 12.8

Table A.7.22 Comparative composition of persons residing in the occupied territories who worked for one month or more the previous year and "non-Jewish" and Jewish employed persons in Israel by type of work and economic sector

	Resident in the occupied territories working in the occupied territories (FAFO 1992)	Resident in the occupied territories working in Israel (FAFO 1992)	"Non-Jews" in the Israeli labour force (CBS 1990)	Jews in the Israeli labour force (CBS 1990)l
Type of work				
Professional, academic, administrators, clerical	19	-	20	51
Vocational and traditional craft	26	33	42	21
Mercantile	17	-	9	9
Agriculture/fishing	16	12	7	3
Service work	13	23	13	13
Unskilled work	7	30	10	2
Economic branch				
Construction	13	50	19	3
Industry	8	(10)	22	22
Commerce, hotels, restaurants etc.	19	-	15	15
Public Services	30	(12)	20	31
Farming/fishing	16	14	6	4
Transport and communication	5	(6)	6	6
Other sectors	9	(7)	13	19
N (UNW)	676	244	*	*
N (NIW)	707	244	*	*

Sources CBS data: "Statistical abstract of Israel 1991", tables 12.10, 12.18 and 12.19

Table A.7.23 Labour force participation ratios for working women by location of work

	Occupied territories			All women		
	All women	Percent of these women in labour force	Percent of these women not in labour force	Gaza	West Bank	Arab Jerusalem
Job outside home	10	85	(15)	(4)	12	(14)
Professional job	4	85	(15)	(3)	4	(8)
Factory	(2)	(95)	-	-	-	-
Agricultural	(1)	-	-	-	-	-
Domestic paid work	-	-	-	-	-	-
Other	1	(63)	-	-	-	-
Serving	6	40	60	(4)	8	-
Beauty care	(1)	-	-	-	-	-
Food processing	-	-	-	-	-	-
Raising animals	2	-	69	(3)	(2)	
Selling consumer goods	(1)	-	35	-	-	-
Piece work	1	-	89	-	-	-
Other incomegenerating activity	(2)	-	-	-	(3)	-
N (UNW)	1228			483	503	24?
N (NIW)	1199			419	675	105

Table A.7.24 Labour force members by sex, main region, refugee status, religion and age

	Male labour force in the occupied territories	Female labour force in the occupied territories
Main region		
Gaza	30	(15)
Gaza without camps	20	(13)
West Bank	62	74
West Bank without camps	57	70
Arab Jerusalem	8	(11)
Refugee camps	15	(7)
Refugee status		
Non-refugees	64	75
UNRWA refugees	35	23
-in camps	15	(7)
-outside camps	20	(17)
Religion		
Moslem	96	94
Christian	4	(6)
Age		
15-19	9	18
20-29	35	30
30-39	25	20
40-49	15	18
50-59	8	8
60 or more	8	7
N (UNW)	955	168
N (NIW)	994	171

Table A.7.25 Labour force members by sex, region, education and occupation

	Male labour force in the occupied territories	Female labour force in the occupied territories
Years of education		
0	4	21
1-6	24	(17)
7-9	23	23
10-12	30	18
13 or more	19	22
Type of education		
Apprenticeship	(1)	-
Primary/kuttab/preparatory	46	37
Secondary general	21	(13)
Secondary vocational/agricultural	(2)	-
Post-secondary course/nursing/teaching/laboratory etcetera	9	14
Bachelors Academic University	5	-
Academic B.A. for engineering/medicine	(2)	-
Academic University degree above B.A.	(1)	-
Non-specified education	(2)	-
No education	5	21
Still studying	6	(7)
Occupation		
High professional	5	-
Mid professional	12	24
Business Administration/related professional work/4 years at University	(2)	-
Skilled worker/vocational	20	(11)
Sales worker	5	-
Farmer/fisher	12	-
Traditional	4	(10)
Other	15	(13)
No training	25	37
N (UNW)	955	168
N (NIW)	994	171

Table A.7.26 Labour force members who worked at least one month the previous year by gender, type, and economic branch of work, employment stability and average daily two-way travel time

	Male	Female		Male	Femal
Type of work			**Number of jobs last year**		
High professional	(3)	-	1 job	81	97
Mid professional	9	38	2-4 jobs	14	-
Vocational	23	14	5 jobs or more	5	-
Mercantile	14	-	**Number of jobs last 2 years**		
Agriculture/fishing	16	(11)	1 job	73	90
Traditional craft	4	(18)	2-4 jobs	18	-
Service work	16	(11)	5 jobs or more	8	-
Unskilled work	15	-	**Number of working weeks last 2 months**		
Economic branch			0 weeks	5	-
Construction	25	-	1-2 weeks	8	-
Industry	9	-	3-4 weeks	19	-
Commerce, hotels, restaurants etc.	15	-	5-6 weeks	19	(9)
Public Services	22	54	7-8 weeks	49	67
Farming/fishing	16	(11)	**Daily two-way travel time to place of work**		
Transport and communication	6	-	Less than 15 min	21	(27)
Other sectors	6	(28)	16-30 min	26	33
Main place of work			31-60 min	21	(24)
Arab Jerusalem	9	(10)	61-120 min	21	-
West Bank	43	67	More than 120 min	11	(9)
Gaza	19	(16)	N (UNW)	826	108
Israel	28	((6))	N (NIW)	857	104

Table A.7.27 Labour force members who worked at least one month the previous year by sex, region, education and occupation

	Male	Female		Male	Female
Years of education			**Occupation**		
0	4	(14)	High professional	5	-
1-6	24	(17)	Mid professional	12	37
7-9	22	(20)	Business Administration/ related professional work/4 years at University	(2)	-
10-12	30	(18)	Skilled worker/vocational	22	(17)
13 or more	20	31	Sales worker	6	-
Type of education			Farmer/fisher	12	-
Apprenticeship	-	-	Traditional	5	(13)
Primary/kuttab/preparator	47	39	Other	15	(15)
Secondary general	22	(15)	No training	22	(12)
Secondary vocational/agricultural	(2)	-	N (UNW)	826	108
Post-secondary course/ nursing/teaching/	10	22	N (NIW)	857	104
laboratory etcetera	10	22			
Bachelors Academic University	5	-			
Academic B.A. for engineering/medicine	(2)	-			
Academic University degree above B.A.	(2)	-			
Non-specified education	(2)	-			
No education	5	(14)			
Still studying	(2)	-			

Table A.7.28 Weekly time use for women by labour force status

	Occupied Territories		
	All women	In labour force	Not in labour force
Weekly hours of "economic" activity			
0	68	(8)	77
1-7	13	-	13
8-35	12	30	8
36 or more	7	58	(2)
Average hours	6	36	3
Weekly hours of housework			
0-28	19	46	17
29-49	28	36	26
50-70	32	(12)	35
71 or more	21	(5)	23
Average hours	51	34	53
Weekly hours of studying			
0	87	91	88
1-21	3	-	3
22-42	5	-	6
43 or more	4	-	4
Average hours	4	1	4
Weekly hours of relaxing and other activity			
0-21	40	40	40
22-28	14	(15)	14
29-42	34	39	34
43 or more	12	(7)	13
Average hours	27	26	27
Total	88	97	87
N (UNW)	1228	168	1060
N (NIW)	1199	171	1028

Table A.7.29 Weekly time use for women in Gaza and the West Bank by labour force status

	Gaza			West Bank		
	All women	In labour force	Not in labour force	All women	In labour force	Not in labour force
Weekly hours of "economic" activity						
0	81	-	85	59	-	71
1-7	10	-	11	15	-	16
8-35	7	-	(4)	15	(25)	11
36 or more	(2)	-	-	11	67	(3)
Average hours	3	30	1	9	38	4
Weekly hours of housework						
0-28	14	-	13	21	53	18
29-49	23	-	22	31	(33)	29
50-70	41	-	43	27	(10)	31
71 or more	22	-	22	21	-	25
Average hours	55	42	55	49	31	52
Weekly hours of studying						
0	87	-	87	89	94	89
1-21	(2)	-	-	(4)	-	(4)
22-42	8	-	8	4	-	(4)
43 or more	(3)	-	(3)	(3)	-	(4)
Average hours	4	5	4	3	0	4
Weekly hours of relaxing and other activity						
0-21	43	-	41	38	35	37
22-28	16	-	16	13	(16)	13
29-42	27	-	28	38	41	37
43 or more	15	-	15	11	(7)	12
Average hours	28	23	29	27	27	27
Total	90	100	89	88	96	87
N (UNW)	483	32	451	503	96	407
N (NIW)	419	25	394	675	127	548